BEING WITH GOD

BEING WITH GOD

Trinity, Apophaticism, and Divine-Human Communion

ARISTOTLE PAPANIKOLAOU

University of Notre Dame Press

Notre Dame, Indiana

University of Notre Dame Press
Notre Dame, Indiana 46556
undpress.nd.edu
All Rights Reserved

Copyright © 2006 by University of Notre Dame
Published in the United States of America
Reprinted in 2008, 2015

Material from "Divine Energies or Divine Personhood: Vladimir Lossky and John Zizioulas on Conceiving the Transcendent and Immanent God," *Modern Theology* 19, no. 3 (July 2003): 357–85, appear throughout the four chapters of this book and are reprinted with the permission of Blackwell Publishing.

A revised version of "Is John Zizioulas an Existentialist in Disguise? Response to Lucian Turcescu," *Modern Theology* (October 2004): 587–93, appears in chapter 4. Material from that article is reprinted with the permission of Blackwell Publishing.

Library of Congress Cataloging in-Publication Data

Papanikolaou, Aristotle.
Being with God : Trinity, apophaticism, and divine-human communion / Aristotle Papanikolaou.
    p. cm.
Includes bibliographical references (p.   ) and index.
ISBN-13: 978-0-268-03830-4 (cloth : alk. paper)
ISBN-10: 0-268-03830-9 (cloth : alk. paper)
ISBN-13: 978-0-268-03831-1 (pbk. : alk. paper)
ISBN-10: 0-268-03831-7 (pbk. : alk. paper)
1. Deification (Christianity)—History of doctrines—20th century.
2. Trinity—History of doctrines—20th century.
3. Orthodox Eastern Church—Doctrines—History—20th century.
4. Lossky, Vladimir, 1903–1958.
5. Zizioulas, Jean, 1931– . I. Title.
BT767.8.P37 2006
231.092′2—dc22
2005036071

∞ *This book is printed on acid-free paper.*

To

DENA

Truly, Madly, Deeply

Contents

Acknowledgments — ix

Introduction — 1

chapter 1   Ontology and Theological Epistemology   9
    Lossky's Apophaticism   12
        Incarnation as Revelation   12
        Cataphatic and Apophatic Theologies   13
        Knowledge as Union   20
        Essence/Energies Distinction   24
        Theology as Antinomy   27
    Zizioulas's Eucharistic Epistemology   30
        Truth, Eucharist, and Eschatology   31
        Pneumatological Christology   32
        Icon: The Unity of History and Eschatology   38
    Divine-Human Communion: Knowledge or Ignorance?   44

chapter 2   Trinity: Antinomy or Communion?   49
    Lossky on Apophaticism and Trinity   50
        Oikonomia and *Theologia*   50
        The Person/Nature Antinomy   53
        The *Filioque*   65
    Zizioulas on Ontology and Trinity   71
        Truth as Life   71
        The Ontological Revolution   73
        Apophaticism versus Ontology   89

chapter 3 Knowing the Triune God — 91

The *hopos esti* of Trinitarian Existence 94
The Economic and the Immanent Trinity 99
Ontology and Epistemology 102
Divine Energies or Divine Personhood? 106

chapter 4 Trinity and Personhood — 129

Person as *Ekstasis* and *Hypostasis* 129
Zizioulas's Philosophical Argument for an Ontology of Personhood 142
The Problem of 'Freedom' in Zizioulas's Thought 148
'Person,' Patristic Interpretation, and the Hermeneutics of Retrieval 154

Notes — 163

Bibliography — 207

Index — 223

Acknowledgments

The completion of this project is both a culmination and a beginning. It is the beginning of what I intend to be continuous reflection in one form or another on the most fundamental existential questions which impinge on all of us. It is a culmination of a lifelong journey of learning and formation. In that I am who I am and know what I know through my relationships with friends, colleagues, teachers and professors, priests and hierarchs, to each of them I owe a debt of gratitude. There are others who more directly contributed to the realization of this project. I am thankful to Father Emmanuel Clapsis, my professor in Dogmatics and the current Dean at Holy Cross Greek Orthodox School of Theology, from whom I have learned and continue to learn much about systematic theology. He encouraged my further studies and inspired in me an even deeper love for theology. I am also indebted to Bernard McGinn and David Tracy for their patient and wise counsel throughout my academic career at the Divinity School of the University of Chicago. I'm especially grateful to McGinn for his immediate response to my many requests for all types of support after I graduated from the Divinity School. Where others may have questioned this type of project, McGinn and Tracy wholeheartedly supported it. Among the many things that I learned from them, an even greater appreciation for my own tradition stands as the most important. I consider it a blessing to have worked with them. My koumbaro and friend, John Fotopoulos, has been an indefatigable source of support throughout our shared academic journeys and a valued conversation partner in all things ecclesial and theological; I thank both him and my colleague Christophe Chalamet for reviewing portions of this text. A Fordham University Junior Faculty Fellowship generously funded the sabbatical time that allowed me to complete the manuscript. I am also grateful to the Ames Fund for Junior Faculty, granted through Fordham University Graduate School of Arts and Science, which subsidized, among other things, the use of the stunning icon of Moses at the Burning Bush as the book cover. Saint Catherine's Monastery graciously permitted the use of the icon, and I thank Father Justin, together with Mr. and Mrs. Michael Jaharis, for helping me obtain the permission granted by Archbishop Damianos. Finally, I consider myself blessed to have worked with Barbara Hanrahan, Director of the University of Notre Dame Press. I cannot overstate my appreciation for her openness, interest, encouragement, and guidance throughout the publication process. This book has benefited from the comments of many reviewers, and I can only hope that they see the fruits of their own labor in the final product. Whatever may be lacking, which I am sure is much, is my own doing.

My family has always been a constant source of strength and support. My brother and sister, Evans and Sultana, have always challenged and encouraged their little brother in ways too numerous to mention; I could not have asked for more loving and supportive siblings. It is difficult to express my feelings about my parents, the Reverend Byron Stylianos and Presbytera Xanthippe Papanikolaou. Their life has been one continuous sacrifice for others, but mostly for their children. Through their various forms of support, but more importantly, through their constant and incessant love they provided the conditions which made possible my education and my happiness. In many ways, this work is a reflection of their many sacrifices. How I feel about them is best expressed by St. Augustine's own sentiments about his mother Monica: "In the flesh [they] brought me to birth in this world: in [their] hearts [they] brought me to birth in your eternal light" (*Confessions* 9.8.17). I feel compelled to mention also my grandmother, Panagiota Kassos, who recently celebrated her hundredth birthday. She survived Turkish Occupation, two World Wars, Civil War, poverty, and adversity. If it were not for her strength of character, her determination, her faith in God, in humanity, and in the future, I would not be the recipient of the many blessings I presently enjoy. In my relationship with her I understand what it means to receive a gift that cannot be returned. Of the many gifts she made possible for me to receive, the greatest of these are my children, Byron Theodore and Alexander Panagiotis, and my wife, Constantia (Dena) Tolios, Esq. In them I have experienced all the virtues and joys of life that are alone truly meaningful. Byron and Alexander by simply existing are a constant, daily source of happiness. Dena's strength, support, and unconditional love allowed me to see this project through to the end. A close friend of mine once described her as "my sacrament." In her presence I have indeed come to understand and experience God's unconditional love; I have learned what it means to be loved not because of who I am, but in spite of who I am. I am indebted to her for much more than simply the completion of this project.

Introduction

This book is about 'being with God,' about the realism of divine-human communion as it is expressed in the work of Vladimir Lossky (1903–58) and John Zizioulas (1931–), arguably two of the most influential Orthodox theologians of the past century.[1] Since it discusses divine-human communion through these two figures, it is also a small window into contemporary Orthodox theology. In addition to their impact on twentieth-century Orthodoxy, each has served in their own time as a spokesperson for Orthodoxy to the non-Orthodox world. Vladimir Lossky was one of the many Russian émigrés to Paris, where he lived and taught after the Bolshevik revolution until his tragically sudden death. Zizioulas studied at the University of Athens and at Harvard, worked with renowned Orthodox patristic scholar and church historian Georges Florovsky, and was a part of a group of young Orthodox theologians in Greece who were determined to heed Florovsky's call for a "neo-patristic synthesis" in Greek theological studies.

In spite of being separated by a generation, both theologians shared a commitment to a return to the fathers for contemporary Orthodox theology. Lossky, together with Florovsky, was instrumental in initiating this paradigm shift in contemporary Orthodoxy against what he perceived to be the philosophically tainted Russian sophiology best represented in the person of Sergius Bulgakov. Zizioulas was reacting to a Greek theology that he considered inherently influenced by the neo-scholastic models of the 'West.' Both also taught in non-Orthodox institutions and worked within the ecumenical movement, Zizioulas more formally in the World Council of Churches (WCC), and Lossky more informally through a theological working group that included such figures as Gabriel Marcel. Lossky also counted among his friends such notable Catholic theologians as Yves Congar, Jean Daniélou, and Henri de Lubac and was active in the English Fellowship of St. Alban and St. Sergius.

Both Lossky and Zizioulas, however, are united by something more substantial than simply formal characteristics of their academic life and work. The two theologians identify as the heart and center of all theological discourse the realism of divine-human communion, which is often understood in terms of the familiar Orthodox concept of *theosis,* or divinization. The Incarnation, according to Lossky and Zizioulas, is the event of a *real* divine-human communion which is made accessible to all; God has become human so that all may participate fully in the divine life. This book will show how an ontology of divine-human communion is at the center of both Lossky's and Zizioulas's theological projects. It will also show how, again, for both theologians, this core is also used as a self-identification marker against 'Western'[2] theologies, which they see as excessively rationalistic and therefore a threat to the very heart of theological discourse defined in terms of the realism of divine-human communion. On these two points, the affirmation of the realism of divine-human communion and the rejection of the so-called 'Western' rationalism, Lossky and Zizioulas share much in common with other contemporary Orthodox theologians. There exists an identifiable consensus in contemporary Orthodox theology that is united around these two principles, particularly that of the realism of divine-human communion.

The similarities between the theologies of Lossky and Zizioulas do not extend much further than this affirmation of the realism of divine-human communion as the central core of theological discourse. Theology for both theologians attempts to give expression to this core of theological discourse, to unpack the implications of this central axiom. The theologies of Lossky and Zizioulas give witness to the fact that shared premises do not lead necessarily to the same conclusions. In fact, the shared premise of the realism of divine-human communion resulted, in the case of Lossky and Zizioulas, in two distinct theologies. This is nowhere more evident than in their trinitarian theologies.

For both Lossky and Zizioulas, the doctrine of the Trinity is rooted in the Christian affirmation of the realism of divine-human communion in Jesus Christ by the power of the Holy Spirit. The doctrine of the Trinity is the Christian expression of the God who is simultaneously transcendent and immanent, who offers the gift of God's very life to that which is 'other' than God—the non-divine. The God who offers and realizes this divine-human communion is the trinitarian God; on this both Lossky and Zizioulas concur. On what the affirmation of the realism of divine-human communion means in conceptualizing God as Trinity, Lossky and Zizioulas have substantial and profound differences. The central debate is over the use of apophaticism in theology in general, but especially the relation of apophaticism to the doctrine of the Trinity. For Lossky, apophaticism is the central precondition for a trinitarian theology, i.e., there can be no non-apophatic doctrine of the Trinity; for Zizioulas, apophaticism has a much more restricted role in theological discourse and the God experienced in the eucharist is not the God beyond being but the immanent life of the trinitarian God. In a way, one could frame the debate between Lossky and Zizioulas over the relation between apophaticism and trinitarian theology as one over Karl Rahner's famous axiom, "*The 'economic' Trinity is the 'immanent' Trinity and the 'immanent' Trinity is the 'economic' Trinity.*"[3] Lossky would reject the identification of the economic and the immanent Trinity, while Zizioulas would accept Rahner's axiom with qualifications.

The central task of this book then is a critical comparison of the trinitarian theologies of Lossky and Zizioulas as expressions of the core axiom that they both share—the realism of divine-human communion. Insofar as the most substantial debate between the two theologians is over the relation between apophaticism and trinitarian theology, it will explore the relation between their theological epistemologies and trinitarian theologies. Both Lossky and Zizioulas develop theological epistemologies that are rooted in their affirmation of an ontology of divine-human communion. In their theologies, ontology precedes epistemology. Their particular understanding of the implications of an ontology of divine-human communion for theological epistemologies then impacts their respective trinitarian theologies. These initial moves in their theologies then explain the substantive differences in other aspects of their theologies. The "critical" component of this exercise will be to judge the adequacy of their theologies based on their consistency with the central premise that they both share—the realism of divine-human communion.

Chapter 1 will begin this critical comparison by analyzing Lossky's and Zizioulas's theological epistemologies. The question of the knowledge of God is a perennial theological and philosophical problem. During the modern period, this question, together with questions of epistemology in general, shaped theological discourse. The content of central Christian theological themes was often dependent on and derivative of the answers theologians gave to the questions of epistemology. In modern theological discourse epistemology preceded ontology.

For Lossky and Zizioulas the relation is reversed. This chapter will show how for both theologians ontology precedes epistemology, i.e., that their theological epistemologies presuppose an ontology of divine-human communion. Both agree that knowledge of God is experiential, given only in union with God; however, they disagree over the nature and locus of such a union and on the limits of God-talk. For Lossky, an ontology of divine-human communion entails an apophatic theological epistemology. I will argue that Lossky's turn to apophaticism is driven by a concern to safeguard the realism of divine-human communion, i.e., apophaticism is the only means to divine-human communion. For Zizioulas, divine-human communion is an event realized in the eucharist and, as such, is a communal event of communion with the divine life. Lossky's and Zizioulas's affirmation of this realism of divine-human communion leads in two different, and in part, mutually exclusive directions. These distinct theological epistemologies account for the differences in other aspects of their theologies, in particular, their trinitarian theologies. At the heart of their differences is the debate over the conceptualization of divine-human communion.

Chapter 2 will analyze Lossky's and Zizioulas's trinitarian theologies and will argue that for both theologians the doctrine of the Trinity is essentially the Christian affirmation and conceptualization of divine-human communion, and correlatively, of the nature of God as immanent and transcendent. Substantive disagreement exists, however, on how to conceptualize this trinitarian God, which, in part, can be traced to distinct theological epistemologies.

Lossky's apophatic epistemology shapes his understanding of God's trinitarian life. For Lossky, knowledge of God in terms of union, i.e., as an event of divine-human communion means that theology must be 'antinomic' in method. Lossky defines an antinomic theology as the affirmation of two contradictory principles to the being of God. Divine-human communion means that God is knowable and unknowable, transcendent and immanent, and the nature of God as such is best expressed for Lossky in the antinomic essence/energies distinction. The essence of God is that which is transcendent and unknowable, while the energies of God are that through which humans participate in the divine life.

The notion of antinomy further guides Lossky's trinitarian theology and his understanding of the use of central trinitarian categories. For Lossky, the Trinity is "a fact" that is revealed in the Incarnation. The categories of person/nature are not meant to indicate anything about God's trinitarian being, but are meant to express the antinomy of unity and distinction within the triune life. What is important for Lossky is the antinomic expression of theology, because it is only through an antinomic theology that one can go beyond human limitations toward an *ekstatic* union with the divine energies. In this sense, Lossky adheres to a strict separation between the immanent and the economic Trinity, or between *oikonomia* and *theologia*.

For Zizioulas, the eucharistic event is a communion with the immanent life of God and reveals God's being as personal and relational. The eucharist is the experience not of the apophatic God beyond being but of the immanent, trinitarian life of God. As such, it is the source for a trinitarian theology that is 'revolutionary' in its ontological implications. The doctrine of the Trinity is then not a rejection of the link between God and being, but a Christian expression about the way God *is* as Trinity. The 'revolutionary' aspect of trinitarian theology is that ontology gives priority to categories that were within a metaphysics of substance considered to have no ontological import. Implicit in the doctrine of the Trinity is a relational ontology of trinitarian personhood, where being is best understood in terms of such notions as 'difference,' 'otherness,' 'relationality,' and 'person.'

In this sense, trinitarian theology is itself an attempt to give expression to the being of God as personal and relational. The patristic theology of the fourth century, particularly that of Athanasius of Alexandria and the Cappadocian fathers, is the era in which, according to Zizioulas, trinitarian theology receives its clearest expression. I will analyze Zizioulas's use of these patristic figures with special attention to his interpretation of the category of *hypostasis* and the trinitarian notion of the monarchy of the Father. As with Lossky, it will be shown that guiding Zizioulas's interpretation is the claim that the doctrine of the Trinity is essentially a Christian understanding of divine-human communion. The chapter will thus make clear the differences between Lossky and Zizioulas over what the realism of divine-human communion means for conceptualizing the Trinity and how their own epistemological claims influence such a conception.

The third chapter will focus on the two main theological differences between Lossky and Zizioulas: the relation between *oikonomia* and *theologia*, or the immanent and economic trinity; and, the conceptualization of theosis, or divine-human communion, in terms of person/hypostasis or the "energies" of God. I will demonstrate how Zizioulas answers the challenge of justifying a trinitarian ontology against Lossky's rendering of the Trinity in apophatic terms. For Lossky, the distinction between the uncreated and the created, between God's transcendence and immanence leads to the further positioning of two realms in his trinitarian theology, *theologia* and *oikonomia*. God is known in God's economy but not in *theologia*, or God's immanent life. A trinitarian ontology would thus be impossible since God's trinitarian life lies beyond being in non-being. In order to justify an ontology of personhood based on the Trinity, Zizioulas will need to account for an experience not simply of the economic trinity, but of the immanent trinity, i.e., of the way God truly exists. He does so by interpreting the patristic category *tropos hyparxeos,* or mode of existence, in a way absent in Lossky (and in most Orthodox theologians). For Zizioulas, three distinctions are needed to adequately account for God's trinitarian existence: *hoti esti* (that God is), *ti esti* (what God is), and *hopos esti* (how God is). Though God's essence, the *ti esti* of God, cannot be known, the *hopos esti* of God, the way in which God exists, is known insofar as it is revealed in the eucharistic experience of the triune life. It is this experience of God's way of existence that forms the condition for the possibility of a theological ontology. This ontology is rooted in God's very being and is the basis on which Zizioulas interprets other theological doctrines. The substantive differences, then, which exist between the theologies of Zizioulas and Lossky, between their theologies of person, christologies, doctrines of creation and soteriologies, can ultimately be traced to a debate over the priority of ontology or apophaticism in theological expression.

This chapter will further develop the implications of Zizioulas's trinitarian theology by arguing that Zizioulas's trinitarian ontology is internally more consistent than Lossky's apophaticism. The latter prioritizes God's hyperessence and, in so doing, it leads Lossky ironically to affirm an ontology of substance that he claims is the mistake of 'Western' theology and which threatens the realism of divine-human communion. Lossky, in the end, affirms that which he finds most menacing in theology. In addition to arguing for the necessity of experiencing the immanent trinitarian life of God if divine-human communion is to be real, Zizioulas offers the distinctions necessary for a doctrine of a triune God who is simultaneously transcendent and immanent. Zizioulas's trinitarian ontology of personhood also suggests something equivalent to a paradigm shift in Orthodox theology, in that it affirms a more humble role for the traditional Eastern Christian category of God's 'energies.' Such a shift is especially evident in a comparative analysis of Lossky's and Zizioulas's Christology and creation theology.

The final chapter will critically compare Lossky's and Zizioulas's theologies of personhood. Given their own disagreements over the epistemological logic of divine-human communion, the two theologians construct theologies of personhood that are strikingly similar. For both theologians, the theological concept of 'person' as *ekstatic* and *hypostatic* emerged from the trinitarian discussions of the early church, though each gives distinct interpretations of the development of the concept. This chapter will continue reflection on the inherent tension between Lossky's apophaticism and theology of personhood. It will also illustrate how Zizioulas's understanding of the importance of the monarchy of the Father for theological personhood and his amplification of person as relation could be considered developments of Lossky's own theology of personhood, even though there is never an indication in Zizioulas's work of a reliance on Lossky. Zizioulas's own philosophical grounding of a relational notion of person will also be considered. It will analyze the philosophical undercurrent to Zizioulas's ontology of personhood, and examine the relation between philosophy and theology in his thought.

This chapter will also offer a critique of Zizioulas's theology of trinitarian personhood, especially his emphasis on the monarchy of the Father and its implications for 'freedom' within the life of God. I will offer suggestions for constructive resolutions to the problems inherent in his ontology of person that will draw in part on Lossky's understanding of the relation between *kenosis* and personhood.

Finally, I will conclude chapter four by looking at Lossky's and Zizioulas's patristic hermeneutic, i.e., at their use of the patristic texts in their theology, showing that both Lossky and Zizioulas construct a history of Eastern Christian thought that reflects their own theological emphases; for Lossky a theological apophaticism, and for Zizioulas a relational ontology of trinitarian personhood. Though I will not offer a thorough assessment of their interpretation of the fathers, of whether they 'get the fathers right,' a task well beyond the scope of this study and much better left in the hands of patristic scholars, I will argue that Lossky and Zizioulas are consistent with the Eastern patristic tradition. I will also examine the charge against both Lossky and Zizioulas that their theologies owe more to modern personalism and existentialism than patristic theology.

In the end, this book is a window into the state of contemporary Orthodox theology in that it attempts to make sense of the consensus and debate between two of the leading Orthodox theologians of the past century on the realism of divine-human communion. The whole of contemporary Orthodox theology of the past century is a tradition of consensus and debate over this central axiom. Insofar as my discussion on Lossky and Zizioulas's understanding of divine-human communion leads to their trinitarian theologies, this book also hopes to contribute to the larger, revived discussion on trinitarian theology. Both Lossky and Zizioulas, quite rightly I would argue, remind us that the doctrine of the Trinity emerges in the Christian attempt to give expression to the realism of divine-human communion in Jesus Christ by the power of the Holy Spirit. In spite of their differences, these theologians challenge much contemporary trinitarian theology that misses this 'point' of the doctrine of the Trinity. Their thought is a resource for the never-ending reflection on the God who is transcendent, but who in transcending all things is not the remote God, but rather the God who is everywhere present and fills all things.

chapter 1

Ontology and Theological Epistemology

Since the seventeenth century, theology has dealt with, and often obsessed over, the question of epistemology. Challenges by modern thought to traditional Christian notions of revelation and knowledge of God have compelled some Christian theologians to give an account for how a revelation from God or 'knowledge' of God, either revelatory or natural, is possible, and whether these concepts are still meaningful. In modern theological discourse, epistemology usually precedes ontology and usually determines whether so-called ontological questions are relevant.

For Vladimir Lossky and John Zizioulas, however, the reverse is the case; an ontology of divine-human communion is the basis for their understandings of theological epistemology. Both also agree that *real* knowledge of God is experiential. This shared starting point, however, leads to two, somewhat mutually incompatible, theological epistemologies. In turn, their theological epistemologies shape the content of their theologies and, hence, the form of their theological ontologies.

It should come as no surprise to the theologically literate that as Eastern Orthodox theologians Lossky and Zizioulas share a methodological commitment to thinking within a particular tradition, which means to draw on the patristic writings of the tradition. Both theologians locate themselves within the movement in contemporary Eastern Orthodoxy which called for theology to return to the fathers of the church, or what Georges Florovsky coined as a "neo-patristic synthesis."[1] Lossky and Florovsky together can be considered founders of this movement, while Zizioulas considers himself a student of Florovsky.

The return to the fathers parallels the movement named *ressourcement*, which occurred within Roman Catholic theology of this century, associated with such notable twentieth-century Catholic theologians as Henri de Lubac, Jean Daniélou, Yves Congar, and Hans Urs von Balthasar.

The motivation for the return to the fathers was, in part, a reaction to existing trends within contemporary Orthodox theology. Lossky was reacting to Russian religious philosophy, best represented in the person of Sergius Bulgakov.[2] Russian religious philosophy, according to Lossky, was simply the Eastern Orthodox version of the intellectualization of theology that he thought was characteristic of Thomistic theology. The same could be said of Zizioulas's problems with his Greek predecessors and his ecumenical colleagues. As he sees it, "the German Protestant and Roman Catholic Universities of the last century acted as the pattern and the prototype in the establishment of the theological Faculties in the Universities of Athens and Salonica in Greece."[3] The structure of dogmatic manuals, such as those of Christos Androutsos and Panagiotes Trembelas, indicates the "Scholastic Captivity" of Orthodox theology in the early part of the century in which the content of Orthodox thought was determined by a "scholastic methodology."[4] For our purposes, Zizioulas's rejection of the theological content of these early manuals is not as important as his claim that a particular way of doing theology determines the content of theology. The problem with both Russian religious philosophy and the Greek Orthodox manuals of the twentieth century is that they give priority to reason over experience in theological epistemology. Such a priority for Zizioulas is inconsistent with the Eastern patristic approach to theology and is the source of substantial theological differences between Eastern and Western Christianity.[5]

The return to the Eastern patristic texts authoritative for Eastern Orthodox Christianity reveals that at the core of these texts is the principle of the realism of divine-human communion that theological models in Russian religious philosophy and Western 'scholasticism' cannot adequately express. The danger of such models, for both theologians, is that they tend to obfuscate the fact that at the core of theological discourse is this principle of the realism of divine-human communion. Both Lossky and Zizioulas agree, formally, that having such a principle at the center of theology led the Eastern patristic writers of the Orthodox tradition to do and think theology in ways that are mutually exclusive with Russian religious philosophy and Western 'scholasticm.'

To illustrate that the realism of divine-human communion is at the center of Eastern patristic theology, both Lossky and Zizioulas construct a history of

Eastern and Western patristic thought. This history, for both, has two trajectories. The first trajectory is what both interpret as the rationalization or intellectualization of theology, with the truth of theology understood in terms of reason. In this trajectory, both Lossky and Zizioulas draw a line from Justin Martyr through Clement of Alexandria, Origen, and Augustine. This particular movement within the tradition culminates in the scholasticism of Thomas Aquinas.[6]

The other trajectory is that which maintains at the center of theology the principle of the realism of divine-human communion. For both theologians, this trajectory begins with Ignatius and runs through Irenaeus, Athanasius, the Cappadocian fathers, Dionysius the Areopagite, Maximus the Confessor, John of Damascus, and Gregory Palamas. Irenaeus is the one who, according to both theologians, breaks with the Justin-Clement-Origen tradition by linking truth not with *nous* but with, according to Lossky, "the incorruptibility of eternal life,"[7] or, according to Zizioulas, the "incorruptibility of being."[8]

The differences between the two histories of Eastern and Western patristic thought are in terms of emphasis. For Lossky, the emphasis is on Dionysius and Gregory Palamas as the two great synthesizers of theological apophaticism and the essence/energies distinction, both demanded by a theology that attempts to express the realism of divine-human communion in the Incarnation. For Zizioulas, the emphasis is clearly on the Cappadocian fathers and their clarification of a trinitarian, relational ontology of personhood that is grounded in the eucharistic experience of God in Christ by the power of the Holy Spirit, an experience that he attempts to trace back to an early Christian eucharistic consciousness.

The core, however, of both their theological systems remains an ontology of divine-human communion and each theologian interprets the implications of this ontology for theological epistemology differently. For Lossky, an ontology of divine-human communion results in a theological epistemology that is apophatic and an understanding of theology as 'antinomic' that is rooted in the very being of God, which itself is a being-in-antinomy insofar as God is simultaneously transcendent and immanent. For Zizioulas, divine-human communion is experienced in the eucharistic Body of Christ by the power of the Holy Spirit and, as such, is a communion with the personal being of God. Their shared presupposition of an ontology of divine-human communion does not preclude the development of distinct understandings of the nature and locus of experiential knowledge of God and, more importantly, of the degree to which God is known.

Lossky's Apophaticism

Incarnation as Revelation

Revelation is, according to Lossky, the condition for the possibility of knowledge of God. The meaning of revelation, however, is a source of controversy in theology both in terms of its possibility and its content. For Lossky, knowledge of God in terms of revelation means that in order for humans to know God, God must take the initiative. Humans cannot know God unless God allows such knowledge to be possible.[9]

Such knowledge requires that God reveal Godself. This revealing, according to Lossky, may assume many forms, each of which entails an encounter between humans and God. The type of revelation determines the degree of knowledge. For example, creation is a revelation of God in which, among other things, humans learn of God's goodness. *The* revelation of God occurs in the incarnate Christ, who makes known God's trinitarian being and makes possible a deeper knowledge of God through union with God. It is not simply a revelation of God but "the revelation of God the Holy Trinity—the Father, Son and Holy Spirit," that forms "the basis of all Christian theology; it is, indeed, theology itself, in the sense in which that word was understood by the Greek fathers, for whom theology most commonly stood for the mystery of the Trinity revealed to the Church."[10] This type of revelation, however, would not be possible if it were not for the Incarnation, which, for Lossky, makes "theology possible."[11] The Incarnation reveals God as Trinity as "a primordial fact,"[12] i.e., a word or proclamation about God's being. The Incarnation, however, is more than revelation as descriptive information about God's being. It is the event of the giving of God's very being in creation, of divine-human communion. As such, the Incarnation is the starting point of all theology, but also the *telos* of all theological discourse. The Incarnation makes possible a theology that does not simply state facts, but expresses a mystery in order to lead one toward a deeper union with God as Trinity.

This understanding of the Incarnation as the event of divine-human communion, as both the starting point and end of all theological discourse, leads necessarily for Lossky to two types of knowledge of God, *cataphatic* and *apophatic*. Cataphatic knowledge, in its simplest terms, is positive knowledge of God. An example of cataphatic knowledge is the affirmation "God is good." Apophatic knowledge is negative knowledge of God; it is knowledge of God in terms of what God is not. For example, God is not a stone. The significance of the two types of knowledge for Lossky are not what they say about God, for even apophatic theology is a kind of saying something about God, but their role as means to what is considered the only real knowledge of God, which is union with God's very life. One could read Lossky as saying that the only legitimate forms of knowledge in light of the Incarnation are cataphatic and apophatic theologies, since they are the only means to union with God. Since the history of theology has seen a variety of understandings of revelation and knowledge of God in light of the Incarnation, it remains to be seen how Lossky argues for the priority of cataphatic and apophatic theologies and how, in fact, his particular interpretation of the Incarnation as the event of divine-human communion leads necessarily to cataphatic and apophatic theologies as means toward union with God. Lossky's arguments are interwoven in his retrieval of two important Greek patristic figures, Dionysius the Areopagite and Gregory Palamas.

Cataphatic and Apophatic Theologies

Dionysius the Areopagite has enjoyed somewhat of a revival in recent contemporary theology, due in no small part to recent interest in apophaticism.[13] Very early in Lossky's career, however, Dionysius was a prominent figure in Lossky's work. His first major publications focused on the thought of Dionysius, who remained central to Lossky's thinking throughout his life.[14] It is unclear why Lossky turned to Dionysius early in his career. What is clear is that from the beginning and throughout his life Lossky was determined to offer an alternative interpretation of Dionysius than the prevailing Thomistic and neo-thomistic interpretations of the time. What is also clear is that Lossky attempted to establish the thought of Dionysius as pivotal to the Greek patristic emphasis on *theosis,* or divine-human communion, and to the understanding of *theosis* in terms of the divine energies of God. Evident throughout Lossky's analysis of Dionysius is his own concern to affirm the centrality of divine-human communion in theological discourse and his understanding of cataphatic and apophatic theologies in light of divine-human communion.

The thought of Dionysius represents for Lossky the clearest and most coherent expression of the insights of the earlier patristic texts with regard to the question of knowledge of God. Lossky is also quick to emphasize that Dionysius's synthesis is christological and not neo-platonic.[15] Its foundation is not the neo-platonic understanding of the One but the unity of the created and the uncreated in the person of Christ.

Lossky further stresses that his interpretation of Dionysius is in sharp contrast to that of 'Western' thinkers, especially Thomas Aquinas.[16] This contrast is especially clear in the Areopagite's understanding of 'negative theology,' which Lossky argues is not simply a corrective to the *via eminentia,* but an attitude of the mind resulting in a knowledge of the God beyond being. Referring to Dionysius's use of cataphatic and apophatic theology, Lossky asserts that "this is not the way of eminence, whose outlines can be found in Middle Platonism—the way towards which Thomas Aquinas wished to channel the Areopagite's apophasis in order to restore an affirmed signification to God, denying merely the human mode of signifying Him. *Dionysius's negations triumph over affirmations.*"[17] Thomas attempts, according to Lossky, "a synthesis of the two opposed ways" of knowing, in order to

> bring them together as a single method of knowing God. It is thus that St. Thomas Aquinas reduces the two ways of Dionysius to one, making negative theology a corrective to affirmative theology. In attributing to God the perfections that we find in created beings, we must (according to St. Thomas) deny the mode according to which we understand these finite perfections, but we may affirm them in relation to God *modo sublimiari.* Thus, negations correspond to the *modus significandi,* to the always inaccurate means of expression; affirmation to the *res significata,* to the perfection which we wish to express, which is in God after another fashion than it is in creatures. *We may indeed ask how far this very ingenious philosophical invention corresponds to the thought of Dionysius.*[18]

In the background of Lossky's own reading of Dionysius lies what Lossky would describe as the traditional 'Western' one, which is primarily a Thomistic reading and one that he attempts to refute.

What will become clear from his analysis of Dionysius is Lossky's own theological agenda. For Lossky, divine-human communion is the center of all theological discourse and the central significance of the Incarnation. Lossky's theology is thus christologically grounded, but in a particular understanding of Jesus Christ as the person in whom is realized the event of divine-human communion. The realism of divine-human communion in Christ leads necessarily to cataphatic and apophatic forms of theologies. According to Lossky both apophatic and cataphatic theologies are "implied in the paradox of the Christian revelation: the transcendent God becomes immanent in the world, but in the very immanence of His economy. . . . He reveals Himself as transcendent, as ontologically independent of all created being."[19] Cataphatic and apophatic forms of theology are rooted in God's very being as transcendent to and immanent in created being. These forms of theologies are given their clearest explication, according to Lossky, in the thought of Dionysius. In order, then, to understand Lossky's arguments for the priority of cataphatic and apophatic theologies, and what he means by these forms of knowledge, it is necessary to look at his analysis of Dionysius, realizing throughout that this analysis reflects much of Lossky's own theological presuppositions.[20]

Cataphatic theology for Dionysius is a positive form of knowledge of God. As a form of knowledge, it expresses itself through divine names or the names of God. According to Lossky, Dionysius's *Divine Names* is a treatise arguing for the possibility of naming God. He adds that the basis for Dionysius's understanding of cataphatic theology and the condition for its possibility lie in a particular understanding of an *ekstatic* God who transcends being, but in whose very transcendence is immanent in the incarnate Christ, "the central event of revelation."[21]

In a sense, cataphatic theology is one side of the Incarnational coin, the side of immanence. It is the form of theology that gives expression to the positive form of knowledge given in the Incarnation. The flip side is the transcendence of God, the affirmation that God is simultaneously unknowable. In contemporary Eastern Orthodox theology the simultaneity of God's transcendence and immanence, of the God who is both known and unknown, is expressed in the well-known essence/energies distinction. God is unknowable in God's essence, which is really "*hyper*-essence" to express its transcendence beyond any created essence, beyond being. God, however, is also knowable or immanent to creation through God's energies. The essence/energies distinction is rooted in the realism of divine-human communion in Christ and expresses the God who is transcendent and immanent. According to Lossky, this distinction, though present in the tradition from the beginning, is first given its clearest expression in the thought of Dionysius. And it is the presence of the energies of God in creation and in the Incarnation that allows for the possibility of cataphatic theology.

Lossky identifies the two terms that Dionysius uses to discuss the energies of God as *proodoi* or *dunameis*. This distinction is based on a prior one between the 'unions' (*enoseis*) and the 'distinctions' (*diakriseis*) in God. "The 'unions' are . . . the superessential nature of God" that remain eternally inaccessible. As Lossky clarifies, "[t]he 'distinctions,' on the other hand, are the processions (*proodoi*) beyond Himself, His manifestations (*ekphanseis*), which Dionysius also calls virtues or forces (*dunameis*), in which everything that exists partakes, thus making God known in His creatures."[22] Though the literal meaning of these two categories means 'going forth' or 'powers,' Lossky often refers to them as 'energies' or *energia*.[23] By doing this, he is identifying Dionysius's two categories with the notion of 'energies' that received its clearest and most developed expression in the thought of Gregory Palamas, and which has become, in no small part due to Lossky's influence, the central category in contemporary Eastern Orthodox theology for expressing divine-human communion. Throughout his work, Lossky is attempting to link the thought of all the Eastern patristic writers, but especially that of Dionysius and Gregory Palamas. He is intent on showing that Dionysius's *dunameis* is equivalent in meaning to Gregory's *energia,* and that both are grounded in the centrality of divine-human communion for theological discourse.

The concept of the energies of God is not difficult to grasp. It basically means the activity of God as opposed to the essence of God.[24] It implies that God is not a static essence or a motionless 'what.' The *proodoi* or *dunameis* of God, to use Dionysius's language, are the activity of God. They indicate a going forth of God outside Godself toward an other. The created cosmos is the product of this activity of God and is the activity of God insofar as it participates in the *proodoi* of God. This participation, however, does not imply an emanationism or a necessary link between God and creation. The *proodoi* are eternal, but creation is contingent since it is based on God's freedom. Created being is a product of the divine *proodoi* and, in order to exist, must participate in these *proodoi.*

If creation is a product of God's free activity and participates in the energies of God, then it manifests something real about God. The possibility for cataphatic theology results from the fact that creation itself participates in the energies of God, which are God. The type of knowledge depends on the degree of participation. As thought, through reflection on creation, produces names for the sake of knowledge, it is also able to name God through reflection on God's glory manifested in creation. Such names as goodness, wisdom, and life indicate something real in God without exhausting who God is. Thus human reasoning has a positive role according to Lossky in Dionysian epistemology. Cataphatic theology is like a ladder whose steps are "images or ideas intended to guide and to fit our faculties for contemplation of that which transcends all understanding."[25] The problem for Lossky is not so much the role of thought and positive theology, but the failure to recognize the limits of thought in the face of the Incarnation.

Cataphatic theology does not end with reflection on creation. Lossky often says that the revelation of the Holy Trinity is the "summit of cataphatic theology."[26] He adds that "The Incarnate Word represents the fullness of the divine manifestation and the summit of all the theophanies in creation . . . being, thus, the foundation of cataphatic theology."[27] These two statements, though seemingly contradictory, are in fact complementary. The Incarnation is the summit of cataphatic theology insofar as it reveals the fact that God is Trinity.[28] For Lossky there is no clearer proof that Dionysius's system is christologically grounded than in the latter's affirming Trinity as the primary name of God.[29] Unlike the Good, Being, or the One, Trinity is a name which lies beyond thought and can only be known through revelation. It is the name that surpasses all names in that it indicates the very being of God as both one and many, as transcendent and immanent. It is ultimately this name that one must contemplate in order to attain the highest possible knowledge of God.

Cataphatic theology is thus, for Lossky, a real possibility because of the initiative of God in creation and in the Incarnation. The Incarnation reveals that God is a knowable God who comes toward creation in order to be known. Creation is itself a product of the going forth of God from Godself toward an other that is the product of God's own energies. Real, positive knowledge of God is possible because these energies are God. The Incarnation is the summit of cataphatic theology in revealing the fact of the trinitarian God. With cataphatic theology, Dionysius affirms, according to Lossky, the positive side of the theology of Clement of Alexandria and Origen; not, however, without the caution of the Cappadocians. Much more clearly than the Cappadocians, Dionysius affirms the real content of divine names, while affirming the limits of names and of thought that produces the names. To cataphatic theology one must add apophatic theology, which prevents cataphatic theology from becoming idolatrous.

That the most perfect form of knowledge is ignorance is one way of expressing Lossky's affirmation that apophatic theology is not a denial of any knowledge of God, but a form of knowing itself. This second form of knowledge of God has for Dionysius "a greater perfection" than cataphatic theology.[30] Paradoxically, "the ignorance (agnosia) to which it leads would be higher than science."[31] Unlike cataphatic theology, which as science discerns a positive knowledge of God through reflection on created being, apophatic theology leads to an ignorance more superior than cataphatic theology. To understand this argument, attention must be given to Lossky's distinction, more implied than stated, between apophatic theology and the apophatic method in theology. Apophatic method is the negation of all positive names of God based on the affirmation that God is beyond being and thus beyond all positive knowledge, which is inherently linked to being. Apophatic theology is the fruit of such an exercise in the form of an *ekstatic* union with God beyond affirmation or negation, beyond being itself.

Where does the negation begin? According to Lossky, Dionysius's *Mystical Theology* directs the negation to begin with those names of God that are least likely to express God's nature. Apophatic theology in itself is a process of knowing God by affirming what God is not. For example, God is not a rock. In eliminating those names one begins the assent in isolating those names which more closely express positive knowledge of God. Accompanying this negation is contemplation because in the process of negation one is contemplating the appropriateness of names vis-à-vis God and thus contemplating God. The more appropriate the names, the higher the contemplation. One negates a set of names in order to ascend to names that are more appropriate and thus a higher form of knowledge. In its reliance on names, apophatic theology relies on cataphatic theology. In contemplating the names of God, given through reason and Scripture, one must both affirm the name and negate it. For example, to negate the name Good in relation to God is not to affirm that God is not Good. Such a negation admits that the concept of Good is inexorably linked to thought, which is itself linked to created being. To negate the name is to affirm that God lies beyond being, and thus beyond thought. Though the contemplation of names brings one closer to God, ultimately one must go beyond contemplation to union, the highest possible knowledge of God. Union is not contemplation, and therefore it lies beyond names which are linked to thought. The goal of apophaticism is not to conclude that nothing can be known of God; it is rather to propel the aspiring Christian to a deeper union, which lies beyond being and thus beyond thought. Such a union is the highest form of knowledge, which is not a knowledge per se since knowledge is strictly linked to created being. Such a union is paradoxically an 'unknowing' or ignorance, both of which are understood metaphorically to affirm a form of knowledge which lies beyond thought.

One way to clarify Lossky's understanding of apophatic theology is to examine his interpretation of Dionysius on this subject and how he distinguishes Dionysius from earlier forms of apophaticism, particularly that of Origen and Augustine. For Origen and his Alexandrian predecessor, Clement, negative theology had a positive ring to it. Lossky argues that both are closer to Plotinus. The result of this apophaticism for Clement is to deny any positive content to divine names; the purpose of this apophaticism for Origen is to reject "any notion obstructing the knowledge of the divine nature defined positively as the *One*."[32] Lossky sees Origen's naming of God as "One" as resulting in an apophaticism in the service of cataphaticism. The latter becomes superior to the former, especially when, as with Origen, the locus for the encounter with God is *nous*. For Lossky, neither theology should be prioritized since both are necessary for union with the God who is beyond distinctions, beyond opposites.

Similarly, Augustine's use of apophaticism, Lossky argues, does not deny a positive knowledge of God's essence. It takes on the form of "learned ignorance" for Augustine: "if no one is permitted to know God as He is, *ut est*, it is equally true that no one can be ignorant of His existence: God is a mystery but He is revealed to all, *ubique secretus, ubique publicus (Enarr. in Ps. 74)*."[33] The problem for both Origen and Augustine is that apophaticism is limited and fails to negate any link between God and created being. Dionysian apophaticism is based on different theological presuppositions insofar as, for Dionysius, God is beyond being. This difference is made clear in Augustine's notion of "spiritual touching," which, although it excludes comprehension, "is not the transcendence of a thought in mystical ignorance 'beyond the intellect.'"[34] Though both Augustine and Dionysius draw a "line of demarcation" between the Trinity and "its created effects," the difference lies in Dionysius's insisting on "the 'superessential' character of the Thearchy, whereas St. Augustine saw the excellence of 'Being-itself.'"[35]

Lossky's criticism of Origen's and Augustine's understanding of apophaticism is part of a broader critique of what Lossky considers 'Western' understandings of apophaticism, in which he includes the thought of Thomas and his interpreters. One could almost read Lossky as defining the difference between 'Western' and 'Eastern' Christian approaches to theology by their different understandings of apophaticism, seen in the 'West' primarily in the thought of Augustine and Aquinas, and in the 'East' in the thought of Dionysius and Gregory Palamas. As it will become clear, however, it is not, for Lossky, simply about apophaticism but about the nature and goal of theology itself. Origen's and Augustine's, and also Aquinas's, understanding of apophaticism in the service of cataphatic theology betrays what Lossky describes as a rational approach to theology, which understands knowledge of God in terms of ideas and propositions. According to Lossky, this understanding of apophaticism and, hence, theology, does not get beyond the created intellect and, thus, creation itself. It falls short of real knowledge of God, which is nothing less than full union with the God who is beyond all being. Union with God, however, is union with that which is 'other' to created being, which means that God must be beyond being, ontologically distinct from creation itself. Thus, union with God implies a transcendence, but not obliteration, of all that is created, including created intellect, toward communion with the radically transcendent God. The God who is beyond all being is radically transcendent to creation, but in whose radical transcendence is radically immanent to creation. For this reason, apophaticism cannot simply be a corrective to positive forms of knowledge, but an affirmation of the inadequacy of all forms of positive knowledge of God. For Lossky, apophaticism does not lead to agnosticism, but is a kind of necessary spiritual exercise to avoid complacency with 'rational' knowledge of God that keeps one within the sphere of the created. Apophaticism is thus the logical consequence of the notion of knowledge of the God who is radically 'other' to created being, since knowledge of this God can only be a form of union in which creation itself is transcended, but not obliterated, toward a communion with that which is beyond creation, and hence, beyond being.[36]

Knowledge as Union

Lossky describes knowledge in the form of union with God as an 'unknowing.' It is neither a negation of the apophatic and cataphatic forms of knowledge, nor is it a type of agnosticism. It is an affirmation of both cataphatic and apophatic theologies in that both are necessary means to achieve union. God is both good and non-good in that God transcends both the Good and the not-Good, a state of being which Dionysius refers to as *hyperagathos*. Humans can know that God is good by virtue of the energies of God, which descend toward created existence. But since God is beyond being in that God is uncreated, and since the name 'Good' is a product of thought which is linked to being, the name Good is both applicable and non-applicable to God. The tension is meant to preclude *stasis* or rest in conceptual understandings of God and to maintain the momentum of *kinesis* (movement) toward God.

The goal is not so much knowledge or the lack of knowledge as it is participation that leads to union. In this sense, apophatic theology for Lossky is not simply the negation of the positive predicate, for this negation still lies within the realm of thought and, hence, finite existence. The ascent toward union requires a negation of the negation, a *hyper*-negation,[37] to the God who is beyond all affirmations and all negations. As Lossky himself puts it, "the uncreated surpasses all oppositions, notably those of the intelligible and the sensible, of the temporal and the eternal."[38] Apophatic theology, then, for Lossky, is not simply about the 'transcendence' of God. Yes, apophatic theology is about negating positive affirmations about God to assert this transcendence from all forms of human knowing. But, insofar as negation is a necessary means in the ascent toward union, and insofar as the *hyper*-negation of the negation toward the God leads one to the experience beyond all affirmations and negations, then apophatic theology is also about God's radical immanence to all things created. What the notion of *hyper*-negation signifies is the antinomy between cataphatic and apophatic theology, the necessity of always keeping them together and of seeing them as mutually conditioning each other. It is, thus, not accurate to say that cataphatic theology is simply about God's immanence while apophatic theology is simply about God's transcendence; each, always in relation to the other, is about the simultaneity of both God's immanence and transcendence, about God's ever-present presence and absence.[39]

Union with God is not knowledge of God as an object but an experience of God, a mystical experience that surpasses all understanding and description. This does not, however, keep Christian thinkers such as Dionysius and Lossky from attempting to describe the nature of such a union. The analysis of Lossky's interpretation of Dionysius makes clear that for Lossky knowledge in terms of union is non-intellectual. Gone from Dionysius, according to Lossky, is any "trace of Origen's spiritualism. It is the whole man, not just the spirit or intellect (*nous*), who enters into communion with God."[40] Knowledge of God lies beyond the mind. The Dionysian understanding of God as non-being determines the nature of thought. Theology grounds epistemology. The fact that God is uncreated means that God is transcendent and, hence, ontologically distinct from the created realm, which is the realm of being. The distinction between non-being in Dionysius parallels, or rather, is identical to the uncreated/created distinction in Athanasius of Alexandria and the Cappadocian fathers. If mind or *nous* is created, then its sphere of activity is linked to the created realm or the realm of being. Thus mind's knowledge is that of being, and for this reason, "The particular character of Dionysian theology consists in the principal fact that for Dionysius the pseudo-Areopagite God is not an object, much less an object of knowledge, as he would be for St. Thomas and for all other scholastic theologians."[41] This last sentence is indicative of Lossky's attitude toward the 'Western' understandings of knowledge of God, particularly that of Thomas Aquinas and the neo-scholastics of Lossky's own time.

Lossky sees 'Western' thinkers as isolating the locus for the union with God in the *nous*, and ultimately continuing the mistakes of Clement, Origen, and Evagrius. For Lossky, this understanding misreads Dionysius for whom union lies beyond the *nous*. For Dionysius, "[a]ll knowledge refers to that which is; it is limited to that which is." Knowledge (la connaissance) is linked to mind, whose sphere of activity is that which *is*. God is not an *is,* and therefore cannot be known fully by the *nous*. God is then "beyond all essence" and, thus, "is unknowable."[42]

Though he is not often consistent with his use of terms, inherent to this epistemology is the distinction between *gnosis* and "mystical experience."[43] For Lossky, *gnosis* (la gnose) is knowledge (la connaissance). It results from the activity of the mind. Throughout his work, Lossky contrasts this *gnosis* with "l'expérience mystique." He does not define "experience" other than to distinguish it from *gnosis*. His main use of the term is to indicate that union with God is not an intellectual knowing that results in *gnosis,* knowledge of created being. God lies beyond being and, thus, God is experienced in a union that remains inexpressible. Such a union involves the whole person, not simply the mind. It is an experience where both "knowledge and love" are one, where both the intellectual and affective aspects of the human person are united in union with God.[44] Since the experience is "unutterable"[45] no further definition of "experience" can be given. The category, like others which related to God's being, is shrouded in an apophatic cloud. It is used simply to distinguish union with God from intellectual knowledge and to indicate that union is beyond being and, hence, beyond intellect.

Since *nous* is limited, the approach to God requires an "apophatic attitude." As Lossky himself explains, "apophaticism is an attitude of the mind which refuses to form concepts about God."[46] Moreover,

> the existence of an apophatic attitude—of a going beyond everything that has a connection with created finitude—is implied in the paradox of the Christian revelation: the transcendent God becomes immanent in the world, but in the very immanence of His economy, which leads to the incarnation and to death on the cross, He reveals Himself as transcendent, as ontologically independent of all created being.[47]

This apophatic attitude forms the basis for the negative way or method that "eliminates all positive attributes of the object it wishes to attain, in order to culminate finally in a kind of apprehension by supreme ignorance of Him who cannot be an object of knowledge."[48] It is the revelation of the Trinity through the Incarnation that "forces us to appeal to apophatic theology in order to rid ourselves of concepts proper to human thought, transforming them into steps by which we may ascend to the contemplation of reality which the created intelligence cannot contain."[49]

On the part of the human being such a union requires a transcendence or an *ekstasis* of the limits of nature, including the limits of *nous*.[50] Created being is marked by limits and finitude. To unite with the uncreated means to transcend the limits of created being in an *ekstatic* union with God. *Ekstasis* (extase) is the going beyond, the transcending of the limits of one's nature in order to unite with the divine. Union with God through "the knowledge of the divine energies . . . is not possible in our present state of being other than in ecstasy, by the abandonment of all created things and even of oneself."[51]

Lossky qualifies his use of this concept of *ekstasis*. First, the Dionysian notion is, according to Lossky, different from that of Plotinus, for whom *ekstasis* results in "a reduction of being to absolute simplicity."[52] This Plotinian understanding of *ekstasis* also puts into sharper relief the differences between the two thinkers on negative theology. For Dionysius, negative theology preserves multiplicity, distinction, and otherness since negating does not mean eliminating, but transcending toward a higher union in which unity and diversity exist simultaneously. Dionysius, according to Lossky, goes so far as to admit that the superessence of God is one of unities (*enoseis*) and distinction (*diakriseis*). For Plotinus what is discarded "in the negative way . . . is multiplicity, and we arrive at the perfect unity which is beyond being—since being is linked with multiplicity and is subsequent to the One."[53] It is Plotinus's emphasis on the One that leads him to "describe his ecstasy by a name which is very characteristic: that of 'simplification' (*aplosis*)."[54] But the Dionysian God, according to Lossky, is not a One, but Trinity, "which teaches us that God is neither one nor many but that He transcends this antinomy, being unknowable in what He is."[55] As such, union with God is not an absorption into God, a depersonalization into the One, but a personal communion with Trinity, in whom multiplicity coexists with unity.

Although Lossky describes such a union with God as an 'unknowing' in order to emphasize its non-intellectual character, he resists Dionysian metaphors of 'darkness' to describe the union.[56] Here Lossky draws on the thought of Gregory Palamas,[57] whom he shows as departing from Dionysius when discussing the nature of the mystical experience with God, which he describes in terms of 'light' metaphors. Lossky interprets this difference not as substantive, but as a necessary clarification of a Dionysian insight. According to Lossky, 'darkness' would give way to 'light,' especially in late Byzantine thought. Although 'darkness' was used to express the paradoxical nature of union as knowledge-in-ignorance, and to express the fact that such knowledge consists in union with the God beyond created being, it would be used in later patristic literature to express the incomprehensibility of God's essence, the unknowable character of the divine union.[58] This shift does not necessarily betray the thought of Dionysius and other patristic writers who use 'darkness' metaphors.

The Palamite concept of 'light,' more specifically, 'uncreated light,' is clearly the more appropriate, Lossky argues, for understanding the mystical experience with God. It conveys more precisely that union with God, or mystical experience, is a type of knowing. Lossky follows Palamas's own distinction between three kinds of light required for knowing: the perceptual, the intellectual, and the uncreated.[59] There is the light necessary for perception; there is also a higher light needed for the higher truths of reason, which Lossky refers to as the intellectual light. But the truth of God, the mystical experience, is not one of sensual or intellectual light. The 'uncreated' aspect of the divine light is meant to indicate that this light is beyond being, and as such, is neither intellectual nor sensual. Lossky also emphasizes that the experience of such a light involves the whole person. That it is 'uncreated' follows the logic of an early patristic axiom that declares "what is not assumed is not saved." Salvation is not a matter of the body or the intellect, but of the whole person. Insofar as salvation is knowledge it is an experience of light; insofar as it is knowledge of God, this light must be uncreated and beyond being.

More strongly, Lossky asserts that the experience of the 'uncreated light' is not simply meant metaphorically or analogically; such an experience is 'real' and meant literally. The experience is literally an experience of the uncreated light. As Lossky himself puts it, "it is a datum of the mystical experience."[60] Moreover, the vision of the uncreated light is a vision of the last days, of the eschaton. Indeed, the uncreated light is the eschaton. To experience the uncreated light is to experience the 'eighth day,' a moment beyond time and space.[61] Theology is, in the end, an anagogical exercise. It leads the human person upward toward God and makes possible a proleptic experience of the eschaton.

Essence/Energies Distinction

It is evident from his discussion of the nature of mystical union with God that a non-negotiable axiom of theological discourse for Lossky is the realism of human communion with the divine life, or divine-human communion. Mystical union with God is real union and communion with the divine life, with God's very being and nothing less. The realism of divine-human communion is, on the one hand, an affirmation of God's immanence, i.e., the reality of God's presence in and with created being. On the other hand, it is a union with the transcendent God, the God beyond created being, including the created intellect. Mystical union with God is thus the paradoxical event of real communion with the transcendent God who is ontologically 'other' than created being. Cataphatic and apophatic theologies are grounded in and have as their goal this union with the transcendent and immanent God. The challenge for theology is how to conceptualize this divine-human communion with the God who is simultaneously transcendent and immanent.

For Lossky, the Eastern patristic tradition has met this challenge with the essence/energies distinction. One cannot overemphasize the importance of this distinction to contemporary Eastern Orthodox theology, employed by most well-known contemporary Orthodox theologians.[62] According to Lossky's reading of the history of Eastern patristic thought, it is a distinction that is present from the very beginning, which receives further clarification in the thought of Dionysius with his distinction between *enoseis* and *proodoi*, but is given a kind of doctrinal precision in the thought of Gregory Palamas. Palamas did so in the fourteenth century in attempting to refute the Calabrian monk Barlaam, who denied the realism of divine-human communion.[63] Barlaam provoked Palamas to defend "the very essence of the tradition of the Christian East."[64] In fact, "far from being the author of a new doctrine," Palamas "is only a witness of this Tradition, as are, for example, Sts. Athanasius the Great, Basil the Great, Gregory of Nazianzus or Maximus the Confessor."[65]

The impulse to defend this distinction, Lossky argues, stems from Palamas's unwillingness to compromise the Eastern patristic notion of deification. It was "a dogmatic basis for *union with God* which impelled the Eastern Church to formulate her teaching on the distinction between God's essence and His energies."[66] More importantly than the essence/energies distinction, Palamas shares with his predecessors the idea of union with God in terms of a *real* communion between the created and the uncreated. The essence/energies distinction is made necessary in order to protect the *real* character of communion with God, by which Lossky means union of the whole person with the uncreated God.

For the opponents, both in the Middle Ages and in the twentieth century,[67] of the notion of the uncreated energies of God, the distinction made no sense. The problem does not lie with admitting of a communication of God, since creation itself, not to mention the Incarnation, is indicative of such a communication. Agreement would also exist that such a communication is not of God's essence since this constitutes creation as divine and that such a communication is the activity of God. The question lies in the uncreated or created character of such activity. Those who reject the notion of the uncreated character of divine energies would argue that if God's activity is uncreated then what is communicated is God's very essence, and this would obliterate the distinction between uncreated and created essence, a distinction at the heart of Christian ontology. If God's essence is incommunicable, then the activity of God toward creation is itself created. According to Lossky, at stake was a

> philosophical notion of divine simplicity when they affirm the perfect identity of the essence and the energy of God. When they speak of operations and energies as distinct from the essence, they are thinking of created effects of the divine essence. Their notion of God admits of nothing but an essential existence for divinity. What is not the essence itself does not belong to the divine being, is not God. Therefore the energies must be either identified with the essence or separated from it completely as actions which are external to it, i.e. as created effects having the essence as their cause.[68]

Such is the net result when "a rationalistic doctrine of causality is introduced into the doctrine of grace."[69]

To this argument, Lossky, following Palamas, poses the dilemma that if God's energies are not uncreated, either the essence is communicated which results not in deification but absorption, or created existence participates in something less than divine.[70] In either case, there is no real deification that consists of a *real* communion with the divine without an annihilation of the integrity of creation. The question still exists, however, how created existence is, in fact, "created" when it is a product of divine energies that are uncreated. The logical inconsistency notwithstanding, the distinction falls within the bounds of and is demanded by "piety."[71] Barlaam's defense of divine simplicity starts "from a philosophical concept of essence, leads finally to conclusions which are inadmissible for practical piety and contrary to the tradition of the Eastern Church."[72] It is validated doxologically, in that the soteriological principle of deification is a praise of the love of God toward creation.

Lossky further argues that the essence/energies distinction does not obliterate divine simplicity. The difference lies in understanding the divine simplicity by the logic of deification. The essence/energies distinction does not separate or divide God. It is not a distinction that leads to a separation.[73] Unlike the neo-platonic view, God is not diminished in God's natural processions outside the essence.[74] God is *in* the energies and the energies *are* God. Since the energies are God, God is not divided. The energies are simply a distinct mode of existence. Lossky explains that "essence and energies are not, for Palamas, two parts of God, as some modern critics still imagine, but two different *modes of existence* of God, within His nature and outside His nature, the same God remains totally inaccessible in His essence—and communicates himself totally by grace."[75] The essence and energies of God are two modes of God's existence that do not divide the one existence of God, i.e., the divine simplicity.

This explanation did not satisfy Palamas's opponents nor subsequent generations. The main objection is its pantheistic overtones. If the energies are God, then everything is God. If everything is not God, then the energies are less than God. It would be incorrect to characterize the essence/energies distinction as illogical, for the paradoxical nature of the distinction is grounded in the paradoxical event of divine-human communion. It does seem, however, to violate a basic principle of logic, the law of non-contradiction. For Lossky, however, theological discourse, insofar as it attempts to express the realism of divine-human communion, should not be limited by formal rules of logic, whose adequacy may extend to created being but not to the event of divine-human communion with the transcendent God who is beyond being. It becomes clear that for Lossky the essence/energies distinction is "antinomic," used to conceptualize the antinomic reality of divine-human communion and the God who is transcendent and immanent. Deification leads necessarily to antinomy. The distinction then is one that is grounded in the very being of God, and theology, insofar as it attempts to express this being, which is beyond being (essence) and radically immanent (energies), must be antinomic.

Theology as Antinomy

On the margins of the debate over the Palamite notion of divine energies is a different understanding of the relation between theology and philosophy. According to Lossky, there are "two kinds of theology." The first, characteristic of Barlaam and with obvious references to Thomas and his interpreters, sees "in God an eminently simple object, narrows all possible knowledge about the attributes of God to this primordial simplicity, by reason of which the nature of God can be known only by means of analogies."[76] Here philosophy supersedes theology, according to Lossky, and the God of the philosophers replaces the God of revelation.

The other type of theology is "antinomic theology which proceeds by oppositions of contrary but true propositions." Theology then, for Lossky, seeks not to eliminate what he would understand as contradictions within philosophical discourse. If theology ultimately attempts to express a God who is immanent and transcendent and is the condition for the possibility for communion between two distinct ontological realities, then it must be in both form and content 'antinomic.' Lossky adds,

> the goal of this antinomic theology is not to forge a system of concepts, but to serve as a support for the human spirit in contemplation of divine mysteries. Every antinomic opposition of two true propositions gives way to a dogma, *i.e.* to a real distinction, although ineffable and unintelligible, which cannot be based on any concepts or deduced by a process of reasoning, since it is the expression of a reality of a religious order.[77]

Lossky's handling of the challenges to the incoherency of the essence/energies distinction illustrates further the meaning of an "antinomic theology." In response to the obvious question that if the energies of God are eternal and contain the full presence of God, how is creation not necessary or itself divine, Lossky would argue that this type of question results from the philosophical drive for logical consistency, which is at odds with the antinomic character of the Incarnation. In order to preserve the soteriological principle resulting from the Incarnation, God must be affirmed as both a knowable and unknowable God. The Incarnation demands an "antinomic theology which proceeds by oppositions of contrary but equally true propositions."[78] Put another way "the dialectic which governs the game of negations and affirmations" is defined as "an intellectual discipline of the non-opposition of opposites—a discipline which is proper for all discourse about true transcendence, the transcendence which remains 'unimaginable' for non-Christians."[79] The immanence and transcendence of God is an antinomic truth grasped by faith in a way reason cannot.[80] The activities of God make God knowable, but only if such activities are fully God. Yet at the same time, such activities do not make creation God since there are degrees of participation in the energies of God. The goal of salvation and the purpose of the Incarnation is to increase one's participation in these energies in order to penetrate further the divine mystery. To safeguard this mystery of participation in God's being, "one is forced to establish these distinctions . . . to safeguard the antinomy, to prevent the human spirit from being led astray, breaking the antinomy and falling then from the contemplation of divine mysteries into the platitude of rationalism, replacing living experience with concepts. The antinomy, on the contrary, raises the spirit from the realm of concepts to the concrete data of Revelation,"[81] i.e., the Trinity. Thus, the logical inconsistency implied in the Orthodox understanding of the essence/energies distinction is not without purpose. It protects the reality of the mystical experience in theological expression, and prevents the fall into rationalistic complacency that would preclude an ecstatic union with God.

The centrality of an ontology of divine-human communion is further evident in Lossky's rejection of the intellectualization of theological discourse in 'Western' theology, especially the thought of Thomas Aquinas and his interpreters.[82] This intellectualization of theological discourse lies behind the criticism of the Palamite notion of divine energies and is always in the background in Lossky's development of an apophatic epistemology. As early as the seventeenth century, the Jesuit scholar Denis Pétau referred to Palamas's doctrine of divine energies as "absurd," to which Lossky retorts that "it ought to be clearly recognized that it is his own interpretation of Palamas's doctrine of energies which is absurd."[83] More important to Lossky are the critiques by neo-Thomist theologians of his day, in particular M. Jugie and S. Guichardan.[84] Jugie comments on Palamas's notion of divine energies as "a doctrine which one might view as a punishment permitted by God, that has managed to be imposed as official dogma."[85] This criticism and what Lossky would describe as misinterpretation of Palamas stem from an understanding of theology as the attempt to rationally justify propositions of faith through the means of abstraction and formal logic. This understanding of theology and knowledge of God have their roots in the Christian East with Justin Martyr, Clement of Alexandria, Origen, and Evagrius and reach their climax in the Christian West in the thought of Thomas Aquinas. In this strand of intellectualization of theology within the Christian tradition, "[t]he God of the philosophers and savants is introduced into the heart of the living God."[86]

It would be a mistake, however, to see Lossky's criticism in terms of a protection of the turf of theology against the encroachments of philosophy, or as a radical fideism asserting a blind assent to revelation over reason. For Lossky, the problem with the intellectualization of theology is that it precludes *real* union with God, the goal of all theological discourse rooted in the Incarnation. It thus becomes clearer what Lossky means when he argues that in Thomism "a rationalistic doctrine of causality is introduced into the doctrine of grace."[87] The net result is that it reduces knowledge of God to human concepts.[88] For the God who is transcendent and immanent in the creation, this violates God's transcendence insofar as God becomes that which is necessary according to modes of human thought and logical discourse; it also leads to a God who is not immanent insofar as these modes of human thought and logical discourse are limited to created being and do not bridge the gap between the uncreated and the created. The intellectualization of theology, with the introduction of a "rationalistic doctrine of causality," leads necessarily to notions of created grace, which is something less than God.

The main problem with such an approach to theology is that it fails to establish as its first principle the realism of divine-human communion. It attempts to eliminate the paradoxical nature of the Incarnation when the very core of theology is this antinomy. If the very notion of divine-human communion, of the transcendent and immanent God, is antinomic, then theological discourse itself is grounded in the very being of God and must express, not eliminate, the antinomy. Hence, the necessity for both cataphatic and apophatic theologies to be held in a tension that is transcended in the being of God, and not simply for an apophatic corrective to cataphatic theology. The apophatic affirmation of the God who is beyond being is, ironically for Lossky, the only way to affirm that there can be real immanence in created being and, thus, the realism of divine-human communion. The essence/energies distinction is rooted in God's very being as transcendent and immanent revealed in the Incarnation itself. The distinction may seem incoherent in light of the rules of formal logic, but coheres perfectly with the logic of deification. Theological discourse is the attempt to give expression to the antinomy of the Incarnation and all that it reveals about God and God's relation to the world. Much is at stake for Lossky in theological discourse, and an apophatic epistemology for Lossky is what logically follows from the central axiom of divine-human communion. It is more important for existential concerns, insofar as the goal of theological discourse is to elevate one toward that which it attempts to express, *real* union with the divine life. The question is whether the fundamental presupposition of divine-human communion necessarily leads to a theological apophaticism. John Zizioulas, for one, does not seem to think that it does.

Zizioulas's Eucharistic Epistemology

When answering the question of knowledge of God, little separates Zizioulas and Lossky formally. As with Lossky, the revelation of God is, for Zizioulas, the beginning of Christian theological discourse. Lossky and Zizioulas essentially agree that *real* knowledge of God is communion with the living God made possible through the Incarnation of God in Jesus Christ, and that such an experience is not simply a future hope but a present possibility.

Lossky and Zizioulas, however, do not agree on the locus and nature of this union and, more substantively, its implications for conceptualizing the transcendent and immanent God. The most noticeable difference is that while Lossky emphasizes the ascent of the human person toward union with God, for Zizioulas union is a relational event realized within the eucharist.[89] In the eucharist, the baptized faithful are constituted as the Body of Christ and, thus, as participants in the life of the triune God. Noticeably absent in Zizioulas is any reference to apophaticism or to the God beyond being. For Zizioulas, communion in the Body of Christ is *real* participation in the triune life of God. The eucharist makes present not the God beyond being, but the triune God whose being is relation and the ground of a relational ontology of divine-human communion.

While the logic of Lossky's apophaticism is rooted in the divine-human communion of the Incarnation, Zizioulas gives both historical and theological arguments for his eucharistic epistemology. In contrast to Lossky, his case for the eucharist as the locus of experience of the triune God and, hence, the source of theological knowledge is not strictly incarnational. For Zizioulas, against Lossky, emphasis on the Incarnation is too one-sided if not clarified with a pneumatologically conditioned Christology.

We will thus begin where Zizioulas begins, with his attempt to establish the centrality of the eucharist in the early Christian consciousness. This eucharistic consciousness or spirituality is evident in the early Christian identification of the eucharistic event with the eschaton, or the Kingdom of God, and with the Body of Christ. I will end by showing how Zizioulas's emphasis on the centrality of the eucharist for theology is held together by an understanding of icon and pneumatology, which are both informed by an eschatological vision of the recapitulation of all in Christ. 'Why the eucharist' finds its answer in a particular soteriological vision in which all are united in Christ by the power of the Holy Spirit.

Truth, Eucharist, and Eschatology

For Zizioulas, the eucharist is the locus of the experience of the triune God and, thus, the source of theological knowledge because the eucharist is the event of the proleptic presence of the eschaton in history. Such an understanding of the eucharist is evident, argues Zizioulas, from the very origins of Christianity. Zizioulas avers further that the 'eschaton' for early Christians meant something other than the culmination of history. The 'eschaton' is nothing less than God's eternal life, and, as such, the eschaton is truth insofar as truth is God's being.[90] In early Christianity, then, eucharist, truth, and eschatology are all identified: the eucharist is an event of the eschaton and, hence, of truth. Zizioulas gives both historical and theological reasons for this identification.

Zizioulas's first book, published in 1965 in Greek,[91] tries in part to establish the centrality of the eucharist in early Christian spirituality.[92] The early Christians had a "eucharistic consciousness"[93] that shaped the way they understood the God of Jesus Christ and, in turn, their own self-understanding. This eucharistic spirituality is manifested in the early Christian understanding of the eucharistic event as the fullness of the presence of God in history.[94] This identification, Zizioulas argues, emerges from early Christian sources in which truth is understood eschatologically and the eucharistic event is the event of the eschaton.[95] Constitutive of the early Christian "eucharistic consciousness" was this identification of the eucharist with the eschaton. The eucharist is not the eschaton, but in the eucharistic event is manifested the presence of the eschaton in history, which is nothing less than communion with the triune God. In the eucharist one "knows" truth, i.e., God, insofar as one participates in truth and, by so doing, *is* truth, i.e., acquires God's mode of being. From the very beginning of Christian existence this eucharistic spirituality, which identifies the eucharist with the eschaton, is evident.[96] This identification continues through the patristic period and will form the basis, according to Zizioulas, for the patristic understanding of God as Trinity.[97]

The eschatological identity of the eucharist in early Christian spirituality, moreover, has its basis in Christology. The eucharist as the event of the Body of Christ does not signify, according to Zizioulas, a merely moral identity. It is not the Body of Christ by virtue of the gathering together in Christ's name people who work together in unity as the various parts of a body. The eucharist *is* the Body of Christ for Zizioulas in an ontological sense. It is the real, eschatological Body of the Risen Christ, which forms the basis for the identification of the eucharist with the eschaton, and which further allows Zizioulas to refer to the eucharist as an event of the Body of Christ which is the eschaton. The link between the eucharist and the eschatological Body of Christ is why early Christians identified "the Church," *ekklesia,* with the eucharistic community.[98]

The link between the risen Body of Christ and the eucharist is possible, however, only through the Holy Spirit. What roots the "experience" of God in the eucharistic event is what Zizioulas calls a "pneumatologically conditioned christology." Such a Christology for Zizioulas entails an inherent unity between ecclesiology, eschatology, Christology, and pneumatology.

Pneumatological Christology

Over the past century, the ecumenical discussions of ecclesiology have not given sufficient attention, in Zizioulas's opinion, to the role of the Holy Spirit in the church. In both the Roman Catholic and Protestant churches ecclesiology is understood within a christological framework, at the expense of pneumatology. Orthodox theologians are also guilty of this overemphasis of Christology in ecclesiology, due in large part to the eucharistic ecclesiology of Nicolas Afanasiev in the early twentieth century.[99] Afanasiev's eucharistic ecclesiology[100] maintains that the church is understood eucharistically, that is, from the perspective of the eucharist. According to Zizioulas, Georges Florovsky reaffirmed ecclesiology as "a chapter of christology" without providing a solution to the problem of synthesis between Christology and pneumatology.[101] Lossky's work was the only serious attempt by an Orthodox theologian to synthesize Christology and pneumatology in ecclesiology.[102] For reasons that we shall see later, Zizioulas rejects this synthesis. In short, Lossky attempted to curb the christomonistic tendencies of ecclesiology by stressing the independence of the Spirit from Christ. By contrasting an economy of the Spirit against an economy of the Son he pushed ecclesiology more or less toward the side of pneumatology. This priority given to pneumatology in ecclesiology brings Lossky closer to his Russian forebear A. S. Khomiakov, who promotes, according to Zizioulas, a charismatic ecclesiology.[103] More recently, Orthodox theologians such as Nikos Nissiotis and Boris Bobrinsky continue this priority of pneumatology in ecclesiology.[104] The key to ecclesiology, for Zizioulas, is understanding the correct relation of Christology to pneumatology, since both are related to the church. An understanding of this relationship demands a proper knowledge of the role of the Holy Spirit, which, I will argue, is the theological linchpin that binds together in Zizioulas's thought Christology, ecclesiology, and trinitarian theology.

The Holy Spirit accomplishes the identification of eucharist, church, and the eschatological Body of Christ. It is by the power of the Holy Spirit that the eucharistic community becomes conscious of their unity in Christ and of their participation in the triune life of God. It is Zizioulas's theology of the Holy Spirit that provides the theological justification for the identification of the eucharist with the Body of Christ, and hence, with the eschaton which is communion in the triune life *in* Christ and *by* the Spirit. The Holy Spirit is the epistemological foundation for knowledge of God, though not in a way which separates the Holy Spirit from the Trinity, but rather renders the triune life present. It is the presence of this triune life in the eucharist that is the source of theological knowledge and the mystery that theological reflection attempts to express.[105]

Though present throughout his writing, two important articles set forth clearly Zizioulas's pneumatology: "Implications ecclésiologiques de deux types de pneumatologie,"[106] and "Christ, the Spirit, and the Church."[107] In the former, Zizioulas distinguishes between "two types" of pneumatologies in the early church: the missionary-historical type and the eucharistic eschatological type. Moreover, both types imply a certain Christology and ecclesiology.

In the missionary-historical type, the Son sends the Holy Spirit into history. In this sense, the Spirit is an "agent of Christ" whose purpose is to accomplish "the mission of Christ and to glorify him." In this type, Christology becomes "the source of pneumatology," which thus becomes for Zizioulas a pneumatology "conditioned by Christology."[108] In the framework of this type of christologically conditioned pneumatology the church is defined in terms of mission. The chief aim of the church is to expand (*exige*) the dispersion. Further, the Spirit leads the church on a pilgrimage in the direction of the Kingdom of God. Since the Spirit's work follows that of Christ, "the church becomes the 'body of Christ' in the sense where the head (Christ) *proceeds* and *leads* the body, and the body follows in obedience."[109] The church proceeds toward the Kingdom, the Spirit guides the church with Christ as leader. Moreover, this christologically conditioned pneumatology leads to a linear conception of history, "a sort of *Heilsgeschichte* in the sense in which Oscar Cullman, for example, has familiarized us."[110] As a final analysis, Zizioulas asserts that this type of pneumatology implies a certain "*distance* between the head and the body."[111]

The second type of pneumatology, often neglected by exegetes of the early Christian texts, is the eucharistic-eschatological type.[112] Instead of following Christ or being sent by Christ, the Spirit realizes (*conduire*) the Resurrection of Christ.[113] The Spirit is responsible for the resurrection and without the Spirit there is no resurrection. Moreover, other passages in the New Testament reveal that without the Holy Spirit there is no Christ. In the birth narratives of Mark and Luke, the Spirit realizes the birth of Christ. Further, the baptism of Christ, considered the start of his ministry on earth, is constituted "in and by the Spirit."[114] Contrary to the first type, in this type of pneumatology "the pneumatology is the source of Christology," thus leading to "*a Christology conditioned by pneumatology.*"[115]

This pneumatologically conditioned Christology has several implications for ecclesiology. For one, the church is not simply that which is dispersed through mission, but is reassembled in one place. The reassembly of the people of God in one place is a fundamental characteristic for Zizioulas of the eschaton.[116] Second, this eschatological function of the Holy Spirit vis-à-vis the church suggests that the Holy Spirit's role is not simply one of aiding and assisting individuals, but one of communion.[117] The Spirit constitutes the people of God as the eschatological community. In the New Testament, relative to its missionary purpose the Spirit is called 'power' (*dunamis*—Luke 4:14; 24:49; Acts 1:8; 10:38; Rom 15:13; 1 Cor 2:4; 1 Thess 1:5), whereas the Spirit's eschatological function is described as 'communion' (*koinonia*—2 Cor 13:13; Phil 2:1; see John 1:6).[118] Third, the church is not comprised of individuals, but it is only "in and through the community" that one acquires a true identity and personal distinction. Fourth, if the Spirit realizes the event of Christ in history, then the community formed by the communion of the Holy Spirit iconically realizes the presence of Christ. Unlike the missionary-historical approach, there is no distance between the head and the body, but an identity so that Christ is always present in the world "*with* his Church if not, quite simply, *as* his Church."[119] Finally, the identity of church is Christ. Put another way, "the *I* of the Church *is* Christ."[120] This is not to deny the sinfulness of the church in history, but only to affirm the priority of its holiness as the presence of Christ in history.[121]

Though seemingly contrary, the two types of pneumatologies existed as a synthesis in the early Christian consciousness. The fact that the types can co-exist without difficulty in the same texts (Luke and Acts) evinces a consciousness not of contradiction, but of synthesis.[122] The only question for Zizioulas is that of priority, which was naturally given to the eucharistic-eschatological type. This priority coheres with Zizioulas's logic that history is illuminated by truth which is made present in the end; the future gives meaning to the past and the present.[123] This does not abolish the missionary-historical approach, but only gives it an eschatological meaning. The early Christians simply understood their missionary endeavor as an extension of the eschatological event.

At this point, I wish to make clear an important theological move already hinted at in this presentation of the two types of pneumatologies. The first move concerns the simultaneity of Christology and pneumatology; both are the condition for the possibility of the other's presence in relation to history. There is no Spirit without Christ, who makes present the Spirit in relation to history at Pentecost. There is no Christ, however, without the Spirit; "christology is not autonomous: but is conditioned constantly by pneumatology, and as such it is to be organically related to ecclesiology. This brings Trinitarian theology itself into ecclesiology."[124] Not only is pneumatology a necessary element in ecclesiology, but the Spirit is constitutive of the church as the Body of Christ. Pneumatology brings ecclesiology into relation to Christology by conditioning Christology. Since ecclesiology is a chapter of Christology in that it is the Body of Christ, it is so pneumatologically. One might say that the church is a christological-pneumatological event.[125] As such, it is a trinitarian and an eschatological mystery.

A second theological move is the particular eschatological role which Zizioulas attributes to the Spirit and on which he elaborates in "Christ, the Spirit and the Church."[126] In this article, Zizioulas articulates that the two most important aspects of pneumatology are *"eschatology* and *communion."*[127] These two aspects of pneumatology are inseparable and simultaneous moments in the work of the Holy Spirit. Zizioulas elaborates on the former aspect by way of a critique of Lossky's understanding of an 'economy of the Spirit.'

Lossky speaks of an economy of the Son and the Spirit, by which he distinguishes their work in creation as opposed to their immanent life.[128] It is precisely this eschatological role of the Spirit in terms of communion which Lossky's 'economy of the Spirit' endangers. To speak of an 'economy of the Spirit' confuses for Zizioulas the roles of the persons of the Trinity, particularly that of the Son and the Spirit. Economy refers to God's salvific work in history. But "only the Son becomes history."[129] This 'becoming history' involves the Son in created existence in a way that does not confuse them ontologically. The union within his person is such that creation shares in the personal life of God. Creation possesses the same relation that the Son has with the Father and as a result is deified. Deification is this unity in the Son. No other person shares such a relation with created existence as does the Son incarnate. It is then impossible to speak of an economy of the Spirit.

If the Son's role is to become history, according to Zizioulas, then the Spirit's role is the exact opposite. The role of the Spirit is eschatological, which means it is the fulfillment of history. To then speak of an 'economy of the Spirit,' as Lossky does, is to threaten the eschatological role of the Spirit, and thus, any hope for communion with the triune God. There is 'no economy of the Spirit' since the Spirit is not related to history in the same way as the Son. The Son becomes history, while the Spirit fulfills history by bringing into history the eschata. In this way, "[t]he Spirit is the *beyond* history, and when he acts in history he does so in order to bring into history the last days, the *eschaton.*"[130] Zizioulas would not agree with Lossky that the Spirit is sent to complete the work of Christ.[131] This view stems from a missionary-historical understanding of the Spirit who leads us to the eschaton. The fact that the Spirit is sent does not constitute a special economy of the Spirit, though it does put the Spirit in a specific relationship with history. This relationship consists less in inspiring and sanctification than in making present the eschatological person in history. If where the Spirit is there is the eschaton, then the same principle applies in the Spirit's relationship with history. The Spirit brings the Kingdom into history, and in this sense, does not become history, but fulfills it. The Spirit does not simply lead us to the Kingdom, but makes it present. The church as the eucharistic *synaxis* is filled with the presence of the Spirit that is the presence of the eschatological unity of all in Christ.[132]

The 'communion' aspect of pneumatology consists in constituting this 'eschatological unity of all in Christ.' Zizioulas amplifies that "because of the involvement of the Holy Spirit in the economy, Christ is not just an individual, not 'one' but 'many.' "This 'corporate personality' of Christ is impossible to conceive without Pneumatology."[133] In this way, "Pneumatology contributes to Christology this dimension of communion. And it is because of this function of Pneumatology that it is possible to speak of Christ as having a 'body,' i.e., to speak of ecclesiology, of the Church as the Body of Christ."[134] It is important to note here that the eschatological and communal aspects of the pneumatology are not separate moments, but, as with Christology and pneumatology, simultaneous. In pneumatology, the eschatological is the communal and the communal, in the true sense of the unity of the 'one' and the 'many,' is the eschatological.

Zizioulas's use of 'economy' is not always consistent. On the one hand, he insists on rejecting an 'economy of the Spirit,' suggested by Lossky, arguing that only the Son "*becomes* history," thus, implicitly arguing that 'economy' is linked to the person of the Son.[135] On the other hand, he often speaks of "God's economy" or will insist on a distinction between the "economic Trinity" and the "immanent Trinity." Moreover, he argues with an obvious reference to Lossky that "it is extremely dangerous for the *unity of the economy* to speak of a special 'economy of the Spirit.'"[136] But he then argues that "[t]o be involved in history is not the same as to *become* history."[137] There is, then, God's economy in relation to history and the economy *of* the Son who alone *becomes* history.

The notion of 'economy of the Spirit' makes Zizioulas nervous for two reasons. First, it implies an involvement in history that diminishes the eschatological role of the Spirit. Second, it confuses the roles of the Son and Spirit insofar as it is the Son alone who is immanent in every respect in created existence. A closer analysis of the logic governing Zizioulas's distinction between the *economy* of the Son and the eschatological role of the Spirit will reveal that at the core of his pneumatological Christology is the realism of divine-human communion. The distinction of roles in Zizioulas's theology is what allows for the possibility of a *real* communion with the divine life. The challenge for the notion of divine-human communion is how to conceptualize God as transcendent and immanent without leaning too heavily to one side. If there were an economy of the Spirit such that the Spirit is "involved" in history as the Son is, this implies, according to Zizioulas, that history becomes part of God's very being. If this were so, then the result is either pantheism, which does not secure the integrity and 'otherness' of created existence, or an immanence with no real hope for salvation which Zizioulas defines as freedom from the giveness of our created, historical situation. The Christ event reveals, for Zizioulas, the transcendent and immanent God who is fully immanent in all aspects of created existence in the Son. Through the power of the Spirit, the incarnate and crucified Son becomes the eschatological Body of Christ who unites within himself created existence and the divine life without negating the 'otherness' of creation itself. In some sense, one could argue that the eschatological role of the Spirit, the 'non-economy' of the Spirit, is creation's hope for communion with the divine life, although this freedom depends on the work of the Son.[138]

In summary, it is the eschatological-communion role of the Holy Spirit that justifies theologically Zizioulas's identification of the eucharist with the eschaton. This identification constitutes the eucharist as the space of divine presence, and hence, as the source for theological knowledge. On my reading of Zizioulas, it is not that the Spirit was never active in creation before the birth of Christ, but with the 'Christ event' the Spirit is active in a new way. The activity of the Holy Spirit is now linked with the resurrection of Christ, the fruits of which the Spirit makes present. There is also a particular understanding of the resurrection which informs this pneumatology, which in its simplest form is unity of the divine and the human in Christ, and hence, the sanctification of the latter by the former. The resurrected Christ is the 'corporate personality,' who recapitulates all creation in himself. The Spirit's 'new' activity renders the resurrected Christ present, and this not simply anywhere; but rather in the eucharistic worshipping community, where the people are gathered in praise and offer the world to be sanctified. It is in this act of the people, this *leitourgia,* that the Spirit breaks through history and *constitutes* the church as the Body of Christ, i.e., as the eschatological presence of the triune life.[139] But how can the eschaton break through history without destroying history? Is history abolished by the Spirit? How can the church be simultaneously an eschatological and a historical reality? The answer, says, Zizioulas lies with the concept of icon.

Icon: The Unity of History and Eschatology

Zizioulas begins his series of articles entitled "The Eucharist and the Kingdom of God" saying: "The Divine Liturgy [*Theia Eucharistia*—"Holy Eucharist"] is an image [*eikona*—"icon"] of the Kingdom of God, an image [*eikona*] of the last times [*ton eschaton*—"the eschaton"]. There is nothing so clear as this in the Orthodox Liturgy [*Leitourgia*]."[140] The objective here is to analyze his understanding of 'icon,' of which the following passage gives us a glimpse: "The symbolism in the liturgy is not parabolic or allegorical; it is iconic with the meaning it had in the Fathers of the Church, and where it meant ontologically participation in the prototype."[141] With an icon, as with most art, there is the artwork and there is that which it signifies. Inherent in the artwork is a presence of the idea or event that it represents, but also of the artist's interpretation. This presence exists with absence which it cannot erase, since there exists with the artwork an inevitable distance between the viewer, the artwork, and the artist.[142] Moreover, icon involves some symbolic similarity between the art and that which it signifies. The similarity is not to historical realities but to eschatological realities.[143] The liturgy as icon is symbolically similar to the heavenly liturgy. For this reason Zizioulas argues for a normativity of the fourfold structure of ministry, since it is symbolically similar to the vision of the eschaton discussed in some detail above. An elimination of any one of these ministries would destroy the iconic character of the liturgy.[144] Moreover, icon is symbolism that eliminates the distance between the viewer and that which is represented so that the former participates in the latter. They are 'windows to heaven' as many Orthodox theologians would say, and for Zizioulas they open the present to the future and make the future present without exhausting the future or reducing it to history.[145]

Like with most concepts, Christians transformed the Greek concept of *eikon*. For the ancient Greeks, icon rendered present the heavenly realm through symbol.[146] For the Christians, however, "it is not a platonic vision that the icon brings."[147] The relation between the earthly and the heavenly is less vertical than it is horizontal insofar as Christians introduced the concept of time into their understanding of icon. The icon reflects not the earthly reality which already exists but that which is expected.[148] It makes present the future, the eschaton that fulfills history. The eucharist as icon makes present not a reality which already exists but which is yet to come, without destroying time. The liturgy as icon moves one toward the eschaton without taking one out of history.[149] For Zizioulas, icon not only makes present another reality, but also overcomes the opposition between two realities while maintaining their integrity. In Lossky's terms, icon transcends the 'antinomy' between the uncreated and created. History and the eschaton, two mutually exclusive realities, are brought into relation in the liturgy without being destroyed.

Though the presence of the eschaton through the icon does not destroy history, priority in the dialectic is given to the eschaton.[150] The icon itself is "not a product of history."[151] Moreover, "the truth of history is paradoxical: determined by its end while the end is a part of its unfolding."[152] Truth for the Greek fathers is "not as a product of the mind, but as a 'visit' and 'dwelling' (cf. Jn. 1:14) of an eschatological reality entering history to open it up in a communion event."[153] This truth is communicated iconically without being manipulated or conceived, but manifested. The icon "liberates truth from our 'conception,' 'definition,' 'comprehension' of it and protects it from being manipulated and objectified," and opens the way for its presence in history. Icon thus becomes the "final truth of being communicated in and through the event of communion (liturgical or sacramental), anticipating the 'end' of history from within its unfolding."[154]

The icon, however, manifests without destroying history. History is the arena for change, corruption, destruction, and death. In the eschaton, union with the life of God liberates creation from death and results in incorruptibility and eternal life. Icon makes present this gift of eternal life without destroying the flux of history. Through the icon, the eschaton transforms creation and deifies it in the one Body of Christ.[155] Icon is thus the "truth of history,"[156] as the means through which God becomes present in history. Iconically "Christ makes history into truth and truth into part of the unfolding of history."[157] Eschaton and history are brought into relation, the former fulfilling the latter, without losing their otherness. In the icon, history is transcended "within and through history and this sanctifies history even more."[158]

Zizioulas's rejection of a linear conception of history is evident. Christianity, for Zizioulas, is not salvation-history. The whole point of his "Eschatology and History" was to defend the Orthodox against accusations within the ecumenical movement that the Orthodox do not take history seriously enough.[159] His response is that history needs to be viewed iconically in which it is conditioned eschatologically. The iconic view of history, however, does not wait for the eschaton; through the icon the eschaton bursts through history and becomes present. It does not simply interrupt sameness, the status quo, political ideologies, or meta-histories; it sanctifies history with God's presence and transforms its being. History continues to march toward the truth which lies ahead, but whose presence through the icon continuously bursts through history. Insofar as the church is "an *eikon* of the Kingdom to come,"[160] it is in "the eucharistic community, where the past and the future are through the Holy Spirit perceived in one and the same reality of the present, history and time are fully accepted and eternal life is not opposed to them but enters into them and transcends them as they affect man's destiny and salvation."[161]

Icon affects the meaning of other liturgical categories in Zizioulas's thought. The concept of *anamnesis* or memory is interpreted according to the iconic character of the liturgy and, thus, eschatologically. Memory makes present that which is remembered. In the liturgy, according to Zizioulas, it is usually linked with the past: the events of Christ in the past are remembered. If the eucharist iconically represents the eschaton then, Zizioulas argues, the memory of those gathered is not simply that of the past but of the future. In fact, the past is remembered in light of the future, or as Zizioulas puts it, "the *anamnetic* faculty of the eucharistic community involves precisely a 'remembrance' not only of the past but also of the future in the present."[162] The eucharistic anamnesis "lets the future open the past to become present."[163] The church in liturgy remembers the future thereby making it present. This memory of the future is clear not only in the structure of the liturgy, but in its prayer: "Therefore, remembering this command of our Savior and all that He had endured for us: the cross, the tomb, the resurrection on the third day, the ascension into heaven, the seating at the right hand of the Father, and *second and glorious coming*."[164] In liberating memory from the past, the eucharist as icon also liberates time and nature from the determination of causality: "The causality of the consequences of a fact constitutes the bondage of man's historical existence in the same way that the causality of natural law keeps him a slave to death."[165] Both are affected and liberated by the introduction of liturgical time. The liturgy liberates time from the sequence of the past, present, future, and "lets the future open the past to become present."[166] Finally, in addition to time, nature is liberated from death and becomes immortal and incorruptible. What is remembered and made present is nothing less than the Body of Christ which sanctifies creation: "In this sense the eucharistic *anamnesis* becomes not a mere mental operation but an existential realization, a *re*-presentation of the Body of Christ."[167]

Sacrament is also understood iconically, and hence, eschatologically. It becomes for Zizioulas synonymous with icon. Sacraments are constituted by the presence of the Holy Spirit, who is "linked to the last days." They are events in which history and the eschaton are brought into a dialectical relation, the latter conditioning the former. Being conditioned eschatologically, the ecclesial rituals, such as baptism, ordination, etc., become sacramental in the sense of being placed in the dialectic "between history and the eschaton, between the already and the not yet." They constantly depend on the Holy Spirit, which makes them sacramental, "which in the language of Orthodox theology may be called 'iconic.'"[168]

A brief comparison with a recent, phenomenological approach to the understanding of icon by the Roman Catholic theologian, Jean-Luc Marion, will further clarify Zizioulas's own meaning of icon.[169] For Marion, the concept is rooted in phenomenology while for Zizioulas in Christology. Icon can only make sense of the phenomenology of "the gaze" in Marion's thought. The icon is not an idol which gives "the gaze its stopping point and measures out its scope" and "results from the gaze that aims at it."[170] The idol precludes from going beyond it thus binding it to the finite. In the case of the icon, however, the gaze does not rest on the icon, but "rebounds upon the visible, in order to go back in it up the infinite stream of the invisible."[171] In answer to the question of whether a concept can serve as an icon Marion replies that "the only concept that can serve as an intelligible medium for the icon is one that lets itself be measured by the excessiveness of the invisible that enters into visibility through infinite depth, hence that itself speaks or promises to speak this infinite depth, where the visible and the invisible become acquainted."[172] Like Zizioulas, the icon, for Marion, is the medium for the 'acquaintance' between the finite and the infinite, or as Zizioulas puts it, between history and the eschaton.

For Zizioulas the icon is grounded not so much phenomenologically but christologically. The Spirit's role, of course, is paramount. The Spirit is the one who makes "the Church through her sacramental structures both a presence of the eschaton in history and a pointer beyond history, since pneumatology constantly points to the unobjectifiable, uncontrollable, extraordinary 'beyond.'"[173] The condition for the possibility of sacrament is the *epiclesis,* or the invocation of the Holy Spirit. The present-day form of the *Liturgy of St. John the Chrysostom* "begins with the invocation of the Kingdom . . . and ends with . . . our union and communion with the life of God in Trinity." For the Orthodox East, the important moment is not the words of institution, but "the invocation of the Holy Spirit, whose presence is necessarily linked with the coming of the 'last day' (Acts 2:18)."[174] When the Spirit breaks through history, it transforms history in that eschatological event without destroying it.[175] We find ourselves still in time and subject to the necessity of its conditions (i.e., corruption, decay, death). In the event of the eucharist, with the *epiclesis* of the Holy Spirit these conditions are suspended. The *epiclesis* acts as a "disolvent of historical determinism."[176] Thus, the Kingdom is present in the moment of the eucharist as event. In between eucharistic gatherings it is anticipating the coming of the Kingdom in its fullness, which is present epiclectically in the eucharist. As Zizioulas argues, "when the Church lives epiclectically, she cannot but long for what already is. The synthesis of the historical with the eschatological in this epicletical conditioning of history constitutes what we may properly—and not in the distorted sense—call the *sacramental* nature of the Church."[177]

If pneumatology realizes the icon, then Christology is the condition of its possibility. The icon is the symbol through which the event of our salvation is realized proleptically. This salvation is defined in terms of the union of the uncreated with the created realm, two ontologically distinct realities. The icon is thus not possible without the event, or person, which unites the created with the uncreated. This event is the person of Christ; not simply the incarnate Christ, but the resurrected Christ in whom all of creation reaches its fulfillment. Christ is not only the condition for the possibility of icon, but is icon in that in his person, or *hypostasis,* the uncreated and created are united without confusion. Thus Christ is icon as person, and defines as true icon that *hypostasis* which unites within itself the created and the uncreated. The Holy Spirit constitutes the liturgy as icon, because it constitutes the Church as the body or *hypostasis* of Christ.

Marion lists the criteria by which certain media, including the concept, painting, or sculpture, are determined as valid icons.

(a) Valid as icon is the concept or group of concepts that reinforces the distinction of the visible and the invisible as well as their union, hence that increases the one all the more that it highlights the other.... (b) The icon has a theological status, the reference of the visible face to the intention that envisages, culminating in the reference of the Christ to the Father: for the formula *eikon tou theou tou aoratou* concerns first the Christ. It would remain to specify in what measure this attribution has a normative value, far from simply constituting just one application of the icon among others.... (c) As much as idolatry, because it measures the divine according to the scope of a gaze that freezes, can nevertheless attain to an actual experience of the divine only at the cost of being reduced to one of the 'so-called gods' (René Char), so the icon, as it summons to infinity—strictly—contemplation in distance, could not but overabundantly subvert every idol of the frozen gaze—in short, open the eyes of the frozen gaze, open its eyes upon a face.[178]

Though they share much in common with regard to the meaning of icon, Marion grounds such meaning phenomenologically, while for Zizioulas, icon has no meaning outside of Christology. This phenomenological approach allows Marion to determine criteria by which a particular medium is deemed a valid icon. I would argue that for Zizioulas there is only one valid icon—the person of Christ who alone unites the divine and the human, the eschaton, and history. Consequently, the media in the liturgical context are iconic in that they form visible signs that convey the event of the icon, i.e., the constitution of the *laos* as the body (person) of Christ. In this sense, icon is more an event than a medium.

Like Marion, Zizioulas sets criteria for determining the validity of identifying concepts as icons. In the sense that the *hypostasis* of Christ is the only true icon, then *hypostasis* becomes the only valid concept as icon. But, as we shall see in the following chapters, *hypostasis* is not valid as icon as concept, but as being.

Divine-Human Communion: Knowledge or Ignorance?

Theological epistemology, for both Lossky and Zizioulas, is incarnational. This means that for both theologians, knowledge of God is defined in terms of divine-human communion. The Incarnation, or the Christ event, is the presence of the fullness of the transcendent God in history and, thus, the condition for the possibility of communion. Knowledge of God is the experience of communion with God. Although there can be no separation between the two, the Incarnation gives priority to ontology over epistemology. The divine-human communion revealed and realized in the Incarnation is the answer to the questions of how and in what way knowledge of God is possible.

If, however, their theological epistemologies share this grounding in an ontology of divine-human communion, their similarities end here. The implications of an ontology of divine-human communion for epistemology, and for other aspects of theology, are radically different for both theologians. For Lossky, the revelation and realization of divine-human communion in the Incarnation is also the manifestation of the transcendent and immanent God, the God beyond all contradictions and logical opposites. The very being of God as transcendent and immanent, who brings that which is not God into communion with God, demands a theological discourse that is antinomic and keeps in tension apophatic and cataphatic theologies. Since God is that which is 'other' than creation and in this 'otherness' is a being who can be united with creation without absorbing or obliterating it, such a God can only be described in apophatic terms. God, thus, in God's essence is unknowable and as such is *hyperousia,* but is fully present in that which is not God through God's energies, which are God.

For Zizioulas, the person of the resurrected Christ is made present in the eucharist through the power of the Holy Spirit, whose eschatological role is to unite the participants of the eucharistic gathering as the Body of Christ. The person of Christ is the icon through which the two ontological others are united while remaining 'other,' and where creation goes beyond itself in communion with the divine. The eucharist as the locus of the experience of the divine and, thus, the source of theological knowledge is attested to historically through the eucharistic consciousness of the early Christians, but, more importantly, theologically through an understanding of the eschatological and communal roles of the Holy Spirit, i.e., through a pneumatologically conditioned Christology.

A difficulty that Lossky faces in his theological epistemology is how to relate the notion of knowledge of God in terms of experience of the divine with Christian dogmas which claim to express true statements about God. In other words, he roots this understanding of knowledge of God in the Incarnation understood as the union of the divine and the human, but he cannot account for how an experience of this unity in Christ forms the basis for understanding the Incarnation in this way. If, for Lossky, experiential knowledge of God is the result of an individual struggle and ascent to God, on what basis can one interpret the life of Jesus as the event of God in Christ? There is no first experience of union with God in Christ by the Holy Spirit that Lossky refers to in order to ground his own interpretation of the Incarnation as the union of the divine and the human. Communication is not sufficient to determine the meaning of dogma since, for Lossky, dogma expresses the knowledge of the 'mystical experience' and in turn shapes one's experience toward union with God.[179] When Lossky affirms the Incarnation as the starting point of theology, it is clear he means the Incarnation as expressed in the Chalcedonian definition. But according to his own logic, this dogma must be rooted in the experience of God that illuminates who God is and what God is doing in Christ.

The type of knowledge that results from union with God is manifested for Lossky in one person immediately after Christ's resurrection—the Theotokos. The "mother of God, by virtue of the unique relationship between her person and God, whom we can call her Son, alone can rise from here below to a complete consciousness of all that the Holy Spirit says to the Church, realizing this plenitude in her own person. But this complete consciousness of God, this acquisition of the fullness of grace appropriate to the age to come, could only happen to a deified person."[180] As a deified person, the Theotokos experiences the fullness of union with God that is the fullness of truth. The nature/person distinction used by Lossky to express the christological and pneumatological aspects of the spiritual journey toward deification also forms the basis for understanding the deified state of the Theotokos. By being united to Christ through the Incarnation, as one is united in Christ through baptism in the church, the Theotokos offered her human nature to Christ and received it purified. "The natural connection which linked her to the God-Man did not yet confer upon the person of the Mother of God the state of a deified creature."[181] Though the Holy Spirit rested upon her at the Incarnation, only the communication of the Holy Spirit at Pentecost provided "the possibility of realizing ... personal holiness—something which will always depend on subjective factors."[182] Not simply individual Christians, but the Church as a whole develops toward this personal holiness.[183] By virtue of her unique role, however, the Theotokos realizes on earth all the fullness of personal perfection.

> Only the Mother of God, through whom the Word was made flesh, will be able to receive the plenitude of grace and to attain an unlimited glory, by realizing in her person all the holiness of which the Church is capable. . . . But if this be so, then the historical development of the Church and the world has already been fulfilled, not only in the uncreated person of the Son of God but also in the created person of his Mother. . . . Alongside the incarnate divine hypostasis there is a deified human hypostasis.[184]

The Theotokos manifests in her person all the glory that is the goal for all individuals, but also the church.

For Zizioulas, the experience of divine-human communion is more immediately communal. In some sense, the difference between the types of experiences of the divine can be traced to distinct pneumatologies. The Holy Spirit, for Lossky, assists and in the process of cooperation transforms the believer progressively in personal holiness. For Zizioulas, the Holy Spirit within the eucharistic context transforms the liturgical context into an event of the eschaton, which is itself the fullness of truth. Zizioulas's arguments do not rest simply on historical proofs of a eucharistic consciousness. They are based rather on a pneumatological Christology in which the Holy Spirit constitutes the eucharistic gathering as the eschatological communion that is the resurrected Body of Christ. More importantly, it is the event itself that forms the basis for Christian self-understanding and for knowledge of God. The earliest Christians may have a testimony of the resurrected Christ and of the descent of the Holy Spirit, but it is only in the event of the eucharist where they 'experience' communion with God in Christ by the power of the Holy Spirit. In this eschatological communion, the Christian community becomes what it was created to be, and, in this sense, 'knows' all that God has accomplished in Christ and the Holy Spirit. In this particular knowing, it knows who God is. Such a eucharistic consciousness does not necessarily mean for Zizioulas an immediate expression in the form of, say, Chalcedonian Christology. This communion does, however, form the basis for subsequent expressions.

It is important to emphasize that the experience of communion of God of the Theotokos and other saints is for Lossky an ecclesial event.[185] There is no mystical experience that, for Lossky, is non-ecclesial. It is also clear that Lossky's model for the church is one of growth rather than as event. The church provides the conditions for the possibility of "this complete consciousness of God, this acquisition of the fulness of grace appropriate to the age to come, [which] could only happen to a deified being."[186] According to Lossky, we are in the midst of the "gradual development of the Church in history."[187] Consequently, the gradual development of the church means the gradual development of its knowledge as an ecclesial body. The church is then not able to fully express the knowledge of divine-human communion in its dogmas. If the dogma cannot fully express this knowledge, one wonders if they can then serve the function Lossky ascribes to them in terms of shaping one's experience toward a mystical union with God. Moreover, though the dogmas as expressions of ecclesial knowledge are rooted in a mystical experience, this mystical experience is not, in some sense, ecclesial in that it is not experienced by the entire community.[188] The dogmas are based on a mystical experience that is ecclesial and occurs only within the church, but there is no way that the proclamation or witness to such knowledge that shapes the "gradual development of the Church in history" can be confirmed ecclesially, that is by appeal to a communal experience of divine-human communion.

These different understandings of the nature of the mystical experience suggest a more substantial difference between the two theologians over the degree in which one knows God. For Lossky, knowledge of God is the progressive participation in the divine energies of God that are made available in the life of the church. For Zizioulas, the church is the eucharistic event of the Body of Christ. In the eucharist, one communes with God and, hence, knows God through participation in the *hypostasis* or person of Christ. In the person of the resurrected Christ, the Son of God, one is participating in the life of the trinitarian God. What Zizioulas's eucharistic epistemology suggests is a real participation in and knowledge of the immanent, trinitarian life of God. Lossky would never deny that God is Trinity and that participation in the divine energies is trinitarian, but it is not clear how such participation is trinitarian or why God as Trinity matters for participating in the divine energies of God. For all their agreement on an ontology of divine-human communion, there exist substantial differences in terms of the implications of such an ontology for theological epistemology, which themselves suggest further differences over the degree to which God is known. Their theological epistemologies have, then, real implications for trinitarian theology.

chapter 2

Trinity: Antinomy or Communion?

In addition to placing the question of epistemology at the heart of theological discourse, modernity also affected Christian theology in another decisive way. Since the seventeenth century, the doctrine of the Trinity was increasingly marginalized in theology and philosophy and, as a consequence, in practical piety. The doctrine of the Trinity might have been relegated to the dustbin of historical artifacts if not for Karl Barth and Karl Rahner who initiated a resurgence in the twentieth century of trinitarian theologies. Contemporary Orthodox theologies are a part of this narrative of the renaissance of trinitarian theologies and their influence is noticeable throughout the wider conversation.

Lossky and Zizioulas have made distinctive contributions to this twentieth-century trinitarian discussion. Both affirm that the doctrine of the Trinity is essentially the Christian expression of the realism of divine-human communion, of the God who is simultaneously immanent and transcendent. But just as this common presupposition did not preclude the development of divergent theological epistemologies, even less did it prevent Lossky and Zizioulas from constructing dissimilar trinitarian theologies. More strongly, the trinitarian theologies of Lossky and Zizioulas are, at points, mutually incompatible.

What accounts for the difference? Much of what is distinct in Lossky's and Zizioulas's trinitarian theologies can be traced to their theological epistemologies. As we saw, for both theologians theological epistemology flows from an ontology of the realism of divine-human communion. Lossky and Zizioulas, however, give different responses to the question of what this ontology of divine-human communion implies for the nature, locus, and degree of knowledge of God. Distinct answers to this question affect how they think about the Trinity. For Lossky, the understanding of theology as 'apophatic' and 'antinomic' is the regulating rule in his trinitarian theology and the understanding of trinitarian categories, such as nature and person; it is also the lens through which he critiques the *filioque*. Later in his career Lossky developed a theology of personhood that is in tension with his apophatic impulses.

For Zizioulas, the experience of God in the Body of Christ by the power of the Holy Spirit is the source for the early Christian development of the doctrine of the Trinity, which 'revolutionized' ontology by placing 'person' rather than 'essence' at the heart of ontology. Zizioulas's linking of Trinity and ontology has, contra Lossky, a decidedly non-apophatic character. What will emerge as a central debate between the two theologians is the importance of apophaticism for expressing an ontology of divine-human communion in the form of the doctrine of the Trinity. Is apophaticism necessary for Christian theological discourse more generally and, more specifically, for the Christian doctrine of the Trinity? The latter question will be explored in more detail in the next chapter.

Lossky on Apophaticism and Trinity

Oikonomia and *Theologia*

For Lossky, there are two ways to speak of God: one has to do with God's relation to the world; the other with God in Godself, i.e., God as if the world did not exist. Lossky designates these two ways with the terms *oikonomia* and *theologia*.[1] The transcendent and immanent God who is (*hyper*-) essence/energies gives rise to these two theological discourses.[2] God's activity or *oikonomia* in the world allows for theological expression of God's relation to the world. This *oikonomia* consists of God's activity in creation and God's incarnation in Christ. Though God is present in God's creation, Lossky does not engage in a type of 'natural theology.' He does not juxtapose natural theology against a revealed theology. For Lossky all knowledge of God is revelation since even created nature itself is permeated with God's energies. More importantly, all possible knowledge of God is clarified through the Incarnation, both God's relation to the world and God in Godself. Whatever can be discerned by reflection on created reality must be measured by the revelation in Christ. As we have seen, the summit of this revelation is the knowledge of God as Trinity: "To the economy in which God reveals Himself in creating the world and in becoming incarnate, we must respond by theology, confessing the transcendent nature of the Trinity in an ascent of thought which necessarily has an apophatic thrust."[3]

The question then centers on the relation between *oikonomia* and *theologia*. The *oikonomia* of God, for Lossky, reveals something of God, but this something is not of God's essence since God's essence is unknowable. The result is that God's *oikonomia* does not lead to a positive knowledge of *theologia*, or God's unknowable essence. It does reveal that God is Trinity, but simply as a "primordial fact."[4] God's *oikonomia* cannot tell us anything more about God's trinitarian life other than the "fact" that God is Trinity. Dogmas attempt to express this revealed "fact" about God's life. In the end, for Lossky, the link between God's *oikonomia* and the *theologia* of God's immanent life is slim, and God's immanent life as Trinity remains shrouded in an apophatic cloud.

Apophaticism is related to trinitarian theology insofar as it is needed not only to preserve God's transcendence but to express adequately this "fact" of God's trinitarian life. The Incarnation reveals not only God as Trinity, but a certain descending order in the economy of the divine persons. "Every act of the divine economy follows this descending line: from the Father, through the Son in the Holy Spirit."[5] To make this descending economy the basis for trinitarian theology would be to fall into subordinationism: "It is an exclusive attachment to the economic aspect of the Trinity, with stress on the cosmological signification of the Logos, which renders Ante-Nicene Trinitarian theology suspect of subordinationism."[6] God would not be a true Trinity. The Son would be lower than the Father and the Spirit lower than both insofar as the Father sends the Son and the Spirit into creation. God would be no different than a monad and the philosophical God would reign over the God of revelation.

This apophatic thrust in relation to the Trinity exists on many levels. For one, the fact that the notion of God as Trinity is not a rational concept, an apophatic divesting of the mind is required for acceptance of the trinitarian God based on faith. Second, the economic manifestation of the Father and the Spirit through the Son, in order to avoid subordinationism and all it implies, makes necessary a divesting of the economic properties in relation to the persons of the Trinity. An example of such divesting is the identification of the properties of 'Wisdom' and *Logos* with the Son. According to Lossky, though all the persons of the Trinity share the divine energies, and the divine will in relation to creation is one, each person has a specific role in relation to creation:

> the Father appears as the possessor of the attribute which is manifested, the Son as the manifestation of the Father, the Holy Spirit as He who manifests. . . . This is why the attribute of Wisdom, common to the

Trinity, designates the Son in the order of the divine economy.... The very name of the Word—*logos*—attributed to the Son is itself primarily a designation of the 'economic' order, proper to the second hypostasis as manifesting the nature of the Father.[7]

Elsewhere, Lossky elaborates:

> To speak of God in Himself, outside of any cosmological link, outside of any engagement in the *oikonomia* vis-à-vis the created world, it is necessary for theology—the knowledge which one can have of the consubstantial Trinity—to be the result of a way of abstraction, of an apophatic decanting by negation of all the attributes (Goodness, Wisdom, Life, Love, *etc.*) which in the plane of economy can be attached to the notions of the divine hypostases—of all the attributes which manifest the divine nature in creation.[8]

Such specificity in relation to the divine persons threatens the unity of the Trinity in creating a personal identity independent from the other persons. The apophatic thrust must move the economic Trinity past its economic manifestations toward a doctrine of the Trinity in which the unity-in-distinction is preserved. Ultimately, "what will subsist beyond all negating or positing, is the notion of the absolute hypostatic difference and of the equally absolute essential identity of the Father, the Son, and the Holy Spirit."[9] What more can apophaticism reveal of God as Trinity? According to Lossky, apophaticism's main purpose is not to reveal the nature of God as Trinity, but to preserve the fact of God as Trinity, a doctrinal purity that leads to the experience of union with the trinitarian God. But to preserve this doctrinal fact, a quest for categories must ensue that can adequately express the unity-in-distinction of God's trinitarian life.

This search for proper categories expressing the unity and plurality of God as Trinity has only one specific goal for Lossky: "to make theological discourse possible."[10] As we have seen, theological discourse is necessary as an anagogical tool in that it guides one toward union. If human destiny is union with the God of the Incarnate Christ, then theological discourse must in some way speak of this God. But since the Triune God is on the level of *theologia* this discourse must remain shrouded in apophaticism. It requires above all a deconceptualization of concepts that have their foundation in human rationality.[11] In the apophatic understanding of the doctrine of the Trinity, "what will subsist beyond all negating or positing is the notion of the absolute hypostatic difference and of the equally absolute essential identity of the Father, the Son and the Holy Spirit."[12] The quest of categories then, especially in the Greek patristic thought, was not a search for a foundational concept, such as love, which identifies the very essence of God and explains its expression as Trinity.[13] If "the incarnation, the point of departure for theology, immediately puts at the heart of the latter the mystery of the Trinity,"[14] then theology, if it is to maintain its apophatic thrust also required by the Incarnation, must express *that* God is Trinity, not *how* God is Trinity. The categories themselves must express the *antinomy* of unity and personal diversity in God, "without giving the preeminence either to the one or to the other."[15]

Lossky rejects the claim that apophasis and trinitarian theology are incompatible.[16] The fact that apophasis leads to the notion of *hyper*-essence in relation to God does not translate into a supratrinitarianism. Such an accusation "would be to misunderstand the dialectic which governs the game of negations and affirmations. One can define it as an intellectual discipline of the non-opposition of opposites."[17] We have already seen this game at work in relation to God's transcendence and immanence vis-à-vis the world. In relation to *theologia* or God as Trinity, this rule, "which presides over utilization of apophasis, excludes every attempt to reduce the Trinity of hypostases to a primordial, transpersonal Unity."[18] In the apophatic understanding of Trinity, "the principle of 'divine fecundity' (*to theogonon*) is upheld at the same level as 'superunity,' which suggests the distinction between nature and hypostasis without submitting the Trinity to Unity."[19] Ultimately, the "new element and peculiar to Christian theology" is the distinction or rather antinomy that expresses the simultaneity of absolute distinction and absolute identity in God as Trinity.[20] This antinomy is that of nature and person/*hypostasis*.

The Person/Nature Antinomy

The trinitarian categories used to express the "fact" of God's trinitarian being, God's unity-in-distinction, were established and defined during the trinitarian controversies of the fourth century. The two primary categories were nature/essence (*physis/ousia*) and person (*hypostasis/prosopon*). Fourth-century patristic writers did not coin these specific terms to express the doctrine of the Trinity; they were already embedded within a tradition of meaning. Lossky does argue, however, that the categories could not adequately express the doctrine of the Trinity without "deconceptualizing" them and substantially altering their meaning: "One is then present, with the Fathers, at a true transmutation of language: Using either philosophical terms or words of the current language, they change their meaning until they are rendered able to encompass this prodigiously new reality which Christianity alone reveals."[21]

When Lossky refers to a "transmutation of language," this seems less the case with the notion of the divine nature or essence. The fourth-century patristic writers, particularly the Cappadocian fathers, defined *ousia* or *physis* as "the reality common to the three."[22] In signifying what was identical among the three persons, its usage was not far from that of the ancient philosophers.[23] The "transmutation" is evident more in the trinitarian categories of *homoousios* and *hypostasis* and the antinomic relation between the two.

The term *homoousios*, "while assuming the diversity of the Three Persons, was meant to express the identity in the Trinity, by stressing the unity of the common nature against all subordinationism."[24] Moreover, the use of *homoousios* "introduced an immense innovation, since the identity of essence which it expressed unified, without reabsorbing them into their own unity, two irreducibly different persons," the Father and the Son.[25] By 'reabsorbing' Lossky has in mind Plotinus and his expression *to homoousion einai*.[26] Plotinus's trinity, on Lossky's reading, "comprises three consubstantial hypostases: the One, the Intelligence, and the Soul of the world. Their consubstantiality does not rise to the *trinitarian antinomy* of Christian dogma: it appears as a descending hierarchy and realizes itself through the ceaseless flow of the hypostases which pass the one into the other, reciprocally reflecting each other."[27] According to Lossky, there is no real Trinity here since the distinctions are absorbed into the essence that is the One. The Christian Trinity is antinomic and the category that expresses the identity of the distinct persons must imply the irreducible distinctions. For Lossky, the difference between the Christian Trinity and Plotinus's is indicative of the abyss that exists between revelation and philosophy: "Revelation sets an abyss between the truth which it declares and the truths which can be discovered by philosophical speculations."[28] Philosophy cannot approach the Christian Trinity. It can only help express it in human language. If *ousia*, with some modifications, expresses the identity of the three persons, then another category must express "the mystery of 'the other'" in the divine being, which was no easy task, since the ancients denounced "in the notion of 'the other' what they took to be a disintegration of being."[29]

According to Lossky's historical account of the trinitarian controversies of the fourth century, the term *prosopon* was too weak a word to affirm otherness in God's being.[30] *Prosopon* denoted "the delimiting, deceptive, and finally illusory aspect of the individual: not the open-face of personal being, but the masked-face of impersonal being. *Prosopon* indeed is the mask or the role of an actor: 'the other' here is all on the surface and as such it has no ontological density."[31] To this "weak and perhaps misleading word," the Greek fathers preferred "a word whose meaning they completely remodeled, that of *hypostasis*."[32]

According to Lossky, "*hypostasis* was a popular word which was beginning to assume a philosophical sense. In everyday language, it designated subsistence, but among certain Stoics, it had assumed the sense of a distinct substance, of the individual. In the final analysis, *ousia* and *hypostasis* were almost synonymous, both relating to being, the first denoting especially essence, the second, singularity, without, however, being able to express this divergence too far."[33] Part of the "genius of the Fathers" was to use two synonyms in order to express the antinomy of God as Trinity.[34] The genius lay not simply in the choice of the categories but in their reworking in order to approximate God's trinitarian being. The philosophical meanings of both categories were not clearly defined. *Ousia,* on Lossky's analysis, means an "individual substance, while being capable at the same time of denoting the essence common to many individuals"; *hypostasis* meant "existence in general, but capable also of application to individual substances."[35] The Greek fathers fixed their meaning so that *ousia* indicated that which is common and *hypostasis* that which is particular. The Father, Son, and Holy Spirit are three *hypostases* each of whom possesses the common *ousia*. The synonymous relation between the two categories allows for the affirmation that "*hypostasis* is the same as *ousia*: it receives all the same attributes—or all the negations—which can be formulated on the subject of the 'superessence.'"[36] The Father, Son, and Holy Spirit *are* the divine *ousia,* and each *is* God.[37]

The real genius of the Greek fathers and their break with ancient thought lies not so much in using *hypostasis* to define the particular; but rather in deconceptualizing *hypostasis* to define it as irreducibility to nature.[38] Each *hypostasis* of the Trinity is particular and that particularity cannot be reduced to the common nature. The only "common definition possible" for the concept of divine *hypostasis* is the "impossibility of any common definition of the three hypostases. They are alike in the fact that they are dissimilar."[39] Theological discourse can affirm that "the Father is neither the Son nor the Holy Spirit; that the Son is neither the Father nor the Spirit; that the Holy Spirit is neither the Father nor the Son."[40] Each of the divine *hypostases* is unique and cannot be reduced to the other two, or to the divine *ousia*. *Hypostasis,* then, is not only that which is individual in relation to nature, but individually unique and irreducible to anything common. But as we shall see below, *hypostasis* is more than *an individual*; it is a person (which is not *prosopon*).

To arrive at the understanding of *hypostasis* as person, theology must go beyond the concept of *hypostasis*. This irreducibility to nature is not necessarily the definition or the conceptual content of the *hypostasis*. To speak in these terms is to forget that the purpose of theological discourse is "to lead the intellect towards the mystery of the Trinity."[41] The Greek fathers availed themselves of these categories for this very purpose, and *ousia* and *hypostasis* "have the value of conventional signs rather than of concepts—in order to point out both absolute identity and absolute difference."[42] Lossky points out the mistake of certain Greek fathers who attempt to understand the relation between *ousia* and *hypostasis* on a conceptual level suggesting that the relation between the two is like that of Aristotle's 'first *ousia*' and 'second *ousia*.' According to Lossky, the 'first *ousia*' indicates individual substances while the 'second *ousia*' is the essence.[43] It is a relation of the specific to the general, "the genus or species to the individual."[44] Theodoret of Cyrus uses this model, and also "the same surprise awaits us in the writings of St. John of Damascus."[45] The main problem with this model is its conceptualization of "that which cannot be conceptualized."[46] Lossky's rejection of concepts stems from their being rooted in human thought. To conceptualize the Trinity is then to give to it a determination based on human thought, on created being. The given, however, is God as Trinity, a "fact" of revelation. Faced with this given, human thought can only approximate not define. Though the understanding of the relation of *hypostasis* to *ousia* is useful in that their identity indicates how the Three are the same, it does not go far enough, and in this sense it is simply inadequate. Applied to Trinity, *hypostasis* goes beyond its conceptual definition to indicate something more profound which is the theological notion of person.

The difference between the non-conceptual and the conceptual *hypostasis* is that between individual and person.[47] The concept of *hypostasis* is that of an individual substance which forms a part of nature. "The individual is part of a species, or rather he is only a part of it: he divides the nature to which he belongs, he is the result of its atomization, so to say.... Individuals are at once opposite and repetitive: each possesses its fraction of nature; but indefinitely divided, it is always the same nature, without authentic diversity."[48] Though in some sense unique, an individual's uniqueness is ultimately reducible to sameness or to nature. The Father, Son, and Holy Spirit are not individuals, since what is unique to their *hypostasis* is irreducible to the common *ousia*. Applied to the Trinity then, *hypostasis* goes beyond its conceptual content to approximate the divine life.⁴⁹ It is this difference from individual that makes *hypostasis* as person a strictly theological notion. Theology reveals to being a "new dimension of the personal" in attempting to give expression to the Threeness in God, and in so doing opens Christian anthropology to this personal dimension.⁵⁰

The difference between person and individual has much to do with the relation of person to nature. As we have seen, person, for Lossky, is irreducibility to nature. But in attempting to define what this irreducibility is, Lossky himself experiences a development in thought.⁵¹ In *The Mystical Theology* Lossky describes this irreducibility as a quality: "Indeed our ideas of human personality, of that *personal* quality which makes every human being unique, to be expressed only in terms of itself, this idea of *person* comes to us from Christian theology."⁵² But in a later article, Lossky moves from defining person as *something*. What is irreducible to nature is a *someone* who remains indefinable. Speaking to the possibilities of human personhood, Lossky explains:

> 'person' signifies the irreducibility of man to this nature—'irreducibility' and not 'something irreducible' or 'something which makes man irreducible to his nature' precisely because it cannot be a question here of 'something' distinct from 'another nature' but of *someone* who is distinct from his own nature, of someone who goes beyond his nature while still containing it, who makes it exist as human nature while still containing it, who makes it exist as human nature by this overstepping and yet does not exist in himself beyond the nature which he 'enhypostasizes' and which he constantly exceeds.⁵³

A person then is not a quality that can be defined and contained within a totality; it is a *someone* excessive to thought. One does not acquire a human person, one grows toward being a person. As we shall see below, the Christian life for Lossky is this growth from individuality to personhood, in which one is free from the limitations of nature. God in Godself is simply the presence of true persons. Being Father is not to possess a thing or a quality, but to be Father is what constitutes the uniqueness of the person of the Father which cannot be reduced to the common nature. Person then is a certain freedom from nature. Lossky might even say that person is the *ekstasis* of nature, "if I did not fear being reproached for introducing an expression too reminiscent of 'the ecstatic character' of the *Dasein* of Heidegger, after having criticized others who allowed themselves to make such comparisons."⁵⁴ Insofar as the uniqueness of the three persons cannot be reduced to the common *ousia*, then this *ousia* in no way determines what each of these persons are to be. "For the

Fathers, indeed, personhood is freedom in relation to nature: it eludes all conditioning."[55] The true person then is one that is free, not so much to do something, but from the limitations of nature.

The trinitarian doctrine must also give an account of the way the persons are distinct in the Trinity. This account, however, must not transgress the bounds set by apophasis. Since person indicates uniqueness, what is it that makes the three persons of the Trinity unique from each other? The answer is indicated in the biblical designations of Father, Son, and Holy Spirit. These names indicate, especially that of Father and Son, relations between the three persons, and "the only way to distinguish the hypostases will therefore be by making precise their relationships." Lossky adds that the only way to make precise these relations is to show how the Son and the Spirit are related "to the common source of divinity, to the 'divinity-source' of the Father."[56] The relations of the Son and the Spirit to the Father are what Lossky terms "the relation of origin" and such a relation is "the only characteristic of the hypostases which we can state to be exclusively proper to each, and which is never found in the others, by reason of their consubstantiality."[57] As we indicated earlier, the relations in the Trinity are understood apophatically in that the Father is not the Son, and so forth. More than this, the relation of origin affirms that the Son and the Spirit respectively have a specific relation to the Father determined by their origin from the Father. Traditionally, the origin of the Son is that of 'generation' while that of the Spirit is 'procession.' The fact that the Son is generated from the Father and the Spirit proceeds from the Father is what makes the Son and the Spirit distinct from each other.[58] The uniqueness of the Father is in being Father, the source of the other two persons. The Father "confers His one nature upon the Son and upon the Holy Spirit alike, while being differently conferred; for the procession of the Holy Spirit from the Father is not identical with the generation of the Son by the same Father."[59]

As the sole source of divinity, the Father is the principle of unity in the Trinity. For Lossky the Father as the principle of unity is what the Greek fathers meant by the *monarchia* of the Father.[60] The *monarchia* of the Father is central, according to Lossky, for a proper understanding of the Trinity. First, if the principle of unity were the common essence, as in the West, the common nature "thus overshadows the persons and transforms them into relations within the unity of the essence."[61] Essence as the principle of unity would give to essence a priority in the Trinity that endangers the antinomy between the one and the Three. The Father as the principle of unity as the source of divinity, i.e., the monarchy of the Father, gives rise to both person and nature simultaneously. In thinking Father, one thinks the other persons of the Trinity together with the common essence. "Thus the monarchy of the Father maintains the perfect equilibrium between the nature and the persons, without coming down too heavily on either side.... The one nature and the three hypostases are presented simultaneously to our understanding, with neither prior to the other."[62] Lossky thus affirms the monarchy of the Father based on the criterion of its suitability to an antinomic theology that attempts to express the antinomy of God's trinitarian being. The monarchy of the Father brings to mind the simultaneity of the unity-in-distinction of God's trinitarian life in a way not possible by locating the unity in the divine essence. It must be remembered that antinomy, for Lossky, is essential in theology not for its own sake, but for the purpose of expressing the antinomy of the transcendent and immanent God that makes possible the event of divine-human communion. According to Lossky's logic, a trinitarian theology that is not antinomic fails to express this central axiom of theological discourse.

The monarchy of the Father also establishes a personal principle as the source and unity of the Trinity. Only such a personal principle can generate persons whose uniqueness is irreducible and absolute. "The origin of the hypostases is not impersonal, since it is referred to the person of the Father; but it is unthinkable apart from their common possession of the same essence, the 'divinity in division undivided.'"[63] One sees in *The Mystical Theology* hints of this argument for the monarchy of the Father based on the axiom that only a personal principal can generate and guarantee the distinctiveness of other persons. The argument there is more negative in that if the monarchy of God were the impersonal divine essence, then personal distinctiveness is identified with the essence, and hence, indistinct.[64] In his "Procession of the Holy Spirit in Orthodox Trinitarian Doctrine," first published only fours years after *The Mystical Theology*, the argument becomes more explicit. The 'causality' within God's being must be a "personal principle" otherwise the alternative is God as monad.

> The Father is the Cause of the other hypostases in that He is not His essence, *i.e.,* in that He does not have His essence for Himself alone. What the image of causality wishes to express is the idea that the Father, being not merely an essence but a person, is by that very fact the cause of the other consubstantial Persons, who have the same essence as He has.[65]

The important phrase here is that the Father is "not His essence." This distinction between the nature and person is present in *The Mystical Theology,* but in affirming here that only a personal principle can be the source of other persons

Lossky is, ironically, saying something positive about God as Father as Person. A person is not identified with the essence. There is a certain freedom from essence that allows for that person to share this essence with other persons. If the Father were identified with the essence, then the Father would be a monad generating individual substances. Thus Lossky concludes that "with reference to the Father, causality expresses the idea that He is God-Person, in that He is the cause of other divine persons—the idea that He could not be fully and absolutely Person unless the Son and the Holy Spirit are equal to Him in possession of the same nature and *are* the same nature."[66] The mark of person is the freedom from nature that allows for the sharing of nature. The reality of the Son and the Spirit testify to the fact of God the Father as person, since they possess equally from the Father the divine nature. If the Father were a monad then the Father would be identified with the essence and not a person, since by definition a person possesses essence, and is then free in relation to the essence.

More forcefully toward the end of his career does Lossky argue for the necessity of a personal principle as source of the Trinity. Only a person can break free from the necessity of nature. "Surmounting the monad: the Father *is* a total gift of His divinity to the Son and to the Spirit. Were He only monad, were He to identify with His essence instead of giving it, He would not fully be a person."[67] Lossky returns to St. Maximus, who refers to "the eternal movement of love" in the Trinity, which he first cited in *The Mystical Theology* in the context of discussing the monarchy of the Father, and which he now further develops.[68] The Father as source begins this eternal movement of love. The Father as monarch means that the "very source of divinity is personal."[69] Lossky adds, in continuity with his previous work, that "the notion of monarchy therefore denotes in a single word the unity and the difference in God, *starting from a personal principle.*"[70]

What is new is Lossky's emphasis on love. In refuting the charge of subordinationism leveled against such an interpretation of the monarchy of the Father, Lossky replies that "in our experience, the cause is superior to the effect. In God, on the contrary, the cause as fulfillment of personal love cannot produce inferior effects: it wishes them to be equal in dignity, and is therefore also the cause of their equality."[71] Moreover, "the Father would not be a true person if He were not this: *pros,* towards, entirely turned towards other persons, entirely communicated to those whom He makes persons, therefore equals, by the wholeness of His love."[72] Not only is person a free existence in relation to nature, but it is freedom as love. The implication of Lossky's progression on this *monarchia* of the Father is that if the Father is person only by virtue of the

Father's relation to the Son and the Spirit, then the Father is person as freedom and love. More importantly, "what subsists beyond all negating or positing" is something substantially more than "the notion of absolute hypostatic difference and of the equally absolute identity of the Father, the Son and the Holy Spirit."[73] Person and nature become more than "conventional signs ... in order to point out both absolute identity and absolute difference."[74] They are ontological terms intimating a personal ontology in which true being is person as freedom and love in relation to nature. Lossky himself may have realized these implications when he affirmed that "the Fathers, by specializing their meaning, came to be able, without external hindrance, to root personhood in being, and *to personalize ontology*."[75] The tension, however, here in Lossky's later writings is that a personal ontology moves us into the realm of *theologia,* which for Lossky is off limits. This is not to suggest an abandonment of the dividing line between *oikonomia* and *theologia*. It is clear, however, that, whether consciously or unconsciously, Lossky gives content to person in the Trinity as freedom and love. In so doing he intimates a personal ontology based on trinitarian theology. The categories of 'person' and 'nature' go beyond simply expressing the "fact" that God is Trinity, the inexpressible antinomy of God's trinitarian life, but say something *about* God's trinitarian life.

Though he affirms the *monarchia* of the Father, Lossky does reject any implication that God as Trinity is dependent on the will of the Father. Lossky interprets this monarchy within the framework of the nature-will distinction which Lossky uses to understand the God-world relation. In short, created existence is an act of will, which means it is contingent, unnecessary, and based on the freedom of God. Given this distinction, Lossky then argues that the Trinity is not a work of the will, but a work of divine nature. According to Lossky, this distinction was first suggested by Athanasius of Alexandria and clarified by John of Damascus.[76] The work of will, Lossky argues, has reference to the created world outside of God; the work of nature refers to the generation and the procession of the Son and the Spirit. By 'work of nature' Lossky means to express that the generation and procession, though in the economic realm, may suggest some type of causality and, hence, contingency, in the realm of *theologia* indicates a "primordial fact," since there is no contingency in the nature of God.[77] Even 'work of nature' can be misleading, since there is no agency involved in God's being as Trinity. Such 'work' "is not a work in the proper sense, but the very being of God, for God *is,* by His nature, Father, Son and Holy Spirit."[78]

Nor does 'work of nature' imply any necessity to God's being as Trinity. Relating Trinity to necessity seems to remind Lossky of Russian sophiologist

Sergius Bulgakov. Contrary to what Bulgakov believed, "God has no need to reveal Himself to Himself, by a sort of wakening of consciousness of the Father within the Son and the Spirit."[79] In referring to God as absolute stability, Lossky is tempted to speak of God as Trinity as "an absolute necessity of perfect being."[80] Instead he argues that "the idea of necessity is not proper to the Trinity, for It transcends the antinomy of what is necessary, and the contingent; entirely personal and entirely nature, liberty and necessity are one, or, rather, can have no place in God."[81] Thus, Lossky seems to suggest that the distinction of nature and will in God is not necessarily that of necessity and contingency. Apophasis precludes making God the flip side of a logical distinction. 'Work of nature' means to convey for Lossky that it is internal to the divine nature, which makes the 'how' of the Trinity incomprehensible. Further, it constitutes the Trinity as a "primordial fact" rather than as a contingent reality. God is always, eternally existing as Trinity. Lossky asserts that "just as the trinitarian existence is not the result of an act of will, it is impossible to see here the process of an internal necessity."[82] Some might think that since God's existence is not an act of will, that there is a certain necessity to God's trinitarian being based on the fact that God is love or wisdom. Lossky rejects these conclusions in order to preserve God's absolute freedom. The apophatic character of theology, which attempts to express the God who is beyond all created being, requires such absolute freedom.

There is a tension in Lossky's thought here between his affirmation of the monarchy of the Father and his affirmation of the non-necessary character of God's trinitarian existence based on the nature/will distinction. On the one hand, the distinctiveness of the persons of the Trinity depends on the Father as source and not an impersonal nature. This notion of the monarchy of the Father leads Lossky, albeit inchoately, to affirm that God as person is freedom and love. Yet the absolute freedom of God is grounded not in the personhood of the Father, i.e., the Father as free and loving source of the Trinity, but in God's super-essence. Ironically, essence becomes the primary metaphysical principle for Lossky, though not as a defined essence, such as being or love, but as an incomprehensible essence. With this as the primary metaphysical principle, Trinity becomes simply a fact of *theologia* to be expressed. Ontologically, though Lossky speaks of the Father's capacity to "personalize ontology," it is the *hyper*-essence of God that determines the character of the trinitarian being of God, thus weakening the ontological import of the theological notion of person. Lossky might resolve this tension between personhood and *hyper*-essence by affirming a free and loving personal will on the part of the Father in relation to the other persons,[83] but for Lossky, this smacks of contingency and choice that have no place in God.

> It is the will—which, for the eastern tradition, never intervenes in the interior relationships of the Trinity, but determines the exterior activities of the divine Persons in relation to the created order—which constitutes the difference between the two aspects (the interior and exterior of God's being). The will is common to the three Persons.[84]

The divine will is an aspect of the divine nature that the three persons have in common.

To return to the distinction between nature and will and specifically the 'work of nature' and the 'work of will,' Lossky argues that this distinction indicates two processions in God. "The processions (*proodoi*) that do not go beyond the essence of God,"[85] those inherent to the divine nature, are the Trinity itself. The other procession flowing from the divine nature is that of the divine energies, which, though, not dependent on creation, in relation to creation become multiple in their effects while remaining in the simplicity of the divine cause. In relation to creation, "[i]t is the procession (*proodos*) of the divine union that multiplies and diversifies itself by the Divine goodness."[86] Both processions in God are eternal, but the processions of the energies, based on the will of God, become multiple in creation without losing their simplicity. As Lossky further explains, "The Son and the Holy Spirit are, so to say, personal processions, the energies natural processions."[87]

One might ask Lossky why, if the Trinity itself is the 'work of nature,' the energies are referred to as the 'natural processions'? The answer of course lies in the fact that the energies are a function of the essence in that they reveal the hidden God. One wonders, however, whether there is a certain imprecision in Lossky's choice of terms. It is one thing to affirm the antinomic character of theology based on the "apophatic attitude" that God is beyond being. But the positing of two processions in God might test the patience of those who already feel that Lossky has obliterated God's simplicity. In other words, the notion of two processions in God intimates a lack of coherent integration of the notion of energies with the notion of a trinitarian God. In relation to creation, Lossky has indicated that the will of God is one, and each person of the Trinity has a specific role in fulfilling this will. The question becomes how the persons of the Trinity are related to the divine energies on the realm of *theologia*? In terms of soteriology, if, as we shall comment below, the image of God in humans is personhood, is Lossky's relating salvation in terms of divine energies a reversion to the primacy of essence, albeit super-essence, over person? If salvation is to become person in the sense of a divine person, does not this mean the necessity of participation in the personal life of God and not simply God's energies?

Another indication of Lossky's lack of sufficient clarity on the relation of divine energies to divine persons occurs with his use of the notion 'mode of existence' (*tropos hyparxeos*).[88] For Lossky, the energies "might be described as that mode of existence of the Trinity which is outside of its inaccessible essence."[89] But the energies are not the only mode of existence in relation to God, the other being that of God's inexpressible essence. "Wholly unknowable in His essence, God wholly reveals Himself in His energies, which yet in no way divide His nature into two parts—knowable and unknowable—but signify *two different modes of the divine existence,* in the essence and outside of the essence."[90] The existence of the two modes of existence corresponds to the nature/will distinction in God, and to the two processions in God insofar as the Trinity is a 'work of nature.' One is then surprised to hear Lossky affirm that "when we say that the procession of the Holy Spirit is a relation which differs absolutely from the generation of the Son, we indicate the difference between them as to *mode of origin (tropos uparxeos* [*sic*]) from that common source in order to affirm that community of origin in no way affects the absolute diversity between the Son and the Spirit."[91] Here *tropos hyparxeos* is "mode of origin" and refers to the persons of the Trinity, and not to essence or energies. It must be said that Lossky does not cite the Greek *tropos hyparxeos* in the earlier quotations from *The Mystical Theology,* and perhaps he did not have this expression in mind when speaking of essence and energies. One could argue, however, that "mode of origin" is indeed a "mode of existing," which leaves one unsatisfied in terms of how Lossky reconciles these various modes of existences in God. In the end, one is left with the Aquinas-like statement that in God there are three distinctions: *hypostases,* essence, and energies.[92] But unlike Aquinas who demonstrates the interconnectedness of the five notions, four relations, three persons, two processions, and one essence, the relation between Lossky's distinctions remains somewhat opaque, especially when he introduces into God two processions and two modes of existence.

There is then a tension in Lossky's thought between his affirmation of an apophatic epistemology in theological discourse and his leanings toward a trinitarian ontology of personhood. The latter is evident in his discussion on the monarchy of the Father, which he develops later in his career, and which indicates an understanding of trinitarian 'person' in terms of love and freedom. It is also clear that trinitarian theology for Lossky is no more than an expression of the "primordial fact" of God as Trinity. In this sense, the goal of trinitarian theology is to express the antinomy of the unity-in-distinction of God's trinitarian being. The categories of *hypostasis* and *ousia* were deconceptualized precisely for this purpose. The monarchy of the Father is affirmed precisely because it brings to mind simultaneously the antinomy of the unity-in-distinction of God's trinitarian being. But in Lossky's discussion on the monarchy of the Father, he 'defines' person (*hypostasis*) as irreducible freedom from nature. 'Person' is a way of existing that is 'defined' in terms of freedom and love based on the monarchy of the Father, i.e., God's trinitarian life. Lossky seems to transgress his own apophatic limits here in relation to the Trinity, which is the summit of *theologia*, by giving positive content to the 'concept' of *hypostasis*. To *be* a trinitarian person is to exist as freedom and love. The apophatic distinction, however, between *theologia* and *oikonomia* leaves such a trinitarian understanding of personhood ungrounded.

Thus, Lossky's own affirmation of the centrality of the theological notion of person is undermined by the primacy of apophaticism in his doctrine of God.[93] One wonders whether to affirm, as Lossky does, that one cannot speak of God in the realm of *theologia*, that God in Godself is shrouded in apophaticism, is, ironically, to continue to make primary 'essence' language in God-talk, and to lean toward one side of the antinomy. Such a leaning effaces the diversity of the Trinity. Lossky, however, argues that prioritizing the unity of God's essence over the diversity of persons is the net result of 'Western' approaches to the Trinity and is most evident in the *filioque*.

The *Filioque*

No treatment of Lossky's understanding of the Trinity would be complete without a discussion of his view of the *filioque*. For Rowan Williams, "it is, of course, Lossky's attack on the *filioque* which is the most immediately striking feature of his polemic against Western theology."[94] It is also a position for which he will receive much criticism by both Orthodox and non-Orthodox alike.[95] Without doubt, Lossky considers the issue of the *filioque* as a serious obstacle to East-West unity. It would, however, be wrong to say, as Zizioulas does, that for Lossky the *filioque* is "*the* most crucial problem between the East and West."[96] The crucial problem for Lossky consists in the differences in theological method, which betray distinct theological epistemologies. As Lossky argues, "It is understandable that a divergence in this culminating point, insignificant as it may seem at first sight, should have a decisive importance.

The difference between the two conceptions of the Trinity determines, on both sides, the whole character of theological thought. This is so to such an extent that it becomes difficult to apply, without equivocation, the same name of theology to these two different ways of dealing with divine realities."[97] The *filioque* is the most evident example of how a faulty theological method can lead to a doctrine that threatens personhood, the independence of the Holy Spirit, and, most importantly, the possibilities for deification.[98] As even Rowan Williams admits, "his [Lossky's] unfairness and inaccuracy in particular criticisms of the West are not of primary significance; the essential complaint about Western intellectualism and subordination to philosophy remains unaffected, raising the whole question of rival conceptions of precisely how God is known, and how His activity is mediated in the world to created subjects."[99]

The controversy between East and West over the *filioque* is essentially a debate over the most adequate expression of the relations between the persons of the Trinity, particularly the person of the Holy Spirit.[100] For the Orthodox, as we saw for Lossky above, the most adequate expression is "relations of origin," while for the West it is "relations of opposition." Those familiar with the history of trinitarian theology will know that "relations of opposition" is not so much a 'Western' phrase as it is Thomistic. It is essentially with Aquinas and his interpreters that Lossky takes issue, as he sees in them the most sophisticated form of a trinitarian theology that ultimately began with Augustine. The Thomists and Neo-Thomists thus represent the sophistication of a theological method rooted in the primacy of reason and philosophy, whose beginning can be traced to Augustine. The "relations of opposition," Lossky argues, is then a consequence of this method.

The mistake of the West consists in attempting to understand the diversity within the Trinity from the perspective of the unified essence. Lossky essentially agrees with Theodore de Régnon, who writes that "Latin philosophy envisages first the nature in itself and then proceeds to the expression; Greek philosophy envisages first the expression and then penetrates it to find the nature."[101] It is the attempt to understand how the simple, unified essence can be diverse that leads the West to affirm that the Holy Spirit proceeds from both the Father and the Son.[102] With an emphasis on logic based on the "process of reasoning," the diversity within the unified essence can be established on this principle of "the relations of opposition." In other words, a relation can only exist between "two terms" that are opposed to each other. The opposition between the Father and Son is not difficult to establish, thus leading to the relations of paternity and filiation. The mutual opposition is more to difficult explain, and Aquinas ultimately concluded that the opposition of the Spirit must be to both the Father and the Son, otherwise there would be no way to distinguish the Son and the Spirit.[103] For Lossky then "this is the meaning of the formula (i.e., the *filioque*) according to which the Holy Spirit is said to proceed from the Father and the Son as from one principle of spiration."[104] Thus, the mutual opposition between the Spirit and both the Father and the Son is that of spiration to procession, leading Thomas to conclude four relations within the Trinity.

Lossky lists three problems with this approach to understanding the diversity within the unified essence. For one, "the relations are the basis of the hypostases, which define themselves by their mutual opposition, the first to the second, and these two together to the third."[105] The "relations of opposition" here for Lossky introduce a type of dependence and necessity in God, especially in terms of the distinctiveness of the *hypostases*. Lossky explains that "the relations only serve to *express* the hypostatic diversity of the Three; they are not the basis of it. It is the absolute diversity of the three hypostases which determines their differing relations to one another, not *vice versa*."[106] The diversity of the *hypostases* is then a "primordial fact" not dependent on relations based on mutual opposition. One could argue with Lossky that diversity must in some sense be based on, or identical with relations, and that even the Orthodox "relations of origin" cannot escape this inevitability since the diversity of the Son and the Spirit is based on the relation to the Father, and that of the Father depends on the relation to the Son and the Spirit. But to this Lossky argues that the "relations" of origin is meant to simply express the fact of and not the *how* of diversity in the Trinity. In affirming the Father alone as the source of the persons of the Holy Trinity no attempt is made to oppose the Spirit to the Son, because, for one, the procession is itself ineffable.[107] More importantly, the "relations of origin in the Trinity—filiation, procession—cannot be considered as the basis for the hypostases, as that which determines their absolute diversity."[108] It is here that Lossky concludes that relations only "*express* the hypostatic diversity of the Three; they are not the basis of it."

No doubt Lossky realized that even the "relations of origin" imply that personal diversity is based on origins. But the determination of personal diversity is not the *purpose* of the "relations of origin," which serve to indicate and not explain diversity in God. The "relations of origin" is, in effect, an apophatic way of explaining the diversity in God. "Here we cannot speak of relations of opposition but only of relations of diversity. To follow here the positive approach, and to envisage the relations of origin otherwise than as signs of the inexpressible diversity of the persons, is to suppress the absolute quality of personal diversity, *i.e.* to relativize the Trinity and in some sense to depersonalize it."[109] The depersonalization results from the attempt at an explanation whose only success would be to subject the Trinity to a totalizing scheme that levels all difference. But what Lossky fails to realize is that not to speak positively, or ontologically according to Zizioulas, of the relations of the persons of the Trinity may also carry with it the threat of depersonalizing the Trinity. The demands of apophaticism simply to *express* the Trinity as fact again indicates the priority of the *hyper*-essence with respect to God and an undermining of any ontological content to personal diversity.

The second problem is this depersonalization of the Trinity. Insofar as the Spirit proceeds from the Father and the Son "the two persons represent a non-personal unity, in that they give rise to a further relation of opposition."[110] Here Lossky is espousing the classic Orthodox argument against the *filioque*. If one accepts that the Holy Spirit proceeds from both persons, then the distinction between the Father and the Son is confused, and the Trinity is in jeopardy. The Father and the Son become "a single principle" and the diversity in the Trinity is "relativized."[111] Moreover, in that the Holy Spirit proceeds from both, the Holy Spirit becomes the bond that unites the Father and the Son, or "the unity of the two in their identical nature."[112] Not only is the personal diversity of the Son and the Father threatened by being "a single principle," but also that of the Spirit in being reduced "to no more than a reciprocal bond between the Father and the Son."[113] In being the love which the Father and the Son share, the Holy Spirit is no longer a person but an attribute. No matter which way one turns, the "relations of opposition" ultimately leads one, for Lossky, back to the essence of God.[114]

The third problem, and really a summation of the previous two, concerns the primacy of essence over the *hypostases*. The "relations of opposition" indicate that "in general the origin of the persons of the Trinity therefore is impersonal, having its real basis in the one essence, which is differentiated by its internal relations. The general character of this triadology may be described as a pre-eminence of natural unity over personal trinity, as an ontological primacy of the essence over the hypostases."[115] The solution does not consist in giving primacy to the *hypostases* over the divine *ousia*.[116] In trinitarian theology the antinomy between the unity and diversity, expressed as that between person and nature must be maintained, and this only through the "relations of origin" which emphasize the *monarchia* of the Father. In the person of the Father the unity and diversity is presented simultaneously.[117] It is the antinomic character above all which distinguishes the Orthodox approach to the Trinity from that of the West. Lossky explains the difference:

The positive approach employed by Filioquist triadology brings about a certain rationalization of the dogma of the Trinity, insofar as it suppresses the fundamental antinomy between the essence and the hypostases. One has the impression that the heights of theology have been deserted in order to descend to the level of religious philosophy. On the other hand, the negative approach, which places us face to face with the primordial antinomy of absolute identity and no less absolute diversity in God, does not seek to conceal this antinomy but to express it fittingly, so that the mystery of the Trinity might make us transcend the philosophical mode of thinking and that the Truth might make us free from our human limitations, but altering our means of understanding. If in the former approach faith seeks understanding, in order to transpose revelation onto the plane of philosophy, in the latter approach understanding seeks the realities of faith, in order to be transformed, by becoming more and more open to the mysteries of revelation.[118]

Thus, "by the dogma of the *Filioque,* the God of the philosophers and savants is introduced into the heart of the Living God."[119] And the fatal existential consequence of this introduction is that it precludes full personal communion with the divine. Lossky's opposition to the *filioque* is not simply because "it introduces a certain rationalization and therefore it is in opposition to the apophatic principle."[120] Lossky does not oppose a "rationalization" of theology because he wants to affirm the primacy of revelation as manifestation. For Lossky, revelation is the event of divine-human communion that is the condition for the possibility of salvation as deification. If theology is to help one toward this goal, it must express this antinomy of divine-human communion and must be antinomic. It must thus resist a rationalization for the sake of divine-human communion. For Lossky, the rationalization of theology precludes an ascent toward union with God insofar as the truth of God is defined in terms of concepts and propositions and not in terms of union with the living God. The rationalization of theology is, in the end for Lossky, idolatrous. It is revelation as divine-human communion that grounds all other antinomic distinctions for Lossky, such as essence/energies and person/nature. For this reason, Rowan Williams's claim that the "unifying theme" in Lossky's theology "might be called 'personalism'" requires further nuancing.[121] Lossky's understanding of 'person' is rooted in the realism of divine-human communion. My argument is that the latter is the unifying theme, and divine-human communion is nothing less for Lossky than a personal encounter.

Given Lossky's understanding of the relation between dogma and mysticism, doctrine is central toward guiding one to the experience of God that is a living of the doctrine. A theology based on a faulty theological method leads one down the wrong path. Perhaps, for this reason Lossky criticizes George Every for not seeing how dogmatic differences lie at the root of cultural and political differences, thus implying that the cultural and political differences point to deeper dogmatic differences, which themselves point to fundamental differences in orientation toward God.[122] The differences in "attitude" toward God form the foundation for differences in dogma and culture. The *filioque* points to a more fundamental difference between East and West, and is not simply the result of cultural and political phenomena.

Though his criticisms on Aquinas may be misleading, as Rowan Williams has indicated, this central insight that the differences between 'Eastern' and 'Western' theologies consist in different conceptions on the role of philosophy and, hence, on the use and limits of reason in theology, remains worth considering.[123] The problem with Lossky's critique of the *filioque*, and perhaps this is one of the "extremes" which Zizioulas refers to, is that he rejects any speculation on the 'how' of the relations in the Trinity for fear of making hypostatic diversity depend on some thing. Ironically, this rejection runs the risk of depersonalization, the one thing Lossky sought to avoid. The Father as the source of the Trinity implies a rich concept of person as freedom and love, one which Lossky himself attempted to clarify later in his career. But such a notion of person is only possible if ontological status is given to this 'how' of the relations in the Trinity. This notion of person becomes empty when Lossky continues to affirm that the "relations of origin" only serve to indicate diversity and not explain it. If such is the purpose of the *monarchia* of the Father, i.e., to only indicate difference, then person lacks ontological content, and thus, loses its power to render human existence meaningful. The issue then is whether one can begin where Lossky begins, a theology based on the experience of the revelation of God that gives to theology an "apophatic thrust," and yet still affirm something ontologically of God, i.e., on the realm of *theologia*.[124]

For Lossky, apophaticism is the precondition for trinitarian theology, since it alone can secure the antinomy of the unity-in-distinction of God's trinitarian life. A non-apophatic approach, as represented in Aquinas and Bulgakov, collapse the antinomy either in favor of the unity or the diversity. Insofar as the antinomy is collapsed, these attempts fail to express adequately the realism of divine-human communion that is grounded in the very being of God who is transcendent and immanent. The question becomes whether apophaticism is the only or most adequate way to express the realism of the divine-human communion and the God who is transcendent and immanent. To this, Zizioulas would respond negatively.

Zizioulas on Ontology and Trinity

Truth as Life

Christians gave further expression, according to Zizioulas, to the eucharistic understanding of truth in terms of the eschatological Body of Christ, the 'corporate personality,' especially in relation to both the Greek and Jewish cultural traditions. The Christian understanding of truth developed against Greek and Jewish conceptions while simultaneously integrating aspects of these forms of thought. Regarding the Greeks, Zizioulas argues that Christians affirmed their concern with ontology while rejecting the necessary link between God and the world implied in Greek thought. Contrary to this notion of 'necessity,' Christians maintained the biblical and, hence, Jewish notion of the absolute freedom of God who acts in history. The eucharistic understanding of truth integrated aspects of two seemingly contradictory notions of truth and did so by linking ontology, freedom, and history in the Person of Christ.[125] The challenge to early Christian thought

> can be summarized in the following question: How can we hold at one and the same time to the historical nature of truth and the presence of ultimate truth here and now? *How*, in other words, *can truth be considered simultaneously from the point of view of the 'nature' of being (Greek preoccupation) from the view of the goal or end of history (preoccupation of the Jews), and from the viewpoint of Christ, who is both a historical person and the permanent ground (the Logos) of being (the Christian claim)—and all while preserving God's 'otherness' in relation to creation?*[126]

The Christian response to such a challenge was the doctrine of the Trinity. Before, however, such a doctrine assumed its fourth-century form, two distinct trajectories emerged within the Christian tradition distinguished by their understanding of the Christian conception of truth.

The first approach is what Zizioulas calls the "*logos* approach" and is represented in the thought of Justin Martyr, Clement of Alexandria, and Origen. Although Zizioulas would not accuse these thinkers of ignoring the biblical roots of Christian thought, their particular identification of Christ with the Greek concept of *logos* did not adequately sever the 'necessary' link between God and the world. As Zizioulas himself puts it, "the idea of *logos* helped to explain the unity of God and creation, but not the difference that there is between the two."[127] In the end, it limits God's freedom and denies the truth of history. It will become clear below that the limitation of God's freedom and the denial of the truth of history are unacceptable, for Zizioulas, on soteriological grounds. A more adequate understanding of God's relation to the world and to history was developed in the "eucharistic approach" to truth represented in the thought of Ignatius of Antioch and Irenaeus of Lyon.

The proponents of the eucharistic approach to truth are those early Christian bishops whose flock was far less educated than the audiences addressed by Justin Martyr or Origen. This context led them to a conception of truth that is, to paraphrase Zizioulas, more 'practical' than rational.[128] Truth involved *life,* interprets Zizioulas, and not concepts or the mind. But its concern with the practicality of truth does not make truth something ephemeral. Truth is that which is eternal and unchanging, i.e., linked with being. The unity of all in the Body of Christ renews creation and bestows it with eternal life. This eucharistic approach to truth led to a seemingly impossible marriage between the practical and the ontological; life was equated with being. This identification is unusual for the Greek mind, particularly Aristotle for whom "life is *a quality added to being.*"[129] In this eucharistic conception of truth, life is not added to being but *is* true being. Truth was equated with that which lives forever; *true life* is *being* forever. For Zizioulas this notion of truth led to the radical reappraisal of Greek thought. As he puts it, "If a Greek mind was unable to say *in the same breath* 'being and life,' the Christian had to say both at once. This identification of being with life affected the idea of truth in a decisive way."[130]

It is in the thought of Ignatius that "we have the first profound identification of being with life."[131] Zizioulas maintains that the "role played by the eucharist in the theology of Ignatius is so decisive that it would be surprising if it had not had an influence on this identification of existence with life."[132] A more elaborate expression of this idea of truth is found in Irenaeus of Lyons. Against Gnostic rationality, Irenaeus interprets Christ as truth not of the mind but of "the *incorruptibility of being.*"[133] What led Ignatius and Irenaeus to identify truth with life was not any intellectual movement, but their shared experience in the eucharistic community.[134] Like Ignatius the eucharist is central to Irenaeus's thought and "and there is no doubt that this is what influenced his conception of incorruptibility, with its ontological implications."[135]

The radical implications of equating truth with life, according to Zizioulas, is that truth must be considered as simultaneously historical and ontological.

The ontological notion of truth as 'being forever' is now paradoxically identified with history.[136] There is no question for Zizioulas that such an understanding of truth has its roots in the eucharist. Speaking of Ignatius and Irenaeus, "if the eucharist is not *truly* Christ in the historical and material sense of the word 'truth,' then truth is not life and existence at the same time, since for both men the eucharist imparts life. Thus truth had to become historical without ceasing to be ontological."[137] The ontological implications of this eucharistic identification of truth with life would receive further clarification in the trinitarian theologies of Athanasius and the Cappadocian Fathers. He adds that this "identification of being with life is so decisive for the history of Christian theology that, in our opinion, it is solely upon this basis that the great achievements of Trinitarian theology of the fourth century can be judged to their full value."[138]

The Ontological Revolution

Further clarification of the God-world relation and of God's inner life within the eucharistic framework of Ignatius and Irenaeus came from Athanasius of Alexandria in the wake of the Arian controversy. "Athanasius' standpoint, which proved crucially important in the Church's struggle against Arianism, was a direct consequence of the ontology of communion formed within the current of eucharistic theology that connected Ignatius, through Irenaeus, up to Athanasius."[139] The eucharistic experience of divine-human communion rooted Athanasius's intransigence concerning the divinity of Christ. By adhering to the full divinity of Christ Athanasius was, according to Zizioulas, rejecting the Greek starting point with respect to God, which is reason. This does not mean that his theology lacked coherency or does not make use of reason.[140] The priority is given not so much to reason, interprets Zizioulas, as to the eucharistic event of the Body of Christ. Zizioulas's reading of Athanasius places the eucharistic experience of communion at the center of his reflection on God and God's relation to the world. This emphasis on 'communion' would alter radically Greek ontology and cosmology.

The first indication, says Zizioulas, of this radical change is Athanasius's distinction between the *nature* and *will* of God.[141] This distinction has profound cosmological and trinitarian implications. In attempting to assert the full divinity of the Son, Athanasius would assert that the Son's generation is a matter of nature, while the creation of the world is a matter of the will. According to Zizioulas, "this distinction was needed in order to make it plain that the being of the Son in his relation to God was not of the same kind as the being of the world. The Son's being belongs to the substance of God, while that of the world belongs to the will of God."[142] The implication is that the Son's being is eternal, while the world's is not only finite, but a product of the free will of God. Athanasius thus introduced otherness, difference, and relationality into the being of God, while affirming God's independence from the world and the latter's dependence on the free will of God, positions foreign to Greek thought. As will be clear below, these are the radical implications of a theology rooted in the eucharistic experience because the eucharist itself is an event of communion with two 'others,' God and the world, but one in which the 'otherness' of both God and the world is affirmed and not negated. According to Zizioulas, Athanasius's nature/will distinction flows logically from the eucharistic experience of communion, freedom, and otherness.

Athanasius was also wary of polytheism and wanted to adhere to the notion of the One God. To affirm the One God together with the divinity of the Son, Athanasius modified the concept of 'substance.' In Aristotle, the meaning of substance was that of a concrete individual thing which could exist in itself or on its own.[143] According to Zizioulas, "it is here that his departure from the cosmological thinking of Justin and Origen appears to be actually an adoption of the eucharistic thinking of Ignatius and Irenaeus." He adds that "to say that the Son belongs to God's substance implies that substance *possesses almost by definition a relational character*."[144] By 'relational character' Zizioulas does not mean the relations between substance, but the divine substance itself being inherently relational. The logic is that if the Son is divine, if the divine is eternal, and if God is signified by 'substance,' then the substance of God is relational and conceived as communion. God's being insofar as it is substance is not a 'thing in itself,' but communion; it is a relational entity.

Athanasius's principle contribution to Christian theology, according to Zizioulas, consists in developing that the "idea of *communion belongs not to the level of will and action but to that of substance*. Thus it establishes itself as an ontological category."[145] By ontological Zizioulas means here that communion is not added to the being of God, or something transitory, but is the being of God and as such an eternal 'being' or reality. As with the Son, communion is not a product of God's free will, but part of God's eternal existence. The development of this idea was aided by "the idea of communion which had acquired an ontological significance in and through the eucharistic approach to being."[146] Athanasius did, however, leave certain problems unanswered such as the nature of otherness within God and the ontological basis of the world created by God's will. Concerning the former, does Athanasius's distinction between substance and will make communion within God's eternal life necessary? As we will see below, the thrust of Zizioulas's thought moves toward the elimination of necessity in God in order to make sense of Athanasius's maxim that God became human so that humans could become gods. For a human being to become 'god,' she must be free from the limitations of created nature. But this freedom is possible only on the condition, argues Zizioulas, that God is free from the necessity of God's nature. Somehow Athanasius leaves unanswered the problem of freedom and communion, the question of how God's communal existence can be a product of freedom. Later Christian thinkers, particularly the Cappadocians, took up this problem.

Athanasius's 'nature/will' distinction resulted in what Zizioulas calls the first 'leavening' of Greek ontology, the second coming with the Cappadocians.[147] This 'leavening' consisted in upholding the biblical principle of God's absolute freedom from the world, while adhering to the Greek concern with ontology. A result of this 'leavening' is the notion of creation *ex nihilo*.[148] Although Athanasius did not use precisely this language,[149] he did affirm both a creation with a 'beginning' and a creation out of 'nothing,' both of which are implied by the creation *ex nihilo*. Concerning the 'beginning' of the world, Athanasius's distinction between generation according to 'substance' and generation according to 'will' identifies the Son with the first generation and creation with the latter. As a product of 'will' the world is, for one, not necessary. Athanasius succeeded in freeing God from the world (though not from the necessity of his own existence), and, consequently, from Greek ontological monism which necessarily linked God and the world.[150] Athanasius also clearly broke with his own Alexandrian tradition which, based on the principle of God's immutability, posited the existence of some type of eternal world.[151] Since it is a product of God's free will and not the substance of God, the world is not eternal since only the divine substance is eternal. If not eternal, then it had a 'beginning.' This is what it means for God to create: it is a free act on the part of God's will, which means the world did not exist eternally, since only God's substance exists eternally and that is not a product of will.[152]

There are several implications, according to Zizioulas, to the affirmation that the world has a 'beginning.' For one, "time and space are categories which come into being *together with creation*."[153] Zizioulas amplifies that "it is meaningless to ask 'what did God do before creating,' for there is no such thing as 'before' and 'after' until creation. Time and space are notions that have to do with beginning, and whatever had no beginning could not be measured with such categories."[154] The consequence of such an understanding of creation is that created existence itself is inherently conditioned by the structures of space and time, which affect "the existence of the universe throughout and decisively."[155] Zizioulas explains that "created being by definition is subject to these conditions, which not only mark the difference between God and the world, created and uncreated being, but also determine the world existentially."[156] It determines the world existentially, as we shall see below with the concept of 'nothing,' in that the world is inherently finite and, as a result, surrounded by death. Left by itself, the destiny of created existence is non-existence.

The second implication is that 'nothing' becomes an ontological category. The concept of creation *ex nihilo*, 'out of nothing' to some degree explains 'how' the world began to be. In fact, the understanding of a world with an absolute beginning "could only be expressed through the formula that the world was created 'out of nothing.'"[157] The creation 'out of nothing' secured for Athanasius God's ontological independence and transcendence from the world.[158] If the world were created from 'something' then the only option would be God's substance, but this would make the world God. The idea of something being made out of nothing of course made no sense to Greek thought and to much of contemporary thought. The logic of deification, however, seems to demand it and for the first time in late antique thought 'nothing' becomes ontologically absolute. Zizioulas himself explains that 'nothing' is

> ontologically absolute, in other words it has no relation to being, it does not have any ontological content whatsoever. When the Greek Fathers speak of creation from nothing they do not mean some decoration of the universe or some derivation of a world. In this way someone can say that the Greek Fathers were the first to introduce to Greek philosophy the meaning of nothing as absolute.[159]

To further elucidate the difference between the Christian and Greek understandings of the God-world relation, Zizioulas opposes the dialectic of 'God-cosmos' to 'created-uncreated.' He identifies the former with the Greeks and the latter with the Christians. The implication is that the first dialectic explains the world in terms of interdependence and necessity. The 'created-uncreated' dialectic presupposes an ontological act of God that brings something into being.[160] It makes the world a product of freedom and love, not of necessity.[161] This has important existential consequences in that created existence results from the love of God and depends on the love of God for its survival.[162] As Zizioulas himself says, "that the Christian God does not create because God loves the beautiful and wishes to give form and beauty to the *cosmos*. God creates because God wishes to exist something other than God's own self, with which . . . God wishes to be in communion."[163]

There are, thus, important existential considerations to the Athanasian understanding of creation and correlative concept of 'nothing.'[164] For one, the fact that the world is a product of God's will means that it is a product of God's love and freedom; it exists not out of necessity but out of God's love. It thus requires the love of God for its survival.[165] This fact may explain why 'God became human,' or more likely for Athanasius, the fact that God became 'human' leads to the conclusion of creation *ex nihilo;* in other words, the christological conditions the cosmological.

Creation out of 'nothing' also indicates that creation can return to nothing. Zizioulas explains that "creation taken *in itself* . . . constitutes an entity surrounded and conditioned by nothing; it came from nothing and will return to nothing . . . it hangs in a void and cannot avoid the threat of death."[166] It is not inherently necessary. God's love is needed but so is the free response of creation.[167] Zizioulas adds that "death amounts to the extinction of particular beings precisely because the world having come out of nothing and being penetrated by it does not possess any means *in its nature* whereby to overcome nothingness."[168] It is this 'nothingness' that is circumvented in the eucharistic communion with the triune God. In such a communion, the created transcends its own condition in relation with the uncreated, which is by nature eternal life.

Third, creation out of 'nothing' is the condition for the possibility of an existence based on freedom and love. If creation were not out of 'nothing,' then not only would creation itself be linked necessarily with God, but also God's existence itself would be faced with a given and, hence, not absolutely free. If God's existence is not one of absolute freedom, especially in relation to creation, then God cannot give what God does not have. If God is not free from necessity then God could not free creation from the necessity of its own finitude. The only way to circumvent this tragedy is to make the world itself eternal. To do so, however, would be to negate the concepts of absolute freedom and love in existence.

The principal contribution, then, of Athanasius was to draw out further the logical implications of the realism of divine-human communion realized in the event of the eucharist. If in the eucharist there is real communion with the divine, then in order for such a communion to be real it must exist in freedom and love. Freedom and love, however, imply that God and creation are ontologically distinct, that they are 'others.' The realism of divine-human communion in the eucharist implies an ontology in which history, freedom, love, otherness, particularity, and relationality become "ontologically absolute," in contrast to the 'closed' monistic ontology of the Greeks. Created existence as 'other' than God *is* forever as 'other' only in communion with the eternally loving and free God.[169] This also means that creation as 'other' is inherently finite and tends toward 'nothing' in the absence of such a communion with God. What Athanasius did not sufficiently clarify, however, is the nature of such a communion with *God*. How is it that God exists in such a way as to ground the realism of such a communion? To address this, the ontological revolution began by Athanasius would have to be continued by the Cappadocian fathers.

According to Zizioulas, heretical challenges forced the Cappadocian fathers—Basil of Caesarea, Gregory of Nazianzus, and Gregory of Nyssa—to think more extensively through the theological implications of the eucharistic experience, especially for God's inner life. Their interlocutors were specifically the Sabellians and the Eunomians. These two sets of conversation partners helped them to work through certain problems Athanasius left unresolved.[170] Sabellianism was a variety of Christian theology stemming from the second or third century that attempts to interpret the divine activity of Christ in relation to the one God. It intended to link Christ somehow with the divine while maintaining the biblical monotheism. The Sabellians rejected certain *logos* approaches, such as that of Origen or the more trinitarian approach of Athanasius, for fear of tritheism. They rejected anything that smelled of 'pagan polytheism.' Their solution was to affirm the one God who appears in three different modes or forms similar to the Hellenistic notion of the epiphany of the gods. Thus Christ and the Holy Spirit are not concrete beings, but manifestations of the one God in order to save the world.[171]

The Cappadocians shared this fear of tritheism, but resisted the Sabellian interpretation.[172] Although the notion of manifestation somehow protected God's transcendence vis-à-vis the world, it is insufficient on Athanasian grounds. The eucharistic event of communion must be maintained in order for there to be a salvation of the world. The Cappadocians agreed with Athanasius, and before him with Ignatius and Irenaeus, that the world in all its materiality could only be saved in communion with the divine. If Christ is truly the savior who *recapitulates* all within himself by the Holy Spirit, the body of which is offered proleptically in the eucharist, then Christ and the Holy Spirit are both true God and not manifestations. Thus the Cappadocians side with Athanasius in maintaining that the divine substance belongs both to the Father and to the Son, and even to the Holy Spirit. Christ and the Holy Spirit must be substantially God in order for the created existence to be saved through communion with God. The issue that the Cappadocians must address is the accusation of tritheism from the Sabellians.[173]

Taking a position similar to the tradition running through Ignatius, Irenaeus, and Athanasius, the Cappadocians, contends Zizioulas, found Greek philosophical categories useful but inadequate to express these eucharistic truths about God and the world. Greek philosophy proved incapable of expressing what was emerging as a trinitarian God who effects a divine-human communion without annihilating the uncreated/created dialectic. Athanasius broke ground for the Cappadocians by interpreting divine substance to be relational. The simplicity of the divine substance is not compromised if it is relational. But this relational divine substance must be further conceptualized in order to avoid tritheism and to protect God's freedom to exist from the necessities of nature.

As a start, the Cappadocians suggested that *ousia* in God "should be taken in the sense of the general category which we apply to more than one person."[174] Zizioulas adds that "with the help of Aristotelian philosophy they illustrated this by a reference to the one human nature or substance which is applied to all human beings, and to the many concrete human beings ... who are to be called *hypostases,* not natures or substances."[175] If, however, one can say three men, why not three Gods? The answer lies in the ontological difference between the human and divine substance. Human *ousia* as created *ousia* is affected by the realities of time and space. As a result, "nature precedes person," which means that when "John or George ... are born, the one human nature precedes them; they, therefore, represent and embody only *part* of the human nature. Through human procreation humanity is divided and no human person can be said to be the bearer of the totality of human nature."[176] As a result, humans become individuals, i.e., entities "independent ontologically from other human beings."[177] God's existence, however, is not subject to the conditions of time and space. Consequently, "the three persons of the Trinity do not share a pre-existing or logically prior to them divine nature, but coincide with it. Multiplicity in God does not involve a division of His nature, as happens with man."[178] The point here is that each of the divine beings of the Trinity is the divine nature in its fullest, not a section or a part of it. But even to "coincide" with the fullness of the divine nature does not obviate the charge of tritheism. More is needed than a modified concept of substance based on the created/uncreated distinction to maintain the ontological integrity of the three persons of the Trinity without destroying the divine unity. This requires, according to Zizioulas, a further distinction between nature and person.[179]

Eunomius, in large part, helped move the Cappadocians toward this distinction together with its resulting implications. The Eunomians took a Neo-Arian position attempting to deny the divinity of the Son by arguing that if the Father is *agennetos* then the Son as *gennetos* is of a different substance than the Father. To counter this Neo-Arian logic the Cappadocians made the distinction between "substance and person in God." This distinction implies substantial and personal names. The former are those names which belong to the divine substance (e.g., Good, Love) and which are applied to all three persons. The latter, however, belong only to the divine persons. For example, God is called Father not "with reference to His substance, but to personhood."[180] The Father is *agennetos* as Father not as divine substance; it is a personal name and does not preclude the Son from possessing the fullness of the divine *ousia*. Moreover, these *idiomata* or hypostatic properties "are incommunicable . . . whereas substance is communicated among the three persons. A person is thus defined through properties which are absolutely *unique,* and in this respect differs fundamentally from nature or substance."[181] Sabellianism and Eunomianism pushed the Cappadocians to clarify the ontology of communion suggested by earlier Christian thinkers especially in relation to the trinitarian God that such an ontology demands. To maintain the integrity of the three persons of the Trinity they modified the Athanasian concept of substance and made the distinction between the proper and common names of God. They needed, however, to clarify even more the concept of person if they were to be successful in developing an ontology in which the one and many coincide in communion.

The important thing for the Cappadocians was to emphasize the distinctiveness of the Father, Son, and the Holy Spirit without destroying the notion of the One God, which is demanded on soteriological grounds. To use strictly the term *homoousios* to affirm the threeness of God could lead to a Sabellian interpretation: God is one substance who manifests Godself in various ways. A category was needed to affirm the concrete existence of the Father, Son, and Holy Spirit. A likely candidate from the Greek philosophical stockpile of categories was *hypostasis*. Its exact meaning in the Cappadocians' philosophical milieu is ambiguous; no one sense is easily discernible.[182] In Christian usage it often carried the meaning of 'common principle,' the "spiritual stuff or substance of the Godhead."[183] It also had the sense of 'individual existent.'[184] Zizioulas does not say clearly in what sense the Cappadocians inherit the category, but given what he will say of their 'revolution' in Greek philosophy in terms of the identity of *hypostasis* and *person,* he would probably agree that they affirmed the latter sense which they probably knew from Origen.[185] As *hypostases* the Father, Son, and the Holy Spirit are concrete individual beings and not simply appearances of the One God.

Hypostasis, however, still leaves this emerging trinitarian understanding of God open to the charge of tritheism.[186] It has the merit of identifying the Father, Son, and Holy Spirit with the divine substance without annihilating their distinctiveness. But something more is needed in order to affirm that there are not three Gods, that the Father, Son, and Holy Spirit are the one God. The Neo-Platonic understanding of *hypostasis* as emanation was also unacceptable in that its link to Greek monism threatened God's transcendence to the world.[187] According to Zizioulas, this was accomplished by uniting the concepts of *prosopon* and *hypostasis.*[188]

Zizioulas gives us a history of the meaning of the concept of *prosopon* in Antiquity and Late Antiquity. Through this history he concludes that *hypostasis* and *prosopon* were never linked in Greek and Roman thought. The former had ontological content in that it was defined in relation to *ousia*. Having ontological content means for Zizioulas that it is real, permanent, and lasting.[189] *Prosopon* (*persona*) in Greek and Roman thought was wanting of ontological content.[190] In Greek thought it was understood as 'mask' and was used mostly in the Tragedies. The *prosopon* was the mask one puts on in order to fight fate, the necessity of the cosmological order. It had no relation to who one really was. It was an attempt to combat one's place within the universe, to free oneself from the necessity of being. The great tragedy, as Zizioulas interprets, is that this desire for freedom from necessity, from fate, is never fulfilled but always thwarted.[191] The 'mask' or *prosopon* has no ontological content in the sense of real, eternal being. It is a fleeting attempt to assert oneself against cosmological necessity but to no avail. In Roman thought the category had a more social content. It meant one's identity within the social-political web of the Roman empire. One's identity is constituted only in virtue of her or his place within the set of relations that constituted a community. What *persona* one assumed was determined by their place within this relational mesh. In addition to the relational aspect, *persona* also implied necessity in that most often in the late antique world, one's identity was predetermined by social conditions.

In the time of the Cappadocians, *prosopon,* according to Zizioulas's historical analysis, was a relational category implying freedom from necessity. Because it lacked ontological content, if it were used in relation to the Trinity it might lead to a Sabellian interpretation.[192] Thus the Cappadocians had to rework both the categories of *hypostasis* and *person* if they wanted to apply these insights to the Trinity. For Zizioulas, this reworking constituted a 'revolution' in both theological and philosophical thinking.[193] Although all the Cappadocians made specific contributions to this 'revolution' in philosophy, what they share in common is a desire to express and defend the trinitarian doctrine of God in the face of various challenges. The motivation for this defense was the adherence to the principle of divine-human communion which the trinitarian doctrine expressed and which is experienced in the eucharist. The result was an ontology of personhood in which *communion, otherness,* and *difference* were no longer absorbed into sameness or totality, but assumed ontological significance. 'Person' assumes priority over substance in this trinitarian ontology, which ultimately means love and freedom become constitutive of being itself. This ontology requires freedom to be constitutive even of God's very being, which, according to Zizioulas, the Cappadocians affirmed through the *monarchia* of the Father.

The shift in ontology is particularly evident in Basil's preference for personal categories over substantial categories when speaking of the Trinity.[194] Ample evidence, according to Zizioulas, exists in his letters and treatises indicating this preference. In his *On the Holy Spirit,* Basil avoids applying *homoousios* to the Holy Spirit.[195] Practical reasons may have fueled this abstention such as the risk of a Sabellian interpretation. In accepting the divinity of the Trinity it made no difference to Basil whether one said that the Holy Spirit was *homoousios* with the Father and the Son or that the Holy Spirit was 'uncreated.'[196] This choice on Basil's part is significant, avers Zizioulas, in that it shows that substantial categories were not 'essential,' so to speak, to trinitarian doctrine. It also shows Basil's restricted use of *ousia* when it comes to the Trinity. For one, the Trinity is not simply *ousia,* nor is the *ousia* the primary category for expressing the Trinity. In that it makes no difference whether to use *homoousios* or 'uncreated,' it would appear that for Basil they are synonymous. Thus *ousia* is used in relation to God to denote God's uncreated existence. As a category it assumes importance more in distinguishing God and the world rather than in expressing the trinitarian being of God.[197] The divine *ousia,* being uncreated, is distinct from the created *ousia.* To say that the Holy Spirit is uncreated is to say that the Spirit is *homoousios* with the Father and the Son, i.e., of the same divine, uncreated, eternal substance. If the Spirit is uncreated, the Spirit is God. Zizioulas points us to Basil's principle of opposites in *Epistle* 52 where he affirms that "piety demands that we proceed on the principle of opposites, and reason that, since mortal things do this, the immortal does otherwise."[198] In terms of *ousia* the created is not the uncreated and vice versa. As Zizioulas himself puts it, "neither in Athanasius nor in any of the Fathers of that century is there any indication that *ousia* was used for any other purpose other than to indicate simply that the Son is God (and not a creature)—not *how* he is so, or what this means for God's being as such, (e.g. its unity etc.)."[199]

The move from substantial to personal categories vis-à-vis the Trinity is buttressed, Zizioulas's argues, by Basil's preference to use *koinonia* instead of *ousia* to express the unity of God as Trinity. This preference was inspired mostly by his fear of mistaken Sabellianism. He wanted to "stress and safeguard the distinct and ontologically integral existence of each of the Persons of the Holy Trinity. . . . The *homoousios* was of little help to dispel such fears, for it could be itself subject to Sabellian interpretations." Thus, "Basil must have seen that the best way to speak of the unity of the Godhead was through the notion of *Koinonia*."[200]

The real 'revolution' of the Cappadocians, and again particularly Basil, is the identification of *prosopon* with *hypostasis*.[201] This identification is consistent with Basil's preference for *koinonia* over *ousia* as a category expressing the unity of God. Although Zizioulas does not state this explicitly, his interpretation suggests that the identification of *prosopon* with *hypostasis* is consistent with Basil's hesitancy to use substantial categories with reference to God. If *ousia* or *homoousios* were avoided by Basil for fear of Sabellianism or tritheism then *hypostasis*, a substantial category, remains inadequate for expressing the distinctiveness of the three for the same reasons. The other problem with *hypostasis* by itself is that it does not express the relational dimension of God or the communion between the Three. A category must express the distinctiveness while emphasizing both the relations between the Father, Son, and Holy Spirit and their transcendence to the world.

Prosopon would have had this potential to express the relational dimension of a concrete being, if it were an ontological category. According to Zizioulas, however, its use in Greco-Roman thought was non-ontological. There was nothing 'real' about the *person* in the theater or in the society. The person was relational but lacked ontological status, and thus could be open to a Sabellian interpretation. The relational dimension of *person* needed to be combined with the ontological character of *hypostasis* and this is precisely, argues Zizioulas, the genius of Basil.[202]

The ontological revolution that Zizioulas speaks of consists of the consequences of this identification of *prosopon* with *hypostasis*. This identification was for Basil the most adequate way to express both the distinctiveness of the Father, Son, and Holy Spirit, and yet their inseparable unity or *koinonia*. As *persons* the three are real ontological beings, i.e., *hypostatic* and are related to one another. The identification of *prosopon* with *hypostasis* protects the trinity from Sabellian or tritheistic interpretations. It affirms a God who is three and one, something that the experience of worship, the eucharist, as the event of the body of Christ demands. The identification of these two categories leads to an ontology of personhood, or a relational ontology, according to Zizioulas, which he argues is uniquely the product of the Greek fathers' interpretation of their experience of the Body of Christ. Suffice it to say that with this identification, for the first time in late antique thought otherness, difference, communion, and relation are ontological realities. The understandings of freedom, love, and the God-world relation also take on new meaning. What Zizioulas wants to stress here is that these insights are given to us for the first time by the Greek fathers in their attempt to give expression to their trinitarian faith with its basis in the communal worship of the eucharist. As we shall see below, this attempt, for Zizioulas, also provided answers to the most fundamental and timeless existential questions.

The Cappadocians affirm further this relational ontology through their insistence on the Father as the *aitia* (cause) of the trinitarian existence, or otherwise put, through their affirmation of the *monarchia* of the Father in trinitarian existence. An analysis of the principle of the *monarchia* of the Father will also clarify the essential features of this trinitarian ontology of personhood. The Father as *aitia* of God's trinitarian existence is the second 'leavening' of Greek thought,[203] or the second presupposition for an ontology of personhood.[204] According to Zizioulas, this insistence is seen mostly in Gregory the Theologian and is consistent with Basil's preference for *koinonia* and *prosopon* over *hypostasis* and *ousia* with respect to God.[205] The Father as *aitia* supports a relational ontology in two ways: for one, it links the unity of God to the person of the Father rather than to the divine *ousia*. *Monarchia,* the one *arche,* in the Greek fathers was identified with the Father. According to Zizioulas, "the 'one God' is the Father, and not the one substance, as Augustine and medieval Scholasticism would say."[206] This sense of *monarchia* means that God is one because of the Father, which evinces the priority for the Cappadocians of personal categories over substantial categories.[207]

Second, God's trinitarian existence is the result of a person, the freedom and the love of the Father, not the necessity of substance.[208] Zizioulas interprets the process of finding the logically highest name for God, such as Good or *Esse,* and trying to understand how the divine substance is trinitarian, as subjecting God's existence to the determinism of substance. The Cappadocian preference for *aitia* over *pege* (source) indicates further their affirmation of the priority of a personal over a substantial ontology: "Whereas *Pege* (source) could be understood substantially or naturalistically, *aitia* (cause) carried with it connotations of personal initiative . . . *freedom*. Divine being owes its being to a *free person,* not to impersonal substance."[209] To affirm the person of the Father as the *aitia* of trinitarian existence is to base such existence on freedom and love. Zizioulas is not speaking of freedom and love with relation to the world but within God's own existence. As Zizioulas himself put it bluntly, "God, as Father and not as substance, perpetually confirms through 'being' His *free* will to exist. And it is precisely His trinitarian existence that constitutes this confirmation: the Father out of love—that is, freely—begets the Son and brings forth the Spirit."[210] The Cappadocians introduced "freedom in ontology, something that Greek philosophy had never done before."[211] They did this by making God's own existence a result of the absolute, personal freedom of the Father.

Before clarifying further Zizioulas's understanding of an ontology of personhood based on the Cappadocian trinitarian theology, we return to the Athanasian nature/will distinction and Zizioulas's interpretation of the Cappadocian contribution to the coherency of such a distinction. Athanasius made such a distinction to distinguish the generation of the Son from that of creation. But as we saw with Lossky's appropriation of this distinction, without a further distinction, it remains unclear how God's trinitarian being is not subject to the necessity of nature.[212] If God's divine nature is necessary, i.e., cannot not exist, and if the Son's generation is a work of nature not of will, then the Son's generation is a matter of necessity. As we saw with Lossky, the nature/will distinction thwarts that which he wishes desperately to affirm: that God is beyond all necessity. Zizioulas himself makes use of the Athanasian nature/will distinction but not uncritically. He recognizes the problem for God's being of freedom and necessity inherent in the distinction, and argues that Gregory the Theologian[213] himself offers a solution based on the principle of the *monarchia* of the Father. If the Son's generation is simply a matter of nature it is necessary; if it is simply a matter of will, it is arbitrary. Thus a further distinction is required which would obviate this dilemma.

> In his *Orat. theol.* III, 5–7 Gregory distinguishes between 'will' (*thelesis*) and 'the willing one' (*ho thelon*). The significance of his position for our purpose here is twofold. On the one hand it implies that the question of freedom is a matter of *personhood*: God's being ultimately depends on a willing *person*—the Father; and on the other hand it indicates, as indeed Gregory explicitly states, that *even the Father's own being* is a result of the 'willing one'—the Father Himself. Thus by making a person—the Father—the ultimate point of ontological reference, the *aition*, the Cappadocian Fathers made it possible to introduce freedom into the notion of being, perhaps for the first time in the history of philosophy.[214]

The Father as *ho thelon* is eternally willing a free and loving communion with Son and the Spirit, and in this eternal willing, the trinitarian existence is neither necessary nor arbitrary, but freely and eternally confirmed.

The two categories that, according to Zizioulas, best express the nature of personal existence are *ekstasis* and *hypostasis*. For personal existence to be authentic, the "*hypo-static* and the *ek-static* have to coincide."[215] The former refers to love and the latter to freedom, which ultimately means that personal existence is one of love and freedom, as the *monarchia* of the Father indicates. Zizioulas defines *hypostatic* existence as one in which the person is "the bearer of nature in totality."[216] In divine existence, the persons of the Trinity possess the fullness, and not simply a part, of the divine nature. The Father, in begetting the Son and the Spirit, gives out of love the divine nature in full to each of the divine persons. The divine persons do not claim a part of the divine nature for their own identity, but possess the fullness of this nature in communion with the other persons. It is in this communion with other persons that what is common is affirmed in a relationship of love that constitutes each of the persons as unique and unrepeatable. It is not any particular qualities of the divine nature that constitute the uniqueness of the divine persons, but rather their particular relationships with each other. Thus, *hypostatic* existence implies a relational existence, in which persons in communion with others possess the fullness of nature uniquely, and in so possessing, share what is common with other persons.[217] The uniqueness of personal existence is not an isolated existence, but constituted in relationship with other persons. *Hypostatic* existence is one in which particularity and community converge through love.[218]

The second aspect of personal existence is its *ekstatic* character. *Ekstasis*, for Zizioulas, is defined ultimately in terms of freedom. *Ekstatic* existence is free existence, freedom from the *given*.[219] As Zizioulas himself puts it, "to be God means to be absolutely free in the sense of not being bound or confronted by any situation or reality *given* to you."[220] But such freedom is not simply from that of an eternally given world. God's freedom is one even from Godself. In other words, God is not subject to the necessity of existing according to the defined qualities of divine nature. In begetting the Son and the Spirit, the Father manifests an ecstatic transcendence from the necessity of divine nature and a freedom to constitute divine existence in a trinitarian way, i.e., as a loving communion of persons. As Zizioulas explains, "personhood implies the 'openness of being' and even more than that, the ek-stasis of being, i.e., a movement toward communion which leads to a transcendence of the boundaries of the 'self' and thus to freedom."[221] The *monarchia* of the Father is a manifestation of *ekstatic* existence, as the Father transcends the boundaries of divine nature and constitutes it in a personal communion of love with other persons.

Though personhood is both *ekstatic* and *hypostatic,* the latter two are not separate moments in personal existence. Trinitarian personhood is *ekstatic* and *hypostatic* simultaneously and eternally. Analytically, *ekstasis* is logically prior to *hypostasis,* which means that freedom is a precondition for love. God the Father must be free from the necessity of nature before expressing such freedom as love. Love depends on freedom, but in the *monarchia,* freedom is defined as love.[222]

Another important category for expressing the relational ontology of personhood implicit in a doctrine of the Trinity that affirms the *monarchia* of the Father is *tropos hyparxeos* or "mode of existence." The revelation of God as Trinity, according to Zizioulas, means that speech about God cannot simply be about the fact "that" God exists or about "what" God is in God's essence; it must also address the "how" of God's existence, i.e., God's *tropos hyparxeos*. To affirm the monarchy of the Father, as the Cappadocians did, means, according to Zizioulas, that God's trinitarian existence, the "how" of God's existence, is a result of freedom and not necessity. God's freedom is absolute even in relation to God's very being. It is not a question about whether God could will Godself not to exist, but rather one about God constituting God's existence in a particular way. As Zizioulas himself explains, "God first *is* God (His substance or nature, His being), and then exists as Trinity, that is, as persons."[223] The monarchy of the Father affirms that God constitutes God's being as trinitarian through freedom and love. Thus, if in the trinitarian life of God it is necessary to express the *tropos hyparxeos* of God's being, and not simply that God exists or what God is, then such an ontology is at its core personal and relational. Being, insofar as it is grounded in God, is grounded in the freedom and love of the person of the Father and, as such, is constituted as relational and personal in terms of its "mode of existence" or *tropos hyparxeos*.

The category of *tropos hyparxeos* is found in its most developed form in the thought of Maximus the Confessor.[224] For one, use of this phrase shows Maximus's continuity with the Cappadocians in preferring the primacy of personal categories over substantial categories when speaking of the trinitarian God.[225] Basil identifies the *tropos hyparxeos* with *prosopon* or *hypostasis* to indicate that no nature exists 'naked' without a 'mode of existence,' i.e., without its *hypostasis*.[226] The implication is that both nature and *hypostasis* are constitutive of existence simultaneously.

Maximus's use of *tropos hyparxeos* indicates that existence is not static but dynamic; existence cannot simply be defined in terms of 'what,' *auto,* or nature. There is no existence in itself without a particular 'mode of existing.' Another way to put this, according to Zizioulas, is that there is no nature without *hypostasis* or *prosopon.* 'Mode of existence' is the personal existence of God. If nature is the 'what' of God's existence, then *tropos hyparxeos* is the 'how' of God's existence. There is no 'what,' according to Zizioulas's reading of Maximus, without the 'how.'[227] Existence itself requires both a 'what' and 'how,' both nature and person. Person is the *hypostasis* of nature, thus it constitutes nature in a particular way. Insofar as *hypostasis* is personal it is relational, which means the particular is constituted in and through the communal.

In the case of God, Zizioulas would conclude, communion does not obliterate distinctiveness; it constitutes it.[228] The *ekstasis* of God is not that of substance but of the *prosopon* of the Father who through a free *ekstatic* love produces the 'other,' i.e., the Son and the Spirit, thus constituting a communion of loving persons. *Ekstasis* related to the trinitarian life of God bears the meaning of freedom of person from the limitations of nature. The Father is *ekstatic* person insofar as the Father's identity is not determined by the necessity of *ousia* but through freely constituted relations of loving persons. The Father is thus *ekstatic* person through love, thus defining the content of *ekstasis* in person in relation to love. The Father's own *tropos hyparxeos* or identity becomes one of person who is *ekstatic,* i.e., who transcends the limits of nature freely through love. The result is the equation of freedom and love. The *ekstatic* person is one whose freedom from the limits of nature is love and whose love is freedom. In the trinitarian life of God, *ekstasis* is linked to *tropos hyparxeos,* which results in defining the concept of true person as one who is *ekstatic,* i.e., transcends the limits of nature in freedom as love and love as freedom.

It would be good at this point to be reminded, by way of summary, that this understanding of God as Trinity in terms of a relational ontology of personhood is implicit in the experience of the eucharist. If the eucharist, according to Zizioulas, is communion with the Body of Christ, then such a communion can only make sense within a trinitarian relational ontology of personhood. The realism of divine-human communion within the eucharist is a union between two ontological 'others,' which presupposes a distinction between the uncreated and the created, the first 'leavening' of the Greek, 'closed' ontology. Created existence is finite and, as such, tends toward 'nothingness' and can *be* only in relation to the uncreated and eternal love of God. This communion with God is realized in the person of Christ, where created existence is affirmed in its 'otherness' and *is* forever as it transcends the limits of its own finitude. Such a communion is trinitarian insofar as in Christ one is in union with the Father of the Son by the power of the Holy Spirit. The eucharist is thus the source of the affirmation of the trinitarian life of God and the correlative concept of the monarchy of the Father. Zizioulas, however, is not arguing for the monarchy of the Father simply to resolve the question of the unity of the God's trinitarian existence. The principle of the monarchy of the Father is justified on existential grounds. If the communion in Christ is one in which created existence transcends its own limits, in which it is free from the necessity of finitude inherent in created existence, then this freedom has as its condition for possibility the absolute freedom of God in relation to creation but also to the 'mode of existence' of God's being. In short, God cannot give what God does not have, and in order for God to give created existence an *ekstatic* freedom from necessity through love, God's very being must be one that is freely constituted through love. This particular linking of the monarchy of the Father to existential concerns of created existence will receive further attention in the last chapter, but for now it makes clear how the realism of divine-human communion, for Zizioulas, realized in the eucharist shapes his trinitarian theology.

Apophaticism versus Ontology

For Lossky and Zizioulas the realism of divine-human communion is at the heart of their theological visions. We have seen how such an ontology informs diverse theological epistemologies that have resulted in distinct trinitarian theologies. For Lossky, apophaticism is a necessary precondition for trinitarian theology. The doctrine of the Trinity is a "fact" of revelation. Its antinomic character of the God who is three and one, unity-in-distinction, is a further revelation of the antinomic God who is simultaneously transcendent and immanent. The goal of trinitarian theology is to preserve the antinomy, which means finding proper categories that bring to mind both the unity and distinction within God's life. For this reason, the monarchy of the Father is to be affirmed as the ground of unity within the trinitarian life over the divine essence since the former recalls to mind at once both the unity and distinction, the antinomic unity-in-distinction, within the trinitarian life. In the end, the goal is to preserve the antinomy whose purpose is to transport our contemplation toward union with the God beyond thought and beyond being. Lossky, however, somewhat transgresses his apophatic limits on theology when he further reflects on the monarchy of the Father as a personalization of ontology and the basis for an understanding of 'person' in terms of freedom and love. There is tension, then, in Lossky's thought between his theology of personhood and his apophatic approach to the doctrine of the Trinity.

For Zizioulas, the God revealed in the eucharist is the trinitarian God and, as such, trinitarian theology does not simply express an antinomic "fact" but rather something real about God. In the eucharist, communion exists not with the God beyond being but with the trinitarian being of God. Hence, trinitarian theology is about this trinitarian being, which has radical implications for ontology. The Christian doctrine of the Trinity 'revolutionized' ontology by prioritizing the 'person' and 'relation' over substance. The details of this revolution are seen in the Cappadocian reworking of the Greek philosophical categories of *hypostasis* and *prosopon*. It is also evident in their affirmation of the monarchy of the Father. The importance of the monarchy of the Father is not for expressing an antinomy but, rather, a relational ontology of trinitarian personhood. Only such an ontology can, according to Zizioulas, make sense of the realism of divine-human communion realized in Christ.

Emerging as the central issue between Lossky and Zizioulas is the relation between *oikonomia* and *theologia* or the immanent and the economic trinity. With his relational ontology of trinitarian personhood, Zizioulas is arguing against Lossky's apophaticism by affirming that the immanent trinity, *theologia*, is experienced and known in the eucharistic. The question becomes how Zizioulas can ground such a claim while meeting Lossky's own possible objections that such an ontology shatters the antinomy of God's transcendence and immanence, or inevitably leads to the rationalization of theology and the understanding of God within the limits of the horizon of creation?

chapter 3

Knowing the Triune God

For both theologians the God who is known through a union (Lossky) or communion (Zizioulas) is a trinitarian God. The doctrine of God as Trinity emerges from this union/communion since all three persons, Father, Son and Holy Spirit, are involved in this saving knowledge. Lossky and Zizioulas agree that the patristic attempt to express the doctrine of the Trinity was not simply an exercise in philosophical speculation. It was rather a sincere effort to express the God encountered in a union/communion. Moreover, the Greek fathers considered the right expression of God an existential necessity. The doctrine of God was the summation of all other doctrines. Implicit in it was God's relation to the world, the nature of creation, the identity of the human being, the character of salvation. To err in relation to a doctrine of God would result in misconceiving the nature of salvation, which itself would create obstacles to that saving union/communion with God. The doctrine of the Trinity is, thus, intimately linked to the event of saving knowledge in the form of union/communion. We know that God is Trinity through this event, and it is the doctrine of the Trinity that points us to the possibility of such a saving knowledge. The search, then, for the proper categories to express the knowledge of God as Trinity is necessary both for a proper understanding of God and to safeguard the possibility for a salvific union/communion with God. For both theologians, the category of "person" becomes crucial to this task.

There is a tension, as I have demonstrated, in Lossky's theology between his emphasis on apophaticism and his theological notion of person. For Lossky, the necessity for apophaticism is based on Christology, i.e., the understanding of Christ as the Person who unites within himself the divine and the human.

This christological principle leads Lossky to affirm the ontological break between the created and the uncreated, a distinction synonymous with that between being and non-being. Christology also affirms God's immanence to creation, which leads for Lossky to a further distinction between God's essence and energies. God is transcendent in God's essence, but immanent in God's energies. The dialectic between transcendence and immanence is also present in Lossky's trinitarian theology. For Lossky there are two realms, *theologia* and *oikonomia*. We know that God is Trinity through the revelation given in *oikonomia*. Through an *oikonomia,* or condescension, God is present in the world and reveals Godself. But all that is revealed is *that* God is Trinity, the "fact" that God is Trinity. With regard to God's inner trinitarian life, which Lossky refers to as *theologia,* silence is the rule. *Theologia* is the realm of non-being, about which no words suffice.

The tension in Lossky's thought between apophaticism and ontology can be seen especially in his theological notion of person. There are passages in which Lossky affirms that the categories of person and nature used to express the unity and plurality of the triune life express nothing about the trinitarian being. They are simply used to express *that* God is Trinity. There is an apophaticism that shrouds the trinitarian categories. As I have indicated, Lossky appears to break through the bright darkness of apophaticism when he begins to speak of person as *ekstasis,* freedom, and love. He gives content to the category of person in such a way that person no longer indicates simply the trinitarian distinctions, but how the Father, Son, and Holy Spirit exist as persons. He is, in effect, expressing something about the trinitarian *being* of God, i.e., about *how* God is as Trinity. The problem for Lossky is that he does not have the conceptual apparatus to link his theological notion of person with his apophaticism, primarily because of the priority given to apophaticism in theological method. Lossky cannot conceive of how any speculation can be rendered on the immanent life of the trinitarian God, apart from a Thomistic rationalism, which for him eviscerates the trinitarian distinctions and, more importantly, threatens the possibility of *theosis* by freezing thought in conceptual idols.

Zizioulas's contribution lies in providing the means to link apophaticism and ontology within trinitarian reflection. Thus, the crucial difference between Lossky and Zizioulas is over the centrality of apophaticism for theological discourse in general, and especially on the doctrine of the Trinity.[1] It must first be remembered that Zizioulas himself is not negating the importance of apophaticism for theology, but affirming the priority of ontology over apophaticism. He argues that "[w]ithout an apophatic theology, which would allow us to go beyond the economic Trinity, and to draw a sharp distinction between ontology and epistemology . . . or between *being* and *revelation,* God and the world become an unbreakable unity and God's transcendence is at stake"[2] For Zizioulas, apophaticism serves two fundamental purposes. One, it qualifies Rahner's axiom, *"The 'economic' Trinity is the 'immanent' Trinity and the 'immanent' Trinity is the 'economic' Trinity,"* so that it is not misunderstood to mean that the world is necessary for God to be Trinity or that God is Trinity only in relation to the world. Zizioulas adds, "With the help of apophatic theology we may say that, although the Economic Trinity is the Immanent Trinity, the Immanent Trinity is not exhausted in the Economic Trinity."[3] The fact that Zizioulas would accept some identification between what Lossky describes as *theologia* (Immanent Trinity) and *oikonomia* is a significant difference, especially in relation to their understanding of apophaticism. Second, Zizioulas is joining other theologians such as John Milbank and Jean-Luc Marion in critiquing "onto-theology," or the inherent link between God, being, and thought. In other words, apophaticism allows one to go beyond a traditional metaphysics of substance toward a trinitarian ontology of relationality and personhood.[4]

In this sense, his thought is not so much a rejection of Lossky's as it is a completion. It is true that Zizioulas himself gives the impression that his thought represents a radical break from that of Lossky. Zizioulas critiques various aspects of Lossky's theology, such as his understanding of the *filioque*[5] and his pneumatology.[6] The impression, however, of a radical break is most evident in Zizioulas's trenchant critique of Lossky's apophaticism and its implications for trinitarian theology. In addressing this critique, it will be shown that Zizioulas's affirmation of the primacy of ontology over apophaticism in Orthodox theology represents not so much a break but a completion of Lossky's thought, inasmuch as Lossky's later writings indicate a move toward affirming the ontological character of person. Although Zizioulas presents a more adequate theological position, his critique of Lossky is often unfair.

This chapter, then, will critically compare Lossky and Zizioulas on the relation between trinitarian theology and theological epistemology. I will argue that at the heart of their differences are different attitudes toward the centrality of apophaticism in trinitarian theology. It will further show how their distinct understandings of the relation between trinitarian theology and theological epistemology are sources of their differences in other aspects of theology. The most notable impact is on their understandings of the nature of divine-human communion and adequacy of the traditional Eastern Orthodox category of divine 'energies.'

The *HOPOS ESTI* of Trinitarian Existence

In responding to certain criticisms made by the Greek Orthodox theologians John Panagopoulos and Savas Agourides,[7] Zizioulas decries what he calls the "allergy to ontology."[8] He feels this antipathy to ontology in contemporary Orthodox theology is due largely to the influence of Vladimir Lossky, whom he calls "a typical representative of the Slavophile tradition of a mysticism of Sobornost."[9] Lossky, according to Zizioulas, advanced an understanding of apophaticism "unknown in the Greek patristic tradition."[10] His understanding of apophaticism is closer to neo-platonism than the Greek patristic theology that Zizioulas interprets as being rooted in the eucharistic communion with the trinitarian God.[11] The biggest danger Zizioulas sees to a Losskian apophaticism is that it ineluctably leads to a "mystical trinitarianism" in which the particularities of the persons of the Trinity are eviscerated. As evidence of this, Zizioulas quotes a passage from Lossky's *The Mystical Theology of the Eastern Church*:

> The goal to which apophatic theology leads ... it is a question of an ascent towards the infinite; this infinite goal is not a nature or an essence, *nor is it a person;* it is something that *transcends* all notion of nature *and person:* it is Trinity.[12]

Zizioulas cites this passage as evidence that the priority given to apophaticism by Lossky weakens, if not obliterates, a doctrine of the Trinity. It is to this understanding of apophaticism that Zizioulas speaks as he attempts to argue for the priority of ontology within Orthodox theology.

This critique is, to say the least, odd and surprising, especially given Lossky's rejection of Russian religious philosophy. It is one thing to say that he may have been influenced by the "Slavophile" tradition in attempting to resolve similar problems, such as uniting collectivity and individuality, the notion of personal freedom, through the Greek patristic tradition, but Lossky's own solutions to these issues clearly place him out of this tradition.[13] Moreover, Zizioulas is not clear on how Lossky's apophaticism is linked to the Slavophile tradition of Sobornost.

Zizioulas also ignores or is simply unaware of Lossky's position that "Negative theology never includes the negation of persons."[14] In fact, Lossky later clarifies that apophaticism for the Cappadocians was a tool to deconceptualize trinitarian concepts of their philosophical meaning in order to ascribe them to the "mystery of a personal God in His transcendent nature."[15] Clearly, Lossky's emphasis on apophaticism was not intended to eliminate the irreducibility of the personal distinctiveness within the Trinity. Ironically, Lossky felt that apophaticism was the only way to preserve this personal distinctiveness, since it constituted the only viable alternative to a Thomistic rationalism and Russian sophiology which, according to Lossky, reduces to God's essence that which is irreducible in God. Nor was it intended to threaten God's freedom from necessity. It is somewhat surprising, if not astonishing, that Zizioulas groups Lossky with Pavel Florensky and other sophiologists who, Zizioulas claims, reduce the Trinity to "logical necessity."[16] Apophaticism and the category of *person* for Lossky were essential to theology precisely because they liberated God from the necessity of being.

Why, then, this gross misreading of Lossky on the part of Zizioulas? It is not so much that Zizioulas is simply responding to his critics' misappropriation of Lossky's apophaticism that is radicalized in ways not present in Lossky. Both Michel Stavrou and Constantine Agoras[17] argue that Zizioulas reads Lossky through John Panagopoulos's interpretation, who radicalizes Lossky's apophaticism. If one reads Panagopoulos, however, there are few references to Lossky, and the two citations to Lossky do not refer to his apophaticism. Apophaticism is a central theme in Orthodox thought and one cannot *de facto* attribute Panagopoulos's use of it to Lossky's influence. To attribute Zizioulas's critiques against Lossky's apophaticism to a misreading of another theologian is to fail to see the increasing tension in Lossky's thought between the apophatic and the ontological. Zizioulas is clearly familiar with Lossky's work to the point where he is able to make his own assessments. Moreover, though he mentions Lossky's influence on his critics, Zizioulas is responding to particular passages within the Losskian corpus. The fact that he bases much of his criticism of Lossky's apophaticism on a reading of *The Mystical Theology of the Eastern Church* says much for Zizioulas's reaction. It is in this, the earliest work of Lossky, where Lossky's theology of person is least developed. In his later work, Lossky was much more willing to argue for, what I would term, an ontological content to the category of person based on its application in trinitarian theology, without abandoning the apophatic foundation to trinitarian theology. Although we may assume that Zizioulas is familiar with Lossky's later work, he clearly does not account for this development in his thought. Given this progression in Lossky's thought, one cannot argue, as Zizioulas did, that Lossky engaged in a "mystical trinitarianism."

The more proper assessment is that there exists an unresolved tension in Lossky between apophaticism, which he sees as the only alternative to a reductive rationalism, and his theology of person that is implicitly an ontology of person.[18] In this sense, Zizioulas could then argue, as he does, that a priority given to apophaticism in theology threatens to undercut an ontology necessary for an adequate expression of God as Trinity. Zizioulas himself is right to argue, in his critique of Lossky, that apophaticism and an ontology of person cannot exist together without giving a priority to ontology. Otherwise, apophaticism yields to an alternative ontology, one of non-being, and not of personhood. Thus, the debate is not so much on whether Lossky's apophaticism reduces the Trinity to a monad, but whether it can sustain an ontology based on the *way the persons of the Trinity exist,* which he himself reflects on in his later work. Instead of a radical break, Zizioulas will succeed in putting the other half of Lossky's theology, that of person, on a firmer foundation. In order to do this, he must reduce the importance of apophaticism. He limits apophaticism not, as Lossky feared, by reverting to rationalism. Zizioulas transcends the Losskian dialectic between apophaticism and rationalism by rooting theology in the liturgical experience of God.

The experience of God in the liturgical context does not simply allow but makes necessary, for Zizioulas, a relational ontology of trinitarian personhood. Ontology, for Zizioulas, means the going "beyond what passes away into what always and truly is."[19] An ontology of God does not simply affirm that God exists, but discerns those attributes of God which have permanence and which define *being* itself. The challenge which trinitarian theology poses to discussions on ontology is the ontological status of the particular. In classical Greek ontology, "particularity is not ontologically absolute"[20] since it was fleeting and transient. Trinitarian theology, for Zizioulas, constituted a revolution in philosophical thinking in affirming the ontological priority of the particular. Even in contemporary philosophical discussions that attempt to ground the irreducible character of the other, Zizioulas is resolute that an ontology of the particular is not possible on "the basis of the world as it is."[21] The irreducibility of otherness and its identification with true being is justified only on theological grounds.

The key argument against Lossky's apophaticism lies in Zizioulas's affirmation that the communion of the created with the uncreated in Christ and made present in the eucharist is an experience of the immanent Trinity, i.e., God's being in itself. To give expression to this affirmation, the crucial distinction is not that between essence and energies, but between the existence of God and the *way* in which God exists. Not surprisingly, Zizioulas attributes this distinction to the Cappadocians.

In their attempt to give expression to God as Trinity, the Greek fathers, especially the Cappadocians, made a threefold distinction in speaking of the existence of God. First they affirmed that God existed (*hoti esti*), which for the Greek fathers is discernible not simply in the experience of God in Christ, but in creation itself. The other two distinctions deal specifically with God's trinitarian existence. In Greek patristic theology, essence or *ousia* indicated what was common to the three persons of the Trinity. According to Zizioulas, the *ousia* of God referred to the *what* (*ti esti*) of God's existence.[22] The personal distinctions in God were expressed, as I have shown, through the category of person. Zizioulas avers that the trinitarian existence of God as persons referred, for the Greek fathers, to the *how* (*hopos esti*), or the *tropos hyparxeos* (the mode of being), of God's being.[23] Zizioulas argues that for the Cappadocians the *what* of God's existence, i.e., God's *ousia,* is completely transcendent and unknowable, and it is there that "theology has nothing to say."[24] Apophaticism has its place in relation to the essence of God, since it is God's *ousia* that is unknowable. Its sphere of influence, however, does not extend over God's trinitarian existence. If theology has nothing to say about the *what* of God's existence, it must necessarily speak about the *how* of God's existence, the personal existence of God, since this personal existence is revealed and, hence known, experientially.[25] It is God's personal existence, i.e., as Trinity, that God "draws near to us, is known . . . only as person."[26] Zizioulas adds that within an Orthodox liturgical context, one prays neither to the *ousia* of God nor to the energies of God, but to the persons. The *hopos esti* or *tropos hyparxeos* of God's existence is knowable, because it is experienced. The implication for Zizioulas is that this knowledge makes possible a theological ontology in which the personal distinctions in God have an absolute character. The trinitarian categories do not serve simply to indicate that God is Trinity, but express an ontology rooted in God's very being and in which otherness and particularity have ontological priority.

It is the identification of the *hopos esti* or the *how* of God's existence with God's trinitarian existence that allows Zizioulas to argue for the priority of a relational ontology of trinitarian personhood over apophaticism within trinitarian theology. He does not argue for this priority simply by an appeal to the *hoti esti* or the fact *that* God exists.[27] Although it is not wrong to say that an ontology of God is possible by virtue of affirming God's existence, Zizioulas is not arguing for the priority of such an ontology. He would argue that such an ontology can be established without appeals to God's revelation in Christ. It would be not only distinct from, but also mutually exclusive with a trinitarian ontology of personhood in that the former would assert the primacy of essence over the trinitarian persons since the latter are only known in the revelation of Christ. Moreover, without the necessary identification of the *hopos esti* with God's trinitarian existence, and without the subsequent argument that this *hopos esti* of God is experienced and, hence known, God's revelation in Christ would simply affirm *that* God is Trinity. It could not form the basis for a trinitarian ontology of personhood which presupposes a knowledge of *how* God exists as Trinity, and thus, according to Zizioulas's logic, an experience of this *how* of trinitarian existence. In order to justify the necessity of a trinitarian ontology of personhood, Zizioulas refers not to the *hoti esti,* but the *hopos esti,* the how of God's existence which is experienced in the Body of Christ.

Lossky nowhere makes the threefold distinction that exists in Zizioulas's thought, though he does refer to the *tropos hyparxeos,* which Zizioulas identifies with the *how* of God's existence. As we saw, he is not consistent in his use of the category, sometimes using it to refer to God's energies, other times to God's triune existence. This inconsistency reveals that it does not have the same import for his theology as it does for Zizioulas. It also indicates that Zizioulas is interpreting the patristic category in a way not seen by Lossky, thus providing further evidence of its importance for understanding the differences between him and Lossky. For Lossky, there are only the two distinctions, *hoti esti,* that God exists, and *ti esti,* what God is. The 'what' of God is Trinity, but since this 'what' is distinct from the 'what' of creation, it is unknowable. The revelation in Christ simply reveals the *fact* that God exists and exists as Trinity and does not eliminate the shroud of apophaticism that surrounds God by virtue of his being uncreated and our being created.

Zizioulas is arguing for the necessity of a further distinction, one that Lossky fails to make, when speaking of God to account for God's trinitarian existence—the *hopos esti*. The particular trinitarian ontology, an ontology of personhood and communion, is rooted in the argument that the *hopos esti* of God is experienced and, hence knowable, in Christ, whose person is the link between the created and the uncreated. Thus, knowledge of God through participation in the *hopos esti* of God's trinitarian existence renders possible and necessary the theological articulation not simply of any ontology, but a trinitarian ontology of personhood. More importantly, Zizioulas is arguing that the distinctions of *hopos esti, tropos hyparxeos,* and *hypostasis,* which Zizioulas interprets as being synonymous, are necessary for conceptualization of divine-human communion in a way not possible within the traditional philosophical distinctions of being/act, being/non-being, and essence/existence. It allows for the possibility of thinking of the experience of the immanent life of God, a conclusion implied in the logic of the realism of divine-human communion.

The Economic and the Immanent Trinity

It is the notion of the *hopos esti* of God's existence that allows Zizioulas to affirm the possibility of a trinitarian ontology and that has implications for reconceiving the traditional distinction between *oikonomia* and *theologia*. It is this trinitarian ontology that provides the framework for Zizioulas to interpret and to systematically relate other theological notions, such as Christology and soteriology. The substantial theological differences between Lossky and Zizioulas can be traced to the absence of such a trinitarian ontology in Lossky. A trinitarian ontology leads Zizioulas to define salvation in terms of personal identity in Christ and not in terms of divine energies as Lossky does. It results as well in a different interpretation of the significance of the Chalcedonian christological formula. Before turning to these substantive theological differences, more must be said on the differences between the two theologians on the limits of God-talk.

As we have seen, Lossky's apophaticism leads him to posit two realms, that of *oikonomia* and *theologia*. According to Lossky, knowledge of God is possible through God's economy, or in the realm of *oikonomia*, which refers to God's action in the created realm. Knowledge of God in Godself, or *theologia*, is not possible according to Lossky, since God's life is eternal and ontologically distinct from created existence and, hence, beyond any human knowing. Not even God's economy can reveal anything positive about *theologia* or God in Godself. Though the revelation of God's economy in Christ reveals *that* God is Trinity, nothing more can be said of God's trinitarian existence since "Trinitarian being belongs to the transcendent nature of God,"[28] i.e., *theologia*.

In contemporary trinitarian discussions, this split between *theologia* and *oikonomia* has been challenged by no less than Karl Rahner. Ironically, Rahner draws on the Eastern fathers in order to affirm his famous axiom, *"The 'economic' Trinity is the 'immanent' Trinity and the 'immanent' Trinity is the 'economic' Trinity."* For Rahner, what God is in God's economy is what God is in God's immanence or *theologia*, though it does not exhaust what God is in Godself. This axiom would define the contemporary trinitarian discussions as most recent trinitarian theologies attempt in one form or another to develop a trinitarian theology based on the economy of God.[29] Although Lossky is not willing to cross the line between *oikonomia* and *theologia*, Zizioulas's understanding of the *hopos esti* of God allows for a rethinking of this traditional Orthodox distinction and for a particular reading of Rahner's axiom.

Through developing a trinitarian theology of personhood based on a participation in the *hopos esti* of God, Zizioulas, in effect, is agreeing with Rahner's axiom.[30] Though Lossky's system does not allow for speaking about *theologia* based on *oikonomia,* Zizioulas's trinitarian ontology is a theology about the *being* of God's immanent life, i.e., *theologia.* The *oikonomia* of God, for Zizioulas, is a trinitarian event in which the Son and the Holy Spirit fulfill the work of the Father. In God's economy, each person of the Trinity conditions the specific work of the other person. To be affected by the specific work of the Trinity is to be in relation with all the persons not simply because the work of the Trinity is one, but the identity of the persons of the Trinity is constituted in relation to the other persons. As we saw in Zizioulas's pneumatological Christology, the Holy Spirit constitutes Christ as the corporate personality, the one and the many in the eucharistic context. To be united in the Body of Christ is not simply to be in relation to the energies of God which are distinct from the non-being of God; it is a unity in the person of Christ. Through this participation one is able to affirm that God is a Trinity of persons. More than this, through salvation in the person of Christ, one is able to know what it means to be a trinitarian person in the sense of absolute freedom, love, and ecstasy. Salvation in the person of Christ is where *theologia* and *oikonomia,* the immanent and the economic Trinity unite.

Although Zizioulas cautions against collapsing the immanent Trinity into the economic Trinity, he is clearly arguing for less of an 'apophatic' distance between the two realms. This is evident in Zizioulas's interpretation of Basil's discussion of the proper doxology in *On the Holy Spirit.* According to Zizioulas's interpretation, the difference between the two prepositions *dia* and *syn* indicate for Basil the distinction between the economic and the immanent Trinity. He adds that "[i]f, on the other hand, one speaks of God in termes (*sic*) of liturgical and especially eucharistic experience, then, Basil argues, the proper doxology is that of *syn.* . . . The existence of God is revealed to us in the Liturgy as an event of communion. . . . This is the deeper meaning—and the merit—of the *syn-* doxology and for that matter of a theology inspired by the Liturgy."[31] Zizioulas then adds, "This language which taken up by *I Const.* opens the way to an argument based on liturgical experience and worship and thus to a theology which does not rest upon *historical or economical experience* [emphasis added]. . . . Nothing however can be said about *the way they exist* on the basis of the way they appear in the Economy."[32] "*The way they exist*" is the *hopos esti* of God that is the immanent life of the Trinity, and this is revealed in the eucharist.

Zizioulas appears to confuse the issue when he argues that "nothing however can be said about *the way they exist* on the basis of the way they appear in the Economy." But his statement has to be understood within the context of his strict definition of "economy" as God's act in history in the work of the Son who 'becomes' history.³³ A strict identification of the economic Trinity, understood as the Son 'becoming' history, and immanent Trinity would mean that God would become "suffering by nature," since the Son suffered on the Cross. It would also mean that God's very being is inextricably linked with creation, i.e., who God *is* depends on God's relation to creation. "This kind of God offers no real hope for Man," whose only hope lies in a God whose being is such that transcends suffering and the 'givens' of created finite existence, as witnessed in the work of the Holy Spirit who resurrects Christ.³⁴ Thus, the experience of God in the eucharist is really that of the 'immanent' Trinity, since the eucharist, as the work of the Holy Spirit constituting the community as the resurrected body of Christ, is a meta-historical or meta-economical work, if 'economy' is understood in the strict sense as the Son's 'becoming history.' The Holy Spirit makes present God's immanent life. Based on this strict definition, Zizioulas seems to be emphasizing a distinction between the economic and immanent realms, with the economic being strictly identified with Christ. If, however, one conceives of economy more broadly, as Zizioulas often does and as I argued above, as God's action in relation to the created realm, then Zizioulas is clearly affirming an identification, though not exhaustive, between the *economic* and the *immanent* Trinity. In other words, what one 'experiences' of God in history, is who God *is*.³⁵

Through the economy of God's saving grace, experienced in Christ, one is able to express the meaning of trinitarian personhood, of what it means to *be* a trinitarian person. A trinitarian ontology is not to be understood on the basis of cataphatic and apophatic theology. In other words, a trinitarian ontology is not a series of cataphatic statements which because of their inadequacy are to be negated in a process of spiritual growth. A trinitarian ontology is itself a negation of the non-being/being ontology which roots the cataphatic/apophatic distinction. The point of a trinitarian ontology is to affirm something absolute about God's inner life based on God's economy.

Such an ontology has ecumenical implications as well. It allows for further speculation on the inner life of God that may provide an ecumenical resolution to the problem of the *filioque*. For Lossky, the *filioque* is the fruit of a bad method that grounds speculation on God in reason rather than revelation. Zizioulas comments, "Lossky's views have led to extremes that are beginning to show the weaknesses of his position. The way he brought out the *filioque* issue as *the* crucial problem between the East and West is a clear example of how much Lossky's trinitarian theology stands in need of revision."³⁶ As I indicated above, Zizioulas does not tell us how Lossky's trinitarian theology is "in need of revision," but perhaps a few suggestions can be offered. For Zizioulas, to speculate how the Spirit may be involved in the procession of the Son is not from the beginning indicative of a rational starting point or a violation of the transcendence of God. Zizioulas already argues that God's inner life, the *hopos esti* or the way God exists as Trinity, is revealed, though not exhausted, in God's economy. The foundation is thus set for speculation on the Son's relationship to the Spirit's procession based on the relationship between the Son and the Spirit in the economy. Zizioulas himself claims that the East can speak of the Spirit coming eternally from the Son.[37] He adds that the Greek fathers affirmed the idea of an eternal mediation of the Son in the procession of the Spirit though they did not speculate on how the Son mediates.[38] It must be clear, however, that the Father alone is the cause or *aitia* of the Spirit's existence. As we saw, the monarchy of the Father is absolute for Zizioulas in that the absolute freedom of God's being is threatened if it is not caused by a person. The Son as mediator but not as cause of the Spirit's procession is a type of *filioque* which, according to Zizioulas, Orthodox theology would find acceptable.

The real issue behind the *filioque* for Zizioulas is, like Lossky, methodological. It concerns the question of whether the ultimate ontological category in theology is person or substance. The source of theological misunderstanding caused by the *filioque* is not so much the idea of whether the Son somehow mediates the Spirit's procession, but rather how this mediation is informed and determined theologically. Unlike Lossky, who reverts to the priority of apophaticism over rationalism, Zizioulas argues for a rethinking of the *filioque* on the basis of the priority of an ontology of person. But such an alternative is itself a step beyond the traditional break between *theologia* and *oikonomia*. Participation in the *how*, the *hopos esti* of God's existence, closes the gap, and even allows for speculation of a type that would affirm a particular understanding of the *filioque*.

Ontology and Epistemology

Implicit in this difference between Lossky and Zizioulas is a debate over the relation between ontology and theological epistemology. Both Zizioulas and Lossky agree that the core of theological discourse is an *ontology* of divine-human communion. Both also reject the traditional metaphysical link between being and thought. An ontology of divine-human communion demands that such a link be severed through, again for both theologians, an apophatic approach to theology.[39] For Lossky, however, an ontology of divine-human communion translates into an apophatic ontology of non-being, which leads to an apophatic epistemology. His apophatic epistemology is developed in direct opposition to "Western rationalism" which he sees, perhaps unjustly, as reductive and threatening to the central tenet of all doctrine—the mystical union of the divine and the human. Rationalism, for Lossky, leads to an ontology of created being, since reason itself never goes beyond itself and encloses God within its own idolatrous concepts. An apophatic epistemology protects the transcendence of God that is constitutive for salvation, since only that which is beyond being can save created being, and allows for the realism of God's immanence in creation.

With apophaticism as the epistemological ground for theological expression, Lossky precludes any speculation on the God of *theologia*, the immanent Trinity, or God in Godself. My argument thus far, however, has been that Lossky seems to transgress this apophatic logic in developing a theology of person based on speculation of trinitarian personhood, especially the *monarchia* of the Father. He concludes that to exist as a trinitarian person is to exist as freedom and love. It seems, however, that such a claim of trinitarian personhood must somehow be grounded epistemologically, and according to Lossky, God's immanent being is unknowable. We are able to speak of God through God's *oikonomia,* but what God communicates in this *oikonomia* is primarily God's energies and not trinitarian personhood, though the persons are the medium for communicating these energies. Moreover, the energies are the communication of God's attributes that, in terms of naming God, belong to the *hyper*-essence of God. Theology could say that God is good, divine, etc., but these names always are pale reflections of God's true essence. In terms of the Trinity, theology, according to apophatic logic, can only say *that* God is Trinity not *how.* The point here is that Lossky gives some reflection on this *how* of Trinitarian existence and takes further steps in attempting to draw an analogy, an identity-in-difference, between this divine personhood and human personhood.[40] But there is no way of grounding this analogy, if, in fact, apophaticism precludes any knowledge of divine personhood.

In his own trinitarian ontology of personhood, Zizioulas makes claims similar to Lossky's own theology of person. For both Lossky and Zizioulas, a trinitarian person exists as freedom and love. Zizioulas, however, more boldly asserts a trinitarian ontology of personhood in a way that Lossky's own apophaticism does not allow. To a certain degree, the ontological differences between the two theologians are slight. Both affirm the radical distinction between uncreated and created being, the unknowability of the divine essence, the energies of God in relation to created being, a divine trinity of persons, a theology of divine personhood as freedom and love, and the realism of divine-human communion. The central difference, however, is that Zizioulas more forcefully asserts for the priority of an ontology of personhood as the most adequate expression of an ontology of divine-human communion based on God's trinitarian existence, and he is able to assert such a priority by grounding this ontology epistemologically.

Both Lossky's and Zizioulas's thought show that ontology and epistemology can never be separated within theological discourse. In order for Zizioulas to give priority to a trinitarian ontology of personhood, he must account for how this divine personhood, God's immanent being, God in *theologia,* is known, in that a trinitarian ontology of personhood is making ultimate claims of *how* God exists immanently. The crucial difference between Lossky and Zizioulas is that the latter is making a claim that God in *theologia* is knowable, thought not exhausted, and it is this knowledge which forms the condition for the possibility of expressing theologically a trinitarian ontology of personhood. The epistemological differences become even more manifest in Zizioulas's treatment of apophaticism and the essence/energies distinction, which will be analyzed below. Apophaticism is no longer foundational in God-talk, but restricted to the essence of God, while person replaces energies as the dominant soteriological concept.

For Zizioulas, knowledge of God's *tropos hyparxeos* does not exhaust the being of God and this inexhaustibility is enough to protect God's radical transcendence. Lossky himself would not necessarily dispute Zizioulas's development of the patristic concept *tropos hyparxeos* to express God's trinitarian existence. What Lossky would dispute is grounding knowledge of this *tropos hyparxeos* of God in God's immanent being. For Lossky, any recognition of knowledge of God's immanent being threatens the radical transcendence and, hence, freedom of God which is the *sine qua non* condition for the mystical union of the divine and the human. The fundamental move Zizioulas makes against Lossky is not one that disputes his theology of personhood, nor even his trinitarian theology, but rather his apophatic epistemology. The experience, and hence, knowledge of God's *tropos hyparxeos* in the eucharistic event of the Body of Christ grounds Zizioulas's trinitarian ontology of person and allows him to claim a priority for 'person' in ontology. The distinction of the *tropos hyparxeos* of God is necessitated by the realism of the divine-human communion in the person of Christ and made present in the eucharist. This priority to person is evident in Zizioulas's understanding of the other aspects of theology, while Lossky, though he develops a theology of trinitarian personhood, continues to understand creation, soteriology, etc., within the framework of an ontology, or more precisely, non-ontology of non-being. In this sense, the substantive theological differences between the two theologians can be traced to distinct expressions of an ontology of divine-human communion, which in the end result in distinct ontologies, or more precisely, an apophatic rejection of ontology versus a trinitarian ontology of personhood. The root cause, however, of their difference lies in distinct understandings of the limits of knowing God, i.e., in diverse epistemologies.

A final word must be said on the inseparable relation between epistemology and ontology. As I argued earlier, a break can never exist between epistemology and ontology and their interdependence is manifest in the thought of Lossky and Zizioulas. For both theologians, however, the two are not linked in the sense that being is that which the mind thinks first and by which the mind understands other things. Nor are they Cartesians, in the sense that they turn to the subject in order to determine what can be known with certainty before expounding a particular ontology based on the conditions that are open to the human subject for the possibility of knowing anything at all. For both Lossky and Zizioulas, all knowledge has one source—God—and, as I have said, in this sense, ontology precedes epistemology. Lossky and Zizioulas challenge the modern, even postmodern, prioritization of the epistemological. For both theologians, there is a coincidence or, to use Zizioulas's word, simultaneity between ontology and epistemology. What one knows of God and the limits of this knowledge coincide with one's ecclesial experience of God. What is interesting to compare between the two theologians is how an axiomatic affirmation of an ontology of divine-human communion leads to distinct ontological expressions rooted in distinct theological epistemologies. In a broad philosophical sense, the debate between Zizioulas and Lossky raises the larger question of how thinking the relation of ontology and epistemology affects the naming and thinking of God. The modern prioritization of the philosophical has led to either a Kantian overemphasis on the transcendence, a Spinozan overemphasis on the immanence, or a Feuerbachian atheism. The Lossky-Zizioulas debate offers alternative resources for thinking the relation between epistemology and ontology toward thinking the God named as transcendent and immanent.

One, then, cannot go so far as Zizioulas to say that Lossky's apophaticism obliterates the trinitarian distinctions, since apophaticism does not necessarily exclude a doctrine of God as Trinity; one could raise the question of whether Lossky's apophaticism results in a trinitarian theology adequate to the logic of divine-human communion.[41] There is also the question of whether Lossky's apophaticism tends to prioritize the *hyper*-essence of God over the trinitarian persons and whether it is this distinction between non-being/being that informs the other aspects of theology rather than trinitarian theology. Such a prioritization might be discerned in Lossky's soteriology, where the primary soteriological concept is the energies of God rather than trinitarian personhood. In this sense, does salvation refer primarily to the *hyper*-essence of God, no matter how Lossky attempts to link the energies with the trinitarian persons? If so, does the essence/energies distinction in the end undermine Lossky's attempt to affirm and express the realism of divine-human communion?

Divine Energies or Divine Personhood?

The difference between Lossky and Zizioulas on the relation between trinitarian theology and theological epistemology leads to distinct understandings of other aspects of theology. The most notable difference is their understanding of the traditional Eastern Orthodox category of divine 'energies.' Lossky joins virtually all other contemporary Eastern Orthodox theologians in expressing the union with God, *theosis,* in terms of participation in the divine energies. Zizioulas, consistent with his relational ontology of trinitarian personhood, breaks with his peers by discussing salvation not in terms of participation in the divine energies, but in terms of the divine 'hypostasis' of the Son. In this sense, although Zizioulas attributes the revolution in ontology to the Cappadocian fathers, he is clearly initiating a revolution of his own in contemporary Eastern Orthodox theology. This section will clarify the nature of this revolution by first discussing in some detail the relation in Lossky's thought between Christology, pneumatology, and soteriology, and then analyzing Zizioulas's own understanding of salvation. It will end with some brief reflections on their theologies of creation.

As Lossky's critique of the *filioque* has revealed, apophaticism precludes any speculation of the relation of the Son and the Spirit on the level of *theologia*. This restriction does not apply to the level of *oikonomia,* where the persons of the Son and the Spirit work toward fulfillment of the loving will of the Father, which is the deification of humankind. Each person has their particular role in the economy while being simultaneously dependent on the other persons to accomplish their specific task. Lossky affirms the interdependence of all the persons of the Trinity in relation to the economy, but he also clearly emphasizes the independence of the Holy Spirit in relation to the Son. The independence of the Holy Spirit, which Lossky refers to as the "economy of the Holy Spirit,"[42] is a reaction to the *filioque,* but not on the level of a confessional polemic. For Lossky the "economy of the Holy Spirit" is needed in order for deification to be personal, that is, based on freedom and love. In terms of the "economy of Christ," the person/nature distinction is used to express Christ's particular role in salvation. Christ's role is the "objective side" of salvation in which humanity is regenerated and able to move toward God. The Spirit's role is the "subjective side" in which he works with the personal freedom of the renewed human being in order to move closer toward God. Both work to restore the image of God in the human being, which is personhood, i.e., freedom from the necessities of nature in loving union with God.

For Lossky there are three main periods in salvation history: "the first is a long preparation for the Saviour's coming. It ranges from the Fall to the Annunciation . . . the second period, from the Annunciation to Pentecost, corresponds to the terrestrial life and Ascension of Christ. . . . Then, with Pentecost, begins a new period when human persons, supported by the Holy Spirit, must freely acquire this deification that their nature has received, once and for all, in Christ."[43] Our present concern is with the second period and with Lossky's description of the Son's particular role in the economy of salvation. This period is central for the experience of God and, hence, for theology, since it is "the incarnation of the Word, the central event of revelation, which makes iconography as well as theology possible."[44]

What happens during this period that makes union with God and, hence, theology, possible is the union of the divine and human natures in Christ. Lossky's Christology is strictly Chalcedonian and much of his work on the "economy of Christ" is to draw out the implications of Chalcedon along with showing its coherence with other aspects of theology, such as the divine energies of God. According to Lossky, Chalcedon's adequacy is judged by the soteriological principle of deification, which Nestorianism and Monophysitism threaten. Chalcedon ultimately affirmed that "if there is no real unity in Christ, a union between man and God is no longer possible. The whole doctrine of salvation loses its ontological foundation. We remain separated from God. Deification is forbidden."[45] The trinitarian distinction between nature and person makes such a union possible. The person is not nature, but possesses nature, which does not preclude the person of the Son to possess human nature. In fact, "it is by his person that the Son of God can enter it [the world]; for His person, Whose nature is divine, 'enhypostasizes' human nature."[46]

The union of the two natures in Christ does not mean the absorption of the human nature into the divine. Lossky is quick to emphasize the *asynchutos* and *atreptos* of the Chalcedonian formula. The two natures are neither confused nor changed. Each maintains their ontological integrity. But they are also united *adiaretos* and *achoristos,* without division and without separation. As we saw Lossky affirm earlier, the union is necessary if the *anthropos* is to experience God. Here the notion of the energies becomes important. In the person of Christ, human nature is deified through the energies of the divine nature. In Christ, then, humanity is regenerated to its original capacity through its unity with the divine nature and the reception of the divine energies.

As with creation, in the person of Christ the divine energies become the means by which human nature participates in God. The difference, which is more implicit than explicit in Lossky, is that this participation occurs *in* Christ, i.e., in a particular *person* of the Trinity. Lossky uses the Greek patristic notion of *perichoresis* to express the energetic relationship between the two natures in Christ. His use here of *perichoresis* is odd, though not without patristic warrant, since its trinitarian meaning has more to do with the indwelling of persons, the one with the other, rather than an energetic exchange between two ontologically distinct natures.[47] The two natures, "being united hypostatically without being transformed into one another, they permeate one another (*perichoresis eis allelas*), according to St. Maximus who reproduces here, in the framework of the Christological dogma, the Eastern conception of energies or processions of the nature."[48] Lossky adds, "this perichoresis, or permeation, for St. John Damascene, is on the whole unilateral: comes from the divine side and not from the fleshly side. However, the Divinity, having once penetrated the flesh, gives to it an ineffable faculty of penetrating the Divinity."[49] Lossky never really explains what this penetrating of the divinity consists in, no doubt due to its ineffable quality. At times, it seems that this appeal to the "ineffability" of certain events is Lossky's way out of a tight spot. In this particular case, he may have cornered himself by using *perichoresis* to explain the deification of the human nature in Christ. *Perichoresis* implies reciprocity, and one wonders in what way the human nature is *perichoretic* in relation to the divine and if this affects the divine nature in any way. That notwithstanding, "the humanity of Christ is a deified nature that is permeated by the divine energies from the moment of the Incarnation."[50]

An important concept to understanding the economy of the Son, and to Lossky's thought in general, is that of *kenosis*.[51] By *kenosis* Lossky means "a prodigious humbling" which consists in the Son's descent "into a self-annihilating condition . . . paradoxically, He unites to the integral fullness of His divine nature the unfullness no less integral to fallen human nature."[52] The *kenosis* of the Son is not a matter of divine nature but of the Son's person. It does not consist in the Son's divesting himself of the divine nature. "The subject of the kenosis is not divine nature, but the person of the Son."[53] This *kenosis* on the part of the Son is the renunciation of the Son's will "in order to accomplish the will of the Father by being obedient to Him unto death and unto the cross."[54] Lossky adds, "the *kenosis* is the mode of existence of the Divine Person who was sent into the world, the Person in whom was accomplished the common will of the Trinity whose source is the Father."[55] *Kenosis* refers to both the actual assumption of human nature on the part of the Son, which implies a renunciation of the eternally blissful trinitarian communion in the realm of *theologia;* it also refers to a renunciation of some kind of personal will which finds its fulfillment in submitting to the other, who is the Father.

What does Lossky means by *kenosis* as the "mode of existence of the Divine Person"? We have seen confusion on the part of Lossky in discussing the notion of "mode of existence." On the one hand it refers to the energies, on the other it is applied to the persons of the Trinity in terms of the mode of origin. Applied to person, it indicates something about the theological notion of person. With respect to the mode of origin, person is that mode of existence that is irreducible to nature. By referring to *kenosis* as "the mode of existence of the Divine Person," could Lossky be implying that to be a person is also to be kenotic? He will categorically affirm, as we shall see shortly, that to be a true human person requires *kenosis*. The question is whether by saying that *kenosis* is a "mode of existence" of the Son, Lossky means that a divine person is not only freedom and love, but kenotic.

In *The Mystical Theology* the affirmation of the kenotic being of divine personhood, though implied, remains undeveloped. One must turn to Lossky's later writings, which show Lossky speaking more forcefully in terms of an ontology of personhood. After affirming that the subject of the *kenosis* is the person and not the nature, he adds that

> the person fulfills himself in the gift of himself: he distinguishes himself from nature, not to 'avail himself' of his natural condition, but to renounce himself totally . . . *which is not a sudden decision, nor an act, but the manifestation of His very being, of personhood, which is no longer a willing of His own, but His very hypostatic reality as the expression of the trinitarian will, a will of which the Father is the source, the Son, the obedient realization, and the Spirit, the glorious fulfillment.*[56]

At this point, one could argue that Lossky is speaking of the Son on the level of *oikonomia*, if it were not for what immediately follows: *"There is therefore a profound continuity between the personal being of the Son as renunciation and His earthly kenosis.*"[57] Though much of the discussion of *kenosis* deals with the Son's descent in order to accomplish the loving will of the Father in creation, these last words intimate that for Lossky the very personal being of the Son, on the level of *theologia*, is kenotic. There is a personal will that the Son renounces in a *kenotic*, loving movement toward the Father and the Spirit. This personal will is clearly not the Greek patristic *gnomic* will, which Maximus the Confessor distinguished from the natural will. The *gnomic* will is the capacity to choose, which is personal as opposed to the natural will which inclines the person toward a natural end. Concerning the *gnomic* will, Lossky affirms that "it does not exist in Christ other than as divine liberty."[58] There is no choice for the person of Christ, who is the divine person, since "the single decision of the Son is kenosis, the assumption of the total human condition, total submission to the will of the Father."[59] The following passage makes clear that kenotic freedom, which is personal, is a matter of the Son's being on the level of *theologia* and not simply *oikonomia:*

> Thus the very attitude of Christ implies freedom, even though St. Maximus denies him free-will. But this freedom is not an everlasting choice that would estrange the Saviour; neither is it the constant necessity for Christ each time to undertake a deliberate choice to submit His deified flesh to the limits of our fallen condition, such as sleep and hunger: for this would make Jesus an actor. Freedom here is regulated by the unique personal consciousness of Christ: it is the definitive and constant choice to assume the unwholesomeness of our condition, even unto the ultimate fatality of death. It is the choice, consented to since eternity, to allow all that makes our condition, that is to say our fallenness, penetrate His self at depth: and this depth is anguish, death, descent into Hell.[60]

The language brings Lossky close to affirming that the Son's economy is determinative of the Son's personal being. It seems more consistent with Lossky to say that the personal being of the Son is eternally *kenotic* in relation to the Father, which means the Son's descent into creation was never a matter of choice.

To summarize, there are more than hints in Lossky's later writings that he affirms a kenotic aspect to the personal being of, at least, the Son. Though this would break his own rule of silence on the level of *theologia*, I argue that the later Lossky was moving toward ontology of personhood based on trinitarian theology. It leaves open the question, however, of whether or how this ontology of personhood can speak of the personal being of the Father and the Son in terms of *kenosis*. An "economy of the Holy Spirit," to which we now turn, may offer further suggestions for a notion of *kenotic* divine personhood, or at very least for the personal being of the Holy Spirit.

The economy of the Son accomplishes the "objective side" of salvation while that of the Spirit accomplishes the "subjective side" of salvation. By "objective side" Lossky means that the salvation in Christ in terms of the deification of human nature is a fait accompli. On the subjective side, the Holy Spirit's role is twofold: first, it makes accessible the deified nature of Christ, and second, it elevates the human person toward union. Both the work of Christ and the work of the Spirit constitute what Lossky refers to as the "two aspects of the Church."[61] Christ united in himself human nature and deified it, and through this work human nature becomes free from the consequences of sin. It is restored to its original capacity to move toward God. It is "in the Church and through the sacraments [that] our nature enters into union with the divine nature in the hypostasis of the Son, the Head of His mystical body. Our humanity becomes consubstantial with the deified humanity, united with the person of Christ."[62] "But our person has not yet attained its perfection," which for Lossky consists in becoming Christ-like by way of uniting in the human person the divine and the human. Instead of uniting divine and human nature, the human person unites the deified nature of Christ with the uncreated energies that the Holy Spirit confers.[63] The church itself consists of human persons united in the one deified human nature of Christ.[64] Personal distinctiveness is not destroyed, because like the Trinity, each of the human persons possesses this deified nature without dividing it. Each, however, grows toward deification according to their own personal appropriation of the divine energies.

Salvation thus has as its object both nature and person, and if the former is accomplished in Christ the latter is accomplished in the Spirit.[65] The Spirit is the one who elevates those human persons possessing the deified nature of Christ toward union. The Holy Spirit confers "the grace which works in persons and through persons as though it were their own strength—the divine and uncreated power *appropriated* by human persons in whom union with God is brought to pass. The Holy Spirit bestows divinity upon human persons called to realize in themselves this deifying union."[66]

It is this personal aspect of the Holy Spirit's economy that Lossky sees threatened by the *filioque*. According to Lossky, the dependence of the Holy Spirit on the Son, which he argues the *filioque* affirms, risks "depersonalizing the Church, by submitting the freedom of her human hypostases to a kind of sacramental determinism."[67] Elsewhere, he explains that if the Holy Spirit, as a divine Person, were to be considered as dependent upon the Son, He would appear—even in His personal advent—as a bond which connects us with the Son. The mystical life would then unfold as a way towards the union of the soul with Christ through the medium of the Holy Spirit. This raises again the question of the place of human persons in this union: either they would be annihilated in being united to the Person of Christ, or else the Person of Christ would be imposed upon them from without.[68]

The independence of the Holy Spirit from the Son, which Lossky expresses as an "economy of the Holy Spirit," protects for Lossky the personal character of mystical union. As personal, it is both free, and thus accomplished through love; it is also unique in that the distinctiveness of the person is not destroyed in the union. If one could argue that the missions inform the procession and lead to the *filioque,* for Lossky immanent trinity informs the economic trinity. But, it is the soteriological principle of union based on freedom and love that ultimately informs trinitarian reflection and leads Lossky to affirm unequivocally the independence of the Holy Spirit from the Son. The *filioque* not only threatens the personal distinctiveness in the Trinity, but also the personal character of salvation.

As we have seen, Zizioulas criticized Lossky for overemphasizing the independence of the Son from the Spirit.[69] These criticisms, however, fail to account for Lossky's affirmation of the interdependence of the "economies" of the Son and the Spirit. It must be remembered that for Lossky the economy of God is one. There is God in Godself, *theologia,* and God in relation to the world, *oikonomia,* and this economy involves the whole Trinity not simply the latter two persons. The "action of the Trinity" is this economy, and "rooted in the Father . . . [it] is presented as the double economy of the Son and of the Spirit: the former making the desire of God come into existence, the latter accomplishing it in goodness and beauty; the one calling the creature to lead it to the Father . . . the other helping the creature to respond to this call and communicating perfection to it."[70] The Father is involved on the level of *oikonomia* both as the sender and as the one to whom all is returned. Moreover, the economy of the each person depends on that of the other. "It will first of all be necessary to establish a double reciprocity in the economy of the two divine persons sent by the Father. On the one hand, it is by the Holy Spirit that the Word is made incarnate of the Virgin Mary. On the other hand, it is by the Word, following His incarnation and works of redemption, that the Holy Spirit descends on the members of the Church at Pentecost."[71] Elsewhere Lossky adds that "both dispensations—of the Son and of the Spirit—are inseparable; they mutually condition one another since one without the other is unthinkable. One cannot receive the Holy Spirit without being a member of the Body; one cannot call Christ 'Lord', i.e. have a consciousness of His divinity other than by the Holy Spirit."[72] It is interesting to note that for Lossky trinitarian theology on the level of *theologia* influences understanding of the work of the Trinity in the economy. But the revelation of the Trinity in the work of the economy, especially that of interdependence of the Son and Spirit given in revelation, has no bearing on trinitarian speculation. The relation of the Son and the Spirit in the economy does not lead to speculation on their relation on the level of *theologia*. Such speculation for Lossky results in a *filioqueism* whose end is depersonalization. It need not, however, result in depersonalization, and in fact may strengthen a theology of person based on trinitarian theology. Lossky's own apophatic restrictions, however, precluded any such overt speculation on the trinitarian relations.[73]

References to an economy of the Son and the Spirit and the economy of God leads to the question of whether "economy" refers to the same thing in both instances. There is no question that all three persons have some sort of economy to the creation. Insofar as *oikonomia* signifies God's relation to creation, the economy of God involves all three persons. But does the fact that Lossky nowhere refers to an economy of the Father give a certain specificity to the "economy" of the Son and the Spirit? It seems likely that Lossky does in fact mean something more by economy in relation to specifically the Son and Spirit than merely a relation to creation. The latter two persons not only relate to creation, but are involved in creation more palpably and tangibly than the Father. This involvement is obvious with the Son incarnate, but not so obvious with the Holy Spirit who "remains unmanifested, hidden, concealing Himself in His very appearing."[74] There is a "coming into the world" which forms part of what Lossky refers to as *kenosis,* both that of the Son and the Spirit. How the Holy Spirit communicates itself and becomes present to each person in the church "remains a mystery—the mystery of the self-emptying, of the *kenosis* of the Holy Spirit's coming into the world."[75] Lossky further explains the difference between the *kenosis* of the Son and the Spirit: "If in the *kenosis* of the Son the Person appeared to men while the Godhead remained hidden under the form of a servant, the Holy Spirit in His coming, while He manifests the common nature of the Trinity, leaves His own Person concealed beneath His Godhead."[76] Unlike the *kenosis* of the Son, Lossky does not suggest that the *kenosis* of the Spirit is *"a manifestation of His very being, of personhood."* This absence together with the fact the he does not speak of a *kenosis* of the Father might make it difficult to unequivocally affirm in Lossky's thought an ontology of person based on trinitarian theology in which each of the divine persons is a free, loving, *kenotic* being. One sees tendencies toward this end without further development that, perhaps, Lossky's untimely death prevented.

Though he may not emphatically affirm *kenosis* as an aspect of personhood on the level of *theologia,* Lossky does not hesitate to make it constitutive of human personhood. It is personhood that forms, for Lossky, the image of God in *anthropos.* The fulfillment of this personhood is in a union with God that is an ekstatic transcendence of nature toward a free loving union with the Other. To be in the image of God is to mirror the life of the trinitarian persons. "Trinitarian theology thus opens us to a new aspect of the human reality: that of personhood. . . . Only the revelation of the Trinity, unique foundation of Christian anthropology, could situate personhood in an absolute manner."[77] Drawing on Gregory of Nyssa, Lossky concludes that "because created in the image of God, man is to be seen as a personal being, a person who is not to be controlled by nature, but who can himself control nature in assimilating it to its divine Archetype."[78] As God is free from any necessity, including the necessity of God's divine nature, in and through being person, so too the human person is one who is free from the limits of nature in loving communion with God.

To be in the image, however, the human person must be kenotic, and, as I have suggested, it is unclear as to whether *kenosis* for Lossky is an aspect of divine personhood. The need for *kenosis* on the part of the human person emerges from an understanding of the Fall and its effect on human existence, and from Christology. In terms of the Fall, the effects of original sin, according to Lossky, were an irreversible individualism. As Lossky explains, human nature became divided into parts, "split up, broken into many individuals."[79] An individual possesses only "a part of nature and reserves it for himself, the subject who defines himself by opposition to all that which is not 'I'."[80] An individual then is one whose identity is defined by relationships of distance rather than love. It is this distance, most especially from God, which leads to the destruction of that identity, i.e., to death. Only God who is Life can bestow life, and an individual as one who claims independence from all things cuts her- or himself from the source of life. "Human nature cannot be the possession of a monad. It demands not solitude but communion, the wholesome diversity of love."[81] This love Lossky refers to as a "paradisiacal 'eros'" that characterizes human sexuality before the fall, and this defines the dominion that the *anthropos* was to have over creation through the command "Be fruitful and multiply." Paradise is a creation ruled by human persons who bring all things into relation with God. After the Fall, "sexuality, this 'multiplying' that God orders and blesses, appears in our universe as irremediably linked to separation and death. This is because the condition of man has known, at least in his biological reality, a catastrophic mutation."[82] Sexuality loses its personal character and is reduced to a necessary impulse of nature. And though "human love, the absolute passion of lovers, has never ceased harbouring, in the very fatality of its failure, a paradisiacal nostalgia where heroism and art are rooted," its ultimate result in the fallen state is individualism, separation and death, since it is an act ultimately between individuals.[83]

In the fallen state, then, there is only individualism that results in death. This individualism leads Lossky to question whether an anthropological notion of the human person exists in the Greek fathers. He admits that "until now I have not found what one might call an elaborated doctrine of the human person in patristic theology, alongside its very precise teaching on divine persons or hypostases."[84] He will say, however, that the anthropology of the Greek fathers was personal only because it was based on a personal God, a trinitarian God who created the *anthropos* in God's image and likeness. Given the distinction between *theologia* and *oikonomia* the question becomes whether one can transfer the meaning of divine persons to human persons.

> We will ask ourselves whether this irreducibility of hypostasis to essence or nature—an irreducibility which forced us to give up equating the hypostasis with the individual in the Trinity by revealing the non-conceptual character of the notion of hypostasis—must take place in the realm of created being as well, especially when one is dealing with human hypostases or persons. By asking this question, we will be asking at the same time whether Trinitarian theology has had any repercussion on Christian anthropology—whether it has opened up a new dimension of the 'personal' by discovering a notion of human hypostasis not reducible to the level of natures or individual substances, which fall under the hold of concepts.[85]

If there is to be a notion of human person based on trinitarian theology, it will not be defined as the Boethian *substantia individua rationalis naturae,* which formed the basis for subsequent Western understandings of person.[86] A person is not a nature but freedom from nature, and a human person must be someone who is free from the limitations of nature.

Needed is a way for individual existence to become personal, to mirror the divine life. Such a means is found in Christology, or rather in Christ. Theology of the image becomes possible after the Incarnation of Christ, the "perfect Image who is of the same nature with Him [the Father]."[87] In the case of Christ, the hypostasis is not reducible to the human nature, but the human nature receives deification within the divine hypostasis of Christ. For this reason Greek patristic Christology rejected the notion of two personal beings in Christ; the assumed human nature is not an individual hypostasis but the fullness of human nature united and deified in Christ. In light of this dogma, Boethius's definition becomes insufficient, since Christ reveals that an individual substance of a rational nature is not a person, since human nature itself, as distinct from the person of Christ, receives its deification in His person.[88] Lossky concludes that "this refusal to admit two distinct personal beings in Christ means at the same time that one must also distinguish in human beings the person or hypostasis from the nature or individual substance."[89] It is thus in and through Christ that the personhood of human existence is revealed and realized. Christ fulfills the image of God which "in the last analysis is to be a personal being, that is to say, a free responsible being."[90] To be in the image is ultimately to respond to the call for a free loving communion with God. "A personal being is capable of loving someone more than his own nature, more than his own life. The person, that is to say, the image of God in man, is then man's freedom with regard to his nature . . . and his dignity consists in being able to liberate himself from his nature, not by consuming it or abandoning it to itself, like the ancient or oriental sage, but by transfiguring it in God."[91] To be a human person is not only, however, freedom and love, but *kenosis*. Given the fallen state of individualism, in order to be person one must reject one's own will, both natural and *gnomic,* and be united to God's will. This human *kenosis* mirrors the *kenosis* of Christ who was obedient to the Father even unto death.

> The human hypostasis can only realize itself by the renunciation of its own will, of all that governs us, and makes us subject to natural necessity. The individual, i.e., that assertion of self in which person is confused with nature and loses its true liberty, must be broken. This is the root principle of asceticism; a free renunciation of one's own will, of the mere simulacrum of individual liberty, in order to recover the true liberty, that of the person which is the image of God in each one.[92]

The true human person is, thus, the one who exists in kenotic freedom and love. At this point, however, Lossky's understanding of the relation between Christology, pneumatology, soteriology, and anthropology raises a few questions in relation to this trinitarian theology. One wonders that if *kenosis* is not an aspect of divine personhood, whether the human person is then only in the image of Christ and not of God the Trinity as Lossky asserts. Moreover, it would seem that Christ not only reveals the distinction of person and nature on the level of person, but also manifests that this nature receives its fulfillment only in a *divine* person. This would imply that humanity is fulfilled only in a type of personal relationship with God that the Son has with the Father. A personal salvation would imply something more than an openness toward receiving the divine energies. In this sense, personal being as freedom is only the means of deifying the nature. A truly personal salvation consists in sonship, that is, when a human person is a son in relation to the Father in and through *the* Son. The question, then, is, can Lossky's understanding of salvation in terms of divine energies adequately express all that Lossky says salvation is?

Zizioulas does not define salvation in terms of the divine energies of God. The centrality of the concept of 'person' for expressing divine-human communion is evident in Zizioulas's understanding of Chalcedonian Christology. He interprets the Chalcedonian "two natures in one person" through the lens of a trinitarian understanding of personhood as *hypostatic* (unique) and *ekstatic* (freedom). For Zizioulas, "it emerges that in Christology the crucial thing for our subject is not the *communicatio idiomatum* but the hypostatic union."[93] The Incarnation is not the event in which the divine energies are communicated in their fullness to the human nature; it is the event in which human nature itself exists, *is,* in the person of Christ. "What enables Man in Christ to arrive at a personal identity in ontological terms is that in Christ the natures *are,* only because they are particularized in one person."[94] What Christ offers for salvation for human existence is not so much the divine energies as his own *hypostasis*.

> For Man to acquire this ontology of personhood it is necessary to take an attitude of freedom *vis-à-vis* his own nature. If biological birth gives us a hypostasis dependent ontologically on nature, this indicates that a 'new birth' is needed in order to experience an ontology of personhood. This 'new birth', which is the essence of Baptism, is nothing but the acquisition of an identity not dependent on the qualities of nature but freely raising nature to a hypostatic existence identical with that which emerges from the Father-Son relationship.[95]

Thus, the significance of the union in Christ is not the communication of divine energies, but becoming a 'son' of God by transforming one's hypostasis through a relationship identical with that of the Son. Christ is the 'one' and the 'many' in whom our *hypostases* are not merged or absorbed, but transfigured, or rather constituted in the relationship which Christ has with the Father. It is within this relationship that the human person becomes or exists eternally as a unique and unrepeatable being.

It must also be remembered that for Zizioulas the Christ event is a trinitarian event insofar as Christ is the Son of the Father, but also insofar as the Spirit actualizes the Christ event. Salvation is the result of the *simultaneous* working of the Son and the Spirit. Divine-human communion is the constitution of the community of faithful as the Body of Christ by the power of the Holy Spirit. This understanding of the interdependence of the Son and the Spirit in terms of simultaneity is distinct from Lossky's more developmental model in which baptism is defined as a reception of the deified nature of Christ which gives one the capacity to grow toward personal deification through the bestowal of the divine energies by the Holy Spirit. It is not that Lossky denies the co-working of the Son and the Spirit, but he does not conceptualize divine-human communion as the simultaneous co-presence of the Son and the Spirit. Furthermore, whereas Lossky sees the Spirit's dependence on the Son as threatening personal freedom, for Zizioulas, becoming a child of God is to exist in the way the Son relates to the Father. The work of the Spirit and the Son are mutually conditioning realities.

The significance of understanding Christology through the trinitarian understanding of 'person,' is at least, twofold. For one, Zizioulas is claiming against those who may reject the use of 'person' in trinitarian theology that the concept is the most adequate for expressing not simply the distinction between the Father, Son, and Holy Spirit, but the divine-human communion through the person of the Son.

The other point of significance is directed specifically to the Orthodox tradition, though, again, reverberations can be felt in the wider Christian discussion of divine-human communion. With his trinitarian ontology of personhood Zizioulas is, in effect, arguing against the use of 'energies' as the central soteriological concept. In fact, he argues that to make 'energies' the controlling theological concept tends to make "superfluous, if not suspect, any *logos* on person."[96] This line of argumentation becomes especially clear when one considers Lossky's own understanding of divine-human communion in Christ.[97] For Lossky salvation of the human person involves a personal reception of the energies of God. Within the ecclesial context, one receives a deified human nature by being baptized into Christ. In being united to the Body of Christ, the church, one participates in the work of Christ in receiving a deified human nature. Reception of this deified human nature, however, is only one part of the equation in a process of salvation that must involve both nature and person. Upon being united to the Body of Christ, one is then able, has the capacity, to grow toward perfection. This perfection is a process of growth toward personhood in the energies of God. Personhood is the goal; the means are the energies of God conveyed through the person of the Holy Spirit. One assimilates more fully in personal existence the energies of God already present throughout creation. Personal existence in the end for Lossky is one which mirrors that of Christ: as Christ is one person who possesses a divine and human nature, the deified person is one who possesses a deified *human* nature and the *divine* energies. This process of salvation also makes clear Lossky's understanding of the importance of Chalcedonian Christology. For Lossky, human nature is united to the divine in the one person of Christ in order to be deified. This human nature is then offered to humanity within the church.

What is centrally at issue is how to conceptualize divine-human communion. Both Lossky and Zizioulas would reject the use of divine essence for such conceptualizations, since it results in pantheism. Lossky, however, would also reject the use of *hypostasis,* which indicates exclusively distinction within God's being. Moreover, the hypostatic union itself, the union of the divine and human natures, is "proper to the Son alone, in whom God becomes man without ceasing to be the second Person of the Trinity." He continues, "Even though we share the same human nature as Christ and receive in Him the name of Sons of God, we do not ourselves become the divine hypostasis of the Son by the fact of the Incarnation. We are unable, therefore, to participate in either the essence or the hypostasis of the Holy Trinity."[98] The reality of divine-human communion, therefore, requires, according to Lossky, another distinction within God's being. "This distinction is that between the essence of God, or His nature, properly so-called, which is inaccessible, unknowable and incommunicable; and the energies or divine operations, forces proper to and inseparable from God's essence, in which He goes forth from Himself, manifests, communicates, and gives Himself."[99] Zizioulas thus seems to depart from what some would argue is identifiably "Eastern Orthodox," the centrality of the concept of 'energies' for expressing a realistic notion of divine-human communion. He also argues against Lossky that the distinction necessary to conceptualize divine-human communion is that between *hypostasis* and essence and not that between essence and energies.

The concept of divine energies is not as central to Zizioulas's soteriology as it is to Lossky's. There are two important qualifiers which Zizioulas places on this patristic concept that are not as clearly stated in Lossky. For one,

Zizioulas emphatically affirms that an energy is never apersonal.[100] The energies of God are communicated only through the persons of the Trinity. This emphasis on the personal character of energies is indicative of the primacy of an ontology of personhood and communion in Zizioulas's thought. Second, salvation is not described for Zizioulas as an increase in participation in the divine energies, but as the transformation of being into true personhood *in* the person of Christ. For Zizioulas, the essence/energies distinction is "nothing else essentially, but a device created by the Greek Fathers to safeguard the absolute transcendence of God without alienating Him from the world."[101] The energies are God's actions in the world and are saving events. The ultimate saving event, though not excluding the divine energies, is not simply a matter of God's action, but a relational event of communion that constitutes human personhood as true personhood *in the image* of Christ. The important point here is that the ontology of personhood and communion which emerges from Zizioulas's understanding of the eucharist as a communion event in the Body of Christ forms the basis for Zizioulas's understanding of the God-world relation, and more importantly, the Eastern patristic notion of energies. Such an ontology leads Zizioulas to affirm a much more humble role for 'energies' in his theology than that of Lossky.

The difference between Lossky and Zizioulas on the centrality of the concept of 'energies' for theological discourse is also evident in their respective creation theologies. On the one hand, the understanding of God's relation to created existence is not a source for substantial differences between Lossky and Zizioulas. For both the divine-human communion that forms the basis for knowledge of God is raised to a theological principle. On the basis of this principle, both Lossky and Zizioulas make similar conclusions concerning God's relation to the world. For one, the notion of a divine-human communion leads both to affirm the ontological distinction between the created and the uncreated. Such an ontological break serves two purposes. For one, it protects God's radical freedom or transcendence. There is no necessity on God's part either to create or to be involved in the world. It also protects the freedom of created existence to either reject or affirm such a communion. Creation is not forced to be in communion with God, but only freely enters into such a communion. The existence of such a freedom on the part of created being affirms also the uniqueness and distinctiveness of creation. Though it depends on God it is not God; it is ontologically 'other' than God. The relation between God and the world is a relation between two others.

The two theologians, however, conceive differently the relation between the Creator and the created. These different conceptions clearly evince how the substantial differences between Lossky and Zizioulas stem from the former's emphasis on apophaticism and the latter's emphasis on ontology. For Lossky, the uncreated is ontologically distinct from the created. God's becomes immanent in the created realm through God's energies. In fact, God creates through God's energies and is ever present since creation itself exists only in relation to the energies of God. He takes up traditional theological concepts such as the notion of the divine ideas and interprets them within the framework of the essence/energies distinction.[102] Lossky further argues that creation itself is a result of the love of God, which leads to advance, at least implicitly, a metaphysics of love, in which love is the beginning, middle, and end of creation.[103] As a result, Lossky appears to endorse the theological notion of *apokatastasis*, in which all of creation will be saved.[104] The important point here is that the theological notion of person, based on the doctrine of the Trinity, does not play a substantial role in conceptualizing God's relation to creation.

The ontology of person becomes from the start the controlling factor in understanding God's relation to the world. For Zizioulas, the traditional concept of creation *ex nihilo* can only make sense within the framework of a personal ontology.

> Now it is all too easy to admit on a doctrinal level that for Christians things are different because the world was created *ex nihilo*. But I venture to suggest that unless we admit on a philosophical level that personhood is not secondary to being, that the mode of existence of being is not secondary to its 'substance' but itself primary and constitutive of it, it is impossible to make sense of the doctrine of creation *ex nihilo*.[105]

An ontology of person validates theologically the traditional Christian doctrine of creation *ex nihilo*. Zizioulas's ontology of person is ultimately an affirmation of the permanence of personal being in and through a reality beyond created being, which is the love of God. Such a communion based on love and freedom is only possible if God is not necessarily linked to an eternal world. Creation *ex nihilo* expresses a God-world relation based on freedom and love, one in which God is not so much transcendent as other than created being. The link between the two realms is personhood. Nowhere in his discussions on creation does the concept of energies become central. Zizioulas does not speak of a permanent, unbreakable bond between God and creation through the energies. As a result, he rejects any notion of an *apokatastasis*, affirming that created reality, as totally other than the uncreated, is surrounded by death.

If we take the world as a 'whole,' as an entity in itself, which we *can* do if we regard it, as we do, as *finite* and as *other* than God.... All this means that creation *taken in itself* (this condition is of decisive importance for, as we shall see, things are different if creation is not taken 'in itself') constitutes an entity surrounded and conditioned by *nothing*: It came from nothing and will return to nothing.[106]

Creation is not surrounded by God's energies, as with Lossky, but by nothing. In affirming this, Zizioulas is veering away from the notion of degradation of being which is implicit in Lossky's understanding of God's energies. For Lossky, the love of God is constant in the form of God's energies, but being is less authentic the less it responds to this love. For Zizioulas creation depends on God's love, which is the meaning he attributes to Maximus the Confessor's notion of creation as the *idea thelemata* of God. Creation, however, is an event of love because it is other than the uncreated. It is, however, inherently created and finite and, thus, permeated and affected by death and nothingness.[107] It exists eternally through love, but such love is not a matter of receiving God's energies, but of being constituted as true persons. The important point here is that in terms of describing God's relation to creation, the two theologians affirm the foundational distinction between the created and the uncreated. Lossky explains the relation between the two in terms of the essence/energies distinction, which, especially with his notion of, or perhaps hint of *apokatastasis*, leans his system toward a monistic necessity, which he adamantly rejects with his understanding of person. Zizioulas interprets this relation, as well as other doctrines, consistently through the eye of personhood.

Given this substantial difference between Lossky and Zizioulas, whose thought is judged more adequate and on what grounds? Lossky's and Zizioulas's theologies can be comparatively judged on the basis of their shared central commitment, divine-human communion. On this criterion, Lossky's own theology suffers from internal incoherencies. More substantially, apophaticism itself cannot express the divine-human communion as Lossky himself argues and, in effect, collapses into an ontology of substance, which Lossky has consistently attributed to "Western rationalism."

The first internal inconsistency is seen in the tension that exists between Lossky's epistemological apophaticism and his theology of person. As was indicated, Lossky affirms a theology of person based on the doctrine of the Trinity and which he defines in terms of freedom, irreducibility, and love. Though he tends toward a trinitarian ontology of personhood in which to *be* a trinitarian person is to exist as freedom and love, the apophatic distinction between *theologia* and *oikonomia* leaves such a trinitarian understanding of personhood ungrounded. How can one know that God exists as trinitarian persons as freedom and love if God in Godself is shrouded in the apophaticism of the *hyper*-essence? Thus, Lossky's own affirmation of the centrality of the theological notion of person is undermined by the primacy of apophaticism in his doctrine of God. If he is to maintain the theological concept of person as irreducibility, freedom, and ecstatic love, then apophaticism must have a more restricted role in his theological scheme, and the gap between *theologia* and *oikonomia* must be bridged. A theology of person based on the doctrine of the Trinity must somehow give an account for how God's trinitarian existence as a communion of persons is known, i.e., it requires a knowledge of *theologia* based on God's *oikonomia*. To affirm, however, any degree of knowledge of God in *theologia* is to move away from apophaticism as the epistemological foundation for theology.

There is also the question of whether Lossky's apophaticism, and theological apophaticism in general, tends to prioritize the *hyper*-essence of God over the trinitarian persons and whether it is this distinction between non-being/being which informs the other aspects of theology rather than trinitarian theology. To affirm, as Lossky does, that one cannot speak of God on the realm of *theologia*, that God in Godself is shrouded in apophaticism, is, ironically, to continue to make primary 'essence' language in God-talk. Lossky's criticism of the West is that to understand the trinitarian God based on a metaphysics of substance is to efface the diversity in the Trinity. Lossky himself, however, continues to make essence, albeit hyper-essence, primary in God-talk by affirming that one cannot speak of God as Trinity other than to express it as a "primordial fact." Such a prioritization is also discernable in Lossky's soteriology, where the primary soteriological concept is the energies of God rather than trinitarian personhood. In this sense, salvation refers primarily to the *hyper*-essence of God, no matter how Lossky attempts to link the energies with the trinitarian persons.

For Lossky, however, speaking of God in terms of non-being, or *hyper*-essence, is the only way to secure the 'freedom' of God vis-à-vis creation and, thus, to affirm the freedom of God to be in communion with this non-divine other of God. A metaphysics of being necessarily links God to creation and leads to idolatrous discourse. But Lossky's apophatic solution leads to a radical break between *oikonomia* and *theologia,* between the immanent and economic Trinity. But the logical implication of this break is that the God who is experienced in the economy is not the God who is free to be in communion with the non-divine other. In an effort to maintain the freedom of God in relation to creation and to commune with creation, Lossky's apophaticism results in a break such that there is no experience of God's immanent life, i.e., of the God who is free to commune with creation. This freedom is conceptualized in terms of God's energies, and whatever Lossky's immanent Trinity is, it is not the God who is free to be with what is other than God. Zizioulas's argument is almost the reverse of Lossky's: only the experience of the immanent life of the triune God is an experience of the God who is free to be in union with the non-divine other. This experience is the foundation for conceptualizing the doctrine of the Trinity in terms of the freedom of God in relation to creation and within God's very life. The latter is grounded in the monarchy of the Father and is the condition for the possibility of God's freedom to be in communion with creation. Lossky's strict apophaticism leads not simply to a God without being but to a God beyond all being, and, thus, a God not free to commune with created being.

Lossky's attempt to analogize personal growth in the divine energies to Christology also manifests this primacy of 'essence' in his theology. He explains that as in the person of Christ where two natures are united in one person, so in the human person progressing toward deification, the human (nature) and the divine (energies) are united in one person. The analogy breaks down in several respects. First, what is divine in Christ, i.e., the nature, is distinct from what is divine in the human person. Moreover, one wonders how this analogy coheres with the analogy of deified personhood to divine personhood as freedom from nature. If, according to Lossky, in baptism one receives the deified nature of Christ, and if this deified nature is the basis for personal growth toward deification, then Lossky is suggesting that personal growth is freedom from a deified nature. Lossky defines personal growth in the Holy Spirit as a greater participation in the energies of God, but why should such a greater participation be necessary if one receives in baptism the nature that Christ deified in his own person? In that in Christ human nature is the recipient of the divine energies, there is no clear sense of what relation the divine energies has to the human 'person' other than a vague sense of greater participation. Although he defines 'person' in terms of freedom and love, in Lossky's soteriology and his Christology, 'person' simply becomes a space that houses divine and human natures (Christology), or divine energies and human nature (anthropology). The point is that in spite of his intentions, 'person' becomes a superfluous category and Lossky's apophatic logic consistently betrays a primacy of essence over person.

This all leads to the related question of how salvation in Lossky's soteriology is trinitarian.[108] If the primary purpose of the Incarnation is to communicate the divine energies to human nature in order to deify it, why must God be conceived as trinitarian to communicate God's energies to human nature? The Son and Spirit simply become conveyors of the divine energies, but one could easily conceive of a non-trinitarian God who communicates the divine energies. If, in fact, creation is a result of the divine energies of God, as Lossky asserts, then creation is already participating in God's divine energies. One would then need more practical wisdom on how to participate more fully in the divine energies, but not necessarily an incarnation of the divine person of the Son. If Lossky were to retort that we need to receive a deified human nature to renew our capacity for holiness, deified human nature becomes the beginning and the goal of the Christian life. If the deified human nature we receive at baptism needs constant regeneration because of the continued existence of sin in the world, how does it still provide the capacity for holiness? In the end, the issue is whether salvation itself in Lossky is conceived in terms of participation in the triune personal existence of God. Though the divine persons communicate the divine energies, the issue is whether participation in the divine energies is something less than participation in the triune personal existence of God, especially since divine personhood is itself something more than a participation in the divine energies. More than this, however, the question becomes not simply whether apophaticism makes the Trinity superfluous, but whether in fact, according to Lossky's own criteria, apophaticism is a form for conceptualizing divine-human communion that is compatible with the doctrine of the Trinity understood as an expression of the realism of divine-human communion.[109] In other words, what is not clear in Lossky is not simply what role do the trinitarian persons have in salvation, but why would the realism of divine-human communion necessitate both apophaticism and the affirmation of God as Trinity? For Lossky, the doctrine of the Trinity is a primordial fact and requires antinomic expression in light of the antinomy of divine-human communion. But is the antinomy of Trinity necessary for expressing the antinomy of divine-human communion? Why would one need the antinomy of the trinitarian God in addition to antinomy of God's essence/energies?

Although one can locate weaknesses in Zizioulas's theology, it does not suffer from the kind of internal inconsistency present in Lossky. One weakness in Zizioulas's theology is lack of attention to the notion of the person's particular relation with God. In his attempt to emphasize salvation as an event that is the simultaneous constitution of the one and the many, Zizioulas almost completely neglects that particular, ascetical struggle of a person in their particular relationship with God. It is as if Zizioulas is ignoring this dominant aspect of the Eastern tradition for fear of insinuating that salvation is individualistic.

Personal and communal notions of spirituality need not be mutually incompatible. Here there is perhaps room for integrating aspects of Lossky's theology in Zizioulas's thought, where greater attention is needed to account for the person outside the eucharist, in their struggle for living daily a Christian life. Such an integration is necessary to avoid the impression that notions of communion and community are prioritized at the expense of the particular relationship each has with God through Christ by the power of the Holy Spirit.

A more substantial issue in Zizioulas's theology is the emphasis he gives to the monarchy of the Father. The whole notion of a relational ontology of trinitarian personhood rests on Zizioulas's affirmation of the monarchy of the Father. The latter, however, is not an indisputable point in contemporary trinitarian theology. The traditional critique to the monarchy of the Father is that it is inherently subordinationist. The problem is not with subordinationism per se, but that a subordinationist understanding of the Trinity leads to something less than full communion with God, a central theological axiom for Zizioulas. Furthermore, the monarchy of the Father has been challenged by recent feminist theologies of the Trinity, a critique to which Zizioulas gives little attention. The question is whether Zizioulas's relational ontology of trinitarian personhood can still be affirmed without the monarchy of the Father, particularly as Zizioulas understands it in terms of 'causality.' Zizioulas would answer 'no,' but in the next chapter I will suggest that a modified understanding of the monarchy of the Father would more adequately ground Zizioulas's intentions and, hence, his trinitarian ontology.

The adequacy of Zizioulas's thought over that of Lossky's, and over theological apophaticism more generally, lies in giving an interpretation of the doctrine of the Trinity as a doctrine of salvation, i.e., that deification is trinitarian through unity in the *hypostasis* of Christ, in a way not possible within Lossky's thought. It consists also in the types of distinctions needed in order to conceptualize divine-human communion, particularly that *in* Christ. Both Lossky and Zizioulas rightly agree that the language of "essence" fails in regard to conceptualizing divine-human communion. It either leads to pantheism or, in the end and somewhat ironically, a God incapable of real communion. For Lossky, the answer lies in identifying God's energies as divine. As I have argued, however, this does not allow him to escape the language of essence in the way he thinks it does, and hence, he unwittingly undercuts his own attempts at affirming the realism of divine-human communion.

For Zizioulas, the realism of divine-human communion requires a further distinction other than that between God's essence and God's action/energies/ *dunameis*. This distinction is given with the Cappadocian reworking of *hypo-*

stasis. The many detractors of Zizioulas's interpretation of the Greek fathers notwithstanding, what is suggestive about Zizioulas's theology is his claim that *hypostasis* both in its trinitarian and christological developments must imply more than simply identifying the fact of irreducible distinction in God, or the means for uniting divine and human natures. *Hypostasis* is that in and through which divine-human communion is realized, and is a distinction necessary not simply for conceptualizing how such a communion is possible *in* Christ, but how it is possible at all. In this sense, Zizioulas's "ontology," though not explicit in the Greek fathers, may be interpreted to be consistent with their own logic. For Athanasius, the affirmation against Arius that Christ is divine has as its basis the claim that for God to be transcendent and immanent in a way that saves creation from 'nothing' and protects human freedom there needs to be a mediator that is fully divine and fully human.[110] If this is the case, then *hypostasis* becomes not simply a way of indicating what is distinct in God or a philosophical way of showing how it is reasonable to claim that God is one and three without threatening God's simplicity. The reworking of *hypostasis* itself has as its basis the realism of divine-human communion in Christ, who is fully God and fully human. In this sense, Zizioulas is correct in thinking that *hypostasis* is the category through which to think divine-human communion, especially if such a communion is to be trinitarian, i.e., *in* Christ. The language of *hypostasis* allows for a conceptualization of the realism of such a divine-human communion in a way not open to language of essence or of *hyper-essence*.[111]

Zizioulas's theological synthesis is thus more coherent than Lossky's in that he provides a theological argument for a how one knows the trinitarian God, which is necessary if one is to, in fact, affirm a trinitarian God and that salvation itself is trinitarian. He is able to ground epistemologically his trinitarian ontology in the eucharistic experience of the personal existence of the Triune God. Zizioulas also is able to account for why Christians affirm a trinitarian God, i.e., to explain the link between a trinitarian God and deification. More substantially, however, Zizioulas provides the kinds of distinction not present in Lossky needed for conceptualizing the realism of divine-human communion. Though Lossky develops a trinitarian ontology of person similar to that of Zizioulas, the apophatic thrust to his theology cannot sufficiently ground such an ontology. It also shapes his understanding of other theological dogmas in ways that do not easily cohere with his trinitarian theology of person and which affirms that which Lossky feared most, an ontology of substance.

chapter 4

Trinity and Personhood

Given the substantial differences between the theologies of Lossky and Zizioulas, one is surprised to see that they both develop theologies of 'person' that are strikingly similar. This chapter will sketch their respective theologies of person in the attempt to highlight these points of similarity. It will also indicate the minor points of dissimilarity in their theologies of person. I will then focus explicitly on Zizioulas's attempt to philosophically ground the notion of person, an aspect completely missing in Lossky's thought. Attention will then be given to the critique leveled against Zizioulas's emphasis on the monarchy of the Father as inherently subordinationist. While showing that aspects of this critique are misplaced, Zizioulas's claim that the Father is the sole cause of the Son and Spirit does give the Father a kind of freedom that the Son and the Spirit do not possess. I will offer my own resolution to this problem by modifying Zizioulas's understanding of causality within God's life and through an appropriation of Lossky's understanding of *kenosis*. Finally, I will offer an assessment of the charge that both Lossky and Zizioulas have been influenced by modern personalism and existentialism, particularly that leveled most recently by Lucian Turcescu. In so doing, I will offer my own reflections on the hermeneutics of retrieval of the patristic tradition by a contemporary theologian.

Person as *Ekstasis* and *Hypostasis*

For both theologians the theological concept of person emerged from the trinitarian discussions of the early church. 'Person' was co-opted from the ancient Greek philosophical categories and infused with a new meaning in order to express the trinitarian God. The process by which this christianizing of Greek philosophical categories occurred is given different interpretations by each theologian. To simply summarize what we saw earlier, Zizioulas describes the trinitarian concept of person as an 'ontological revolution.' For both Lossky and Zizioulas, the concern of the Greek fathers, particularly the Cappadocians, was to avoid tritheism or Sabellianism. *Ousia* was clearly not the answer to expressing the threeness of God, since three *ousiai* would be equivalent to three gods. *Ousia* expressed that which was common to the three persons. What Lossky and Zizioulas disagree over is how the Greek fathers arrived at the concept to express the threeness of God. For Lossky there were two moves: the rejection of *prosopon* and the selection of *hypostasis* to express the threeness of God, since the latter was a synonym of *ousia;* and the reconceptualizing of *hypostasis* to express irreducibility to nature. *Hypostasis* as a category to express the threeness of God and as a synonym of *ousia* indicates that the Father, Son, and Holy Spirit are each identical with the common *ousia*. But the category itself required reconceptualization in a Christian form in order to indicate irreducibility to nature. Even though each of the three *hypostaseis* is identical to the common *ousia,* they are not reducible to this essence. The christianizing of *hypostasis* protects the doctrine of the Trinity from a reductionistic monism. *Hypostasis* in a Christian form is what Lossky understands to be the theological concept of person (which, again, is not *prosopon*).

For Zizioulas, the genius of the Greek fathers comes in the form of an ontological revolution that unites the concepts of *hypostasis* and *prosopon*.[1] As we saw, this ontological revolution resulted in giving ontological content to difference, otherness, and particularity. In the doctrine of the Trinity, difference and otherness were not given simply ontological content, but ontological priority. *Person* becomes the primary ontological category insofar as true being itself is personal existence. What constitutes being in an authentic sense is understood in light of trinitarian existence. Important here is not so much the historical accuracy of these accounts (however important historical accuracy is) but rather the distinct theological frameworks that their two interpretations indicate. In both Lossky and Zizioulas one detects an underlying theological argument woven into a historical interpretation of primarily Greek patristic texts. Lossky sees history with apophatic eyes, which leads him first to reject any significance to the category of *prosopon* in the trinitarian discussions of the fourth century. *Prosopon* could in no way express the *fact* that God is three and one and would only lead to Sabellianism. *Hypostasis* expressed particularity, but it needed to be reconceptualized to express irreducibility to nature. The concern for Lossky was to find the proper categories that would signify the *fact* that

God is three and one, without implying any ontological implications in a trinitarian sense.

For Zizioulas, the revelation of the *tropos hyparxeos* of God makes necessary the affirmation of a revolutionary ontology in which communion, otherness, and particularity assume priority over sameness. The concern of the Greek fathers, according to his interpretation, was to express this new trinitarian ontology. In this regard, *hypostasis* was reconceptualized, but only by uniting it with *prosopon*. The latter, for Zizioulas, was the only category in the repertoire of Greek philosophical categories that signified true difference as relationship distinct from individuality. The reconceptualization occurred not with *hypostasis* for the purpose of expressing an irreducibility to nature, but with *prosopon*, which already signified particularity through relation but lacked ontological content. *Prosopon* linked with *hypostasis* was the adequate category to express the new trinitarian ontology. Moreover, the use of *prosopon* represents for Zizioulas the radical break with an ontology of substance. A trinitarian ontology demands such a break. To identify the theological concept of person with a reconceptualized *hypostasis* is to continue to work within an ontology of substance, since *hypostasis* itself is derivative of essence or nature. To make *prosopon* the primary ontological category meant not simply to express the threeness of the Trinity, but to indicate a radical break with traditional understandings of being.

Whether it be signified by *hypostasis* or *prosopon*, the doctrine of the Trinity for both theologians forms the basis for a theological understanding of 'person.'[2] Given their differences over epistemology and ontology, it is, admittedly, surprising to witness broad agreement over the theological understanding of person. This agreement is explained, in large part, by the simple fact that, for both theologians, the category of person emerges from or has as its basis in the patristic attempt to express a God who is three and one, and who is simultaneously transcendent and immanent. Nature or *ousia* proved insufficient, since the one would be emphasized at the expense of three. *Ousia* remains, however, a central category for the doctrine of the Trinity in expressing the oneness of God, not in the sense of unity but in terms of what is common to the three persons. What is common, however, is not what makes them distinct. The Father, the Son, and the Holy Spirit are each distinct from each other and from their common *ousia*.[3] For both theologians, 'person' becomes the category that most adequately expresses the distinctiveness or threeness of God, but also, as we have seen, the realism of divine-human communion.

Whether it be a reconceptualizing of *hypostasis* or the linking of *hypostasis* with *prosopon*, the patristic attempt to express the threeness of God gives rise to the theological understanding of 'person' in terms of *ekstasis* and *hypostasis*.[4] Given that the Father, Son, and Holy Spirit are not three natures, but three *hypostaseis,* or persons, they are distinct from nature. Both Lossky and Zizioulas translate such a distinction from nature into a freedom, or *ekstasis* from nature.[5] To be a person is then to be free from nature, to have one's identity not be determined by the content of one's nature. A person is free vis-à-vis his or her nature, and thus, free to determine one's own destiny or identity.

Personal freedom according to Lossky and Zizioulas is better understood in the context of their reaction against Greek or Scholastic monism. According to their interpretation, Greek and Scholastic thought, in the context of a metaphysics of substance, subject both the world and God to necessity. In the attempt to determine the 'essence' of God's being, God's identity becomes identified with God's nature. It is God's nature which then determines God's being, thus subjecting the being of God to what is necessarily determined to be God's nature. If, for example, God is in God's essence love, then God necessarily loves, and the logic of love then explains God's trinitarian existence. The trinitarian distinctions are derived from the divine essence. If God's being is determined by the fact that God in God's *ousia* is love, then God is not absolutely free, but subject to the determination of God's essence which, according to some theologians, is love. 'Person' as *ekstasis,* or freedom from nature, signifies that God's trinitarian being is not linked to the necessity of an impersonal substance. God is not trinity because God's nature is necessarily identified with an attribute such as love or goodness. To be person, then, for both Lossky and Zizioulas, is to be free from the necessary determinations of nature. It signifies the absolute transcendence of God from any necessity. For Zizioulas, this translates into the priority of person over nature, and to the affirmation of an ontology of the particular. It is person that gives existence to nature, and not nature which forms the basis for personal existence. It is not that one *is* and is then person; one simply *is* as person. What is ultimately maintained with the priority of person over nature is the absolute freedom of God.

The importance of the concept of person for maintaining the absolute freedom of God in theology can be clearly seen in the emphasis both theologians give to the *monarchia* or monarchy of the Father. The monarchy of the Father, insist both Lossky and Zizioulas, is necessary for preserving the absolute freedom of God, despite criticisms which argue that this *monarchia* gives a pre-eminence to the Father that threatens the trinitarian equality of persons. As was discussed above, if the Father, for Lossky, were not the source of the other two persons of the Trinity and, hence, the principle of unity in the Trinity, then the only alternative would be the common essence. As the principle of unity, the common essence would overshadow the persons and transform "them into relations within the unity of the essence."[6] Lossky adds that the antinomy between nature and person collapses with the common essence as the principle of unity. The monarchy of the Father "maintains the perfect equilibrium between the nature and the persons, without coming down too heavily on either side. . . . The one nature and the three hypostases are presented simultaneously to our understanding, with neither prior to the other."[7] Thus, in thinking the *monarchia* of the Father, one thinks of both person and nature together, the one and the three simultaneously, rather than the one first and then the three. The antinomy of person and nature functions as any antinomy in precluding a reduction of God to any particular concept. As a central aspect of apophaticism, antinomy both frees the mind from itself in order to transcend itself in union with God, but it also affirms the transcendence of God from anything created, including a rational concept. Thus, nature is not sufficient to express the trinitarian God, who lies beyond any rational calculus. In thinking Trinity, one must think both person and nature together, and affirming the monarchy of the Father protects this antinomy.

Lossky further argues that only a personal principle can generate persons who are themselves unique and irreducible. The Father as source and principle of unity preserves the integrity, distinctiveness, and irreducibility of the Son and the Holy Spirit. If the 'cause' of trinitarian existence were the impersonal essence, then each of the divine persons would be derivative beings. God the Father as *aitia* or 'cause' of trinitarian existence means that God the Father is not simply identified with God's essence.[8] God the Father 'causes' the existence of the Son and the Holy Spirit, who are themselves distinct from the Father, but possess the fullness of the divine nature. Thus, the meaning of person is to be distinct from one's nature, but also to be in relation with other persons who possess the fullness of this nature. Lossky adds that God the Father "could not be fully and absolutely Person unless the Son and the Holy Spirit are equal to Him in possession of the same nature and *are* the same nature."[9] If God were, as Eunomius affirmed, identified with God's essence, then the Father could not share the fullness of this essence without fundamentally altering God's identity. The sharing of the fullness of this nature is what constitutes God as Father, as distinct though not separate from this nature and relation with other persons who possess this nature fully. The monarchy of the Father alone is able to maintain this personal freedom from nature.

Zizioulas would not disagree with the main thrust of Lossky's insistence on the monarchy of the Father. He would disagree, however, with Lossky's insistence on preserving, on the basis of apophaticism, the antinomy between nature and person. As we have seen, Zizioulas affirms the priority of person over nature and such a priority must be given to person to maintain God's absolute freedom. Thus, for Zizioulas the monarchy of the Father is not necessary in order to maintain the person/nature antinomy, which itself is rooted in the apophatic character of theology. God the Father as *aitia* is the logical consequence of his ontology of personhood, which is nothing less than an ontology of divine-human communion.

Zizioulas more forcefully and explicitly argues that God the Father as *aitia* of trinitarian existence is the only way to maintain God's absolute freedom. As we saw above, for Zizioulas, the eucharistic communion with the trinitarian God forms the basis for affirming an ontology of personhood in which otherness, communion, and freedom are given, for the first time, ontological significance. Such an ontology gives priority to person over nature with regard to the 'cause' of personal existence. In terms of God's own trinitarian existence, God's existence itself is a free existence, not subject to necessity, only if God the Father is *aitia* of such existence. Zizioulas argues *pege* or source was not adequate enough for the Cappadocians to express the relation of the Son and the Spirit to the Father, because it "could be understood substantially or naturalistically" and thus, link God's existence to necessity.[10] *Aitia* needed to complement *pege,* since the former "carried with it connotations of personal initiative . . . of *freedom.* Divine being owes its being to a *free person,* not to impersonal substance."[11] In rooting the source and unity of God's existence to the person of the Father, "when we say that God 'is,' we do not bind an ontological 'necessity' or a simple 'reality' for God—but we ascribe the being of God to His personal freedom."[12] Zizioulas adds that "in a more analytical way this means that God, as Father and not as substance, perpetually confirms through 'being' His *free* will to exist. And it is precisely His trinitarian existence that constitutes this confirmation: the Father out of love—that is freely—begets the Son and brings forth the Spirit."[13] In a personal ontology in which person is the ultimate ontological category, freedom itself becomes the presupposition of being, even of God's being.[14]

Zizioulas's logic for affirming the monarchy of the Father, which some might interpret as introducing a certain arbitrariness into God's being, is simple. If the eucharistic experience reveals salvation to be a communion with the divine, one that bestows eternal life, then this salvation is personal in the sense that it is a freedom from the giveness of created nature inherent in which is the reality of death. Evident here are the profound existential concerns that underlie Zizioulas's theology. Salvation is defined in terms of absolute freedom which for Zizioulas is a freedom from the given.[15] This given for created beings is created nature itself and the necessity of death. In communion with God, one transcends this giveness and is affirmed in his or her unique identity in an eternal relationship of love with the triune God. If, however, Zizioulas argues, God's own existence is not a result of freedom, then God cannot give what God does not have.[16] Freedom becomes the precondition for love, the possibility for an unforced communion with the other. Though Zizioulas roots the ontology of personhood in God's being, and though God's trinitarian existence gives meaning to 'person,' the 'necessity' of absolute personal freedom in God's existence for personal salvation from death reveals the extent to which existential concerns inform his theology. That notwithstanding, Zizioulas and Lossky, despite their subtle differences, identify person with freedom based on trinitarian theology. The monarchy of the Father for both theologians protects the reality of personal existence within the triune life and maintains God's freedom from the necessity of monism inherent in Greek and Scholastic metaphysics. Zizioulas more forcefully than Lossky, based on his ontology of personhood, argues that the monarchy of the Father is essential if God's being is to be one of absolute freedom, and if such absolute freedom is the condition for the possibility of transcending death.[17]

The other aspect of personhood on which the two theologians share agreement is its hypostatic element. Person is *hypostasis* for Lossky and Zizioulas, which in itself is a bit confusing since *hypostasis* was the category used by the Greek fathers to express the diversity within God's being. 'Person,' however, is not strictly *hypostasis,* in that person for Lossky is the reconceptualization of *hypostasis* and for Zizioulas is the uniting of *hypostasis* and *prosopon*. A person is hypostatic, but an *hypostasis* in and of itself is not a person. What it means to be hypostatic for both theologians is distinct from the classical understandings of *hypostasis*. Its meaning is based on the doctrine of the Trinity, and, in short, a person is *hypostatic* by possessing the fullness of nature. The persons of the Trinity do not share the nature, or participate in the nature, or possess a part of the divine nature; within each divine *hypostasis* is the fullness of the divine nature.[18] Person is the *hypostatization* of nature, and the Father as the *aitia* of the Son and the Spirit, constituting their distinctiveness, bestows the fullness of the divine nature. It could not be otherwise if the Son and the Spirit are to be truly persons, for to be 'person' is uniquely distinct, and such uniqueness is possible only if one were to possess the fullness of nature. Each person possesses this nature in a unique and distinct way, the Father as Father, etc.

The notion of God being simultaneously person and nature, in which person is neither derivative of nature nor an identity-in-distinction with the common nature, but rather the *hypostatization* of nature, is one unique to the Greek patristic tradition, and one which emerges from the attempt to give expression to a God who is one and three.[19] By affirming person as being distinct from nature but fully possessing nature, the Greek fathers wish to signify that personal existence is itself an existence of love and uniqueness. In terms of love, as *hypostasis* of nature the person is not isolated, but in communion with other persons who share this nature.[20] The Father as person gives the common essence to other persons, so that he *is* the person of the Father, not by possessing the common essence for Godself, but by giving it to the Son and the Spirit. Thus, a person possesses the fullness of nature in communion with other persons and such a communion is one of love. The communion itself is a *perichoretic existence,* in which the persons co-inhere, the one in the other, each affirming both the common identity and the otherness of the other. In possessing the fullness of nature, the otherness of the person is not absorbed but constituted. To be *hypostatic* is, thus, to be unique, as each person is not defined by what is common, but possesses what is common in a unique way. Furthermore, if *hypostatic* existence is one of loving communion, then love itself is the condition of such uniqueness. One becomes uniquely person only in loving communion with other persons. Communion, thus, does not threaten otherness; it constitutes it.[21]

For both theologians, the person as the *hypostasis* of nature, i.e., possessing the fullness of nature is contrasted with individuality, which is the division of nature. According to Lossky, "as for *hypostasis* . . . it no longer contains anything individual. The individual is part of a species, or rather he is only a part of it: he divides the nature to which he belongs, he is the result of its atomization."[22] Elsewhere he explains that

> men have therefore a common nature, one single nature in many human persons . . . individual and person mean opposite things, the word individual expressing a certain mixture of the person with elements which belong to the common nature, while person, on the other hand, means that which distinguishes it from nature . . . When we wish to define, 'to characterize' a person, we gather together individual characteristics, 'traits of character' which are to be met with elsewhere in other individuals, and which because they belong to nature are never absolutely 'personal'.[23]

Zizioulas likewise contrasts person with nature, identifying the latter with division: "At the same time, and in contrast to the partiality of the individual which is subject to addition and combination, the person in its ecstatic character reveals its being in a *catholic,* i.e., integral and undivided, way, and thus in its being ecstatic it becomes *hypostatic,* i.e. the bearer of its nature in its totality."[24] Zizioulas uses Maximus's distinction between *diaphora* (difference) and *diairesis* (division) to contrast personhood with individuality. "Different beings become distant beings: because difference becomes division, distinction becomes distance. St. Maximus makes use of these terms to express this universal and cosmic situation. *Diaphora* (difference) must be maintained, for it is good. *Diairesis* (division) is a perversion of *diaphora,* and is bad."[25] Elsewhere, Zizioulas says, "individualisation is precisely the fact that accounts for the impossibility of real communion, because it implies distance and hence division instead of difference."[26]

For both theologians there are at least two distinguishing characteristics of individuality: isolation and repeatability. Concerning the latter, an individual, who is not the *hypostasis* of the fullness of nature and, thus, not distinct or free from nature, receives its identity from the common nature. In this sense, the individual is a derivative of the common nature, a combination of common traits of human nature that are repeatable. The individual is isolated in the sense that his or her identity is constituted over against the other individual who is constituted through natural qualities. The individual is a static reality,[27] not relating in love in relation to those who possess the fullness of nature, but a self-possessed thing in itself, defined over-and-against those who 'possess' natural qualities different from his or her own. Thus, if personhood, according to the trinitarian model, is the hypostatization of the fullness of nature, then the non-person or individual is the division of nature into isolated beings who are unable to transcend their created nature in loving communion with God and others.

Thus, for both theologians, personal existence is one in which, as Zizioulas puts it, "the *hypo-static* and the *ek-static* have to coincide."[28] Freedom and love, communion and otherness, the one and the many exist simultaneously in the person. As Zizioulas explains,

> Thus personhood implies the 'openness of being', and even more than that, the *ek-stasis* of being, i.e. a movement towards communion which leads to a transcendence of the boundaries of the 'self' and thus to *freedom.* At the same time, and in contrast to the partiality of the individual which is subject to addition and combination, the person in its ekstatic character reveals its being in a *catholic,* i.e. integral and undivided way, and thus in its being ekstatic it becomes *hypostatic,* i.e. the bearer of its nature in its totality.[29]

As we saw above, analytically freedom is the condition for the possibility of love; however, ontologically love and freedom are simultaneous. Zizioulas is able to say that the Father "confirms through 'being' His *free* will to exist,"[30] but the Father exists as Father eternally as freedom and love. In 'freely' willing to exist as Trinity, the Father identifies this freedom with love. Though lacking the ontological import, we see Lossky's thought in fundamental agreement with Zizioulas in saying that, "'person' signifies . . . *someone* who is distinct from his own nature, of someone who goes beyond his nature while still containing it."[31] The implication of this convergence of love and freedom in personal existence further implies for Lossky as well as for Zizioulas the mutual conditioning of the one and the many, of unity and multiplicity, of otherness and communion. According to Lossky,

> it is precisely because each one opens itself to the others, because they share nature without restriction, that the latter is not divided. And this indivisible nature gives every *hypostasis* its depth, confirms its uniqueness, reveals itself in this unity of the unique, in this communion in which every person, without confusion, shares integrally in all the others: the more they are one the more they are diverse, since nothing of the communal nature escapes them; and the more they are diverse the more they are one, since their unity is not impersonal uniformity, but a fertile tension of irreducible diversity, an abundance of a 'circumincession without mixture of confusion' (St. John Damascus).[32]

Equally, Zizioulas, responding to the emphasis on the 'one' in ontology, affirms that "the 'one' not only does not precede—logically or otherwise—the 'many', but, on the contrary, requires the 'many' from the very start in order to exist. This, therefore, seems to be the great innovation in philosophical thought, brought about by the Cappadocian Trinitarian theology."[33] Person is, for Zizioulas, "otherness in communion and communion in otherness."[34] He adds that communion without otherness is nothing but "an arrangement for careful co-existence,"[35] while otherness without communion is non-existent. What both theologians seem to be implying is that love and communion are the precondition for otherness and difference. It is only in loving communion with others that true difference is not simply respected, but constituted. One becomes other as one relates to the other, but this difference or otherness is given permanence, or as Zizioulas puts it, ontological significance, in a relationship of love. In an eternal communion of love, the persons of the Trinity confirm the other's identity. Otherness, however, is also the precondition for communion and not community that is simply a fellowship of individuals. Communion or unity requires real difference, otherwise the unity is less a union than an absorption into sameness. Love, which is the force of communion and unity, requires freedom or an *ekstasis* from oneself toward the other. This freedom in communion does not become division but true diversity or otherness.

Personhood, for both Lossky and Zizioulas, is existence in which otherness and communion, freedom, and love coincide. It is the fulfillment of the image of God in the human. Given their epistemological differences and methodological differences, it is somewhat surprising to find such broad agreement on the theological notion of person. This agreement leads one to suspect that Zizioulas may owe more to Lossky's thought than he admits. Another explanation, however, could be that at the heart of both theological systems lies the basic Orthodox axiom of salvation in terms of the unity between the divine and the human. Though this union may take different forms for both theologians, the two theologies, and I would venture to say most of Orthodox theological tradition up to the present age, seem to be rooted in the famous Athanasian dictum "God became *anthropos* so that the *anthropos* can become God." It is this soteriological principle that leads to the rejection of a metaphysics of substance as inadequate to express this truth. The this-that, either-or, created-uncreated oppositions simply prove incapable of expressing a communion with the divine in which otherness—of God, within God, of the human—and freedom are simultaneously affirmed. Another category is needed, and person ultimately becomes, for both theologians, the means of expressing this reality of divine-human communion. If Zizioulas did not in fact rely on Lossky for the basis of his theology of personhood, then perhaps the two theologians, attempting to clarify the patristic insights in light of contemporary questions, simply followed the logic of divine-human communion that affirms true existence as the simultaneity of freedom and love. In either case, certain features of Zizioulas's theology of personhood, besides its ontological import already discussed, indicate a break with Lossky's thought.

The single most distinguishing factor of Zizioulas's theology of personhood from that of Lossky's is his emphasis on relationship. This is not to imply that Lossky's understanding of person does not include relations. As we saw, a person, for Lossky, exists "not by excluding others, not by opposition to the 'Not-I,' but by a refusal to possess the nature for himself. . . . Personal existence supposes a relation to the other; one person exists 'to' or 'towards' the other."³⁶ Even in the realm of trinitarian existence, Lossky argues that the monarchy of the Father does not confer upon the Father any hypostatic primacy since the Father "is a person only because the Son and the Holy Spirit are also."³⁷ The Father is person, i.e., not identified with the divine essence, since, as person, the Father gives the fullness of this essence to other persons. He could not give the divine essence in this way if the Father were not distinct from the essence, i.e., a person.

Since, for Lossky, to be a person is to relate, one encounters confusion when reading "the (trinitarian) relations only serve to *express* the hypostatic diversity of the Three; they are not the basis of it."³⁸ What Lossky is referring to here is the 'relations of origin' that he contrasts with the Thomistic 'relations of opposition.' The 'relations of origin' in Greek patristic trinitarian theology indicate, for Lossky, that the Son and the Spirit have a different mode of origin from the Father. This difference in the mode of origin is what protects their hypostatic diversity, otherwise if they originated in the same way from the Father, they would not be hypostatically diverse.³⁹

Lossky adds, alluding to the Thomistic 'relations of opposition,' "no attempt is being made to establish a relation of opposition between the Son and the Holy Spirit . . . because relations of origin in the Trinity—filiation, procession—cannot be considered as the basis for the hypostases, as that which determines their absolute diversity."⁴⁰ Thomistic trinitarian theology, according to Lossky, affirmed that the diversity within the Trinity must be based, logically, on 'relations of opposition' between the persons of the Trinity. For a person to be person there must be a relation opposite that of another person. In trinitarian theology, the relation between the Father and the Son is easily explained in terms of generation. The difficulty lies in establishing the relation of opposition to the Holy Spirit. If it is only to the Father, then the Holy Spirit is no different than the Son; hence, the relation of opposition must be to the Father and to the Son as one principle of spiration. For Lossky, this emphasis on 'relation of opposition' in order to establish hypostatic diversity is to make the latter depend on the Aristotelian concept of relation. This attempt runs contrary to Lossky's apophatic thrust, which affirms that God lies beyond all concepts. To base the hypostatic differences on a particular concept is to reduce God's trinitarian existence to the necessity of relations. Furthermore, the attempt to logically conceive how the one divine essence can be logically differentiated through the Aristotelian concept of relation is, for Lossky, to break the antinomy between person and nature and to prioritize the divine essence over trinitarian diversity. This priority not only threatens the personal diversity within the Trinity, but it reflects the precedence given to the rational over the mystical in theological method in undertaking to give a rational explanation to that which is beyond rationality. Thus, when Lossky says that the relations do not serve as the basis for hypostatic diversity, he has in mind the Thomistic 'relations of opposition' which he interprets as making the trinitarian God dependent on the logic of the concept of 'relation.' But in order to affirm that a person is person only in relating, Lossky cannot escape the conclusion that relations do form the basis for personhood. Words such as 'basis' or 'dependence' smack of rational necessity and fly in the face of Lossky's apophaticism. In order for his theology of personhood to be coherent, the relation must be constitutive of person without undermining the freedom of personal existence.

Not being caught between the either-or of essence and superessence, between mystical and rational theology, Zizioulas is able to affirm that even for the divine life, relations are constitutive of personhood. Zizioulas's argument for the notion of the *tropos hyparxeos* in expressing God's existence allows him to close the gap between the immanent and economic Trinity. This distinction allows for ontological statements in relation to God's existence without effacing God's transcendence. Moreover, the eucharistic participation in the *tropos hyparxeos* of God's existence demands the affirmation of an ontology of particularity or of personhood. Inherent in this ontology of personhood is relation: relations constitute personhood. For Zizioulas, a person *is* "only as it *relates to*."[41] He adds that in a personal ontology, "the particular is raised to the level of ontological primacy, it emerges as *being itself* without depending for its identity on qualities borrowed from nature and thus applicable also to other beings, but solely on a relationship in which it is inconceivable for the rest of beings to *be* outside a relationship with it."[42] Moreover, it is this relationship or communion with others which constitute an identity that is personal, i.e., unique and unrepeatable.[43] It is not, however, any relationship which constitutes personhood, but only those defined as love: "The more one loves ontologically and truly personally, the less one identifies someone as unique and irreplaceable for one's existence on the basis of such classifiable qualities."[44] Thus, for Zizioulas, "personal identity is totally lost if isolated, for its ontological condition is relationship."[45] Relationship as love does not simply constitute the person as person, but gives that person the uniqueness inherent in personal identity: "It is the other and our relationship with him that gives us our identity, our otherness, making us 'who we are', i.e. persons; for by being an inseparable part of a relationship that matters ontologically we emerge as *unique* and *unrepeatable* entities."[46] With the framework of his ontology of personhood, Zizioulas is able to affirm that the Father is particularly Father because of the Father's relation to the Son and the Spirit. Thus, the Father's fatherhood is constituted in and through particular relations of love; the Father's identity 'depends' on relations.

This affirmation, however, does not necessarily slide trinitarian theology into a metaphysics of substance; Zizioulas is not saying that the one divine essence first is and then relates, and in relating is three persons. Integral to Zizioulas's theology and his ontology of personhood is the notion of 'simultaneity.' Person and relation are simultaneous events. Personal identity, love, relationship, freedom are all concurrent. They are marks of divine existence, which is eternal existence, and hence simultaneous existence. Thus, God's being is all at once love, freedom, and relationship, though analytically, one could state that the "ontological condition of personal identity is relationship." Though he shares Lossky's rejection of a metaphysics of substance in order to express the doctrine of the Trinity, Zizioulas also avoids the apophatic turn. Within an ontology of personhood, Zizioulas is able to affirm that relation is, in fact, constitutive of personal identity, even those personal identities within the triune life.

Zizioulas's Philosophical Argument for an Ontology of Personhood

A second difference, though more methodological than substantive, has to do with Zizioulas's philosophical justification for an ontology of personhood. Zizioulas himself is adamant that 'person' as *ekstasis* and *hypostasis* is a strictly theological concept: "The Orthodox understanding of the Holy Trinity is the only way to arrive at this notion of personhood."[47] His writings, however, betray a philosophical argument for 'person' as the only means to fulfill a fundamental drive in human existence. This drive is one away from death toward life realized in communion with others. According to Zizioulas if such a drive is left unfulfilled, then non-existence defines the meaning of existence.

This philosophical argument for the centrality of the concept of 'person' for human existence appears for the first time in his seminal article, "Human Capacity and Human Incapacity: A Theological Exploration of Personhood." In arguing "for an approach other than the 'substantial' one to the human being,"[48] which, of course, is the personal approach, Zizioulas outlines the constitutive elements of his theology of personhood which he develops throughout his career. Early in the article, after discussing the difference between substantial and personal understandings of the human being, Zizioulas illustrates "the greatness and tragedy of man's personhood" through what he terms the "presence-in-absence paradox"[49] inherent in all creaturely existence. The human being's personhood and the tragedy of the presence-in-absence paradox are most evident, for Zizioulas, in the human capacity to create. For Zizioulas, to create as an individual is different from creating as a person. The former is a process of *"seizing, controlling and dominating* reality." Beings are turned into things, and insofar as such manufacturing is more often than not "a collective effort," the human being turns him- or herself into a thing, "an instrument and a means to an end."[50] To create as a person is to imbue the created object with the uniqueness and irreducibility of the person. Zizioulas uses art as an example of such personal creativity, in which the artist "becomes 'present' as a unique and unrepeatable *hypostasis* of being and not as an impersonal number in a combined structure." Reminiscent of Lossky's reference to artists to illustrate the uniqueness of person,[51] Zizioulas argues that "when we look at a painting or listen to music we have in front of us . . . a 'presence' in which 'things' and substances (cloth, oil, etc.) or qualities (shape, colour, etc.) or sounds become part of a personal presence."[52] Thus, a personal 'presence,' which is one of uniqueness, irreducibility, freedom, is inherent in a work of art.

If art is a manifestation of personal existence, it is also a revelation of the 'tragedy' inherent in creaturely existence. 'Tragedy' is an important concept for Zizioulas's understanding of personhood, especially with regard to its philosophical justification. Concerning our present discussion, the tragedy of all works of art consists in the fact that art itself manifests the absence of the artist as much as his or her presence. "If we take again our example from the world of art, the fundamental thing that we must observe with regard to the 'presence' it creates, is that the artist himself is absent."[53] Art is just an example of the "paradoxical fact" which plagues all creaturely existence, namely, "that the presence of being in and through the human person is ultimately revealed as an *absence.*"[54] It must be remembered that Zizioulas is speaking here of a 'presence' which is personal. When a person is present, he or she is present as a unique, irreducible, free, relational being. 'Pure presence' is a personal existence without absence, i.e., an existence in which the marks of personal existence are immediate and permanent. This 'pure presence' is not possible so long as it is mediated or limited by the boundaries of the body.[55]

What ultimately constitutes this presence-in-absence paradox as tragic, for Zizioulas, is the fact that it indicates a fundamental *drive* for personal presence in created existence that is thwarted by the co-existence of absence. "All this means that the ekstatic movement towards communion which is part of personhood, remains for man an unfulfilled longing for a presence-without-absence of being as long as there is no way of overcoming the space-time limitations of creaturehood."[56] This "unfulfilled longing" is one for personal presence or personhood and it is on this 'longing' which Zizioulas bases his philosophical argumentation for the validity of an ontology of personhood. The longing for pure presence is, in effect, a desire to eradicate absence, and the definitive form of absence is death. Inherent in all creaturely existence is death and, consequently, all creaturely attempts for a personal presence without absence will always be reduced to the absence which is death. The important point here, however, is that Zizioulas isolates in human existence a fundamental 'longing' for personhood, for an existence that is free, unique, and unrepeatable. Such a longing is, in the end, a longing to escape death: "All this means that the overcoming of death represents a longing rooted in the *personhood* of man."[57] Since death is inherent in all creaturely existence, "personal presence *quâ presence* is something that *cannot be extrapolated from created existence*."[58] What Zizioulas means here is that the longing for personal existence can only be affirmed by uncreated existence. Personal existence, one which is both *ekstatic* and *hypostatic*, which attempts to transcend the boundaries and limitations of creaturely existence, namely death, through personal relations, becomes a reality only in an *ekstatic* and *hypostatic* movement and communion with the uncreated, with that which does not die. It is only in communion with that which is not-created that created being can fulfill its longing for personal existence. Implicit here is a proof for God's existence: "Personhood, understood in its terrifying ontological ultimacy to which I have tried to point in this Paper, leads to God—or to non-existence."[59] Either there is God who fulfills this 'longing' for personhood and gives meaning to life; or there is death which envelopes all existence, and the only way to affirm one's personhood, one's freedom from the given, is to commit suicide, which, however, negates the very freedom one seeks in committing the act. For Zizioulas such meaninglessness is not an option, which leads him to conclude that this fundamental 'longing' "reveals that there is a future, an *eschaton* or a *telos*, a final goal in creation, which must resolve the problem created by personhood."[60]

Zizioulas never speaks to this 'presence-in-absence' paradox in his later work, though the basic thrust of this philosophical argument for personhood as the fundamental longing of all human existence remains intact. In the first chapter of *Being as Communion*,[61] Zizioulas describes what he terms "the *hypostasis of biological existence*." This existence "suffers radically from two 'passions' that destroy precisely that towards which the human *hypostasis* is thrusting, namely the person."[62] The first passion Zizioulas calls 'ontological necessity,' and consists of the inevitable link between the *hypostasis* and natural instinct. The second passion is that of *"individualism,* of the *separation* of the hypostases."[63] Both passions as well as the drive to personhood are intertwined in erotic love, which conceals "the deepest act of communion a tendency towards an ecstatic transcendence of individuality through creation."[64] This new creation, a human being, bears both the marks of personhood and of individuality: "He is born as a result of an *ecstatic* fact—erotic love—but this fact is interwoven with a natural necessity and therefore lacks ontological freedom. He is born as a *hypostatic* fact, as a body, but this fact is interwoven with individuality and with death."[65] Zizioulas's focus has shifted from the creation of an artist to that of an erotic couple. There is no mention of the presence-in-absence paradox, but the drive toward personhood manifested in the creative act of erotic communion indicates both the capacity for personhood and the inability to fulfill such a longing. "All this means that man as a biological *hypostasis* is intrinsically a tragic figure."[66] Human existence in its longing for personhood, expressed in the act of communion, manifests aspects or degrees of personhood, but such a longing is inherently tragic since it confronts death, which negates all uniqueness. It is not simply either personhood or individuality, but that within the horizon of created, finite existence, all human longing for communion can only lead, in the end, to individuality, as Zizioulas defines it, because of death. Zizioulas is simply arguing that given the limits of finitude the only way that such a drive can be fulfilled is through an eternal relationship of freedom and love with God.

In his "On Being a Person. Towards an Ontology of Personhood," Zizioulas explores how the personal and the particular can have ontological import. He analyzes the question "Who am I" from an ontological perspective, indicating that "'Who' is a call for *definition* or 'description' of some kind. . . . The ingredient 'am' or *to be* . . . is a cry for security, for ground to be based on, for fixity. . . . The ingredient 'I' or 'Your' or 'He/She' . . . is a cry for *particularity,* for *otherness.*"[67] In this basic question is the cry, for Zizioulas, for 'particularity' and 'otherness' to be permanent or to be grounded ontologically. In characteristic fashion, Zizioulas then argues how an ontology based on substantial categories is inadequate to secure the permanence of otherness. Zizioulas explains that "the inability of Greek thought to create a personal ontology is not due to a weakness or incapacity of Greek philosophy as *philosophy*. . . . Otherness cannot acquire ontological primacy as long as one begins with the world as it is, as did the ancient Greeks and all philosophy does, if it wishes to be pure philosophy. The observation of the world cannot lead to an ontology of the person, because the person as an ontological category cannot be extrapolated from experience."⁶⁸ Elsewhere Zizioulas explains that "the *ekstasis* of beings towards humanity or towards creation alone leads to 'being-into-death.'"⁶⁹ Zizioulas reiterates here what we saw in his earlier work, namely, that an ontology of personhood and the particular needs a beyond, an uncreated realm, since creation itself is inherently ridden with death. The particular is not ontologically absolute if it dies.

Besides the necessity of a beyond, Zizioulas posits other presuppositions for an ontology of personhood and the particular. The first of these is that "in order to give to the particular an ontological ultimacy or priority it is necessary to *presuppose* that being is *caused* and cannot be posited as an axiomatic of self-explicable principle." The second is related to the first, in that the *cause* of being must be a person.⁷⁰ These two presuppositions are required for Zizioulas for the simple reason that freedom is inherent in an ontology of personhood. By definition, a person for Zizioulas is a free, i.e., *ekstatic* being. This personal existence itself must be a result of freedom and not necessity. Personal existence itself is freely constituted only if it is caused by another free being, i.e., a person.⁷¹ If human persons exist as a result of a person, then their personal existence depends on the continuing relationship with this person. Such a relationship is not possible, however, with the first or any human being since death destroys the permanency of any human relationships. "In God it is possible for the particular to be ontologically ultimate because *relationship is permanent and unbreakable*," otherwise put, "the conditions that we have set out for this ontology of personhood exist only in God."⁷² It is within God's life that the ontology of the particular is affirmed, and personal existence on the level of created existence is affirmed only through communion with this divine life, i.e., only through a relationship that is "permanent and unbreakable." As we saw above, such a relationship occurs through a union with Christ.

Before concluding, it is necessary to ask Zizioulas why an examination of the presuppositions of an ontology is important or even necessary? If an ontology of personhood is given in the eucharistic communion with the triune God, why attempt to examine the question of personhood from the reverse direction, i.e., from an observation of the human condition? Zizioulas provides an answer in "On Being a Person":

> The ontology of personhood with all the conditions we have just outlined cannot be extrapolated from history or nature. If it exists and *is not wishful thinking on man's part*, it is the only 'analogy' or *proof we have that God exists*. If it does not exist, then our faith in God is untrue. Ontology in this situation is not applicable to personhood. *We are left with a drive*

towards personal identity, which will never be fulfilled. Even so, it is worth keeping it at all costs. For without it Man ceases to be human.[73]

Zizioulas offers a sort of phenomenological argument in identifying a fundamental fact of human existence, which requires a particular understanding of God, if human existence is to have any meaning at all. All this raises the question of the relation between philosophy and theology in Zizioulas's thought.

Zizioulas is adamant that the concept of person is itself a theological concept that emerges only through the eucharistic communion with the triune God. One wonders, however, along with Alan J. Torrance, "whether a foundational (ist) ontology of personhood together with attendant notions of personal freedom, creativity and, in particular, causality do not threaten to become the driving force (or 'critical control') in his exposition of the doctrine of God.... There remains ... the suspicion that his exposition of the Trinity is, perhaps, over-conditioned at points by a 'personalist' ontology."[74] Certainly in intent, one must give the benefit of the doubt to Zizioulas, who absolutely rejects the possibility of a non-theological personalist ontology. He argues that "the meaning of person is not borrowed from philosophy ... but philosophy is able, if it wishes, to borrow this meaning from theology."[75] Zizioulas elsewhere amplifies this statement through a series of rhetorical questions:

> is a philosophical justification of patristic theology possible? Or does patristic theology in its essence constitute the converse, that is, a *theological justification of philosophy,* a proclamation that philosophy and the world can acquire a true ontology only if they accept the presupposition of God as the *only* existent whose being is truly identified with the person and with freedom?[76]

The answer for Zizioulas is clearly yes, and it helps explain more clearly such statements as "the person as an ontological category cannot be extrapolated from experience."[77] Philosophy can identify the fundamental drive to personhood, but only theologically can such an implicit ontology be validated. Such a personal ontology requires not simply any God, but the trinitarian God who is experienced within the eucharistic communion. Specifically, it requires a God whose own existence is personal, i.e., a result of freedom. These conditions are achieved for Zizioulas in the monarchy of the Father, and it is this latter principle, more than any other that confirms for Zizioulas that the notion of person is a strictly theological and not philosophical concept.[78] What gives Torrance's suspicion some validity, however, is when Zizioulas claims that, theology must seek ways of *relating* the Gospel to the existential needs of the world and to whatever is human. Instead of throwing the Bible or the dogmas of the Church into the face of the world, it would be best to seek first to feel and understand what every human being longs for deep in their being, and then see how the Gospel and doctrine can make sense to that longing.[79]

This statement places Zizioulas further from Barth and closer to Tillich, in that, for Zizioulas, theological knowledge must be correlated to the existential needs of the human condition. Thus, it is quite justifiable to wonder whether a particular philosophy is shaping Zizioulas's theology. Given, however, that Zizioulas's early work is strictly theological, for the most part ecclesiological, it is more likely that Zizioulas developed his theology of person within a theological framework. The explicitly theological character of his notion of personhood is especially clear in Zizioulas's understanding of personal freedom.

The Problem of 'Freedom' in Zizioulas's Thought

Alan Torrance offers a more substantial critique, not unrelated to that already discussed, in which he argues that Zizioulas's understanding of the monarchy threatens the doctrine of the Trinity. For Torrance, this insistence on the monarchy of the Father indicates that underlying Zizioulas's trinitarian theology is an *a priori* ontology of communion. It heightens his suspicion of whether a foundational ontology of personhood together threatens to become the driving force in his exposition of the doctrine of God. This foundational ontology drives Zizioulas, according to Torrance, toward endorsing uncritically "the Cappadocian projection of causal notions into the internal life of God."[80] According to Torrance, however, introducing such causal notions into the life of God is "potentially damaging to his [Zizioulas's] identification of being and communion."[81] It violates the Anselmian axiom for divinity in that it suggests that the Son, as well as the Spirit, is that "than which something greater can be conceived." As a result, Torrance suggests that Zizioulas subordinates the Son and the Spirit to the Father.[82]

Torrance further questions Zizioulas's consistency when the latter claims that God as Trinity is the primordial reality. With the Father as causal principle of divine existence, Torrance asks rhetorically, "does *the* exclusively primordial reality not actually become the person of the Father?"[83] Torrance's point is that causality within the divine life threatens the very thing Zizioulas wishes to defend, a trinitarian communion. This communion is affirmed only when the intra-divine communion "is not only a primordial concept but an eternal 'given', that is ontologically primitive and original."[84] Torrance is aware of Zizioulas's rejection of the "'structure of communion existing by itself'" as the ultimate ontological category.[85] He adds that

> given that what is being referred to is not some contingent existent or mere 'structure' conceived as 'existing by itself', but nothing less than God, it seems to us that he fails to offer sufficiently compelling arguments as to why it should be of 'incalculable importance' that we do *not* conceive of the intra-divine communion of the Trinity as the ground of all that is, that is, as sufficient in itself and as indeed 'capable' of existing by itself.[86]

But as we have already seen, Zizioulas does give both theological and existential reasons for rejecting Torrance's suggestion.

The answer to Torrance's query about why Zizioulas does not "conceive of the intra-divine communion of the Triunity as the ground of all that is" is, quite simply, Zizioulas's rejection of linking the divine life to any form of necessity. For Zizioulas, the price for making the intra-divine communion the primordial concept is the negation of absolute freedom. God's existence is not absolutely free if it is necessarily one of intra-divine communion. Linking the unity of God with the Father as the causal principle of divine life constitutes divine existence as a reality resulting from freedom and not necessity. It is ironic that Torrance himself argues for the intra-divine communion as an "eternal 'given,'" since the 'given' is that which defines absolute freedom for Zizioulas. Freedom, according to Zizioulas, is precisely freedom from the given. 'Givenness' is what constitutes "the greatest provocation to freedom."[87] Existential reasons constitute the importance of absolute freedom in God's life, in that if God's life is not free from any 'given,' then creation cannot free itself from the givens inherent in created nature, the ultimate given being death. God cannot give what God does not have, and without the possibility of this freedom then there is no possibility for personhood, or more importantly, for salvation. Perhaps one can accuse Zizioulas here of allowing an a priori ontology of communion to define salvation and with Torrance ask how does "this causal series of chain of contingency in God integrate with the eucharistic experience that Zizioulas perceives as the context of trinitarian articulation?"[88] But it is precisely in this eucharistic communion that creation experiences this freedom from the ultimate 'given' that is death. It experiences this reality only in mirroring the divine life, in the image of this divine life, through communion with the trinitarian life. It receives what God has by being united to the 'person' of Christ, and in this union lives eternally as a son or daughter of God, i.e., as an *ecstatic* and *hypostatic* person.[89]

If the above criticism offered by Torrance seems misplaced, he does set forth another which, in our estimation, is not sufficiently addressed by Zizioulas. This criticism is addressed in the form of a rhetorical question: "is the freedom of the Father to be conceived as *qualitatively* distinct from that of the Son and the Spirit?"[90] Torrance further asks, "Does the ontological freedom of the *arche vis-à-vis* the hypostases of the Son and the Spirit parallel the cosmological freedom of the Father *vis-à-vis* the created order as a whole?"[91] Torrance's point is that if creation results from a freedom from the given, then how is freedom inherent in the act of creation different from that of the generations of the Son and the procession of the Spirit? Though the Son and the Spirit may be eternal, their relationship to the Father, who alone constitutes existence, divine and created, through a freedom from the given, appears to be parallel to that which exists between creation and the Father. Zizioulas would, of course, counter that the only way the Son's and the Spirit's life could parallel created existence is by introducing notions of time and space within divine existence, which, for Zizioulas, is prima facie absurd. He would add against his critics of divine causality that the very notion of divine causality liberates the latter from the constraints of time and space. The only way the divine causality could imply subordination of the other persons, as Torrance suggests, is if one continues to link causality with time and space. The cause does not produce an effect that is distinct from the cause in terms of time and space. In the divine causality of the triune life, cause and personhood are a simultaneous event and subordination arises only if one links this causality with the conditions of time and space.

Analytically,[92] however, Zizioulas cannot escape the fact that if the Father "perpetually confirms through 'being' His *free* will to exist," or put another way, if "the Father out of love—that is freely—begets the Son and brings forth the Spirit," then the Father has a type of freedom which the Son and the Spirit do not possess. The Son and the Spirit do not possess the freedom to constitute their existence as communion. They may possess the freedom to confirm this existence of communion, but not to constitute it in the way that the Father as the exclusive causal principle is able. If freedom is defined by the person of the Father as freedom from the given, then freedom which the Son and the Spirit possess is qualitatively different, since they are faced eternally with the given of the Father. If freedom from the given is the mark of true personhood, then the Son and the Spirit are not persons in the true sense. The causality of the Father is so crucial to Zizioulas in defining existence as person, as one of freedom and love, yet it alone cannot guarantee such an existence for the divine being. In short, it cannot secure a true trinitarian being.

If Zizioulas's understanding of the *monarchia* of the Father tends toward a subordinationist understanding of the Trinity, the solution is not necessarily to eliminate causal notions in the divine life and affirm the Trinity as a "structure of communion existing by itself" or to locate the divine union in the divine *ousia,* as the Torrances have suggested. Such solutions continue to link God's triune existence with necessity, which Zizioulas rejects for both theological and existential reasons. I will argue below that causality within the divine life, while being able to preserve the notion of absolute freedom within the Trinity, does not necessarily lead to subordinationism, especially if this notion of divine causality is extended to all the trinitarian persons. I will also suggest that Lossky's notion of *kenosis* could also help resolve the tension between freedom and subordinationism in Zizioulas's understanding of the Trinity.

Concerning the problem of freedom within the divine existence, if the Son and the Spirit are to be on an equal footing with the Father in terms of freedom, then they must 'cause'[93] the Father's existence as much as the Father is the cause of their existence. In a certain sense, Zizioulas is already affirming this very principle through the notion of 'communion' or *koinonia,* and 'relation' or *schesis.* As we have seen, Zizioulas affirms that communion and otherness are mutually constitutive. Based on his argument for the necessity of theological ontology, this mutually constitutive relationship between communion and otherness means for the Trinity that the Son *causes* the Father and the Spirit to be; that the Spirit *causes* the Father and the Son to be; as much as the Father *causes* the Son and the Spirit to be. The identity of each person is dependent on the other persons. On the level of freedom, each person being the *cause* of the existence of the other persons means that each person freely confirms their free will to exist in communion with other persons, and by so doing, *causes* the existence of the other as person.

Zizioulas argues that introducing the notion of cause within the divine existence is the only way for God's existence to be a result of freedom, but in order for this freedom not to be possessed by only one person, each person must somehow be a causal agent within the divine life. By extending the notion of causality to the three persons, the act of freedom to affirm God's existence as trinitarian is one attributable to all three persons rather than simply one person. The existence of each of the trinitarian persons is an act of freedom insofar as each affirms their being-in-relation to the other. If the Father's being-in-relation to the Son is an act of freedom, this means that Father both causes the Son to exist as Son, since the Son exists as Son only in relation to the Father. But the Son is Son only through an act of freedom of being-in-relation to the Father. Put another way, a person is person only through an act of freedom of being-in-relation. If this being-in-relation is reciprocal, one both causes the existence of the other, is caused by the other, but also causes oneself insofar as one exists as person through the act of freedom of being-in-relation. Causation in relation to creation, though an act of freedom, is distinct from causation within the divine life. In relation to creation, *that* creation exists is result of the will of God. In the divine life, it is not a question of whether God exists since God is an eternal reality; it is rather a question of *how* God exists. In trinitarian theology, the question arises whether one can extend the notion of causality to the other persons of the trinity and maintain the Father as source (*pege*). I would argue that though the Father as source introduces other problems into the doctrine of the Trinity, such as the question of whether God could be something other than Trinity, it does not necessarily lead to subordinationism if the all the trinitarian persons cause, i.e., through an act of freedom, perpetually affirm God's existence as Trinity.

Within the divine life, the notion of causality itself is reconceptualized in that causality is freed from space-time limitations. Causality within divine existence does not lead to separation and division that inevitably results within the limits of space and time; divine causality results in distinctions in communion, and eternal event of love and freedom. One might raise the objection that such an understanding of the Trinity is no different than three Zeus's who decide to live in loving communion together. It is not this, however, in that it is the God who is revealed in the eucharistic communion, and such a God is one that reveals God's being truly, not falsely. The theological knowledge of the Trinity is rooted in the experience of such a God, who freely affirms divine existence as communion and love. To say that each of the divine persons necessarily relates to the other in communion and love is equally as absurd. A necessary communion is not one based on love. Zizioulas is right to point out the necessary link between love and freedom. If God's existence is love then it must result from freedom. Each of the persons as cause of the other persons, and hence, of the divine communal existence, gives to each person the same type of freedom. This free and loving confirmation of the divine existence is itself eternal, but to say that it is eternal does not mean that it is 'given' or necessary.

The Losskian notion of *kenosis* can also strengthen Zizioulas's theology of person here, especially with regard to the problem of freedom. *Kenosis,* which literally means emptying but also conveys the sense of denial, is relevant for Zizioulas on the level of anthropology. He rarely refers to *kenosis* except to convey the necessity of human self-denial for authentic personhood. The *image of God*, i.e., personhood, is possible only through incorporation into Christ, which "implies the following... Communion with the other requires the experience of the cross."[94] Zizioulas amplifies that "since the Son of God, moved to meet the other, his creation—by emptying himself through the kenosis of the incarnation—the 'kenotic' way is the only way that befits the Christian in his or her communion with the other—be it God or the neighbour."[95] Zizioulas adds that "in this 'kenotic' approach to the other . . . the other is not to be identified by his or her qualities, but by the sheer fact that he or she is, and is himself or herself."[96] Thus, for Zizioulas, the incarnation itself is a revelation that true personhood in communion with the other is an event of the cross, a kenotic act of self-emptying for communion with the other.

Kenosis is an important category for Lossky's system. He speaks of the *kenosis* of the Son and the Holy Spirit,[97] whereby *kenosis* and *oikonomia* are understood synonymously. I will focus on the implication of Lossky's claim that *kenosis* is an eternal aspect of divine personhood.[98] Thus, Lossky can affirm without hesitation that *"There is therefore a profound continuity between the personal being of the Son as renunciation and His earthly kenosis."*[99] Making *kenosis* a constitutive aspect of divine personhood in a way that Lossky implies but does not fully affirm would, I propose, strengthen Zizioulas's theology of personhood. First, Zizioulas has the conceptual apparatus to affirm a *kenotic* divine personhood, because his identification of the *tropos hyparxeos* of trinitarian existence allows for reflection on the immanent Trinity based on the economic activity. If what is revealed in the economy is the *mode of existence* of the trinitarian persons, then the Son, by his incarnation and passion, reveals that such a *mode of existence* is *kenotic*. The notion of *kenosis* would also allow Zizioulas to incorporate the Cross into his trinitarian theology, without necessarily linking suffering to God.[100] Consistent with his relating *kenosis* with communion and otherness, *kenosis* becomes an act of freedom and reception: the *kenotic* person, both divine and human, is free from oneself in order to *receive* the other. Such a notion of *kenosis* is consistent with Chalcedonian Christology, in which the divine person Christ is free to receive the utterly other, created being and death.

It would also obviate the problems with divine freedom created by the *monarchia* of the Father. Personal freedom is no longer defined simply by the Father affirming his free will to exist, but becomes a matter both of *ekstatic* movement and reception. Each of the divine persons as persons freely receives the *ekstatic* movement toward their person. Thus, an *ekstatic* movement is not complete without reception, which itself is a *kenotic* act. The Trinity is an existence of *ekstatic* movement and *kenotic* reception. Personal freedom is defined in terms of both and forms a constitutive part of each person of the Trinity, as they move toward and receive the other.

In summary, though Zizioulas's theology of person is more coherent than Lossky's, his insistence on the *monarchia* of the Father creates inconsistencies that an expansion of causality to all three persons and a Losskian understanding of divine *kenosis* would obviate. But Torrance's critique of Zizioulas raises another, implicit question other than the consistency of Zizioulas's trinitarian theology. It is a question that can be posed to both Zizioulas and Lossky and it has to do with the extent to which their theologies of personhood, strikingly similar in many respects, are influenced by contemporary philosophies of personalism. But this question implies a further question about the identity of a contemporary Orthodox theologian and her relation to the Greek patristic tradition. What are the criteria for judging the adequacy of patristic retrieval of contemporary Orthodox theology? In this sense, what is contemporary Orthodox theology? Patristic retrieval or patristic fundamentalism? If the former, how is one to relate the patristic texts to contemporary questions and modes of thought?

'Person,' Patristic Interpretation, and the Hermeneutics of Retrieval

It is beyond the scope of this study to offer a thorough assessment of Lossky's and Zizioulas's interpretations of each of the Eastern patristic writers they reference.[101] Both theologians have been critiqued for their readings of the patristic traditions, both Eastern and Western.[102] Their attempt at constructing a history of Eastern patristic thought does, however, raise important hermeneutical questions for theology, some of which I will attempt to address.

First, the very notion of 'trajectory' in historical studies itself raises many red flags. It conjures up memories of attempts to locate the 'essence' of Christianity, the only difference being that both Lossky and Zizioulas are attempting to isolate two kinds of essences: a kind of Christianity which intellectualized theology and a kind rooted in the principle of the realism of divine-human communion. These histories that attempt to isolate trajectories or essences attempt to clarify that which defies complete clarification. They are often too simplistic and texts are often interpreted in such a way as to be forced into particular trajectories. For example, in the case of both Lossky and Zizioulas, it is debatable whether Origen was primarily influenced by Greek philosophy.[103] He could no more escape the intellectual environment surrounding him than could Lossky and Zizioulas in the twentieth century, but this does not necessarily translate into a Hellenization of Christianity. Others have also disputed the charge that the principle of divine-human communion is not at the center of the theologies of Augustine and Aquinas.[104] It would be more helpful to see the theologies of Augustine and Aquinas as particular attempts to think through the principle of divine-human communion in a specific context and faced with particular challenges, such that their theologies are contributions to the broader Christian attempt to express an understanding of the transcendent God who is radically immanent in Jesus Christ by the power of the Holy Spirit.

For all their problems, the historical constructions of Lossky and Zizioulas are not without their merit. A simple perusal of the Eastern patristic writings of Ignatius, Irenaeus, Athanasius, the Cappadocian fathers, Dionysius, Maximus, John of Damascus, and Gregory Palamas would reveal that the notion of divine-human communion is central to their theologies. Apophaticism, essence/energies distinction, understandings of the eucharist are all related to this principle of divine-human communion. Both have succeeded in highlighting important strands of the tradition. In doing so, they have also shown how a shared premise, i.e., the realism of divine-human communion, does not necessarily lead to conclusions that are mutually consistent or compatible with each other. The challenge for a theology that takes the realism of divine-human communion seriously would be to bring together the apophaticism of Lossky, which its emphasis on the mystical, ascetical components of the Christian tradition, with Zizioulas's concern for ontology and personhood, with its emphasis on the communal and liturgical strands within the tradition.

A final hermeneutical question implied in the patristic interpretations of Lossky and Zizioulas concerns the hermeneutics of retrieval and the issue of a twentieth-century theologian attempting to retrieve the thought of patristic writers from the first through the fifteenth centuries. Lossky and Zizioulas have often been accused of being influenced by one form or another of modern personalism or existentialism.[105] More specifically, the general critique claims that their theologies of 'person' have more to do with modern notions of 'person' rather than patristic thought.

The most recent and sharpest expression of this critique is give by Lucian Turcescu.[106] Since Lossky and Zizioulas agree on essential features of the theological notion of person grounded in trinitarian theology, much of what

Turcescu says of Zizioulas could be applied to Lossky. Turcescu's critique rests on the distinction made by Zizioulas, together with Lossky, between the individual and the person. He summarizes Zizioulas's own understanding of the notion of the "individual" as, first, a complex of qualities that cannot ensure uniqueness. Second, an individual is an entity that can be enumerated whereas the uniqueness and sacredness of the person defies such enumeration. Third, Western theology and philosophy wrongly define 'person' as 'individual' and such an identification has its roots in Augustine and Boethius. Zizioulas further claims, according to Turcescu, that this understanding of 'person' as 'individual' is absent in the Cappadocian fathers. Turcescu then attempts to show that Gregory of Nyssa does in fact speak of 'person' in terms that Zizioulas associates with the concept of 'individual.' By so doing, he hopes to show that Zizioulas's relational understanding of 'person' cannot be attributed to the Cappadocian fathers.

Turcescu proceeds to provide citations from the work of Gregory of Nyssa as supporting evidence in his attempt to illustrate that "the understanding of a person as a collection, congress or complex of properties is found in the Cappadocian texts when the Fathers try to explain what a person is,"[107] and that "the concept of enumeration of individuals (that is, the individuals being subject to addition and combination) was an important feature of the concept of person."[108] He further argues that the distinction between individual and person was one not made at the time of the Cappadocians and that the terms were used interchangeably. In fact, "[t]heirs was a time when the notion of individual/person was only emerging."[109] The thrust of Turcescu's argument can be paraphrased as follows: by looking primarily at the work of Gregory of Nyssa, it can be shown that the Cappadocian fathers do in fact identify person with individual as Zizioulas defines the latter and, therefore, there is no such thing as a relational ontology of person in the trinitarian theology of the Cappadocian fathers.

Though Turcescu may, in the end, be correct that a relational ontology of trinitarian personhood does not exist in the Cappadocian fathers, this particular article does not by itself discredit Zizioulas's (or Lossky's) interpretation. First, Turcescu grounds his critique primarily in an interpretation of passages by Gregory of Nyssa. Of all the Cappadocian fathers, however, Zizioulas's development of his relational ontology of trinitarian personhood relies least on the thought of Gregory of Nyssa. Put another way, if one were to eliminate the references to Gregory of Nyssa in the works where Zizioulas most develops his relational ontology of trinitarian personhood, there would be little, if any, substantive change.[110] This focus on Gregory of Nyssa is understandable given the fact that the volume in which the essay appeared was devoted to "rethinking" Gregory of Nyssa. But it does not warrant the general claim that a relational ontology of trinitarian personhood cannot be found within the thought of the Cappadocian fathers or in the Eastern patristic tradition. It also does not sufficiently address Zizioulas's interpretation of other patristic writers upon which he bases his claim about the link between a relational ontology and the doctrine of the Trinity.

The Cappadocian father that is never mentioned by Turcescu is arguably the one whose thought is most significant for Zizioulas's claims about a relational ontology of trinitarian personhood: Gregory of Nazianzus. Zizioulas cites this Cappadocian father as support for the Cappadocian understanding of the *monarchia* of the Father.[111] As we have seen, if there is an ontology that is personal and relational, in which person has ontological priority over substance, it is because of the monarchy of the Father, which means that God

> as Father and not as substance, perpetually confirms through 'being' His *free* will to exist. And it is precisely His trinitarian existence that constitutes this confirmation: the Father out of love—that is, freely—begets the Son and brings forth the Spirit. Thus God as person—as the *hypostasis* of the Father—makes the one divine substance to be that which it is: the one God. . . . Outside the Trinity there is not God, that is, no divine substance, because the ontological 'principle' of God is the Father.[112]

It is clear that for Zizioulas, the Cappadocian distinction between *ousia* and *hypostasis,* the linking together of *hypostasis* and *prosopon* with the result of giving "ontological content" to the category of the *prosopon,* the distinction between essence and *tropos hyparxeos,* or "mode of existence," express a personal, relational ontology insofar as their meaning is grounded in the principle of the monarchy of the Father. Without the monarchy of the Father, according to Zizioulas, there is no such ontology.

Even a "primordial" communion between the trinitarian persons is not enough to affirm a relational ontology since this communion itself is one of necessity and not freedom. A relational ontology of trinitarian personhood means, for Zizioulas, that freedom is at the heart of ontology insofar as "being" means to be free from the "given." For created existence, this means to be free from finitude and death that are inherent to created existence. To *be* is to exist in an eternal relationship with the loving God and only through such a relationship is created existence 'free' to *be* eternally in loving union with this God.

But in order for God to give this freedom from the 'given,' God's mode of existence, *tropos hyparxeos,* must itself be free from necessity, so argues Zizioulas, and must be freely constituted. This freedom within God's very being is the condition for the possibility of the freedom of created existence from the 'given' of its own nature, and this freedom within God's being can only be affirmed, avers Zizioulas, through the principle of the monarchy of the Father.

Turcescu's reading of Zizioulas's understanding of the relation between individual, person, and uniqueness is also in need of greater nuancing. It is not so much that Zizioulas does not think that a complex of qualities embodied within a particular human being actually contributes to personal uniqueness. It is the case, however, that such a complex of qualities does not guarantee such uniqueness. For Zizioulas, uniqueness is identified with 'irreplaceability.' A particular embodiment of a combination of qualities, which results from the "division of nature" in creation, does contribute to uniqueness but not as irreplaceability. Death ultimately renders all created being as replaceable, destroying a particular, embodied set of qualities, only to be reconstituted again, perhaps in the same way, in a newly created human being who tends toward death. Personal uniqueness can only be guaranteed, according to Zizioulas, in relationship to a being 'other' than created existence, i.e., to the eternally loving God who alone can constitute all human uniqueness as irreplaceable.[113]

Even with the notion of the monarchy of the Father, is Zizioulas's (and Lossky's) thought irretrievably "tainted" by modern thought so as to render it non-patristic? Several things must be said in response to this question. First, for both Lossky and Zizioulas, the core of theological discourse is an ontology of divine-human communion. For Zizioulas, in particular, the monarchy of the Father and, hence, a relational ontology of trinitarian personhood, is rooted in the experience of God in the eucharist understood as the event of the Body of Christ by the power of the Holy Spirit. Notwithstanding the charge of influence by modern personalism, Zizioulas and Lossky self-consciously are attempting to give expression to this core of theology, which is the realism of divine-human communion. For Zizioulas, the "ontological revolution" is not so much the change in the meaning of the words "person" and "*hypostasis,*" but in the Christian affirmation that God in the person of Christ has "become history" and, hence, the need to articulate an ontology in which the notions of history, time, change, particularity, otherness, relationality are integrated. In the end, for Zizioulas, this can only be done through the Christian doctrine of the Trinity that affirms the monarchy of the Father.

Second, Lossky and Zizioulas do not hide the fact that they are attempting to relate traditional Christian dogma to contemporary questions and concerns.

Zizioulas himself is quite explicit when he says that the true task of theology is to "seek ways of *relating* the Gospel to the existential needs of the world and to whatever is human. Instead of throwing the Bible or the dogmas of the Church into the fact of the world, it would be best to seek first to feel and understand what every human being longs for deep in their being, and then see how the Gospel and doctrine can make sense to that longing."[114] Regarding the specific charge of being influenced by "modern personalism" Lossky himself in *The Mystical Theology* admitted as such that *hypostasis* means "*person* in the modern sense of the word," while also affirming that person is a Christian theological notion.[115] There is also no need, as Turcescu does, "to suggest" possible influences on Zizioulas's notion of person as a relational category. Turcescu indicates that Martin Buber and John Macmurray are the most substantial influences. But Zizioulas does not appear to hide the fact that both Buber and Macmurray have influenced his thought.[116] Turcescu himself cites Zizioulas's reference to Buber.[117] Zizioulas has also cited Macmurray.[118] He even gives credit to Pannenberg for helping him to articulate thoughts concerning personhood that he was "struggling to express."[119]

Criticisms of Lossky and Zizioulas being under the influence of "modern personalism" do not give the theologians enough credit of being aware of these various philosophies, nor to their attempt to define their own theologies of personhood over and against the prevailing philosophical understandings. Both Lossky and Zizioulas argue that only a theological notion of "person" can ground the various insights or aspects of contemporary philosophical understandings of personhood. In an article written only three years after *The Mystical Theology,* Lossky qualified his earlier reference to "person in the modern sense of the word," by arguing that "we should resolutely renounce the sense of the word 'person' which belongs to sociology and to most philosophers. We should go to seek our norm or 'canon' of thinking in a higher region, in the idea of person or *hypostasis* as it is found in trinitarian theology."[120] Even if there are similarities, Lossky is at least attempting to differentiate the theological notion of person grounded in the Trinity from what he knows to be the prevailing sociological and philosophical notions.

In "The Being of God and the Being of Anthropos,"[121] Zizioulas responds specifically to this very charge by the Greek theologians John Panagopoulos and Savas Agourides; namely, that his understanding of personhood is influenced by modern personalism and existentialism. Here Zizioulas identifies distinct kinds of philosophical personalism of various thinkers such as J. Maritain, E. Mounier, N. Berdyayev, M. Buber, G. Marcel, as well as the existentialism of S. Kierkegaard. According to Zizioulas, these modern forms of personalism and existentialism, though he recognizes similarities, differ from his understanding of person through either defining the person in terms of consciousness or subjectivity and not in terms of relations; or in giving the notion of communion an ontological priority over 'person.' Zizioulas then lists four ways in which his understanding of 'person' differs from these philosophical approaches. Of the four, Zizioulas refers to the patristic understanding of the monarchy of the Father as providing the most decisive difference between the trinitarian understanding of person and modern, philosophical accounts, and which "precludes any philosophical-personalistic interpretation of God."[122] In establishing the meaning of trinitarian personhood, "the truth is rather that philosophy is used in this situation, in order to disclose a new meaning of person, which appears in front of us, when the 'in what way' (πῶς ἐστιν) of God's existence is revealed in Christ."[123] In the end, it is not a philosophy that justifies or influences the theological, trinitarian understanding of personhood, but rather only a trinitarian theology that affirms the monarchy of the Father that can ground and justify the philosophical notions of person in terms of freedom, uniqueness, and relationality.[124]

There is, thus, no reason to suggest possible influences on the thought of Zizioulas, since Zizioulas himself admits a knowledge of modern forms of personalism, and that some thinkers such as Martin Buber have actually influenced his understanding of person. But Zizioulas also attempts to show how the trinitarian understanding of personhood differs from these forms of modern personalism. He and Lossky are no more superimposing a philosophical system on the Eastern patristic writers than did these same writers Hellenize the teachings of Jesus. Their attempt to give further expression to the realism of divine-human communion through twentieth-century notions of person is analogous to the patristic co-opting of Greek philosophical categories to express the same principle. They are doing exactly what these writers did insofar as thinking about the authoritative texts of the tradition in light of the questions, challenges, and prevailing philosophical currents of their time. The alternative is either the hermeneutically impossible bracketing of all that the interpreter has read and experienced as they approach the patristic texts in the hope of distilling the pure 'essence' of the text itself, or to judge contemporary Orthodox theology as authentic based on its faithful reiteration of patristic texts. The latter, however, is not consistent with the approach of the patristic writers themselves, who did more than simply reiterate their predecessors.

Zizioulas and Lossky are consistent with the Eastern patristic writers in the most substantial way insofar as they affirm as the core of theological discourse the realism of divine-human communion. Zizioulas claims that a personal ontology is the most adequate way to express the realism of divine-human communion. The real issue, then, is not whether they have been influenced by modern personalism, but whether a trinitarian theology that affirms the monarchy of the Father is the only way to ground a personal ontology, and whether such an ontology does correct and justify the various modern, philosophical understandings of personhood.[125] If the core of Christian faith is communion with God the Father, in the person of Christ, by the power of the Holy Spirit, it is difficult to think how such a communion does not imply an ontology that is relational and personal.

Notes

Introduction

1. I will not repeat the excellent biographies that exist on both theologians. For Lossky, see Rowan Williams, *The Theology of Vladimir Nikolaievich Lossky: An Exposition and Critique* (PhD diss., Oxford University, 1975), 1–31; Oliver Clément, *Orient-Occident: Deux Passeurs: Vladimir Lossky et Paul Evdokimov* (Geneva: Editions Labor et Fides, 1985), esp. 94–99; and Nicholas Lossky, "Theology and Spirituality in the Work of Vladimir Lossky," *Ecumenical Review* 51 (1999): 288–93. For Zizioulas, see Gaëtan Baillargeon, *Perspectives Orthodoxes sur l'Eglise Communion: L'oeuvre de Jean Zizioulas* (Montreal: Editions Paulines & Médiaspaul, 1989), esp. 27–62; and Patricia Fox, *God as Communion: John Zizioulas, Elizabeth Johnson, and the Retrieval of the Symbol of the Triune God* (Collegeville, MN: Liturgical Press, 2001), 3–10.

2. I have intentionally placed 'Western' in quotations for several reasons. First, as it will be clear throughout this book, the category of 'Western' Christianity is normally used to identify a tradition represented in the thought of specific thinkers such as Augustine and Aquinas. Second, and more importantly, I would argue that the constructs 'Western' and 'Eastern' Christianity are not so easily identifiable and that rather than illuminate the history of thought within Christianity, they have been used as means of self-identification vis-à-vis the 'other.' Though Lossky and Zizioulas would argue that there are clear boundaries between 'Western' and 'Eastern' Christianity, I think the lines are much more fluid. For an analysis and critique of the attempts of contemporary Eastern Orthodox theologians to self-identify Orthodox theology against 'Western' rationalism, see Aristotle Papanikolaou, "Reasonable Faith and Trinitarian Logic: Faith and Reason in Eastern Orthodox Theology," in *Restoring Faith in Reason,* ed. Laurence Paul Hemming and Susan Frank Parson (Notre Dame, IN: University of Notre Dame Press, 2003), 237–55.

3. Karl Rahner, *The Trinity,* trans. Joseph Donceel (New York: Crossroad, 1997), 22.

Chapter 1. Ontology and Theological Epistemology

1. Georges Florovsky, "Patristics and Modern Theology," in *Procèc-verbaux du premier Congrès de Théologie Orthodoxe* (Athens, 1939), 238–42.

2. For Lossky's debate with Bulgakov and the "Sophia Controversy" see Paul Valliere, *Modern Russian Theology: Bukharev, Soloviev, Bulgakov: Orthodox Theology in a New Key* (Grand Rapids, MI: William B. Eerdmans, 2000). See also R. Williams, *Theology of Vladimir Lossky,* 1–31; also, idem, *Sergii Bulgakov: Towards a Russian Political Theology* (Edinburgh: T&T Clark, 1999). On Russian religious philosophy see Frederick C. Copleston, *Philosophy in Russia: From Herzen to Lenin to Berdyaev* (Notre Dame, IN: University of Notre Dame

Press, 1986); and Alexander Schmemann, "Russian Theology: 1920–1972: An Introductory Survey," *St. Vladimir's Theological Quarterly* 16 (1972): 172–93.

3. "The Ecumenical Dimensions of Orthodox Theological Education," in *Orthodox Theological Education for the Life and Witness of the Church* (Geneva: World Council of Churches, 1978), 33.

4. Ibid. For more on theology in twentieth-century Greece, see Christos Yannaras, "Theology in Present-Day Greece," *St. Vladimir's Theological Quarterly* 16 (1972): 195–214.

5. "You cannot return to the Patristic ethos of theology and still keep your scholastic methodology" ("Ecumenical Dimensions of Orthodox Theological Education," 33).

6. For these trajectories see *The Vision of God*, trans. Asheleigh Moorhouse (Crestwood, NY: St. Vladimir's Seminary Press, 1983) and *Being as Communion*, (Crestwood, NY: St. Vladimir's Seminary Press, 1985), esp. ch. 2. What is remarkable is how both theologians single out the same Eastern and Western figures for this trajectory. It should be noted that neither Lossky or Zizioulas claim a direct influence from Origen to Augustine, but simply argue that Augustine's way of understanding theology, and, subsequently, all of Western theology, is similar to that of Origen's.

7. *Vision of God*, 34.

8. *Being as Communion*, 80.

9. "For outside revelation nothing is known of the difference between the created and the uncreated, of creation *ex nihilo*, of the abyss which has to be crossed between the creature and Creator" (*The Mystical Theology of the Eastern Church* [Crestwood, NY: St. Vladimir's Seminary Press, 1976], 31).

10. Ibid., 67.

11. "Apophasis and Trinitarian Theology," in *In the Image and Likeness of God*, ed. John H. Erickson and Thomas E. Bird (Crestwood, NY: St. Vladimir's Seminary Press, 1974), 14. He affirms elsewhere that Orthodox theology takes "as its starting point" not Trinity or Incarnation, but "the initial antinomy of essence and hypostasis" ("The Procession of the Holy Spirit in Orthodox Trinitarian Doctrine," in *Image and Likeness of God*, 84). As we shall see below, this antinomy stems from the Incarnation and as such forms part of the "datum of revelation."

12. *The Mystical Theology*, 64.

13. For a very helpful introduction to apophaticism in the Platonic and early Christian traditions, see Deirdre Carabine, *The Unknown God: Negative Theology in the Platonic Tradition: Plato to Eriugena* (Louvain: Peters Press, 1995). On Dionysius, see Thomas A. Carlson, *Indiscretion: Finitude and the Naming of God* (Chicago: University of Chicago Press, 1999); Bernard McGinn, *The Foundations of Mysticism*, vol. 1 of *The Presence of God: A History of Western Christian Mysticism* (New York: Crossroads, 1991); Andrew Louth, *Denys the Areopagite* (London: Geoffrey Chapman, 1989); and Paul Rorem, *Pseudo-Dionysius: A Commentary on the Texts and an Introduction to Their Influence* (New York: Oxford University Press, 1993). For recent works on apophaticism and the appropriation of the apophatic tradition, see Oliver Davies and Denys Turner, eds., *Silence and the Word: Negative Theology and Incarnation* (Cambridge: Cambridge University Press, 2002); Amy Hollywood, *Sensible Ecstasy: Mysticism, Sexual Difference, and the Demands of History* (Chicago: University of Chicago Press, 2002); Mark A. McIntosh, *Mystical Theology* (Oxford: Blackwell, 1998); Denys Turner, *The Darkness of God: Negativity in Christian Mysticism* (Cambridge: Cambridge University Press,

1995); J. P. Williams, *Denying Divinity: Apophasis in the Patristic Tradition and Soto Zen Buddhist Traditions* (New York: Oxford University Press, 2000). See also the fine essay by Mary-Jane Rubenstein, "Unknow Thyself: Apophaticism, Deconstruction, and Theology after Ontotheology," *Modern Theology* 19, no. 3 (2003): 387–417.

14. See "La Théologie Négative dans La Doctrine de Denys L'Aréopagite," *Revue des Sciences Philosophiques et Théologiques* 28 (1930): 204–21. All contemporary Orthodox theologians do not share the centrality of Dionysius to the Greek patristic tradition. John Meyendorff, for example, has argued that Maximus the Confessor and Gregory Palamas had to subject Dionysius to a "christological corrective" (*Christ in Eastern Christian Thought* [Crestwood, NY: St. Vladimir's Seminary Press, 1975]). For an alternative view to that of Meyendorff, see Alexander Golitzin, "Dionysius the Areopagite in the Words of Gregory Palamas: On the Question of a 'Christological Corrective' and Related Matters," *St. Vladimir's Theological Quarterly* 46, nos. 2–3 (2002): 163–90. Lossky's interest in Dionysius may have been sparked by his study of Meister Eckhart, which was published posthumously by his mentor Etienne Gilson (*Théologie Négative et Connaissance de Dieu chez Maître Eckhart* [Paris: Librairie Philosophique J. Vrin, 1960]), but throughout his career it extended far beyond a relevance to Meister Eckhart. Dionysius was of central significance to a Losskian apology for Eastern Orthodox notions of *theosis* and divine energies.

15. Defending Dionysius against the "common opinion" that sees the thinker as a "Platonist with a tinge of Christianity," Lossky asserts, "here is a Christian thinker disguised as a neo-Platonist, a theologian very much aware of his task, which was to conquer the ground held by neo-Platonism by becoming a master of its philosophical method" (*Vision of God*, 122).

16. Lossky, "La Notion des 'Analogies' chez Denys le Pseudo-Aréopagite," *Archives d'Histoire Doctrinale et Littéraire du Moyen-Age* 5 (1931): 280.

17. "Apophasis and Trinitarian Theology," 26, my emphasis.

18. *The Mystical Theology*, 26, my emphasis. See also Lossky's *Théologie Négative et Connaissance de Dieu chez Maître Eckhart*, 37–39.

19. "Apophasis and Trinitarian Theology," 14–15.

20. This is even more evident when Lossky attempts to give Dionysius a christological reading, which has been and continues to be a much-debated point in Dionysian scholarship. As stated above, even the contemporary Eastern Orthodox theologian John Meyendorff has argued that it was necessary to apply a christological corrective to Dionysius's work.

21. "Apophasis and Trinitarian Theology," 14.

22. *The Mystical Theology*, 72; Lossky quotes Dionysius's *Divine Names*, 2.4.

23. Ibid., 71.

24. For a helpful discussion, see Duncan Reid, *Energies of the Spirit: Trinitarian Models in Eastern Orthodox and Western Theology* (Atlanta: Scholars Press, 1997), esp. 7–26.

25. *The Mystical Theology*, 40.

26. "La Théologie Négative de Denys L'Aréopagite," 220.

27. Ibid.

28. "The Incarnation, the point of departure for theology, immediately puts at the heart of the latter the mystery of the Trinity" (*Orthodox Theology: An Introduction,* trans. Ian and Ihita Kesarodi-Watson [Crestwood, NY: St. Vladimir's Seminary Press, 1978], 36).

29. "Apophasis and Trinitarian Theology," 27.
30. "La Théologie Négative de Denys L'Aréopagite," 213.
31. Ibid.
32. Ibid., 205.
33. "Elements of 'Negative Theology' in the Thought of St. Augustine," *St. Vladimir's Theological Quarterly* 21 (1977): 70.
34. Ibid., 73.
35. Ibid., 68.
36. The recent revival of apophaticism in a variety of discourses, ranging from theology and philosophy to cultural studies and critical theory, has much to do with Martin Heidegger's critique of "ontotheology." Although "ontotheology" has come to mean different things for different people, a consensus of meaning across disciplines is discernible which translates into something like this: "ontotheology" is the attempt toward totalization insofar as it reduces and explains all reality by means of principles which form the condition for the possibility of existence itself. This totalizing impulse results in nothing less than ideological and/or idolatrous forms of knowledge. This critique of totalization lies at the heart of 'apophaticism' in cultural studies and critical theory, and owes much to Jacques Derrida's own development of Heideggerean thought. But theology and philosophy would add something to this definition: the danger of 'ontotheology' is that it conceals or blocks the manifestation or appearance of truth, of Being, or of God. Apophaticism in this sense is a critique of a form of human reason which attempts to answer all questions and in so doing obfuscates the truth. As Mary-Jane Rubenstein has much more eloquently described it, "it is the desire to end desire with the certainty of the Concept" ("Unknow Thyself," 410). In this sense, Lossky's own critique of 'Western' rationalism can be seen as somewhat prophetic. His critique of Aquinas resonates especially with Jean-Luc Marion's own critique of Aquinas as an ontotheologian in *God without Being* (trans. Thomas Carson [Chicago: University of Chicago Press, 1991]), though Marion has since retreated from this interpretation of Aquinas. Insofar as 'apophaticism' is the means through which conceptual idols are subverted so as to make possible union with God who is beyond all language, beyond all being, then Lossky's own understanding shares much in common with the work of Rubenstein, Marion, Turner, McGinn, and the authors who contributed to *Silence and the Word*. One wonders, however, whether Lossky would see Marion's emphasis on the 'gift' as too insufficiently apophatic, especially in his attempts to establish the possibility for Revelation through a phenomenological analysis of 'givenness' (see *Being Given: Toward a Phenomenology of Givenness*, trans. Jeffrey L. Kosky [Stanford, CA: Stanford University Press, 2002]). Regarding the use of apophaticism in post-modern thinkers and their emphasis on difference, Lossky would probably describe it as Rubenstein does: "the aimlessness of *différance*," especially since for Lossky apophaticism is itself grounded in God's (non) being, in the God whose is simultaneously transcendent and immanent insofar as God is beyond the distinction itself, and, as such, is the source of the realism of divine-human communion. The great value of Thomas Carlson's work is to suggest that the apophatic theology of Lossky, Rubenstein, etc., may not be as diametrically opposed to the apophatic anthropology of Derrida and other postmodern thinkers as may appear on the surface, and the "indiscretion" between the two could further our understanding of both (see Carlson, *Indiscretion*).

37. On the meaning of this term, see Carlson, *Indiscretion,* 160.
38. *Orthodox Theology,* 63.
39. Jean-Luc Marion has recently appropriated the apophatic tradition in order to 'liberate' God from ontotheology, so that thought can think the God who "gives Himself to be known insofar as He gives Himself—according to the horizon of the gift itself" (*God without Being,* xxii–xxv). One wonders whether Lossky might see Marion's use of apophaticism as itself still insufficiently liberated from thought insofar as Marion's use is about 'thinking' and not 'experiencing' in union the giving God.
40. *Vision of God,* 126.
41. "La Notion des 'Analogies,'" 280.
42. Ibid. For the same thought, see "La Théologie Négative de Denys L'Aréopagite," 214.
43. His use of "mystical experience" occurs throughout all his works. I list here only a few citations. See *The Mystical Theology,* 8, 221, 224; also, *Image and Likeness of God,* 43, 54, 56, 57; *Vision of God,* 154, 160. He also refers to a "religious experience" (*The Mystical Theology,* 221; *Image and Likeness of God,* 59). It is clear from the context that these expressions are synonymous with "mystical experience" and do not refer to any universal experience of the divine preceding understanding, nor to any experience of an exclusive mystery cult. It is also clear that "mystical experience" is contrasted with *gnosis* and is meant as knowledge of God in the form of union that lies beyond thought.
44. *The Mystical Theology,* 231; see also *Vision of God,* 88.
45. *The Mystical Theology,* 231.
46. Ibid., 38.
47. "Apophasis and Trinitarian Theology," 14.
48. Ibid., 13.
49. *The Mystical Theology,* 45.
50. "La Théologie Négative de Denys L'Aréopagite," 214; for Lossky on transcending the limits of *nous,* see *Vision of God,* 127.
51. "Notion des 'Analogies,'" 286.
52. *The Mystical Theology,* 30.
53. Ibid.
54. Ibid., 31. This understanding of Plotinus in terms of 'absorption mysticism' has been critiqued by A. H. Armstrong, "Plotinus," in *The Cambridge History of Later Greek and Early Mediaeval Philosophy,* ed. A. H. Armstrong (Cambridge: Cambridge University Press, 1967), esp. 258–63; also more recently by McGinn, *Foundations of Mysticism,* 53–55; also Kevin Corrigan, "'Solitary' Mysticism in Plotinus, Proclus, Gregory of Nyssa, Pseudo-Dionysius," *Journal of Religion* 76 (1996): 28–42.
55. *The Mystical Theology,* 31.
56. I would, thus, not agree with Alar Laats's claim that "Lossky, following the old Byzantine apophatic tradition, describes it as darkness and absolute ignorance" (*Doctrines of the Trinity in Eastern and Western Theologies: A Study with Special Reference to Karl Barth and Vladimir Lossky* [New York: Peter Lang, 1999], 136).
57. For other studies on Palamas and the Palamite controversy, see John Meyendorff, *A Study of Gregory Palamas,* 2d ed., trans. George Lawrence (London: Faith Press, 1974) and Georges Florovsky, "St. Gregory Palamas and the Tradition of the Fathers," in *Bible,*

Church, Tradition: An Eastern Orthodox View, vol. 1, of *The Collected Works of Georges Florovsky* (Belmont, MA: Nordland, 1972), 105–20. See also Anna Williams, *The Ground of Union: Deification in Aquinas and Palamas* (New York: Oxford University Press, 1999).

58. "Darkness and Light in the Knowledge of God," in *Image and Likeness of God*, 38.

59. *The Mystical Theology*, 222.

60. "The Theology of Light in the Thought of St. Gregory Palamas," in *Image and Likeness of God*, 59.

61. Ibid., 60.

62. To name a few: Paul Evdokimov, *La connaissance de Dieu selon la tradition orientale* (Paris: Desclée de Brouwer, 1988); Georges Florovsky, *Creation and Redemption*, vol. 2 of *The Collected Works of Georges Florovsky* (Belmont, MA: Nordland, 1976); Georgios I. Mantzaridis, *The Deification of Man*, trans. Liadain Sherrard (Crestwood, NY: St. Vladimir's Seminary Press, 1984); Meyendorff, *Study of Gregory Palamas;* idem, *Christ in Eastern Christian Thought;* Panayiotis Nellas, *Deification in Christ: The Nature of the Human Person*, trans. Norman Russell (Crestwood, NY: St. Vladimir's Seminary Press, 1987); John Romanides, *The Ancestral Sin*, trans. George S. Gabriel (Ridgewood, NJ: Zephyr, 2002); Dumitru Staniloae, *Orthodox Dogmatic Theology: The Experience of God*, vol. 1, trans. and ed. Ioan Ionita and Robert Barringer (Brookline, MA: Holy Cross Orthodox Press, 1998); Christos Yannaras, *Elements of Faith: An Introduction to Orthodox Theology*, trans. Keith Schram (Edinburgh: T&T Clark, 1991); idem, "The Distinction between Essence and Energies and Its Importance for Theology," *St. Vladimir's Theological Quarterly* 19 (1975). Absent from this list is John Zizioulas, discussed below.

63. For more on the controversy see *Vision of God*, 153–56; "Theology of Light in Gregory Palamas," 45–49; and Meyendorff, *Study of Gregory Palamas*.

64. "Theology of Light in Gregory Palamas," 48.

65. Ibid., 46. Curiously absent is Dionysius, though throughout his work Lossky's link of Palamas to Dionysius is evident.

66. *The Mystical Theology*, 71.

67. See *Vision of God*, 11–24. See also below, note 84.

68. Ibid., 158. For references to a Thomistic influence on Barlaam's notion of divine simplicity, see *The Mystical Theology*, 77: "The philosophy of God as *pure act* cannot admit anything to be God that is not the very essence of God.... Thus, according to Barlaam and Akindynus, the energies are either the essence itself, understood as pure act, or are produced by the outward acts of the essence, that is to say, the created effects which have the essence for their cause—creatures, in other words."

69. *Vision of God*, 158.

70. Ibid., 159.

71. Concerning God as communicable and incommunicable Lossky quotes Palamas as saying: "'We must affirm both things at once and must preserve the antinomy as the *criterion of piety*'" (ibid., 156, my emphasis).

72. *The Mystical Theology*, 77–78.

73. See "Theology of Light in Gregory Palamas," 55.

74. Ibid.

75. *Vision of God*, 157.

76. "Theology of Light in Gregory Palamas," 51.

77. Ibid., 52.

78. Ibid., 51.

79. "Apophasis and Trinitarian Theology," 26. As we shall see in the next chapter, this principle of the 'non-opposition of opposites' is significant for Lossky's understanding of the relation of apophasis to Trinitarian theology.

80. *Orthodox Theology,* 38–39; for antinomy, see also *The Mystical Theology,* 68–69.

81. "Theology of Light in Gregory Palamas," 52.

82. It is important to note that Lossky's review (*Sobornost* [1950]: 295–97) of E. L. Mascall's *Existence and Analogy* contains a rare praise of Aquinas: "Indeed, since the publication of the latest books of M. Etienne Gilson, there can be no doubt about the authentic Thomism of S. Thomas and his immediate predecessors, a thought rich with new perspectives which the philosophical herd, giving in to the natural tendency of the human understanding, was not slow in conceptualizing, and changing into school Thomism, a severe and abstract doctrine, because it has been detached from its vital source of power." Lossky knew the difference between the thought of Aquinas and neo-Thomism and his main contention was with the neo-Thomists of his time, though his respect for Thomas was not uncritical. Lossky adds, "Thomist 'existentialism', the re-evaluation of which is the indisputable merit of M. Gilson, gives back the vital spark to a doctrine long 'de-existentialized' *by most Thomist commentators and authors of compilations.*" The review also indicates a willingness to see a possible *rapprochement* between Gilsonian Thomism and his own Palamism. "With Fr. Mascall, I ask myself to what extent that God of S. Thomas Aquinas, knowable in His cosmological relation, i.e., on the plane of His creative energy, can be made to resemble the God of S. Gregory Palamas, unknowable in His essence, as distinct from His energy." Though such a possibility must "resolutely make our way outside the boundaries of Natural Theology, and that would oblige us to leave the subject of Fr. Mascall's book," he clearly did not dismiss the possibility. This small but significant review clearly evinces recognition on Lossky's part of the affinities between Aquinas and Palamas, a point that is completely absent in his extant works. Though his later works continue to criticize a Thomistic understanding of the *filioque* and a Thomistic way of doing theology, it is hard to believe that he surrendered this appreciation for Aquinas. It is a loss that his tragic, early death cut short his attempt to discover in what way "the God of S. Thomas Aquinas . . . can be made to resemble the God of S. Gregory Palamas."

83. *Vision of God,* 166.

84. "Theology of Light in Gregory Palamas," 46n2. Lossky refers to Jugie's articles on Palamas and the Palamite controversy in *Dictionnaire de théologie catholique* II, cols. 1735–1776 and 1777–1818; to his "De theologia Palamitica," in his *Theologia dogmatica christianorum orientalium* II (1933): 47–183; and to various articles in *Echos d'Orient*. Concerning Guichardan, Lossky refers to his work *Le problème de la simplicité divine en Orient et en Occident aux XIV siècles: Grégoire Palamas, Dun Scot, Georges Scholarios* (Lyons, 1933). Another article critical of Palamas's thought is that of Dom Clément Lialine, "The Theological Teaching of Gregory Palamas on the Divine Simplicity," *Eastern Churches Quarterly* 6 (1946): 266–87. For a review of the Palamite debate together with additional references, see Rowan Williams, "The Philosophical Structure of Palamism," *Eastern Churches Review* 9 (1977): 27–44. For a critique of the use of the essence/energies distinction in Lossky's thought, see Dom Illtyd Trethowan, "Lossky on Mystical Theology," *The Downside Review* 92 (1974): 242–44.

85. "Theology of Light in Gregory Palamas," 46.

86. "Procession of the Holy Spirit," 88.

87. *Vision of God*, 158.

88. Lossky's critique here of the rationalization of theology in Thomistic metaphysics is similar to Jean-Luc Marion's critique of ontotheology and his discussion of the latter in terms of the 'idol.' "Thus the idol consigns the divine to the measure of a human gaze" (*God without Being*, 14). "To take seriously that philosophy is foolishness [. . .] means first (although not exclusively) taking seriously that the 'God' of onto-theology is strictly equivalent to an idol" (*L'Idole et la distance* [Paris: Grasset, 1977], 36–37; as quoted in Carlson, *Indiscretion*, 195). For an excellent analysis of Marion's thought, including his progression from a theological to a phenomenological account of gift and the tension between the two, see Carlson, *Indiscretion*, 191–214.

89. 'Event' is Zizioulas's word and as such will be used throughout the chapter instead of 'ritual' or 'worship.' What he means by 'event' will hopefully be made clear in the analysis of his thought. In short, its meaning is christological and it refers to the church as the pneumatologically constituted Body of Christ which occurs in and through the eucharist.

90. One could say that Zizioulas's 'eschatology,' his 'logos' of the 'last things,' has less to do with the final event in history and more with "the fulfillment of God's creative intent in humanity and in the world of God's creation" (Zachary Hayes, *Visions of a Future: A Study of Christian Eschatology* [Wilmington, DE: Michael Glazier, 1989], 69). Though not necessarily his motivation, the basic thrust of Zizioulas's eschatology is similar to that of the post–Vatican II shift in Roman Catholic eschatology from a "physical style to a more anthropological style" (ibid, 69; see also 11–14; as Hayes points out, this contrast between a 'physical' and 'anthropological' style belongs to Yves Congar).

91. *Eucharist, Bishop, Church: The Unity of the Church in the Divine Eucharist and the Bishop during the First Three Centuries*, trans. Elizabeth Theokritoff (Brookline, MA: Holy Cross Orthodox Press, 2001).

92. "The Early Christian Community," in *Christian Spirituality: Origins to the Twelfth Century*, ed. Bernard McGinn and John Meyendorff in collaboration with Jean Leclerq (New York: Crossroad, 1985), 23–43: "The great source of spirituality is . . . the eucharist."

93. *Being as Communion*, 146.

94. For a recent discussion on the eucharist in the New Testament, see Eugene LaVerdiere, *The Eucharist in the New Testament and the Early Church* (Collegeville, MN: Liturgical Press, 1996). LaVerdiere's argument is similar to Zizioulas's in arguing that "From the very beginning, there was no separating the Eucharist from the Church and the local assembly," and, he adds, from the risen Christ (see 186–91). See also Oscar Cullman and F. J. Leenhardt, *Essays on the Lord's Supper*, trans. J. G. Davies (Richmond, VA: John Knox Press, 1958); Edward Kilmartin, *The Eucharist in the Primitive Church* (Englewood Cliffs, NJ: Prentice-Hall, 1965); G. D. Kilpatrick, *The Eucharist in Bible and Liturgy* (Cambridge: Cambridge University Press, 1983); and Jerome Kodell, *The Eucharist in the New Testament* (Wilmington, DE: Michael Glazier, 1988).

95. *E Ktise os eucharistia* (Creation as Eucharist) (Athens: Akritas, 1992), 20; also *Being as Communion*, 209–46, esp. 213, 235. This 'act' and 'event' language seems to have in mind debates over 'real presence' which, Zizioulas feels, reduces the eucharist to a *pragma* defined in terms of substance categories and which itself is the product of a rational approach to truth. Zizioulas implies that to argue whether the early Christians believed in

the 'real presence' is anachronistic and imposes philosophical models foreign to the early Christian mindset. Further, it forgets the early Christian understanding of truth as eschatological in contrast to a supposedly Greek rational understanding. Finally, it approaches the eucharist apart from other aspects of theology such as Christology, pneumatology, and even ecclesiology; for the latter together with an assessment of its ramification, see "The Ecclesiological Presuppositions of the Holy Eucharist," *Nicolaus* 10 (1982): 333–49, esp. 337–40.

96. Zizioulas gives textual support for this identification in *Eucharist, Bishop, Church*, 45–53, but also more recently in "The Eucharist and the Kingdom of God" (Part 1), *Sourozh* 58 (November 1994): 1–11; (Part 2) 59 (February 1995): 22–38; and (Part 3) 60 (May 1995): 32–46; see also "L'eucharistie: quelques aspects bibliques," in *L'eucharistie,* ed. J. Zizioulas, J. M. R. Tillard, and J. J. von Allmen, église en dialogue 12 (Mame, 1970), 15–30, and "Some Reflections on Baptism, Confirmation, and Eucharist," *Sobornost* 9 (1969): 651.

97. Zizioulas makes the claim that Athanasius's affirmation of the full divinity of Christ against the Arians was "a direct consequence of the ontology of communion formed within the current eucharistic theology that connected Ignatius, through Irenaeus, up to Athanasius" (*Being as Communion*, 83). See also "The Teaching of the 2nd Ecumenical Council on the Holy Spirit in Historical and Ecumenical Perspective," in *Credo in Spiritum Sanctum,* ed. J. S. Martins (Roma: Libreria Editrice Vaticana, 1983); also, in its entirety, "The Eucharist and the Kingdom of God."

98. See *Eucharist, Bishop, Church*, esp. 53–58 and 108–28. Central to Zizioulas's argument is the use of the category 'corporate personality.' According to Zizioulas, the New Testament speaks of Jesus "as the Messiah in terms of 'corporate personality' (servant of God, Son of Man, etc.), and the Fathers, following that, describe him as recapitulation of all humanity, even of creation" ("The Pneumatological Dimension of the Church," *International Catholic Review* 2 [1974]: 145). As 'corporate personality' Jesus is the One in whom the Many are united and who is simultaneously defined by the Many. For Zizioulas on 'corporate personality,' see *Eucharist, Bishop, Church;* "Informal Groups in the Church," in *Informal Groups in the Church: Papers of the Second CERDIC Conference, University of Strasburg, 1971,* ed. R. Metz (Pittsburgh: Pickwick Press, 1975); "The Mystery of the Church in the Orthodox Tradition," *One in Christ* 24 (1988) and *Being as Communion*. Ignatius's understanding of 'catholicity' further supports the link between church, eschaton, and Body of Christ. For the latter, see *Eucharist, Bishop, Church*, 107–62; *Being as Communion;* and "Ecclesiological Presuppositions of the Holy Eucharist." For an excellent analysis of Zizioulas's understanding of 'corporate personality' and 'catholicity,' see Paul McPartlan, *The Eucharist Makes the Church: Henri de Lubac and John Zizioulas in Dialogue* (Edinburgh: T&T Clark, 1993).

99. *Being as Communion*, 23, 132, 155n57. For a helpful overview of the relation between pneumatology and Christology in contemporary Orthodox theology, see Jaroslav Z. Skira, "The Synthesis between Christology and Pneumatology in Modern Orthodox Theology," *Orientalia Christiana Periodica* 68, no. 2 (2002): 435–65.

100. See Nicholas Afanassieff, "The Church Which Presides in Love," in *The Primacy of Peter,* John Meyendorff et al. (London, Faith Press, 1963), 57–110; also, "Una Sancta: To the Memory of John XXIII, the Pope of Love," in *Tradition Alive: On the Church and the Christian Life in Our Time: Readings from the Eastern Church,* ed. Michael Plekon (New York:

Rowman & Littlefield, 2003), 3–30. For a good study on Afanasiev, see Aidan Nichols, O.P., *Theology in the Russian Diaspora: Church, Fathers, Eucharist in Nikolai Afanas'ev* (Cambridge: Cambridge University Press, 1989); also, for a critical assessment of Zizioulas's reading of Afanasiev, see Michael Plekon, *Living Icons: Persons of Faith in the Eastern Church* (Notre Dame, IN: University of Notre Dame Press, 2002), esp. 149–77.

101. *Being as Communion*, 124; Zizioulas takes the Florovsky quote from "Le corps du Christ vivant," in *Le sainte Eglise universele* (Neuchâtel, 1948), 12.

102. *Being as Communion*, 124–25.

103. See Khomiakov's *The Church is One*, rev. trans. Nicholas Zernov (London, 1968). For more on Khomiakov, see J. Romanides, "Orthodox Ecclesiology According to Alexis Khomiakov," *Greek Orthodox Theological Review* 2 (1956): 57–73; and more recently, P. O'Leary, *The Triune Church: A Study in the Ecclesiology of A. S. Khomiakov* (Dublin, 1982).

104. *Being as Communion*, 126. See Nissiotis, "The Importance of the Doctrine of the Trinity for Church Life and Theology," in *The Orthodox Ethos*, ed. A. J. Philippou (Oxford: Holwell Press, 1964); and "Pneumatologie orthodoxe," in *Le Saint-Esprit*, ed. F. J. Leenhard et al. (Geneva: Labor et Fides, 1963). See Bobrinksy, "Le Saint-Esprit dans la liturgie," *Studia Liturgia* 1 (1962): 47–60; "Présence réelle et communion eucharistique," in *Revue des Sciences philosophiques et théologiques* 53 (1969): 402–20; and more recently, *The Mystery of the Trinity: Trinitarian Experience and Vision in the Biblical and Patristic Tradition*, trans. Anthony P. Gythiel (Crestwood, NY: St. Vladimir's Seminary Press, 1999).

105. "In the ancient Church itself the term 'theology' was not based on creeds or propositions of faith; it was used to define a grasp of the mystery of divine existence as it is offered to the world and experienced in the ecclesial community" ("Ecumenical Dimensions of Orthodox Theological Education," 33).

106. "Implications ecclésiologiques de deux types de pneumatologie," *Communio Sanctorum: Mélanges offerts à Jean-Jacques von Allmen* (Geneva: Labor et Fides, 1981), 141–54.

107. Chapter 3 of *Being as Communion*. This chapter was first published as "Cristologia, pneumatologia e instituzioni ecclesiastiche: un punto de vista ortodosso," *Cristianesimo nella storia* 2 (1981): 111–27.

108. "Implications ecclésiologiques de deux types de pneumatologie," 141.

109. Ibid., 142.

110. Ibid.

111. Ibid.

112. With regard to the eschatological role of the Spirit, Zizioulas cites Acts 2:17; Rom 8:23; 1 Cor 15:44–45; 2 Cor 1:22; Eph 1:14.

113. "Implications ecclésiologiques de deux types de pneumatologie," 142.

114. Ibid.: "That which appears to be the most primitive christological form (including the Gospel of Mark) is that the event of Christ *is constituted by his baptism*, i.e., *in and by the Spirit*."

115. Ibid., 142–43.

116. Ibid., 143.

117. "When the Holy Spirit blows he does not create good individual Christians, individual saints, but an event of communion" ("Communion and Otherness," *Sobornost* 16 [1994]: 14). Although Zizioulas attributes the understanding of the Spirit in terms of 'inspiration' to Lossky, the difference between Lossky and Zizioulas on this point should not be exaggerated. For Lossky, the Spirit does have the role of assisting and aiding the

individual Christian toward a fuller realization of personhood that culminates in deification. One must remember, however, that to be a true person for Lossky is to be in relation to other persons. Though he does not use Zizioulas's language, the Holy Spirit's role in assisting Christians toward personhood is one of communion. And since such a communion is characteristic of the eschaton, the Holy Spirit's role is thus eschatological. What Lossky does not argue for is that the Holy Spirit constitutes the eucharist itself as an event of this communion. This is an important epistemological difference with Zizioulas that I will explore in detail below.

118. "Implications ecclésiologiques de deux types de pneumatologie," 143.

119. Ibid., 144.

120. Ibid. "The Person of Christ is automatically linked with the Holy Spirit, which means with a *community*" ("Ecclesiological Presuppositions of the Holy Eucharist," 342).

121. Ibid.

122. Ibid., 147.

123. "It is not on the basis of one's past or present that we should identify and accept him or her, but on the basis of one's future" ("Communion and Otherness," 14).

124. "Ordination—A Sacrament? An Orthodox Reply," *Concilium* 4 (1972): 34. See also "Mystery of the Church in Orthodox Tradition," 295–99.

125. "Pneumatological Dimension of the Church," 146. See also "Ecclesiological Presuppositions of the Holy Eucharist," 342: "In order to find the deeper roots of this coincidence between Church and Eucharist we must again go back to the question of the relation between Christology and Pneumatology. . . . The Eucharist is the only occasion in history when these two coincide."

126. See also "Pneumatological Dimension of the Church," 142–58, esp. 155–56; "The Theological Problem of 'Reception,'" *One in Chris*t 21 (1985): 3–6; and "Communion and Otherness," 14.

127. *Being as Communion*, 131.

128. *The Mystical Theology*, 156–73. Elsewhere, Zizioulas explains that Lossky argues for this 'economy of the Spirit' in order "to stress the independence of the Spirit with regard to Christ" as an argument against the *filioque*, but offers the criticism that with this understanding of the Spirit, "ecclesiology has been more or less pushed towards the side of pneumatology" ("Pneumatological Dimension of the Church," 144). It is understandable that Zizioulas would think that Lossky wished to stress the independence of the Spirit from Christ, especially in light of Lossky's criticism of the *filioque*, which I will clarify in the next chapter. But it is clear that Lossky did not, in fact, see the Spirit's activity as separate from that of the Son's. On the economic level, the work of the Spirit and the Son are interdependent. See Clément, *Orient-Occident: Deux Passeurs*, 65n191, where he attributes this understanding of Lossky's pneumatology to Florovsky.

129. *Being as Communion*, 130.

130. Ibid.

131. See *The Mystical Theology*, 159: In relation to the Incarnation, the economy of the Holy Spirit "is its sequel, its result."

132. Gaëtan Baillargeon criticizes Zizioulas for trivializing the historical church through this identification of the church with the eschatological Christ (see *Perspectives Orthodoxes sur l'Église Communion*, 256; also, "Jean Zizioulas, porte-parole de l'Orthodoxie contemporaine," *Nouvelle Revue Théologique* 111 [1989]: 193). Paul McPartlan is right to

correct this criticism by pointing to the fact that for Zizioulas the eschatological nature of the church is experienced only *"momentarily,* namely in the Eucharist" (*The Eucharist Makes the Church,* 266). The discussion below on Zizioulas's understanding of "icon" will also illustrate how for Zizioulas the Church is "icon" in the sense of being the presence of the eschaton *in* history. Baillargeon's criticism, however, has some merit, since for Zizioulas the *true* church is the eschatological church. If this is experienced *momentarily,* as McPartlan rightly indicates, Zizioulas could elaborate more fully on the relationship between this eschatological church, realized in the moment of the eucharist, and the institutional, or purely historical church—the community outside of the context of worship—or, put another way, between the missionary and eschatological roles of the Spirit. To some degree, Zizioulas draws out this relationship, especially in his discussions on the structure of councils. He leaves other questions, however, unresolved, such as power structures within the institutional church, or the church's responsibility to social problems.

133. *Being as Communion,* 130.

134. "The Church is the body of Christ, because Christ is a pneumatological being, born and existing in the *koinonia* of the Spirit" ("The Church as Communion," *St. Vladimir's Theological Quarterly* 38 [1994]: 6). See also *Being as Communion,* 130.

135. "The economy, therefore, in so far as it assumed history and has a history, is *only one* and that is the *Christ event*" (*Being as Communion,* 130).

136. "Pneumatological Dimension of the Church," 144, my emphasis. See also *Being as Communion,* 129–30: "We must bear in mind that according to patristic tradition, both Eastern and Western, the activity of God *ad extra* is *one* and indivisible . . . the contributions of each of these divine persons to the economy bears its own distinctive characteristics which are directly relevant for ecclesiology in which they have to be reflected."

137. *Being as Communion,* 130.

138. In the chapters that follow, discussion of Zizioulas's understanding of the distinction between the 'economic' and the 'immanent' Trinity will further clarify his understanding of 'economy.'

139. The difference between the role of Christ and the Spirit in ecclesiology is indicated, according to Zizioulas, by the distinction between *constitute* and *institute.* Christ *institutes* the Church and the "eucharist realizes in the course of history the continuity that links each Church to the first apostolic communities and to the historical Christ: in short, all that was *instituted* and is *transmitted.*" Through the work of the Holy Spirit, "the eucharist . . . manifests the Church not simply as something instituted, that is, historically *given,* but also as something *con-stituted,* that is constantly realized as an event of free communion, prefiguring the divine life and the Kingdom to come" (*Being as Communion,* 22). Later in the work, Zizioulas explains: "Christ *in-stitutes* and the Spirit *con-stitutes.* . . . The 'institution' is something presented to us as a fact, more or less a *fait-accompli.* As such, it is a provocation to our freedom. The 'con-stitution' is something that involves us in its very being, something we accept freely, because we take part in its very emergence" (*Being as Communion,* 140).

140. "The Eucharist and the Kingdom of God (Part 1)," 1. Elizabeth Theokritoff is right to translate *Theia Eucharistia* as "Divine Liturgy" from the point of view of eliminating confusion in Zizioulas's thought. For Zizioulas, "Holy Eucharist" refers not primarily to the concecrated elements, but to the communal worship as an event of the Body of Christ.

141. Ibid., 18. One may raise the obvious point here that in the iconoclastic controversy over the use of icons in the eighth and ninth centuries, those who supported icons explicitly rejected the notion that the eucharist is an icon. When Zizioulas speaks of the eucharist as an icon he is not referring to the body and blood of Christ, which are consumed by the faithful and which, clearly, is the referent for Orthodox denials of the eucharist as icon. Zizioulas is referring to the whole of the liturgical act, which for him is a presence of the eschaton as the Body of Christ, and, as such, properly an icon. For this interpretation he appears to have considerable patristic support, especially in Maximus the Confessor's *Mystagogy*.

142. For a discussion of the concepts 'presence' and absence' see "Human Capacity and Human Incapacity," *Scottish Journal of Theology* 28 (1975): 412ff.

143. "Eschatology and History," in *Cultures in Dialogue: Documents from a Symposium in Honor of Philip A. Potter*, ed. T. Wieser (Geneva, 1985), 35–36: "The liturgical or iconic language, on the other hand (i.e., in comparison with Protestant and Roman Catholic religious art), does not derive from what has happened, but strives to present what will happen"; "What one sees in the icon is not the state of things as they have been in history but as they will be in the end." See also Douglas Knight, "John Zizioulas on the Eschatology of the Person," in *The Future as God's Gift: Explorations in Christian Eschatology*, ed. David Fergusson and Marcel Sarot (Edinburgh: T&T Clark, 2000), 189–97.

144. *Being as Communion*, 229–46. See also "Eucharist and the Kingdom of God" (Part 3), 32–37; also, *Eucharist, Bishop, and Church*.

145. The classic text on icon for the Orthodox remains John Damascene's *Three Treatises on the Divine Images*, trans. Andrew Louth (Crestwood, NY: St Vladimir's Seminary Press, 2003); for other Orthodox interpretations on icon, see Leonid Ouspensky, *Theology of the Icon*, 2 vols., trans. Anthony Gythiel (Crestwood, NY: St Vladimir's Seminary Press, 1992); also Paul Evdokimov, *The Art of the Icon: A Theology of Beauty*, trans. Father Steven Bigham (Torrance, CA: Oakwood, 1990).

146. *Being as Communion*, 100. See also "Symbolism and Realism in Orthodox Worship," *Sourozh* 79 (2000): 3–17.

147. "Eschatology and History," 34.

148. Ibid.: "this image or icon, what we see, is not of this world. It is clearly eschatological both in origin and in content."

149. Ibid.: "The eucharistic image of the kingdom does not leave history behind it, it involves it."

150. Ibid., 36; see also *Being as Communion*, 99–101.

151. Ibid., 34.

152. *Being as Communion*, 92.

153. Ibid.

154. Ibid.

155. "Eschatology and History," 36: "The eschaton respects history not by copying it but by transforming it, and transcending especially the antinomies and limitations of history."

156. *Being as Communion*, 99.

157. Ibid.

158. "Pneumatological Dimension of the Church," 146.

159. There are still some in the ecumenical movement that he has not succeeded in convincing. Miroslav Volf in his recent work, *After Our Likeness: The Church as the Image of the Trinity* (Grand Rapids, MI: William B. Eerdmans, 1998), offers a sustained reflection

on Zizioulas's thought (73–123) in which he, following Gaëtan Baillargeon, accuses Zizioulas of an "overrealized eschatology." Such an eschatology requires "that the historical character of the church, if the latter genuinely is to be a church, be transcended eschatologically" (101–2). Though it is true that Zizioulas lacks an adequate account of the relation between the church as a eucharistic event and the historical church, to transcend history eschatologically does not mean to obliterate history. Otherwise, following Zizioulas's logic, 'icon' would be meaningless. The fact that the eucharist is the locus of the eschatological presence in history does not necessarily mean that the historical church, i.e., the non-eucharistic church, is empty of this presence. Zizioulas's understanding of icon, however, might be strengthened conceptually if he were to demonstrate how the eschaton can be experienced in the eucharist as a moment that transcends history while remaining somehow present within history.

160. "Mystery of the Church in Orthodox Tradition," 301.
161. *Being as Communion,* 169.
162. Ibid., 240. See also "The Eucharist and the Kingdom of God" (Part 2), 29–37.
163. "Eucharistic Prayer and Life," *Emmanuel* 81 (1975): 469.
164. *The Liturgy of St John the Chrysostom* (Brookline: Holy Cross Press), my emphasis.
165. "Eucharistic Prayer and Life," 469.
166. *Being as Communion,* 161.
167. Ibid.
168. Ibid., 138.
169. It would also be of interest to compare Zizioulas's understanding of icon with Paul Tillich's concept of symbol as participation; see *Dynamics of Faith* (New York: Harper and Brothers, 1958), esp. 41–54. For an opposite understanding of symbol, see Sallie McFague, *Models of God* (Philadelphia: Fortress Press, 1987). In her judgment of the models of God throughout the Christian tradition as being primarily "triumphalist, imperialistic, (and) patriarchal" (20), McFague is either unaware of or chooses to ignore this particular Christian concept of icon.
170. Marion, *God without Being,* 12, 17.
171. Ibid., 18.
172. Ibid., 123.
173. "Pneumatological Dimension of the Church," 156.
174. "The Eucharist and the Kingdom of God" (Part 1), 1–2.
175. "Eschatology and History," 38: "The eschatological overcomes the historical reality; it does not destroy history but transforms it."
176. "Eucharistic Prayer and Life," 466.
177. *Being as Communion,* 187.
178. *God without Being,* 23–24.
179. "The eastern tradition has never made a sharp distinction between mysticism and theology; between personal experience of the divine mysteries and the dogma affirmed by the Church . . . [t]o put it another way, we must live the dogma expressing a revealed truth" (*The Mystical Theology,* 8).
180. "Panagia," in *Image and Likeness of God,* 196.
181. Ibid., 205.
182. Ibid., 206.
183. Ibid., 207.

184. Ibid., 207–8.

185. "Therefore it is through her Son, and in His Church, that the Mother of God could attain the perfection reserved for those who bear the image of the 'man of heaven'" (ibid., 205).

186. Ibid., 200.

187. Ibid., 208. This understanding of the church in terms of 'growth' rather than event has much to do with Lossky's own understanding of the relation of Christology and pneumatology to ecclesiology, which will be explored below more fully.

188. Lossky does say that the Mother of God has a "complete consciousness of all that the Holy Spirit says to the Church," implying that by virtue of the presence of the Holy Spirit the church experiences the fullness of truth. True knowledge, however, which Lossky identifies with "a complete consciousness of God . . . could only happen to a deified being" (ibid., 200). Thus, when Lossky speaks of a "gradual development of the Church in history," he means a communal consciousness of God analogous to that of a deified being.

Chapter 2.   Trinity: Antinomy or Communion?

1. "Apophasis and Trinitarian Theology," 15.

2. "The distinction between the unknowable essence of the Trinity and its energetic processions . . . allows Orthodox theology to maintain firmly the difference between tri-hypostatic existence in itself and tri-hypostatic existence in the common manifestation outside the essence" ("Procession of the Holy Spirit," 93).

3. "Apophasis and Trinitarian Theology," 15.

4. "Here apophaticism finds its fulfillment in the revelation of the Holy Trinity as primordial fact, ultimate reality, first datum which cannot be deduced, explained or discovered by way of any other truth; for there is nothing which is prior to it" (*The Mystical Theology*, 64).

5. "Apophasis and Trinitarian Theology," 16.

6. Ibid.

7. *The Mystical Theology*, 83.

8. "Apophasis and Trinitarian Theology," 16.

9. Ibid.

10. "The three hypostases, decanted, stripped of all economic attribution, maintain only the relative properties of paternity, filiation and procession, necessary only to make theological discourse possible" (ibid., 24).

11. "A movement of apophasis therefore accompanies the Trinitarian theology of the Cappadocians and, in the last analysis, deconceptualizes the concepts which are ascribed to the mystery of a personal God in His transcendent nature" (ibid.).

12. Ibid., 16.

13. "There is no interior process in the Godhead; no 'dialectic' of the three persons; no becoming; no 'tragedy in the Absolute', which might necessitate the trinitarian development of the divine being in order that it might be surmounted or resolved. These conceptions, proper to the romantic tradition of nineteenth century German philosophy, are wholly foreign to the dogma of the Trinity. . . . Again we are forced to appeal to

apophatic theology in order to rid ourselves of concepts proper to human thought, transforming them into steps by which we may ascend to the contemplation of a reality which the created intelligence cannot contain" (*The Mystical Theology*, 47).

14. *Orthodox Theology*, 36.

15. *The Mystical Theology*, 50.

16. Made recently by Catherine Mowry LaCugna in *God for Us: The Trinity and Christian Life* (New York: HarperCollins, 1991), esp. 333.

17. "Apophasis and Trinitarian Theology," 26.

18. Ibid., 27.

19. Ibid.

20. "The Theology of the Image," in *Image and Likeness of God*, 134.

21. *Orthodox Theology*, 40.

22. Ibid.

23. Christopher Stead, *Philosophy in Christian Antiquity* (Cambridge: Cambridge University Press, 1994), 196.

24. "Procession of the Holy Spirit," 75; same thought in *The Mystical Theology*, 48–49.

25. *Orthodox Theology*, 40.

26. *The Mystical Theology*, 49.

27. Ibid., my emphasis. For a critique of this reading of Plotinus, see above, ch. 1, n. 54.

28. Ibid.

29. *Orthodox Theology*, 40.

30. Ibid., 40–41.

31. Ibid., 41; also *The Mystical Theology*, 51–54. As we shall see below, Zizioulas gives the same historical interpretation for the ancient understanding of *prosopon*.

32. Ibid. For preference of *hypostasis* over *prosopon*, see also "The Theological Notion of the Human Person," in *Image and Likeness of God*, 112. As we shall see later, it is at this point that Lossky and Zizioulas's historical interpretation disagree. If for Lossky the weakness of *prosopon* led to *hypostasis*, for Zizioulas the "ontological revolution" of the Greek fathers was to identify *hypostasis* with *prosopon* thus giving *prosopon* ontological content.

33. Ibid.; for *ousia* and *hypostasis* as synonyms, see also *The Mystical Theology*, 51.

34. *The Mystical Theology*, 51.

35. Ibid.

36. "Theological Notion of the Human Person," 113.

37. Two quotes from Gregory the Theologian help express this fact for Lossky: "When I say *God*, I mean Father, Son and Holy Spirit" (*Oration* 42.8); "No sooner do I conceive of the One than I am illumined by the splendour of the Three; no sooner do I distinguish them than I am carried back to the One. When I think of any One of the Three, I think of Him as the whole, and my eyes are filled, and the greater part of what I am thinking of escapes me. I cannot grasp the greatness of that one so as to attribute a greater greatness to the rest. When I contemplate the Three together, I see but one torch, and cannot divide or measure out the undivided light" (*Oration* 40.41; both quotes from *The Mystical Theology*, 46–47).

38. "Theological Notion of the Human Person," 113.

39. Ibid.

40. *The Mystical Theology*, 54.
41. Ibid., 50.
42. "Theological Notion of the Human Person," 112.
43. *The Mystical Theology*, 50.
44. "Theological Notion of the Human Person," 113.
45. Ibid., 114. It is interesting to note that in *The Mystical Theology*, 51, Theodoret of Cyrus's use of Aristotle is quoted without any criticism which indicates that originally Lossky did not find this use of Aristotle objectionable, though he does indicate that the theological notion of person required that *hypostasis* be "purged of its Aristotelian content" (53).
46. "Theological Notion of the Human Person," 113.
47. "Purged of its Aristotelian content, the theological notion of *hypostasis* in the thought of the eastern Fathers means not so much *individual* as *person*, in the modern sense of this word" (*The Mystical Theology*, 53).
48. *Orthodox Theology*, 41–42.
49. There exists in the Trinity "an irreducibility which forced us to give up equating the hypostasis with the individual in the Trinity by revealing the non-conceptual character of the notion of hypostasis" ("Theological Notion of the Human Person," 115).
50. Ibid.
51. I owe this insight to Michel Stavrou, *L'Approche Théologique de La Personne chez Vladimir Lossky et Jean Zizioulas: à L'Image et à La Ressemblance de Dieu* (masters thesis, Institut de Théologie Orthodoxe Saint-Serge, Paris, April 1996), 37–38.
52. "Theological Notion of the Human Person," 53; Lossky adds that "when we say that 'this is by Mozart', or 'this is by Rembrandt', we are in both cases dealing with a personal world which has no equivalent anywhere." Also, 121: "person . . . means that which distinguishes it from nature. . . . Finally, we admit that what is most dear to us in someone, what makes him himself, remains indefinable, for there is nothing in nature which properly pertains to the person, which is always unique and incomparable." In *The Mystical Theology*, Lossky also suggests that *hypostasis* means "*person* in the modern sense of the word," while affirming that person is a Christian theological notion (53). The implication is that the affinities notwithstanding, person is first a patristic theological notion. In a later article, he moves away from such comparisons and suggests that "we should resolutely renounce the sense of the word 'person' which belongs to sociology and to most philosophers. We should go to seek our norm or 'canon' of thinking in a higher region, in the idea of person or hypostasis as it is found in trinitarian theology" ("Redemption and Deification," in *Image and Likeness of God*, 106).
53. "Theological Notion of the Human Person," 120.
54. Ibid.
55. *Orthodox Theology*, 42.
56. Ibid., 43.
57. *The Mystical Theology*, 54.
58. "These two persons are distinguished by the different mode of their origin: the Son is begotten, the Holy Spirit *proceeds* from the Father. This is sufficient to distinguish them" (*The Mystical Theology*, 55).
59. Ibid., 60.
60. *The Mystical Theology*, 59; "Procession of the Holy Spirit," 71; *Orthodox Theology*, 46.

In *The Mystical Theology*, 59, Lossky relies heavily on Gregory the Theologian's *Orations* 20.7, 31.14, and 42, for this interpretation of the *monarchia* of the Father.

61. *The Mystical Theology*, 58.
62. "Procession of the Holy Spirit," 81.
63. Ibid.; quote from Gregory the Theologian, *Oration* 31.14.
64. *The Mystical Theology*, 58.
65. "Procession of the Holy Spirit," 83.
66. Ibid.
67. *Orthodox Theology*, 44. As is explained in the Bibliography, this text contains translations of articles which Lossky wrote late in his life, and which were first published posthumously in *Messager* 46–48 (1964); 49–50 (1965).
68. *The Mystical Theology*, 44; *Orthodox Theology*, 45.
69. *Orthodox Theology*, 46.
70. Ibid.
71. Ibid., 47.
72. Ibid. For support Lossky quotes Gregory the Theologian: "The Father 'would only be the Principle (*arche*) of petty and ignoble things, but more than this, He would be the Principle of divinity and goodness which one adores in the Son and the Holy Spirit: in the one as Son and Word, in the other as Spirit proceeding without separation.'" Unfortunately, no citation is given.
73. "Apophatic Theology and Trinitarian Theology," 16.
74. "Theological Notion of the Human Person," 112.
75. *Orthodox Theology*, 41.
76. *The Mystical Theology*, 45; *Orthodox Theology*, 48.
77. "If the creature is contingent by nature, the Trinity is an absolute stability" (*The Mystical Theology*, 45).
78. *Orthodox Theology*, 48.
79. Ibid.; he adds that "revelation is thinkable only in relation to the other-than-God, that is to say, within creation."
80. *The Mystical Theology*, 45.
81. Ibid.; the English translation has a semi-colon after "entirely nature," but I have here followed the French which has simply a comma.
82. *Orthodox Theology*, 48; elsewhere Lossky says: "If the Father shares His own essence with the Son and the Holy Spirit and in that sharing remains undivided, this is neither an act of will nor an act of internal necessity. In more general terms, it is not an act at all, but the eternal mode of Trinitarian existence in itself. It is a primordial reality which cannot be based on any notion other than itself, for the Trinity is prior to all qualities—goodness, intelligence, love, power, infinity—in which God manifests Himself and in which He can be known" ("Procession of the Holy Spirit," 85).
83. Which is what Zizioulas affirms.
84. *The Mystical Theology*, 85.
85. "Notion des 'Analogies,'" 283.
86. Ibid.
87. *The Mystical Theology*, 86; also 158.
88. One of the key differences between Lossky and Zizioulas is the use of this term, which I will argue Zizioulas uses in a more coherent way.

89. *The Mystical Theology*, 73.
90. Ibid., 86, my emphasis.
91. "Procession of the Holy Spirit," 79. Lossky adds in a note that *tropos hyparxeos* is "more exactly, 'mode of subsistence'" and indicates that the expression is found first in Basil's *On the Holy Spirit*, 18. Zizioulas also cites this very text, and relates it to the "mode of origin," as Lossky puts it, but interprets the expression differently than Lossky.
92. *The Mystical Theology*, 85–86.
93. For this reason, when Olivier Clément says that "Only a theology that includes the ontological in the personal is able to unite the fullness of the personal freedom to the fullness of life and being" (*Orient-Occident: Deux Passeurs*, 33), one cannot so easily agree with Clément that such a theology is that of Vladimir Lossky. Clément does not consider the tension in Lossky's thought between a personal ontology and an epistemology rooted in apophaticism.
94. R. Williams, *Theology of Vladimir Lossky*, 129.
95. For a thorough critique of Lossky's own criticisms of the West, especially in relation to the *filioque*, see ibid., 129–56. On the Orthodox side, Zizioulas comments that "Lossky's views have led to extremes that are beginning to show the weaknesses of his position. The way he brought out the *Filioque* issue as *the* crucial problem between the East and West is a clear example of how much Lossky's trinitarian theology stands in need of revision" ("The Doctrine of God the Trinity Today: Suggestions for an Ecumenical Study" in *The Forgotten Trinity* [London: British Council of Churches and Council of Churches of Britain and Ireland, 1991], 110). Zizioulas, however, fails to elaborate and clarify for us what he means by Lossky's "extremes" and "weaknesses," while giving us no hint as to what specifically in Lossky's thought is "in need of revision."
96. An indication that the *filioque* in itself was not *the* most crucial problem for Lossky is indicated by the fact that he himself was open to an alternative understanding of the *filioque*. Olivier Clément argues that Lossky advanced such an alternative in course lectures given on 11 July 1955. See Clément, *Orient-Occident: Deux Passeurs*, 61n175.
97. "Procession of the Holy Spirit," 80.
98. Concerning the necessity of the independence of the Holy Spirit from the Son for deification, see "Redemption and Deification," 109–10.
99. R. Williams, *Theology of Vladimir Lossky*, 156.
100. The *filioque* is not exclusively a debate over the mode of origin of the Holy Spirit, since a determination of the mode of origin of the Holy Spirit affects an understanding of the relations of the persons of the Trinity in general.
101. As quoted in "Procession of the Holy Spirit," 78n10; the de Régnon citation comes from *Études de théologie positive sur la Sainte Trinité* I (Paris, 1892), 309. Michel René Barnes's claim that de Régnon influenced Lossky's trinitarian theology, although it cannot be disputed, needs careful qualification (see his "De Régnon Reconsidered," *Augustinian Studies* 26, no. 2 [1995]: 51–79). Barnes argues that de Régnon's paradigm that Latin trinitarian theology begins with the unity of nature and that Greek trinitarian theology begins with the diversity of persons had considerable influence on trinitarian theology in the twentieth century, Lossky included. He cites chapter three of *The Mystical Theology* as evidence. Yet in the same chapter Lossky says, "Nevertheless, the two ways were both equally legitimate so long as the first did not attribute to the essence a supremacy over the three persons, nor the second to the three persons a supremacy over the common nature"

(56). It is clear that Lossky uses de Régnon for support that Latin trinitarian theology, particularly Aquinas, depersonalized the Trinity by starting with the unity of essence. The other tendency of emphasizing the persons over the nature is the mistake of Russian sophiology represented in the person of Bulgakov. What is important to Lossky is the antinomy between nature and person in the Trinity. This is secured by the monarchy of the Father, and the significance of the Cappadocian contribution to trinitarian thought was not where they started, but securing the trinitarian antinomy by affirming the monarchy of the Father. Barnes also mentions how ten citations of de Régnon that were present in chapter three of the original French edition of *The Mystical Theology* were eliminated in the 1957 English translation. It seems, however, a bit presumptuous on Barnes's part to conclude that "there is in fact the appropriation of de Régnon's paradigm by modern Neo-Palamite theology, coupled with a hesitation, if not embaressment (*sic*), at acknowledging its Roman Catholic (indeed, Jesuit) origins." Lossky's own ecumenical interests throughout his life would appear to contradict such an accusation. Furthermore, of the two quotations left in the translation, the one cited in this footnote and that on page 64 acknowledge the use of the paradigm. Throughout the third chapter of *The Mystical Theology,* both in the English and French editions, it is evident that Lossky is not "embarrassed" to acknowledge his indebtedness to de Régnon, citing him in support of certain claims, and qualifying his paradigm with respect to the relation between person and nature within trinitarian theology. The other citations eliminated from the English edition simply indicated the location in de Régnon's book of the Greek patristic texts Lossky cites. Perhaps this information was simply thought redundant or unnecessary for an English-speaking audience, since what is important to Lossky's argument is the patristic text itself.

102. On this point, see Wolfhart Pannenberg, *Systematic Theology,* vol. 1, trans. Geoffrey W. Bromiley (Grand Rapids, MI: 1991), esp. pp. 280–99. Pannenberg argues that Augustine "did not try to derive the trinitarian distinction from the divine unity" (284). He does say, however, that such an attempt is evident in Anselm and finds its culmination in Aquinas. The logical end of such an attempt is a flattening of the personal distinctions within God and, hence, of the Trinity itself, a point on which Lossky would fully concur, though there is much that separates Lossky and Pannenberg. For Pannenberg's critique of the *filioque,* see 317–19. De Régnon is not cited in this volume of Pannenberg's *Systematic Theology.*

103. *Summa Theologia* Ia.36.2. Aquinas argues that since spiration is not a personal property and contains no relative opposition to paternity and filiation, it belongs both to the person of the Son and the Father. Thus, if the mutual opposition is between spiration and procession, and insofar as spiration belongs to both the Father and the Son, then the Spirit proceeds from both the Father and the Son; see ibid., Ia.30.1–2.

104. "Procession of the Holy Spirit," 76.
105. Ibid., 77.
106. Ibid., 79.
107. Ibid., 78.
108. Ibid.
109. Ibid., 79.
110. Ibid., 77.
111. Ibid.

112. Ibid.

113. *The Mystical Theology*, 62.

114. Rowan Williams in dealing with Lossky's misinterpretations of Aquinas strongly disagrees with Lossky's interpretation and ultimately concludes that "the understanding of persona which emerges" from Thomistic trinitarian theology, "is one which *does* allow for a measure of real trinitarian pluralism, a plurality of consciousnesses, and for a genuine analogy between human and divine personality" (*Theology of Vladimir Lossky*, 154). Pannenberg would disagree with Williams; see *Systematic Theology*, 1.295. On the Thomistic tradition, see also Ralph Del Colle, "'Person' and 'Being' in John Zizioulas' Trinitarian Theology: Conversations with Thomas Torrance and Thomas Aquinas," *Scottish Journal of Theology* 54, no. 1 (2001): 70–86.

115. "Procession of the Holy Spirit," 77.

116. This is Bulgakov's mistake; see ibid., 93.

117. "Procession of the Holy Spirit," 81.

118. Ibid., 80.

119. Ibid., 88.

120. Laats, *Doctrines of the Trinity in Eastern and Western Theologies*, 112. Otherwise I am in fundamental agreement with Laats's analysis of Lossky's understanding of the *filioque*.

121. Rowan Williams, "The Via Negativa and the Foundations of Theology: An Introduction to the Thought of V. N. Lossky," in *New Studies in Theology*, ed. Stephen Sykes and Derek Holmes (London: Duckworth, 1980), 112.

122. See his review of Every's *The Byzantine Patriarchate*, in *Sobornost* 3 (Summer, 1948): 108–12.

123. There has been, however, considerable progress since Lossky's time between the Roman Catholic and the Orthodox Churches on the question of the *filioque*. Pope John Paul II has on numerous occasions recited the Creed without the *filioque*. See especially the agreed statement of the North American Orthodox-Catholic Theological Consultation, "The *Filioque*: A Church-Dividing Issue?" *St. Vladimir's Theological Quarterly* 48, no. 1 (2004): 93–123.

124. The tension is evident when, on the one hand, Lossky affirms that "The goal to which apophatic theology leads—if, indeed, we may speak of goal or ending when, as here, it is a question of an ascent towards the infinite; this infinite goal is not a nature or an essence, nor is it a person; it is something which transcends all notion both of nature and of person: it is the Trinity" (*The Mystical Theology*, 44); and on the other hand, "negative theology never includes the negation of persons" (quoted in R. Williams, "Via Negativa and the Foundations of Theology," 102). As Williams notes the citation "comes from transcripts of tape recordings from lecture courses" (96). The date of this particular lecture is 24 November 1955. The fact that it occurs later than *The Mystical Theology* is not insignificant since, as I intimated above, Lossky was moving more toward an ontological understanding of person in terms of freedom, love, and communion.

125. For a good discussion of Zizioulas's interpretation of the Christian understanding of truth in relation to that of the Greeks and Jews, see Constantine Agoras, "Hellénisme et Christianisme: la question de l'histoire, de la personne et de sa liberté selon Jean Zizioulas," *Contact* 44 (1992): 244–69. Zizioulas discusses this understanding of the development of early Christian notions of truth in relation to Greek and Jewish thought throughout much of his work. See *Being as Communion*, 67–72; "Christology and Existence:

The Created-Uncreated Dialectic and the Dogma of Chalcedon" (in Greek), *Synaxe* 2 (1982): 9–20; "Human Capacity and Human Incapacity"; "Preserving God's Creation: Lecture One," *King's Theological Review* 12 (1989): 1–5; "The Contribution of Cappadocia to Christian Thought," in *Sinasos in Cappadocia,* ed. Frosso Pimenides and Stelios Roides (National Trust for Greece: Agra Publications, 1986), 23–37; and "On Being a Person: Towards an Ontology of Personhood," in *Persons, Divine and Human,* ed. Christoph Schwöbel and Colin E. Gunton (Edinburgh: T&T Clark, 1991), 33–46.

126. *Being as Communion,* 72, original emphasis.

127. Ibid., 93.

128. Ibid., 78. 'Practical' does not mean any of the various forms of practical reason. Its meaning is closer to 'existential.'

129. Ibid., 79.

130. Ibid.

131. Ibid., 80.

132. Ibid., 80–81.

133. Ibid., 80. For a similar interpretation of Irenaeus, see Lossky, *Vision of God,* 34. For more on the limitations which Irenaeus places on intellectual speculation, see Robert Grant, "Irenaeus and Hellenistic Culture," in *After the New Testament* (Philadelphia: Fortress Press, 1967), 158–69; and William R. Schoedel, "Theological Method in Irenaeus (*Adversus Haereses* 2.25–28)," *Journal of Theological Studies* 35 (1984): 31–49. Both Schoedel and Grant suggest, however, that Irenaeus's attitude to the use of reason in theology and to his own Greco-Roman context is more complex and less antagonistic than both Zizioulas and Lossky might have us believe.

134. *Being as Communion,* 80

135. Ibid., 81. On this point, see also Jacques Fantino, *La Théologie d'Irénée: Lecture des Écritures en réponse à l'exégèse gnostique: Une approche trinitaire* (Paris: Les Éditions du Cerf, 1994), esp. 209. Fantino fundamentally agrees with Zizioulas that incorruptibility, for Irenaeus, is given in the eucharist which is Church as the Body of Christ: "However, in virtue of the double reading, individual and communal, already mentioned, the body of Christ is the Church, but it is also the body of the resurrected Christ in which commune the faithful in the eucharist" (209; see n. 16 of this page for references of other works which agree with this position).

136. "Ontology in the metaphysical sense of the transcendence of beings by being, i.e. in the sense of going beyond what passes away into what always and truly is, was the primary preoccupation of ancient Greek thought" ("On Being a Person," 35).

137. *Being as Communion,* 80. Elsewhere Zizioulas asserts, "without this foundation of the Church's eucharistic experience, such as exhibited in Ignatius and Irenaeus, the trinitarian theology of the fourth century would remain a problem" (ibid., 82).

138. Ibid., 80.

139. Ibid., 83. For support of the link between Irenaeus and Athanasius, see Khaled Anatolios, *Athanasius: The Coherency of His Thought* (London and New York: Routledge, 1998). In light of this, it is not quite accurate to assert with Volf that to follow the "inner logic of Zizioulas's thinking" one would have to begin with "the Trinity itself, and then . . . make the transition to the eucharistic community" (*After Our Likeness,* 75n15). Volf also adds that it is probably no accident that Zizioulas's widely published and widely translated essay "Eucharist and Catholicity" stands in the middle rather than at the be-

ginning of *Being as Communion*. It should be remembered, however, that this essay was one of the first Zizioulas ever published (see Bibliography). In one sense, Volf is correct, since for Zizioulas logically God defines all reality. But Zizioulas is also trying to make the point that the eucharist was foundational for the formation of the Christian doctrine of the Trinity, and this because it is the event of the presence of the Triune God. Thus, there is also a logic in Zizioulas that flows from the experience of the eucharist to the doctrine of the Trinity. The logic of the eucharist to the doctrine of the Trinity is important to see in Zizioulas since it does not render his theology so easily susceptible to the charge that he is simply reading a relational ontology off a particular, a priori understanding of the Trinity.

140. "The Church Fathers wanted to show that Christian Faith could make sense to a thinking person, and that although a mystery, it was nevertheless not an absurdity for the human mind" ("Contribution of Cappadocia," 25).

141. See *Being as Communion*, 83. For more on this distinction in Athanasius's thought, see Alvyn Pettersen, *Athanasius* (Harrisburg, PA: Morehouse, 1995), esp. 167–73. See also Georges Florovsky, "Creation and Creaturehood," in *Creation and Redemption*, vol. 3 in the *Collected Works of Georges Florovsky* (Belmont, MA: Nordland, 1976), 46.

142. *Being as Communion*, 84.

143. See "Substance," in *The Encyclopedia of Philosophy*.

144. *Being as Communion*, 84.

145. Ibid., 86.

146. Ibid., 85–86.

147. Ibid., 39.

148. For more on this theme in Athanasius, see Anatolios, *Athanasius, the Coherency of His Thought*; Pettersen, *Athanasius*, 22. For a discussion of the development of the doctrine of creation *ex nihilo* before Athanasius, see Gerhard May, *Creatio Ex Nihilo: The Doctrine of 'Creation out of Nothing' in Early Christian Thought* (Edinburgh: T&T Clark, 1994).

149. Though he does say in *On the Incarnation* 20.4: "tou kai ten archen *ex ouk onton* pepoiekotos ta ola" (who [the Saviour] also creates the universe in the beginning from nothing). See Robert W. Thompson, trans. and ed., *Contra Gentes and De Incarnatione* (Oxford: Clarendon Press, 1971), 182; see also 4.15–26 (142–44).

150. For the relation between Greek monism and necessity, see "Preserving God's Creation: Lecture Two," *King's Theological Review* 13 (1990): 42; also, "Christology and Existence," 11.

151. The principle figure in this tradition being Origen: "Thus, Origen argues that, lest it be supposed that God at some time progressed into omnipotence, there must always have been in existence creatures over whom he exercises his omnipotence. By positing a necessarily eternal correlative relationship between God's omnipotence and creation, he protects God's immutability" (Peter Widdicombe, *The Fatherhood of God from Origen to Athanasius* [Oxford: Clarendon Press, 1994], 72). For a different view of the notion of eternal creation in Origen, see McGinn, *Foundations of Mysticism*, 112–13.

152. See "Preserving God's Creation: Lecture Two," 42.

153. Ibid., 43.

154. Ibid.

155. Ibid.

156. Ibid.

157. Ibid.

158. "It took the early Fathers (Irenaeus, Athanasius) a great deal of effort to break down this Greek monism which they thought—and rightly so—endangered the absolute ontological freedom of God, i.e., his transcendence. They produced the doctrine of *creatio ex nihilo* precisely in order to show that God existed *before* and *regardless of* the world" ("Doctrine of God as Trinity," 19–32). The same thought is in *Being as Communion*, 29, and in "Response of John Zizioulas" (in Greek) *Synaxe* 3 (1982): 77–82, where Zizioulas suggests that the problem of the creation of the world is tied to the problem of freedom, of man, and of God. He adds that "a God without freedom is not God according to the Patristic and Biblical Tradition."

159. "Christology and Existence," 13. See also "Preserving God's Creation: Lecture Two," 43.

160. "'*Cosmos*' presupposes a necessary relation with God, the presence of God within it, in order to be *cosmos* while *ktisis* presupposes an act of God which brought into existence something else, something outside of God's self, '*ktisma*' which is found not within God, but opposite of God. Thus the first model '*ktisto-aktisto*' is not the same as '*theos-cosmos*'" ("Christology and Existence," 12).

161. "The fact that the world is '*ktistos*', in other words it is not eternal, but . . . began from 'nothing', means that it was possible for it not to exist. This leads to the conclusion that the existence of the world, our existence, is not necessary, but a product of freedom" (ibid., 14).

162. Ibid., 11–14.

163. Ibid., 11.

164. For a critique of Zizioulas's understanding of 'nothing,' see Philip Sherrard's review of Zizioulas's *E Ktise os Eucharistia* (Creation as Eucharist), *Epiphany* 13 (1993): 41–44.

165. "Preserving God's Creation: Lecture One," 3: "The crucial point, therefore, in the survival of the world lies in the act or the event of its communion with God as totally other than the world."

166. "Preserving God's Creation: Lecture Two," 43.

167. Zizioulas seems to echo Athanasius on this point: "For the transgression of the commandment turned them to what was natural, so that, as they had come into being from non-existence, so also they might accordingly suffer in time the corruption consequent to their non-being. For if, having such a nature as not ever to exist, they were summoned to existence by the advent and mercy of the Word, it followed that because men were deprived of the understanding of God and had turned to things which do not exist—for what does not exist is evil, but what does exist is good since it has been created by the existent God—then they were also deprived of eternal existence. For man is by nature mortal in that he was created from nothing" (*On the Incarnation*, 4.15–26 [Thompson, 142–45]).

168. "Preserving God's Creation: Lecture Two," 44. See also "Christology and Existence," 15.

169. As Zizioulas himself says with regard to creation *ex nihilo*: "Now it is all too easy to admit on a doctrinal level that for Christians things are different because the world was created *ex nihilo*. But I venture to suggest that unless we admit on a philosophical level that personhood is not secondary to being, that the mode of existence of being is

not secondary to its 'substance' but itself primary and constitutive of it, it is impossible to make sense of the doctrine of creation *ex nihilo*" ("Human Capacity and Human Incapacity," 416). As we shall see in Zizioulas, the eucharist ultimately leads to a relational ontology of trinitarian personhood and such an ontology alone can make sense of the Christian affirmation of creation *ex nihilo*.

170. In addition to the problem of freedom and necessity of God, Athanasius's identification of *hypostasis* with *ousia* lent his trinitarian theology vulnerable to charges of tritheism. According to John Lynch, "The Cappadocians were primarily responsible for making Origen's distinction of one *ousia* from three *hypostaseis* in the Trinity achieve permanent ascendancy over Athanasius' identification of *ousia* with *hypostasis*" ("*Prosopon* in Gregory of Nyssa: A Theological Word in Transition," *Theological Studies* 40 [1979]: 732–33).

171. "The Doctrine of the Holy Trinity: The Significance of the Cappadocian Contribution," in *Trinitarian Theology Today: Essays in Divine Being and Act,* ed. Christoph Schwöbel (Edinburgh: T&T Clark, 1995), 44–45.

172. "Contribution of Cappadocia," 26–27.

173. "Doctrine of the Holy Trinity: Significance of the Cappadocian Contribution," 47.

174. Ibid.

175. Ibid.

176. Ibid., 48.

177. Ibid.

178. Ibid.

179. Ibid., 50.

180. Ibid., 47. Zizioulas clearly recognizes that the distinction between nature and person, between common and personal names of God, is implicit in Athanasius, but argues that for Athanasius *hypostasis* and *ousia* were not adequately distinguished conceptually so as to avoid the charge of tritheism. It was left for the Cappadocians to clarify and develop Athanasius's insights.

181. Ibid., 48. Zizioulas adds the qualifier that "we must beware of making this incommunicability the definition of person *par excellence,* as Richard of St. Victor seems to do, for although the hypostatic properties are not communicated, the notion of the person is inconceivable outside a relationship."

182. See Stead, *Philosophy in Christian Antiquity,* 196.

183. Ibid., 194.

184. Ibid.: "Its best-known use is to denote an individual existent, or an individual substance as opposed to a mere action; it is in this sense that Origen insists on three hypostases in the Trinity."

185. Stead supports this interpretation of the Cappadocian use of *hypostasis,* though he adds they are often inconsistent, citing passages which treat *hypostasis* as common principle (ibid., 195).

186. *Being as Communion,* 37; also, "Doctrine of the Trinity: Significance of the Cappadocian Contribution," 47.

187. *Being as Communion,* 37.

188. As we have seen, this historical account differs from that of Lossky, for whom the important step in the development of a theology of person was the reconceptualizing of *hypostasis*.

189. "Ontology of Person," 35; see n. 136 above.
190. For what follows, see *Being as Communion,* 27–35; also, Stead, *Philosophy in Christian Antiquity,* 196.
191. As we will see more fully in the next chapter, Zizioulas identifies the desire of freedom from necessity as a fundamental feature of human existence. Thus, the tragedy of human existence consists in the fact that such a desire, due to the conditions of finitude and death inherent in creaturely existence, is inevitably unfulfilled.
192. *Being as Communion,* 37.
193. "Doctrine of the Holy Trinity: Significance of the Cappadocian Contribution," 44–60, see esp. 47. This interpretation of the Cappadocians in terms of an 'ontological revolution' is not without its detractors, especially among the Greek theologians. See John Panagopoulos, "Ontology or Theology of Person?" (in Greek), *Synaxe* 13–14 (1985): 63–79; 35–47; and Savas Agourides, "Can the Persons of the Trinity Form the Basis for Personalistic Understandings of the Human Being?" (in Greek), *Synaxe* 33 (1990): 67–78; see also André de Halleux, "Personnalisme ou essentialisme trinitaire chez les Pères cappadociens? Une mauvaise controverse," *Revue théologique de Louvain* 17 (1986): 129–55; 265–92; idem, "'Hypostase' et 'Personne' dans la formation du dogma trinitaire (ca. 375–81)," *Revue d'histoire ecclésiastique* 79 (1984): 313–69; 625–70; also, more recently, Lucian Turcescu, "'Person' versus 'Individual', and Other Modern Misreadings of Gregory of Nyssa," *Modern Theology* 18, no. 4 (December 2002): 97–109. To this one could add Rowan Williams's critique of Lossky's understanding of the patristic notion of personhood; see *Theology of Vladimir Lossky,* 107–8 and 122ff.; and John Behr, *The Nicene Faith,* vol. 2 of *The Formation of Christian Theology* (Crestwood, NY: St. Vladimir's Seminary Press, 2004).
194. For a virulent critique of Zizioulas's reading of the Cappadocians, see A. de Halleux, "Personnalisme ou essentialisme trinitaire chez le Pères cappadociens?" 129–55, 265–92. De Halleux argues specifically, among other things, against Zizioulas's thesis that Basil preferred 'personal' over 'essential' categories: "The examination of the term *ousia* in the same treatise on the Holy Spirit confirms that Basil is not showing any hostility to a healthy trinitarian essentialism" (144). See also "'Hypostase' et 'Personne' dans la formation du dogme trinitaire," esp. 318–30. For a detailed analysis of de Halleux's critique of Zizioulas's reading of the Cappadocians, see Baillargeon, *Perspectives Orthodoxes sur l'Église Communion,* 242–53.
195. For what follows see "Teaching of the 2nd Ecumenical Council on the Holy Spirit," 34–36.
196. Ibid., 34.
197. According to Zizioulas, Gregory of Nyssa also affirms this use of substance in *Against Eunomius* 1.22; see ibid.
198. Ibid.
199. Ibid., 33.
200. Ibid., 35. Zizioulas cites other passages from *On the Holy Spirit* such as, *oikea kai somphues kai achoristos koinonia,* or *Koinonia kata phusin* as Basil's way of rendering the meaning of *homoousios* in terms of *koinonia.* He concludes that "*koinonia* unlike . . . *ousia* lends itself to a wider use which includes the *community of glorification and honour,* which is so important to Basil, as well as the *distinctiveness of hypostases* which is, again, fundamental to his particular theological position" (ibid., 35, esp. note 13). On this point see also *Being as Communion,* 134. This interpretation is not quite so clear as Zizioulas would lead us to believe. There are other

references which might indicate that Basil thought of the unity in terms of *ousia*. For example, *On the Holy Spirit* 17.45, speaks of unity in terms of *ousia*: "As unique Persons, they are not one and one; as sharing a common nature, both are one" (*On the Holy Spirit* [Crestwood, NY: St. Vladimir's Seminary Press, 1980], 72). Zizioulas is not, however, oblivious to these citations, but argues that taking the whole of the Basilean corpus, *koinonia* qualifies *phusin* or *ousia* and in that sense assumes an ontological priority ("Teaching of the 2nd Ecumenical Council on the Holy Spirit," 35). Its importance becomes manifest in Basil's reworking of the categories of *person* and *hypostasis*.

201. *Being as Communion*, 36; see also "Doctrine of God the Trinity Today," 30n11; also, "Contribution of Cappadocia," 23–29.

202. "Teaching of the 2nd Ecumenical Council on the Holy Spirit," 38n18: "*Hypostasis* was needed *precisely in order to add to the relational character of prosopon an ontological content*." As proof, Zizioulas cites Basil's *Epistle* 236.6: "Those who say that *ousia* and *hypostasis* are the same, are compelled to confess only different *prosopa* and by avoiding the use of the words *treis hypostasese* they do not succeed in escaping the Sabellian evil" (Zizioulas's translation).

203. *Being as Communion*, 40.

204. "On Being a Person," 37–43.

205. For Zizioulas's citations of Gregory with respect to the Father as *aitia*, see "Teaching of the 2nd Ecumenical Council," 37; "Doctrine of God the Trinity Today," 31n23; "On Being a Person," 42n18; and more recently, "Doctrine of the Holy Trinity: Significance of the Cappadocian Contribution," 50–52. The most quoted passage is *Theological Orations* 3.2; he also cites 3.5–7 and 3.15–16.

206. "Doctrine of the Holy Trinity: Significance of the Cappadocian Contribution," 52 where he quotes Gregory's *Oration* 42.15. For a diametrically opposed reading of Gregory Nazianzus on the unity of God, see T. F. Torrance, *Trinitarian Perspectives* (Edinburgh: T&T Clark, 1994), 21–40.

207. "Doctrine of God the Trinity Today," 24–25. Zizioulas seems to be contradicting himself here by rooting the unity of the Trinity in the person of the Father while elsewhere affirming the unity of God in terms of *koinonia* (as we just saw with his interpretation of Basil). *Koinonia* for Zizioulas is not a "structure . . . existing by itself." In other words, "communion is not a constraining structure for His [God's] existence (God is not in communion, does not love, because He cannot but be in communion and love)" (*Being as Communion*, 18). To root God's unity in *koinonia* is to make the Father the principle of unity, since the Father is the *aitia* of this trinitarian communion.

208. Zizioulas affirms that "since the Person in its identification with hypostasis is an ultimate . . . ontological notion, it must be *a Person* . . . that is the source of divine existence" ("Teaching of the 2nd Ecumenical Council on the Holy Spirit," 37).

209. Ibid.

210. *Being as Communion*, 41.

211. "Doctrine of the Holy Trinity: Significance of the Cappadocian Contribution," 51.

212. Florovsky argues that Athanasius himself was frequently accused of subjecting the generation of the Son to "coercion or involuntariness." Florovsky adds that Athanasius "does not mean to replace free desire by compulsion, but he points out that 'that which is entailed by essence is higher than free choice and antecedes it.'" Florovsky himself interprets Athanasius to be affirming "the free necessity of divine generation." ("St. Athanasius of Alexandria," in *The Eastern Fathers of the Fourth Century*, vol. 7, *The Collected*

Works of Georges Florovsky [Belmont, MA: Notable & Academic Books, 1987], 53). Alvyn Pettersen essentially agrees with Florovsky on this point; see *Athanasius,* 167–73.

213. Who "dealt successfully with this problem" ("On Being a Person," 42n18).

214. Ibid. Aidan Nichols indicates that Maximus the Confessor developed Gregory's distinction even further: "Maximus, however, noticed an important ambiguity in Nazianzen's presentation. . . . In contrast, Maximus considers the willing and the willed to be identical with the will: such simultaneity could not be proposed for human volitional activity, but it may be for the Godhead, which is, as divine, without movement" (*The Byzantine Gospel: Maximus the Confessor and Modern Scholarship* [Edinburgh: T&T Clark, 1993], 73).

215. "On Being a Person," 46. I will review these concepts again in the last chapter in my comparison of Lossky's and Zizioulas's understanding of person.

216. "Human Capacity and Human Incapacity," 407.

217. "Being a person is different from an individual in that a person cannot be conceived in itself as a static reality, but only as it relates to" (ibid.). See also "Preserving God's Creation: Lecture Three," 4.

218. "Love is a *relationship.* . . . It is the other and our relationship with him that gives us our identity, our otherness, making us 'who we are', i.e., persons; for by being an inseparable part of a relationship that matters ontologically we emerge as *unique* and *irreplaceable* . . . it is through this loving relationship that God, too, or rather God *par excellence,* emerges as unique and irreplaceable by being eternally the Father of a unique (*monogenes*) Son" ("Doctrine of the Holy Trinity," 56). See also *Being as Communion,* 46.

219. "Human Capacity and Human Incapacity," 407. For Zizioulas on the notion of the "given," see "Preserving God's Creation: Lecture Three," 2.

220. "Preserving God's Creation: Lecture Three," 2.

221. "Human Capacity and Human Incapacity," 407. See also "On Being a Person," 46; also, *Being as Communion,* 62; also, "Doctrine of the Holy Trinity," 51–54.

222. More will be said on the relation between freedom and love in Zizioulas's ontology of personhood in the last chapter.

223. *Being as Communion,* 40. In a footnote at this point, Zizioulas adds: "The words 'first' and 'then' refer here of course to a priority which is not temporal but logical and ontological" (n. 33). Is this explanation, however, enough to dismiss the question of whether God could not have been otherwise in God's mode of existence? Even if Zizioulas might dismiss such a question as introducing temporal categories into the doctrine of God, it is implied in the notion of God's mode of existence as Trinity being grounded in the freedom of the Father. The issue is not simply logical or ontological, but existential insofar as it raises the question of whether one can trust the God who could be otherwise.

224. On the category of *tropos hyparxeos* in Maximus, its identification with the triune life, and its distinction from God's "*principle of being, ho kat' ousian logos,*" see Nichols, *Byzantine Gospel,* ch. 3, where he analyzes the work of P. Piret, *Le Christ et la trinité selon Maxime le Confesseur* (Paris: Beauchesne, 1983). See also Lars Thunberg, *Man and the Cosmos: The Vision of St. Maximus the Confessor* (Crestwood, NY: St. Vladimir's Seminary Press, 1985), esp. 38, 54.

225. *Being as Communion,* 41n36.

226. Ibid., 88. See also "Doctrine of the Holy Trinity," 55–58.

227. This category has been given considerable attention by scholars, and subsequently, has given rise to conflicting interpretations. Lossky identifies the *tropos hyparxeos* as the 'energies' of God, against the interpretation of Hans Urs Van Balthasar. With Maximus it becomes clear how the conflict of apophaticism and ontology shape Lossky's and Zizioulas's reading of Maximus. As we shall see in the next chapter, reading this category as the 'how' of God's personal existence will be important to Zizioulas's argument for the possibility of an ontology of personhood based on Greek patristic trinitarian theology; see "The Being of God and the Being of *Anthropos*" (in Greek), *Synaxe* 37 (1991): 23. As a result, it is Zizioulas's particular interpretation of this category that separates him from Lossky's apophaticism and accounts for differences between the two theologians in other aspects of theology, such as Christology, creation, and soteriology.

228. "Doctrine of the Holy Trinity: Significance of the Cappadocian Contribution," 55–58.

Chapter 3. Knowing the Triune God

1. In what follows, I am thus disagreeing with André de Halleux, who describes Zizioulas's epistemological approach as apophatic. See "Personnalisme ou essentialisme trinitaire chez les Pères cappadociens?" 129–55, 265–92.

2. "Doctrine of God the Trinity Today," 23–24.

3. Ibid., 24.

4. For a critique of the critique of metaphysics as not being able to sustain an ontology of difference and otherness, see Wayne J. Hankey in "*Theoria versus Poesis*: Neoplatonism and Trinitarian Difference in Aquinas, John Milbank, Jean-Luc Marion, and John Zizioulas," *Modern Theology* 15, no. 4 (October 1999): 387–415.

5. "Doctrine of God the Trinity Today," 20.

6. *Being as Communion,* 125.

7. See Panagopoulos, "Ontology or Theology of Person?" 63–79, 35–47; and Agourides, "Can the Persons of the Trinity Form the Basis for Personalistic Understandings of the Human Being?" 67–78.

8. "Being of God and Being of Anthropos," 22.

9. Ibid., 21.

10. Ibid.

11. Ibid., 21–22.

12. As quoted in ibid., 21; the emphases are Zizioulas's; the translation is from *The Mystical Theology,* 44.

13. See R. Williams, *Theology of Vladimir Lossky,* 1–31; see also Stavrou, *L'Approche Théologique de La Personne chez Vladimir Lossky et Jean Zizioulas,* 157–59.

14. As quoted in R. Williams, "Via Negativa and the Foundations of Theology," 102. See above, ch.2, n. 124.

15. "Apophasis and Trinitarian Theology," 24. One wonders whether the very title of this work does not by itself invalidate Zizioulas's critique of Lossky's "mystical trinitarianism."

16. "Being of God and Being of Anthropos," 32.

17. Stavrou, *L'Approche Théologique de La Personne chez Vladimir Lossky et Jean Zizioulas*, 170; and, Constantin Agoras, "L'anthropologie théologique de Jean Zizioulas: Un bref aperçu," *Contacts* 41 (1989): 19.

18. Zizioulas is also wrong to state that Lossky's "apophaticism of the person" leads him to root his soteriology in the essence/energies distinction (see "Being of God and Being of Anthropos," 26). Lossky attempts to link the doctrine of the energies to the theology of person. The fact that Lossky links salvation to the energies of God rather than to a sharing in the personal existence of God only indicates, again, the tension in Lossky's thought between his apophaticism, on which is based the essence/energies distinction, and his theology of person. The priority of a trinitarian ontology of person would, as Zizioulas does, locate salvation in being united in the personal existence of the Son rather than in the energies of God's essence.

19. "On Being a Person," 35; see also "Being of God and Being of Anthropos," 22.

20. Ibid., 36; see also "Human Capacity and Human Incapacity," 415.

21. "Human Capacity and Human Incapacity," 423–25.

22. "Being of God and Being of Anthropos," 23.

23. Ibid. For the distinction between the *what* and the *how* of God's existence, see also "Doctrine of the Holy Trinity: Significance of the Cappadocian Contribution," 55.

24. "Being of God and Being of Anthropos," 24.

25. Ibid.

26. Ibid.

27. As Michel Stavrou contends (*L'Approche Théologique de La Personne chez Vladimir Lossky et Jean Zizioulas*, 173–79.) The argument that apophaticism cannot be applied to the *hoti esti*, or the fact of God's existence, looks more like one that Aquinas would give rather than Zizioulas, both of whom share in common a certain revised understanding of apophaticism than that given by Dionysius. Furthermore, Zizioulas is not contending against an apophatic agnosticism, but an apophatic theology that limits the knowledge of God as Trinity. Gaëtan Baillargeon, *Perspectives Orthodoxes sur l'Église Communion*, and Paul McPartlan also miss the centrality of the *hopos esti* to Zizioulas's system. McPartlan argues that "the definition of Chalcedon ... may be seen as the kernel of Zizioulas' theological system" (*The Eucharist Makes the Church*, 150). The fact that the Chalcedonian definition is not "the kernel" of Zizioulas's thought will be illustrated below when I argue that Zizioulas interprets this definition in light of a trinitarian ontology of person, which distinguishes his interpretation from the more traditional one offered by Lossky. Similarly, Zizioulas's trinitarian ontology is more than "a radical change of the Greco-Roman *Weltanschauung*" which developed in relation to Greek and biblical understandings of truth, as Constantine Agoras mentions in "Hellénisme et Christianisme," 257. Though Zizioulas himself says that the Greek philosophical worldview or framework did not allow for a personal ontology, the necessary condition for such an ontology is the revelation of the trinitarian being of God in the eucharist, which reveals both the truth and the falsity of the Greco-Roman *Weltanschauung*.

28. "Apophasis and Trinitarian Theology," 15.

29. See Jürgen Moltmann, *The Trinity and the Kingdom* (San Francisco: Harper Collins, 1981); Eberhard Jüngel, *God as the Mystery of the World* (Grand Rapids, MI: Eerdmans, 1983), and Catherine Mowry LaCugna, *God for Us*.

30. Zizioulas does warn against a strict identification between *oikonomia* and *theologia,* or between the immanent and the economic Trinity. He argues that with such an identification, "God and the world become an unbreakable unity and God's transcendence is at stake," or would introduce suffering into God's eternal being ("Doctrine of God the Trinity Today," 23–24).

31. "Teaching of the 2nd Ecumenical Council on the Holy Spirit," 39–40; see also "Doctrine of God as Trinity," 30n20: "The first doxology is based on the economy, whereas the second one, which St. Basil defends, points to God as he is eternally or immanently, and as he is revealed and seen in the eucharistic experience of the *eschata.*"

32. "Teaching of the 2nd Ecumenical Council on the Holy Spirit," 39.

33. See "Doctrine of God as Trinity," 24.

34. Ibid.

35. I thus disagree with McPartlan, who argues that for Zizioulas "how God has come to us historically does not reveal God as He is, and it is God *as He is* who is our destiny" (*The Eucharist Makes the Church,* 253). Zizioulas's very point is that the *hopos esti* of God experienced in the eucharist is God "*as He is,*" and such a revelation is the condition for the possibility of a trinitarian ontology.

36. "Doctrine of God the Trinity Today," 26–27.

37. Ibid., 26.

38. Ibid.

39. Zizioulas and Lossky share this particular understanding of the role of apophaticism in theology. The crucial difference between the two theologians is over the centrality of apophaticism within the theological discourse.

40. In "The Theological Notion of the Human Person," Lossky asks the specific question of whether there exists "a doctrine of the human person among the Fathers of the first centuries" and the more general question, "what is the human person according to theological thought" (111–12). Before answering the question, he feels compelled to "say few words about the divine Persons" (112). After saying these few words, he then concludes that the reality of 'person' as it exists in the Trinity does not exist on the created level. The notion of a 'human person' analogous to the divine person is possible only through Christology, i.e., through the person of Christ. My point is that Lossky has no epistemological ground by which to say a 'few words' about the divine Persons, and hence, to ground the analogy between divine and human personhood.

41. For a view on the compatibility, rather than the mutual exclusivity, of trinitarian theology and apophaticism, see Rowan Williams, "The Deflections of Desire: Negative Theology and Trinitarian Discourse," in *Silence and the Word: Negative Theology and Incarnation,* ed. Oliver Davies and Denys Turner (Cambridge: Cambridge University Press, 2002), 115–35.

42. *The Mystical Theology,* 156. As was mentioned in chapter one, Zizioulas rejects any notion of an "economy of the Holy Spirit."

43. *Orthodox Theology,* 84–85.

44. "Apophasis and Trinitarian Theology," 14.

45. *Orthodox Theology,* 97.

46. Ibid., 99.

47. Verna Harrison has shown that *perichoresis* in the Greek patristic tradition "conveys the simultaneity of rest and movement, of coinherence and interpenetration, among

the persons of the Trinity, between the two natures in Christ, and among God and deified human persons in the transfigured creation" ("Perichoresis in the Greek Fathers," *St. Vladimir's Theological Quarterly* 35 [1991]: 55). This may be true, but it begs the question of whether these diverse uses cohere with one another, and may, in fact, represent conflicting strands of thought within the Greek patristic tradition itself. This question becomes important in light of the tension that I have argued exists in Lossky's thought between an implicit trinitarian ontology of person and apophaticism.

48. *The Mystical Theology*, 145.
49. Ibid., 145–46.
50. Ibid., 146.
51. See Stavrou, *L'Approche Théologique de La Personne chez Vladimir Lossky et Jean Zizioulas*, 34–37.
52. *Orthodox Theology*, 101.
53. Ibid.; *The Mystical Theology*, 144.
54. *The Mystical Theology*, 144.
55. Ibid., 145.
56. *Orthodox Theology*, 101; original emphasis.
57. Ibid.
58. Ibid., 107.
59. Ibid.
60. Ibid., 108.
61. *The Mystical Theology*, 174–95; "In the Church our nature receives all the objective conditions of this union. The subjective conditions depend only upon ourselves" in *synergy* with the Holy Spirit (183).
62. Ibid., 181; see esp. 184–85.
63. Ibid., 182.
64. "The deification of our nature by Christ is only able to be actualized by becoming the living content of our personal communion with the person of Christ" (Clément, *Orient-Occident: Deux Passeurs*, 65, my translation). I fundamentally agree with Michel Stavrou's critique of Clément's description of Lossky's soteriology; see *L'Approche Théologique de La Personne chez Vladimir Lossky et Jean Zizioulas*, 47.
65. "Christ becomes the sole image appropriate to the common nature of humanity. The Holy Spirit grants to each person created in the image of God the possibility of fulfilling the likeness in the common nature" (*The Mystical Theology*, 166).
66. Ibid., 191.
67. "Redemption and Deification," 109.
68. *The Mystical Theology*, 170.
69. *Being as Communion*, 125.
70. *Orthodox Theology*, 55.
71. "Tradition and Traditions," Lossky's introductory essay to *The Meaning of Icons*, included in *Image and Likeness of God*, 153.
72. "Catholic Consciousness: Anthropological Implications of the Dogma of the Church," in *Image and Likeness of God*, 190.
73. I say overt, because his theological notion of person is a result of *theologia*, that is speaking about God in Godself, no matter how much he tries to limit the use of the categories of nature and person to conventional signs.

74. *The Mystical Theology*, 160.

75. Ibid., 168.

76. Ibid. "His Person is hidden from us by the very profusion of the Divinity which He manifests. It is this 'personal kenosis' of the Holy Spirit on the plane of manifestation and economy which makes it hard to grasp His hypostatic existence" ("Procession of the Holy Spirit," 92).

77. *Orthodox Theology*, 42.

78. *The Mystical Theology*, 120. Rowan Williams criticizes Lossky's interpretation of Nyssa's affirmation that the image of God in the human person consists primarily in the "fact that he is freed from necessity, and subject to the domination of nature." Williams argues that "the unambiguous statement that the image of God in man is his personal character, and that this is constituted by self-transcending openness is simply not to be found in the Fathers." He concludes that in the end, "Lossky's appeal to the Greek Fathers for the sources of his personalist understanding of the image of God is doomed: personalism, in anything like the form it takes in Lossky, is a post-Augustinian development of Christian thought, dependent upon Augustine's uncovering of the unique quality of every human soul's relation to God." The same critique could be applied to Zizioulas, since he also identifies the "image of God" with the patristic understanding of 'person.' For Williams's critique, see *Theology of Vladimir Lossky*, 107–8 and 122ff.

79. *The Mystical Theology*, 129.

80. "Catholic Consciousness," 184–85.

81. *Orthodox Theology*, 67.

82. Ibid.

83. Lossky adds: "Paradisiacal sexuality, stemming completely from consubstantial interiority and whose marvelous multiplication, which should fill everything, would certainly have demanded neither multiplicity nor death, is almost entirely unknown to us" (ibid., 77). I mention at length Lossky's understanding of sexuality as a tragic failure toward personhood, because, it is strikingly similar to Zizioulas's understanding of sexuality in terms of "biological hypostasis."

84. "Theological Notion of the Human Person," 112.

85. Ibid., 115.

86. Ibid., 116.

87. "Theology of the Image," 133.

88. "Theological Notion of the Human Person," 118.

89. Ibid.

90. *Orthodox Theology*, 71.

91. Ibid., 72.

92. *The Mystical Theology*, 122.

93. "On Being a Person," 43.

94. Ibid.

95. Ibid. For a similar argument, see *Being as Communion*, 50–65. See also "Human Capacity and Human Incapacity," 437. Miroslav Volf accuses Zizioulas here of essentially absorbing and, thus, effacing the uniqueness of human personhood in Christ. But Zizioulas is not arguing that all human persons become the Son. Having a relationship to the Son "identical" to that of the Father means existing *as* the Son *in* the Son, meaning to

exist in an eternal communion of love and freedom with the Father, the preconditions for uniqueness. The Son is the one in and through whom this relationship is established. On this point, see Volf, *After Our Likeness,* 84–88. It appears that the thrust of Volf's critiques against Zizioulas center around his reading of Zizioulas as overemphasizing the 'one' over and against the 'many.' Zizioulas's entire theology, together with his notion of 'person,' is an attempt to speak about the simultaneity of the 'one' and the 'many.' Such a simultaneity is what 'person' is.

96. "Being of God and Being of Anthropos," 26.

97. See *The Mystical Theology,* esp. 174–95.

98. Ibid., 70.

99. Ibid. Later he adds, "The distinction between the essence and the energies, which is fundamental for the Orthodox doctrine of grace, makes it possible to preserve the real meaning of St. Peter's words 'partakers of the divine nature'. The union to which we are called is *neither hypostatic*—as in the case of the human nature of Christ—*nor substantial,* as in that of the three divine Persons: it is union with God in His energies, or union by grace making us participate in the divine nature, without our essence becoming thereby the essence of God" (87).

100. "Being of God and Being of Anthropos," 26. See also Stavros Giagkazoglou, "Ousia, Hypostaseis, Personal Energies: The Teaching of St. Gregory Palamas on the Uncreated Energies" (in Greek), *Synaxe* 37–38 (1991): 71–78 and 39–48. Reacting to Panagopoulos's statement that the "future of Orthodox theology rests on . . . the distinction between essence and energies" ("Ontology or Theology of the Person?" 46), Zizioulas adds that to make 'energies' the controlling theological concept tends to make "superfluous, if not suspect, any *logos* on person" (26). A larger issue here is whether the Palamite understanding of divine energy is superfluous, or even contradictory to Zizioulas's ontology of person. This is suggested, albeit indirectly, in Dom Illtyd Trethowan's discussion of Lossky's use of the Palamite notion of divine energies: "But to place a real distinction within God himself other than that of the Persons is surely not only uncalled-for but also disastrous. For it seems to destroy God's unity" ("Lossky on Mystical Theology," 243). Although not explicitly stated in Lossky, it is almost assumed in his thought that the energies of God are not apersonal.

101. "Teaching of the 2nd Ecumenical Council on the Holy Spirit," 51. In her discussion of Zizioulas's marginalization of the divine energies and her own critical response that "an understanding of divine energy should be maximized," Nonna Verna Harrison misses the point that Zizioulas is attempting to minimize its use as a soteriological category. See her "Zizioulas on Communion and Otherness," *St. Vladimir's Theological Quarterly* 42, nos. 3–4 (1998): 273–300. What Zizioulas has a problem reconciling here is the fact that though Gregory Palamas admits that the energies are never apersonal, he argues that they are divine as opposed to created for soteriological purposes. The human person becomes god, or achieves *theosis,* because the energies are divine. In attempting to interpret Palamas within the framework of an ontology of personhood, Zizioulas is not necessarily faithful to Palamas's soteriological understanding of the divine energies. This shows more clearly how he attempts to 'fit' the tradition within the horizon of an ontology of personhood. The fact that it is not so easy a 'fit' indicates a lack of coherence to the tradition itself. Zizioulas is identifying one strand of the tradition, an ontology of communion based on trinitarian theology, and interpreting other theological concepts

within that framework. In doing so, he is offering an interpretation from that usually considered 'Orthodox,' as is evident with the concept of divine energies. The other important consideration, however, is the fact that Zizioulas's ontology of person may render a Palamite understanding of divine energies, developed chiefly for soteriological purposes, superfluous. In other words, it appears no longer necessary to maintain this distinction, nor the affirmation that God's energies are God, if salvation is assuming a personal identity equivalent to that of the Son.

102. See *The Mystical Theology*, 95ff.

103. "The two ways in theology correspond to the way of divine love by which God proceeds outside of himself, creating all in order to be manifest in all, and returning all created beings to the divine union by the love that God inspires in them. In this 'eternal circle' of divine Love, God appears as Love, proceeding outside of his essence and creating all things by his energies, and as Beloved, remaining united in himself in his procession, in whom no thing can participate even though he is present in all things [imparticipable même en participations]. As Love, God gives proportionally his infinity to created beings, in defining their 'analogies' (ideas); as Beloved, he produces in created beings the love that is the analogy of the will of beings, making them desire union in the divine energies, according to the pre-established mode for each being" ("La Notion des 'Analogies,'" 304–5).

104. "But though creation is contingent in its origin and began to exist, it will never cease to be; death and destruction will not involve a return to non-being, for 'the word of the Lord endureth forever' (I Pet. 1, 25), and the divine will is unchangeable" (*The Mystical Theology*, 94).

105. "Human Capacity and Human Incapacity," 416. See also *Being as Communion*, 39, where Zizioulas explains that 'first leavening' of Greek philosophy, itself rooted in the attempt to give expression to the trinitarian ontology of personhood, is the creation *ex nihilo*. Also, see lectures Two and Three of "Preserving God's Creation," for the link between an ontology of person and creation *ex nihilo*.

106. "Preserving God's Creation: Lecture Two," *King's Theological Review* 12 (1989): 43. As we saw above, 'nothing' for Lossky, because of the link between the divine energies and creation, is not ontologically absolute. For Zizioulas, however, nothing necessarily has ontological significance in an ontology of personhood.

107. "Preserving God's Creation: Lecture Two," 44.

108. On this point, see Laats, *Doctrines of the Trinity in Eastern and Western Theologies*, 123–25. See also R. Williams, "Philosophical Structures of Palamism." See also Dorothea Wendebourg, "From the Cappadocian Fathers to Gregory Palamas. The Defeat of Trinitarian Theology," *Studia Patristica* 17, no. 1 (1982): 196.

109. On this point, my critique of Lossky differs slightly from that of Laats and Williams, and from Wendebourg's general critique of the essence/energies distinction.

110. For more on this, see Anatolios, *Athanasius*.

111. Here I agree with Robert Turner, who in his excellent analysis of Zizioulas's theology argues, "[a]lthough recognizing the unity which the term substance identifies, Zizioulas goes beyond an understanding of ontology as a totality and assures ontological freedom by elaborating how personhood serves as a principle of otherness and unity for being" ("Foundations for John Zizioulas' Approach to Ecclesial Communion," *Ephemerides Theologicae Lovanienses* 78 [2002]: 441).

Chapter 4. Trinity and Personhood

1. In "*Prosopon* in Gregory of Nyssa," John Lynch refers to H. Wheeler Robinson's *The Christian Experience of the Holy Spirit* (Glasgow, 1962), 228–29, who, like Lossky, argues that the Greek fathers saw *hypostasis* as a synonym of *ousia* and "developed a new usage 'to denote the distinctive being of Father, Son and Holy Spirit, in contrast with *ousia,* their common being'" (Lynch, 728). Lynch agrees with Zizioulas that the meaning of *prosopon* was of equal significance to the Cappadocians in the trinitarian controversies. He illustrates this, however, by referring to Gregory of Nyssa, the least cited Cappadocian in Zizioulas's work.

2. For a critique of Zizioulas's relating trinitarian and human personhood, see Richard M. Fermer, "The Limits of Trinitarian Theology as a Methodological Paradigm," *Neue Zeitschrift fur systematische Theologie und Religionsphilosophie* 41, no. 2 (1999): 158–86. My basic disagreement with Fermer is that he, along with others, assumes that Zizioulas is simply reading off a relational understanding of the Trinity a model for human personhood. I have attempted to show throughout this book that Zizioulas (and Lossky) is not so naïve.

3. In saying that the persons of the Trinity are distinct from their common *ousia,* I am not implying that the divine persons are not the common *ousia.* Each person is the divine *ousia* insofar as they hypostasize or possess it. For both Lossky and Zizioulas, however, there is a clear distinction between person and *ousia* which is meant to convey the freedom of the divine persons in relation to the *ousia.* Both argue that this freedom in relation to *ousia* protects the trinitarian distinctions and precludes the introduction of necessity into the doctrine of the Trinity. To paraphrase Zizioulas, God is not Trinity because God in God's essence is love; God is Trinity because of the person of the Father who freely "constitutes God's substance, makes it hypostases" (*Being as Communion,* 41).

4. Though there are those (as we have seen) who would not necessarily agree that Lossky's and Zizioulas's interpretation of 'person' is explicitly patristic. This dispute becomes important in considering how much Zizioulas actually owes to Lossky for his theology of person. Though Zizioulas criticizes Lossky, giving the impression of radical break with his thought, the similarities in their theology of 'person' raises the query of whether such similarities result from the clarity of the patristic texts or whether Lossky's thought formed the basis for Zizioulas's understanding of person. Such is the case with Christos Yannaras, who has also developed a theology of personhood similar to that of Lossky's and Zizioulas's, and who admitted to me that one of the starting points for his thought was Lossky's theology of person. In a personal conversation with Zizioulas, he indicated to me that one of the influences for his ontology of personhood was Yannaras. In then suggesting to Zizioulas that perhaps Lossky influenced him indirectly, Zizioulas was willing to admit that may be the case, but added that the influence would be slight given the substantial differences between their theologies.

5. Lossky is hesitant to use *ekstasis* to express this personal freedom because of its link with Heideggerean philosophy: speaking of the enhypostatization of nature, "I would have said 'which he ecstacizes,' if I did not fear being reproached for introducing an expression too reminiscent of 'the ecstatic character' of the *Dasein* of Heidegger, after having criticized others who allowed themselves to make such comparisons" ("Theological Notion of the Human Person," 120).

6. *The Mystical Theology*, 58.
7. "Procession of the Holy Spirit," 81.
8. Ibid., 83.
9. Ibid.
10. "Teaching of the 2nd Ecumenical Council on the Holy Spirit," 37.
11. Ibid.
12. *Being as Communion*, 41.
13. Ibid.
14. "Contribution of Cappadocia," 32.
15. "Preserving God's Creation: Lecture Three," 2.
16. *Being as Communion*, 43.
17. One can now understand why Zizioulas acknowledged, in personal conversations with Paul McPartlan, 'freedom' "as his deepest theological preoccupation." See McPartlan, *The Eucharist Makes the Church*, 146. It is, thus, not quite accurate to assert, as Edward Russell does, that "[u]ltimately ecclesiology forms the heart of Zizioulas's theology." In his otherwise insightful analysis and critique of Zizioulas's relational anthropology, Russell fails to elaborate on the link between the monarchy of the Father and a relational anthropology in Zizioulas's thought, both in terms of the monarchy of the Father being the condition for the possibility of a relational anthropology, and in terms of the problem of human freedom being one of the principle reasons Zizioulas insists on the monarchy of the Father. Zizioulas maintains the monarchy of the Father, in part, because without it human longing for personhood is ultimately tragic, and not, as Russell maintains following Miroslav Volf, "for fear of not being able to distinguish between the three persons" ("Reconsidering Relational Anthropology: A Critical Assessment of John Zizioulas's Theological Anthropology," *International Journal of Systematic Theology* 5, no. 2 [2003]: 168–86).
18. "Indeed, each of the three hypostases contains the unity, the one nature, after the manner proper to it, and which, in distinguishing it from the other two persons, recalls at the same time the indissoluble bond uniting the Three" (*The Mystical Theology*, 54); "The personal dimension, as distinct from the individual one, involves what we may call *hypostatisation* and *catholicity* . . . A *hypostasis* is an identity which embodies and expresses in itself the totality of nature" ("Preserving God's Creation: Lecture Three," 4).
19. The difference between "an identity-in-distinction within the common nature" and "the *hypostatization* of nature" can be characterized as one of priority. The first understands personhood from the perspective of the divine *ousia*. It implies the ontological priority of the *ousia* over the divine persons and understands the latter as the differentiated relations of a simple essence. "*Hypostatization* of nature" asserts the ontological priority of the divine persons over the divine *ousia*, and though the divine persons are the divine *ousia*, "*hypostatization* of nature" simultaneously asserts the freedom of the *hypostasis* in relation to *ousia*.
20. See *Orthodox Theology*, 41; see also "Doctrine of the Holy Trinity: Significance of the Cappadocian Contribution," 56–58.
21. Though the notion of 'communion' is not used often by Lossky, he would not disagree that love and uniqueness coincide and are marks of *hypostatic* existence.
22. *Orthodox Theology*, 42.
23. *The Mystical Theology*, 121. For Lossky, this division of nature is itself a product of the fall; see ibid., 129.

24. "Human Capacity and Human Incapacity," 408. For more on this distinction in Maximus's thought, see Lars Thunberg, *Microcosm and Mediator: The Theological Anthropology of Maximus the Confessor,* 2d ed. (Chicago: Open Court, 1995), 50–64. According to Thunberg, the distinction is important to Maximus's doctrine of creation and to his Christology, as well as the relation between the two, and not to explaining the difference between individuality and personal existence.

25. "Communion and Otherness," 11.

26. "Human Capacity and Human Incapacity," 442; see also 425–26, 429, and 434.

27. Ibid., 407. See also "Doctrine of the Holy Trinity," 48.

28. "On Being a Person," 46.

29. "Human Capacity and Human Incapacity," 408. See also *Being as Communion,* 55, and "Doctrine of the Holy Trinity," 56–68.

30. *Being as Communion,* 41.

31. "Theological Notion of the Human Person," 120. Though Lossky is primarily speaking of the relation of the human person to human nature, this relation between person and nature is itself based on that which exists in the Trinity.

32. *Orthodox Theology,* 42.

33. "Doctrine of the Holy Trinity," 49. See also *Being as Communion,* 105: "The significance of the person rests in the fact that he represents two things simultaneously which are at first sight in contradiction: particularity and communion."

34. "Communion and Otherness," 17.

35. Ibid., 10.

36. "Redemption and Deification," 106.

37. "Procession of the Holy Spirit," 93.

38. Ibid., 79.

39. "When we say that the procession of the Holy Spirit is a relation which differs absolutely from the generation of the Son, we indicate the difference between them as to mode of origin (*tropos hyparxeos*) from that common source in order to affirm that community of origin in no way affects the absolute diversity between the Son and the Spirit" (ibid.).

40. Ibid., 78.

41. "Human Capacity and Human Incapacity," 408.

42. "On Being a Person," 41.

43. Ibid.

44. Ibid., 46. See also "Doctrine of the Holy Trinity," 56–58: "The person cannot exist in isolation. God is not alone; He is *communion*. Love is not a feeling, a sentiment springing from nature like a flower from a tree. Love is a *relationship*."

45. "On Being a Person," 46.

46. "Doctrine of the Holy Trinity," 56.

47. "Communion and Otherness," 17. See also "Being of God and Being of Anthropos," 18.

48. "Human Capacity and Human Incapacity," 407.

49. See ibid., 411–33.

50. Ibid., 411.

51. "When we say that 'this is by Mozart', or 'this is by Rembrandt', we are in both cases dealing with a personal world which has no equivalent anywhere" (*The Mystical Theology,* 53).

52. "Human Capacity and Human Incapacity," 412.

53. Ibid., 412. Zizioulas adds, "This is not an entirely negative statement. The tragedy lies in the fact that it is at once positive and negative: the artist exists for us only because he is absent. Had we not had his work (which points to his absence), he would not exist for us or for the world around, even if we had heard of him or seen him; he *is* by *not being there* (an incidental actual presence of the artist next to us while we are looking at his work would add nothing to his real presence in and through his work, which remains a pointer to his absence)."

54. Ibid., 412.

55. "But in so far as the human person is a being whose particularity is established *also* by its boundaries (a body), personhood realises this presence as *absence*" (ibid., 414).

56. Ibid., 421.

57. Ibid., 423.

58. Ibid., 419. See also 424n1: "Christian theology . . . denies the possibility of pure ontology on the basis of the world as it is: and it affirms that there *is* a possibility of a pure ontology of this world, yet only on the basis of the fact that it *will* ultimately exist— of the fact, that is, that being is personal and depends on love." Also, "On Being a Person," 36.

59. "Human Capacity and Human Incapacity," 432.

60. Ibid., 420.

61. Though *Being as Communion* was first published in 1985, this chapter was first published in 1977 in Greek.

62. *Being as Communion,* 50.

63. Ibid., 51.

64. Ibid., 50.

65. Ibid., 52.

66. Ibid. For more on Zizioulas's notion of tragedy, see "Preserving God's Creation: Lecture Three," 2. It is thus not the case, as Miroslav Volf argues, that a human being as "an individual . . . cannot at the same time be a person in Zizioulas's sense" (*After Our Likeness,* 102.)

67. "On Being a Person," 34–35. For an analysis of the same question, which results in ontological conclusions different from Zizioulas, see Charles Taylor, *Sources of the Self: The Making of Modern Identity* (Cambridge, MA: Harvard University Press, 1989), esp. 27–32.

68. Ibid., 37.

69. *Being as Communion,* 107; in a footnote Zizioulas adds that "this observation of M. Heidegger is of great importance for an ontology of the world *taken as it is,* i.e. without reference to a beyond."

70. "On Being a Person," 37–43.

71. This presupposition is not unrelated to the first presupposition, or 'leavening', for an ontology of personhood in *Being as Communion,* 39, which is freeing the world from "cosmological necessity" by affirming the creation *ex nihilo.*

72. "On Being a Person," 42.

73. Ibid., 44.

74. Alan J. Torrance, *Persons in Communion: An Essay on Trinitarian Descriptions and Human Participation, with Special Reference to Volume One of Karl Barth's Church Dogmatics* (Edinburgh: T&T Clark, 1996), 290. Torrance's book is, in part, an interesting attempt to

relate Karl Barth's and John Zizioulas's trinitarian theology, i.e., to interpret Barth's trinitarian theology in terms of communion. For a similar attempt, see Paul M. Collins, *Trinitarian Theology West and East: Karl Barth, the Cappadocian Fathers, and John Zizioulas* (Oxford: Oxford University Press, 2001).

75. "Being of God and Being of Anthropos," 18.
76. *Being as Communion*, 46.
77. "On Being a Person," 37.
78. "Being of God and Being of Anthropos," 18.
79. "Church as Communion," 13; similar thoughts are evident in "Being of God and Being of Anthropos," 13; in "Eschatology and History," 38; and are discernible throughout Zizioulas's work.
80. *Persons in Communion*, 290.
81. Ibid. For this criticism of Zizioulas, Alan Torrance is drawing on T. F. Torrance's criticism of the Cappadocian fathers in *The Trinitarian Life: The Evangelical Theology of the Ancient Catholic Church* (Edinburgh: T&T Clark, 1988), esp. 238, 312ff. T. F. Torrance argues that far from advancing the trinitarian theology of Athanasius with the principle of the *monarchia* of the Father, the Cappadocians actually abolish the equality and the unity of the three persons. He argues that Athanasius, "[w]hile accepting the formulation of *mia ousia, treis hypostaseis* he had such a strong view of the complete identity, equality and unity of the three Persons within the Godhead, that he declined to advance a view of the Monarchy in which the oneness of God was defined by reference to the *Person* of the Father" (312). See also T. F. Torrance, *The Christian Doctrine of God: One Being Three Persons* (Edinburgh: T&T Clark, 1996), esp. 180–93. On the debate between Zizioulas and T. F. Torrance, see Ralph Del Colle, "'Person' and 'Being' in John Zizioulas' Trinitarian Theology," 70–86.
82. *Persons in Communion*, 292.
83. Ibid. See Miroslav Volf on this, who describes the relations between the persons in Zizioulas's theology in terms of an "asymmetrical-reciprocal relationship" (*After Our Likeness*, 78). Volf also questions "why the monarchy of the Father should be necessary for preserving the unity of God, who is, after all, love, or why the only alternative for securing the unity of God is by way of recourse to the 'ultimacy of substance in ontology'" (79). He, like Torrance, argues that the monarchy of the Father is inherently subordinationist. But as I will indicate below, Zizioulas's affirmation of the monarchy of the Father is not simply about the unity of the Trinity, but the only way to express God's being as a unity-in-diversity *in freedom,* the latter being necessary for existential reasons.
84. *Persons in Communion*, 292; this quote is actually in the form of yet another rhetorical question.
85. Ibid. The quotes are from *Being as Communion*, 17–18.
86. *Persons in Communion*, 293.
87. "Preserving God's Creation: Lecture Three," 2.
88. *Persons in Communion*, 291.
89. Torrance also asks what "this causally conceived hierarchical conception of the triune communion suggests about the mirroring of the divine life in the ecclesial communion—given his emphasis on the Christian community as the *image Dei*?" (ibid.). Zizioulas, however, does in fact have a theology of ministry based on trinitarian theology. The hierarchical relationship between the liturgical celebrant and the *laos* mirrors

that between the Father and the other two persons of the trinity. This constitutes hierarchy not as a term of superiority, but as a relational term where the hierarch is the person who unites within himself the 'one' and the 'many.' For a detailed discussion, see *Being as Communion,* 209–46.

90. *Persons in Communion,* 292.

91. Ibid.

92. I am referring here especially to *Being as Communion,* 41: "In a more analytical way this means that God, as Father and not as substance, perpetually confirms through 'being' His *free* will to exist."

93. I am using 'cause' here much in the same way as Zizioulas himself is using it, though he, in fact, does not give any sustained reflection on the problems inherent to the conceptuality of causation. One could easily find in the Christian tradition, broadly conceived, a distinction between the world as a caused being and God as a necessary being. Creation itself is a contingent reality dependent on the will, i.e., the freedom of God. There is no will in relation to God's being since God is a necessary being whose existence is not dependent on the will as an act of freedom. By introducing causation into the doctrine of the Trinity, Zizioulas intends to argue that God's existence is itself a result of absolute freedom. In saying, therefore, that the Father causes the Son and the Spirit to exist, Zizioulas wishes to affirm that God's trinitarian being is not necessary but the result of an act of freedom. Cause, thus, effects through an act of freedom. The causal relationship within the divine life is distinct from that in relation to creation, because what is effected is not a thing, but *the way* in which God exists. In making, however, the Father the sole cause of God's trinitarian existence, Zizioulas cannot escape the inevitable conclusion that the Son and the Spirit, in fact, God's whole trinitarian existence, is based on the person of the Father. In this sense, it seems difficult to avoid the charge of subordinationism, in that the Son and the Spirit, as effects of the Father's act of freedom, are contingent realities much in the same way creation is dependent and contingent on the will of God. With the Father as sole cause, the interdependency within the divine life is not reciprocal.

94. "Communion and Otherness," 14.

95. Ibid. For an interesting and provocative article comparing Zizioulas with Fyodor Dostoevsky on personhood as freedom, love, and suffering, see C. Paul Schroeder, "Suffering towards Personhood: John Zizioulas and Fyodor Dostoevsky in Conversation on Freedom and the Human Person," *St. Vladimir's Theological Quarterly* 45, no. 3 (2001): 243–64.

96. Ibid.

97. Zizioulas rejects a kenosis or economy of the Holy Spirit; see ch. 1.

98. "The person fulfills himself in the gift of himself . . . *which is not a sudden decision, nor an act, but the manifestation of His very being, of personhood, which is no longer a willing of His own, but His very hypostatic reality as the expression of the trinitarian will, a will of which the Father is the source, the Son, the obedient realization, and the Spirit, the glorious fulfillment*" (*Orthodox Theology,* 101, original emphasis).

99. Ibid., original emphasis.

100. For which he criticizes Moltmann among others; see "Doctrine of God the Trinity Today," 24. For a critique of Zizioulas for failing to integrate the cross into his theology of personhood and trinitarian theology, see Alan E. Lewis, "The Burial of God:

Rupture and Resumption as the Story of Salvation," *Scottish Journal of Theology* 40 (1987): esp. 350.

101. But see the brief summary of their patristic interpretation at the beginning of ch. 1 above.

102. On Lossky, see R. Williams, *Theology of Vladmir Lossky*, 107–8 and 122ff; on Zizioulas, see André de Halleux, "'Hypostase' et 'Personne' dans la formation du dogme trinitaire"; also, idem, "Personalisme ou esentialisme trinitaire chez le Pères capadociens?" See also John G. F. Wilks, "The Trinitarian Ontology of John Zizioulas," *Vox Evangelica* 25 (1995): 63–88; and Fermer, "Limits of Trinitarian."

103. See Mark Julien Edwards, *Origen against Plato* (Hampshire: Ashgate, 2002). Also John Behr, *The Way to Nicaea*, vol. 1 of *Formation of Christian Theology* (Crestwood, NY: St. Vladimir's Seminary Press, 2001), 163–206.

104. On Augustine, see Rowan Williams, "*Sapientia* and the Trinity: Reflections on the *De Trinitate*," in *Collectanea Augustiniana: Mélanges T. J. van Bavel*, ed. B. Bruing, M. Lamberigts, and J. van Houlm (Louvain: Leuven University Press, 1990): 317–32; and on Aquinas, see A. Williams, *The Ground of Union*. For a position that interprets the theologies of Aquinas and Palamas as being more similar than different, in addition to Anna Williams, see Bruce D. Marshall, "Action and Person: Do Palamas and Aquinas Agree about the Spirit?" *St. Vladimir's Theological Quarterly* 39, no. 4 (1995): 379–408.

105. Much of the "buzz" in the Orthodox world is that such contemporary theologians as Lossky, Zizioulas, Yannaras, and Nissiotis are corrupting a pure form of patristic thought with modern existentialism. On Zizioulas, see especially Panagopoulos, "Ontology or Theology of Person?" and Agourides, "Can the Persons of the Trinity Form the Basis for Personalistic Understandings of the Human Being?" (I have not seen such an accusation against Lossky in print by an Orthodox theologian, but see R. Williams's critique in *Theology of Vladimir Lossky*, 107–8 and 122ff.).

106. Turcescu, "'Person' versus 'Individual.'"

107. Ibid., 100.

108. Ibid., 101.

109. Ibid., 103.

110. The works I have in mind are: *Being as Communion*, 17, 41n36, 52n46; 228nn55–56); "Teaching of the 2nd Ecumenical Council on the Holy Spirit," 34n12, 37n22, 43–45, 51n62; "Doctrine of God the Trinity Today," 31n23; "Doctrine of the Holy Trinity: Significance of the Cappadocian Contribution," 48. There are no references to Gregory of Nyssa in "On Being a Person" and in the "Being of God and Being of Anthropos." In the article that Turcescu cites most often, "Human Capacity and Human Incapacity," there is only one reference to Gregory of Nyssa (428n1). Zizioulas cites Nyssa's *Great Catechism* in support of the idea that freedom is essential to the Christian notion of the *Image Dei*. Even taking into consideration *Epistle* 38, which most scholars attribute to Gregory of Nyssa but which Zizioulas consistently attributes to Basil, the letter is usually cited in support of the general patristic axiom that "substance never exists in a 'naked' state, that is, without hypostasis, without 'a mode of existence'" (*Being as Communion*, 41; see also 88). Zizioulas also cites the letter to support his interpretation of Basil as understanding the unity of God in terms of *koinonia* (see "Teaching of the 2nd Ecumenical Council of the Holy Spirit," 34–35n12). But this letter is not the central text for this particular reading of

Basil and is used as further support of his interpretation of other texts from Basil, such as *On the Holy Spirit*, 18.

111. See "Teaching of the 2nd Ecumenical Council of the Holy Spirit," 37nn20 and 21; "On Being a Person," 42n18; "Doctrine of God the Trinity Today," 31n23; and "Doctrine of the Holy Trinity," 50–55. Zizioulas does cite one passage from Gregory of Nyssa's *Ad Ablabium* in support of the Greek patristic notion of the monarchy of the Father (see "Teaching of the 2nd Ecumenical Council of the Holy Spirit," 37n22, and again, "Doctrine of God the Trinity Today," 31n23). In both instances, this one passage from Nyssa is cited in further support of Gregory Nazianzus.

112. *Being as Communion*, 41.

113. This understanding of uniqueness in terms of particular relationships can be shown to make sense even without reference to God or the uncreated 'other.' The example of an abandoned baby in the fields especially makes this clear. Is a newborn baby abandoned in the fields unique and, hence, a person? The answer is yes and no. No in the sense that such an abandonment renders this baby a nonperson, and to deny this is not to take seriously the reality of dehumanization. The only hope for a baby to still be person and unique is the fact that she or he is always loved by God. Humans in this sense are not inherently persons, as if they can claim such a dignity for themselves or as part of their essence, but always in relation to the eternal love of God. For this example and more on the relational understanding of person see Aristotle Papanikolaou, "Person, *Kenosis*, and Abuse: Hans Urs von Balthasar and Feminist Theologies in Conversation" *Modern Theology* 19, no. 1 (January 2003): 41–65.

114. "Church as Communion," 13.

115. *The Mystical Theology*, 53.

116. It is surprising not to see the name of Emmanuel Levinas in Turcescu's article, since Zizioulas cites him often, especially his critique of Heidegger.

117. Zizioulas has admitted to me in private conversations that the thought of Martin Buber did influence his understanding of personhood. He did not mention John Macmurray.

118. In "Human Capacity and Human Incapacity," 408n1, and in "Doctrine of the Holy Trinity," 59n14.

119. "It was after struggling to express these thoughts that I came across the following words of W. Pannenberg, which, I find, express the same thing in a clearer way" ("Human Capacity and Human Incapacity," 413n1).

120. "Redemption and Deification," 106.

121. See especially, section 3, pp. 15–19.

122. "Being of God and Being of the Anthropos," 18

123. Ibid., 19.

124. "[I]s a philosophical justification of patristic theology possible? Or does patristic theology in its essence constitute the converse, that is, a *theological justification of philosophy*, a proclamation that philosophy and the world can acquire a true ontology only if they accept the presupposition of God as the *only* existent whose being is truly identified with the person and with freedom?" (*Being as Communion*, 46); elsewhere, "the person as an ontological category cannot be extrapolated from experience" ("On Being a Person," 37); also, "the meaning of person is not borrowed from philosophy . . . but philosophy is

able, if it wishes, to borrow this meaning from theology" ("Being of God and Being of Anthropos," 18).

125. In this sense, Miroslav Volf's claim that "Zizioulas's entire ontology of person—and thus also the foundation of his understanding of salvation and of the church—stands or falls with the claim of ontologically grounding substance through person" is not entirely accurate. According to Zizioulas's own logic, such a grounding is given in the monarchy of the Father. Thus, Zizioulas's ontology of person seems to stand or fall on the adequacy of his understanding of the monarchy of the Father and freedom within God's being. Thus, again, the question is whether such an ontology can be secured without the monarchy of the Father. On Volf, see *After Our Likeness,* 77n26.

Bibliography

The list of primary sources contains an annotated bibliography of Zizioulas's and Lossky's works listed chronologically. It intends to be as complete as possible. For Zizioulas, this list is indebted to Paul McPartlan's "Full Bibliography of Published Writings" in *The Eucharist Makes the Church: Henri de Lubac and John Zizioulas in Dialogue,* 316–21, and to Athanasios G. Melissaris's *Personhood Re-Examined: Current Perspectives from Orthodox Anthropology and Archetypal Psychology*. Readers should consult McPartlan's work for a list of unpublished writings by Zizioulas and for the various translations of the published writings. For Lossky, I am indebted to Rowan Williams's bibliography in *The Theology of Vladimir Nikolaievich Lossky: An Exposition and Critique,* which corrects the bibliography published in *In the Image and Likeness of God,* 229–32.

Primary Sources

Books by Lossky

Spor o Sofii (The Controversy over Sophia). Paris: Confrérie de S. Photius, 1936.
The Mystical Theology of the Eastern Church. Crestwood, NY: St. Vladimir's Seminary Press, 1976. First published as *Essai su la Théologie Mystique de l'Eglise d'Orient*. Paris: Aubier, 1944.
(With Leonid Ouspensky) *The Meaning of Icons*. Translated by G. E. H. Palmer and E. Kadloubovsky. Crestwood, NY: St. Vladimir's Seminary Press, 1989. First published as *Der Sinn der Ikonen*. Bern und Olten: Urs Graf-Verlag, 1952. The introductory essay of this work "Tradition and the Traditions" is by Lossky and forms ch. 8 of *In the Image and Likeness of God*.
Théologie Négative et Connaissance de Dieu chez Maître Eckhart. Paris: Librairie Philosophique J. Vrin, 1960.
The Vision of God. Translated by Asheleigh Moorhouse. Crestwood, NY: St. Vladimir's Seminary Press, 1983. First published as *La Vision de Dieu*. Paris: Delahaux et Niestlé, 1962.
In the Image and Likeness of God. Edited by John H. Erickson and Thomas E. Bird. Crestwood, NY: St. Vladimir's Seminary Press, 1974. First published as *A l'Image et à la Ressemblance de Dieu*. Paris, Aubier, 1967. This work is a collection of articles.
Orthodox Theology: An Introduction. Translated by Ian and Ihita Kesarcodi-Watson. Crestwood, NY: St. Vladimir's Seminary Press, 1978. This work contains primarily a collection of articles that appeared posthumously under the heading *Théologie Dogmatique* in the journal *Messager de l'Exarchat du Patriarche russe en europe occidental* (hereafter, *Messager*) (1964–65), as well as other articles.

Sept jours sur les routes de France: juin 1940. Paris: Cerf, 1998. A journal begun by Lossky in June 1940 when he left Paris as the Germans were advancing on the city.

Articles by Lossky

"La Théologie Négative dans la Doctrine de Denys L'Aréopagite." *Revues des Sciences Philosophiques et Théologiques* 28 (1930): 204–21. This article first appeared in Russian in *Seminarium Kondakovianum* 3 (1929): 133–44.

"La Notion de 'Analogies' chez Denys le Pseudo-Aréopagite." *Archives d'Histoire Doctrinale et Littéraire du Moyen-Age* 5 (1931): 279–309.

"La Dogmes et les Conditions de la Vraie connaissance." *Bulletin de la Confrérie de S. Photius le Confesseur* 1 (1934): 2–9.

"Etude sur la Terminologie de S. Bernard." *Archivum Latinitatis Medii Aevi* 17 (1942): 79–96.

"La Théologie de la Lumière chez S. Grégoire de Thessalonique." *Dieu Vivant* 1 (1945): 94–118. Ch. 3 of *In the Image and Likeness of God.*

"Redemption and Deification." *Sobornost* 12 (1947): 47–56. The French original was actually published later in *Messager* 15 (1953): 161–70. Ch. 5 of *In the Image and Likeness of God.*

"The Spiritual Legacy of Patriarch Sergius." *Diakonia* 6 (1971): 163–71. The Russian original appeared in *Dukhovnoe Nasledstvo Patriarkha Sergiya* (Moscow, 1947), 263–70.

"La Procession du Saint-Esprit dans la Doctrine Trinitaire Orthodoxe." Paris: Éditions Setor, 1948. Ch. 4 of *In the Image and Likeness of God.*

Review of the *Byzantine Patriarchate,* by George Every. *Sobornost* 3 (1948): 108–12.

"Du Troisième Attribut de l'Eglise." *Dieu Vivant* 10 (1948): 78–89. Ch. 9 of *In the Image and Likeness of God.*

"Panagia." In *The Mother of God: A Symposium,* edited by E. L. Mascall, 24–36. London, 1949. Ch. 11 of *In the Image and Likeness of God.*

Review of *Existence and Analogy,* by E. L. Mascall. *Sobornost* 3 (1950): 295–97.

"The Temptations of Ecclesial Consciousness." *St. Vladimir's Theological Quarterly* 32 (1988): 245–54. First published in Russian in *Messager* 1 (1950): 16–21.

"'Ténèbre' et 'Lumière' dans la Connaissance de Dieu." In *Ordre, Désordre, Lumière,* 133–43. Paris: Vrin, 1952. Ch. 2 of *In the Image and Likeness of God.*

"Dominion and Kingship: An Eschatological Study." *Sobornost* 14 (1953): 67–79. The French original was published later in *Messager* 17 (1954): 43–55. Ch. 12 of *In the Image and Likeness of God.*

"L'Apophase et la Théologie Trinitaire." Collége Philosophique. Paris: Centre de Documentation Universitaire. N.d.: 1953. Ch. 1 of *In the Image and Likeness of God.*

"Elements of 'Negative Theology' in the Thought of St. Augustine." *St. Vladimir's Seminary Quarterly* 21 (1977): 67–75. First published in *Augustinus Magister.* Vol. 1, 575–81. Paris: Editions des Etudes Augustiniennes, 1954.

"The Dogma of the Immaculate Conception" and "Lourdes." *One Church* 6 (1971): 277–81. First published in *Messager* 20 (1954): 246–52.

"La Notion Théologique de la Personne Humaine." *Messager* 24 (1955): 227–35. Ch. 6 of *In the Image and Likeness of God.*

"The Problem of the 'Face-to-Face Vision' and the Patristic Tradition of the Byzantines." *Greek Orthodox Theological Review* 17 (1972): 231–54. The French original was published in *Studia Patristica* 2 (1957): 512–37.

"The Theology of the Image." *Sobornost* 22 (1957–59): 510–29. The French original was published in *Messager* 30–31 (1959): 123–33. Ch. 7 of *In the Image and Likeness of God*.

"Obraz I Podobie" (Image and Likeness). *Zhurnal Moskovskoy Patriarkhii* 3 (1958): 53–64. This article is reprinted as the postscript in *Orthodox Theology: An Introduction*.

"Foi et Théologie" (from notes, prepared by Olivier Clément). *Contacts* 31 (1961): 163–76. This article is reprinted as the prologue in *Orthodox Theology: An Introduction*.

"Les Startsy d'Optino." *Contacts* 33 (1961): 4–14.

"Le Starets Léonide." *Contacts* 34 (1961): 99–107.

"Le Starets Macaire." *Contacts* 37 (1962): 9–19.

"Notes sur le 'Credo' de la Messe." *Contacts* 38–39 (1962): 84–86, 88–90.

"Le Starets Ambroise." *Contacts* 40 (1962): 219–36.

"Le Conscience Catholique: Implications Anthropologiques du Dogme de l'Eglise." *Contacts* 42 (1963): 76–88. Ch. 10 of *In the Image and Likeness of God*.

"Théologie Dogmatique" (from notes, prepared by Olivier Clément). *Messager* 46–47 (1964): 85–108; 48 (1964): 218–33; 49 (1965): 24–35; 50 (1965): 83–101. These articles form chs. 1–4 of *Orthodox Theology: An Introduction*.

Books by Zizioulas

Eucharist, Bishop, Church: The Unity of the Church in the Divine Eucharist and the Bishop during the First Three Centuries. Translated by Elizabeth Theokritoff. Brookline, MA: Holy Cross Orthodox Press, 2001. Original Greek version: *E Henotes tes Ekklesias en te Theia Eucharistia kai to Episkopo kata tous treis protous aionas*. Athens: Gregore, 1965. 2d ed. published in 1990.

L'être ecclésial. Geneva: Labor and Fides, 1981.

Being as Communion. Crestwood, NY: St. Vladimir's Seminary Press, 1985. This work contains the articles that were published in *L'être ecclésial,* but also, as John Meyendorff puts it in the foreword, "with important additions" (12). It will be indicated below which articles are included in each work. A new article was added to *Being as Communion* that forms ch. 3 of that work. Ch. 5 of *L'être ecclésial* was replaced with another article that forms ch. 6 of *Being as Communion.*

E Ktise os eucharistia (Creation as Eucharist). Athens: Akritas, 1992. This work contains translations of the three lectures on Creation which were published in *King's Theological Review,* as well as Zizioulas's first theological article, "La vision eucharistique du monde et l'homme contemporain." In the introduction of this work, Zizioulas indicates that the latter article was originally published in Greek in *Christianiko Symposio* (Christian Symposium) 1 (1967): 183–90. This information is absent from McPartlan's otherwise complete bibliography.

Ellenismos kai Christianismos: H Synantese ton duo Kosmon (Hellenism and Christianity: The Meeting of Two Worlds). Athens: Apostolike Diakonia, 2003. This book is a reprint of the article listed below under the same title.

Articles by Zizioulas

"Ignatius I (Saint) Patriarch of Constantinople (846–858, 867–77 A.D.)" in *Encyclopedia of Religion and Ethics* (in Greek).

"Jerusalem," in *Encyclopedia of Religion and Ethics* (in Greek).

"Thyateira—Church of," in *Encyclopedia of Religion and Ethics* (in Greek).

"La vision eucharistique du monde et l'homme contemporain." *Contacts* 19 (1967): 83–92.

"The Meaning of Ordination: A Comment." *Study Encounter* 4 (1968): 191–93.

"The Development of Conciliar Structures to the Time of the First Ecumenical Council." In *Councils and the Ecumenical Movement*, 34–51. Geneva: World Council of Churches, 1968.

"On the Concept of Authority." *The Ecumenical Review* 21 (1969): 160–66.

"Some Reflections on Baptism, Confirmation and Eucharist." *Sobornost* 9 (1969): 644–52.

"The Eucharistic Community and the Catholicity of the Church." *One in Christ* 6 (1970): 314–37. This article was first published in French in *Istina* 14 (1969): 67–88. The English translation forms ch. 4 of *Being as Communion*, while the original French was reprinted as ch. 3 of *L'être ecclésial*.

"God Reconciles and Makes Free—An Orthodox Comment." *Bulletin* 10 (1970): 7–8.

"Ordination and Communion." *Study Encounter* 6 (1970): 187–92. A French translation of this article was published as ch. 5 of *L'être ecclésial*. In *Being as Communion* this article was replaced by an English translation of "Priesteramt und Priesterweihe im Licht der östlich-orthodoxen Theologie" as ch. 6. For the latter reference, see below.

"L'eucharistie: quelques aspects bibliques." In J. Zizioulas, J. M. R. Tillard, and J. J. von Allmen, *L'eucharistie*, 11–74. Eglises en dialogue 12. Marne, 1970.

"Ecclesiological Issues Inherent in the Relations between Eastern Chalcedonian and Oriental Non-Chalcedonian Churches." *The Greek Orthodox Theological Review* 16 (1971): 144–62.

"Informal Groups in the Church." In *Informal Groups in the Church: Papers of the Second CERDIC Conference, University of Strasbourg, 1971*, edited by R. Metz. Pittsburgh: Pickwick Press, 1975.

"Reflections of an Orthodox (on common witness and proselytism)." *The Ecumenical Review* 23 (1971): 30–34.

"Ordination—A Sacrament? An Orthodox Reply." *Concilium* 4 (1972): 33–39.

"Priesteramt und Priesterweihe im Licht der östlich-orthodoxen Theologie." In *Questiones Disputatae 50, Der priesterliche Dienst—V. Amt und Ordination in ökumenischer Sicht*, edited by Karl Rahner and H. Schlier, 72–113. Freiburg-Basel-Vienna: Herder, 1973. The English translation of this article forms ch. 6 of *Being as Communion*, and replaces ch. 5 of *L'être ecclésial*, which is a French translation of "Ordination and Communion."

"The Pneumatological Dimension of the Church." *International Catholic Review—Communio* 1 (1974): 142–58.

"La continuité avec les origines apostoliques dans la conscience théologique des églises orthodoxes." *Istina* 19 (1974): 65–94. This article forms ch. 4 of *L'être ecclésial*. The English translation was first published in *St. Vladimir's Theological Quarterly* 19 (1975): 75–108 and reprinted as ch. 5 of *Being as Communion*.

"Human Capacity and Human Incapacity." *Scottish Journal of Theology* 28 (1975): 401–48.

"Orthodox-Protestant Bilateral Conversations: Some Comments." In *The Orthodox Church and the Churches of the Reformation*, 55–60. Geneva: World Council of Churches, 1975.

"Eucharistic Prayer and Life." *Emmanuel* 81 (1975): 462–70.

"Hellenism and Christianity: The Meeting of Two Worlds." In vol. 6, *History of the Hellenic Nation* (in Greek), 519–59. Athens: Akritas, 1976.

"Die Eucharistie in der neuzeitlichen orthodoxen Theologie." In *Die Anrufung des Heiligen Geistes im Abendmahl*, 163–79. Frankfurt am Main: Otto Lembeck Verlag, 1977.

"The Local Church in a Eucharistic Perspective." In *In Each Place, Towards a Fellowship of Local Churches Truly United*, 50–61. Geneva: World Council of Churches, 1977. This article was reprinted as ch. 7 of *Being as Communion*, and a French translation was reprinted as ch. 6 of *L'être ecclésial*.

"From Prosopeion to Prosopon: The Contribution of Patristic Theology to the Concept of Person." In *Charisteria: Studies in Honor of Metropolitan Meliton of Chalcedon* (in Greek), 287–323. Thessaloníki: Institute of Patristic Studies, 1977. This article was published in French as ch. 1 of *L'être ecclesial* and in English as ch. 1 of *Being as Communion*.

"Verité et communion dans la perspective de la pensée patristique grecque." *Irenikon* 50 (1977): 451–510. This article was reprinted as ch. 2 of *L'être ecclésial* and in English as ch. 2 of *Being as Communion*.

"(Communal Spirit and Conciliarity:) A Comment." In *Procés-Verbaux du Deuxième Congrès de Théologie Orthodoxe*, edited by Savas Agourides, 140–46. Athens, 1978.

"Conciliarity and the Way to Unity—An Orthodox Point of View." In *Churches in Conciliar Fellowship*, 20–31. Geneva: Conference of European Churches, 1978.

"The Ecumenical Dimensions of Orthodox Theological Education." In *Orthodox Theological Education for the Life and Witness of the Church*, 33–40. Geneva: World Council of Church, 1978.

"Ortodossia." In *Eniclopedia del Novecento*.

"The Synodal Institution: Historical, Ecclesiological and Canonical Problems." In *Studies in Honor of Metropolitan Barnabas of Kitros* (in Greek), 1–30. Athens, 1980.

"Episkopé and Episkopos in the Early Church: A Brief Survey of the Evidence." In *Episkopé and Episcopate in Ecumenical Perspective*, 30–42. Geneva: World Council of Churches, 1980.

"Cristologia, pneumatologia e istituzioni ecclesiastiche: un punto di vista ortodosso." *Cristianesimo nella storia* 2 (1981): 111–27. This article was published in English as ch. 3 in *Being as Communion*, and is missing from *L'être ecclésial*.

"Duo Archaiai Paradoseis Peri Apostolikes Diadoches kai e Semasia ton" ("Two Ancient Traditions Concerning Apostolic Succession and Their Theological Significance"). In *Studies in Honor of Prof. G. Konidaris*, 683–712. Athens, 1981.

"God and the World: The Problem of Transcendence in Greek Philosophy and Patristic Thought." In *Epopteia, Studies in Memory of Prof. N. Karmiris*. Athens, 1981.

"Implications ecclésiologiques de deux types de pneumatologie." In *Communio Sanctorum: Mélanges offerts à Jean-Jacques von Allmen*, 141–54. Geneva: Labor et Fides, 1981.

"Christology and Existence: The Created-Uncreated Dialectic and the Dogma of Chalcedon" (in Greek). *Synaxe* 2 (1982): 9–20.

"Response of John Zizioulas" (to reactions to the above article) (in Greek). *Synaxe* 3 (1982): 77–82.

"The Ecclesiological Presuppositions of the Holy Eucharist." *Nicolaus* 10 (1982): 333–49.
"The Teaching of the 2nd Ecumenical Council on the Holy Spirit in Historical and Ecumenical Perspective." In *Credo in Spiritum Sanctum,* edited by J. S. Martins, 29–54. Rome: Libreria Editrice Vaticana, 1983.
"Déplacement de la perspective eschatologique." In *La chrétienté en débat,* 89–100. Paris: Cerf, 1984.
"The Ecclesiology of the Orthodox Tradition." *Search* 7 (1984): 42–53.
"The Bishop in the Theological Doctrine of the Orthodox Church." In *Kanon VII: Der Bischof und sein Eparchie,* ed. Richard Potz, 23–35. Vienna: Verlag des Verbandes der wissenschaftlichen Gesellschaften Osterreichs, 1985.
"Orthodox Ecclesiology and the Ecumenical Movement." *Sourozh* 21 (1985): 16–27.
"The Theological Problem of 'Reception.'" *One in Christ* 21 (1985): 187–93.
"Eschatology and History." In *Cultures in Dialogue: Documents from a Symposium in Honor of Philip A. Potter,* edited by T. Wieser, 30–39. Geneva, 1985. See also *Whither Ecumenism?* (Geneva: World Council of Churches, 1986), 62–71, 72–73, which contains extracts of "Eschatology and History" together with comments of Zizioulas in the discussion which followed the presentation of this paper.
"European Spirit and Greek Orthodoxy" (in Greek). *Eythine* 163 (1985): 329–33; 167 (1985): 569–73.
"Die eucharistische Grundlage des Amtes." In *Philoxenia,* edited by Reinhard Thöle and Ilse Friedeberg. Fürth: Flacius-Verlag, 1986.
"The Contribution of Cappadocia to Christian Thought." In *Sinasos in Cappadocia,* edited by Frosso Pimenides and Stelios Roïdes, 23–37. N.p.: Agra Publications, 1986.
"The Mystery of the Church in Orthodox Tradition." *One in Christ* 24 (1988): 294–303.
"'Discours du métropolite Jean de Pergame,' La célébration du millénaire du 'baptême' de la russie au siège du Patriarcat oecuménique." *Istina* 33 (1988): 197–203.
"The Nature of the Unity We Seek—The Response of the Orthodox Observer." *One in Christ* 24 (1988): 342–48.
"The Institution of Episcopal Conferences: An Orthodox Reflection." *The Jurist* 48 (1988): 376–83.
"The Early Christian Community." In *Christian Spirituality: Origins to the Twelfth Century,* edited by Bernard McGinn and John Meyendorff in collaboration with Jean Leclerq, 23–43. New York: Crossroad, 1989.
"Address to the 1988 Lambeth Conference." *Sourozh* 25 (1989): 29–35.
"Preserving God's Creation: Three Lectures on Theology and Ecology." *King's Theological Review* 12 (1989): 1–5, 41–45; 13 (1990): 1–5.
"Tradition liturgique et unité chrétienne." *Revue de l'Institut Catholique de Paris* 36 (1990): 157–70.
"The Doctrine of God the Trinity Today: Suggestions for an Ecumenical Study." In *The Forgotten Trinity. 3 A Selection of Papers Presented to the BCC Study Commission on Trinitarian Doctrine Today,* edited by Alasdair I. C. Heron, 19–32. London: British Council of Churches and Council of Churches for Britain and Ireland, 1991.
"On Being a Person: Towards an Ontology of Personhood." In *Persons, Divine and Human,* edited Christoph Schwöbel and Colin E. Gunton, 33–46. Edinburgh: T&T Clark, 1991.
"Come, Holy Spirit, Sanctify Our Lives!" *Sourozh* 44 (1991): 1–3.

"Orthodoxy and the Contemporary World" (in Greek). In *Oikodome kai Martyria. Ekfrasis Agapes kai Temes eis ton Sevasmiotaton Metropoletin Servion and Kozanis Kyrion Dionysion*, 226–29. Kozani, 1991.

"The Experience of the Mystery of the Church." In *Tomos Afieromenos ston Metropolete Attikis Dorotheo Giannaropoulo*, 31–40. Athens, 1991.

"The Being of God and the Being of the *Anthropos*" (in Greek). *Synaxe* 37 (1991): 11–36.

"Orthodoxy and the Problem of the Protection of the Natural Environment" (in Greek). In *Gia na Zese e Demiourgia tou Theou—So that God's Creation Might Live*, 20–32. Ecumenical Patriarchate of Constantinople, 1992.

"The Practice of Orthodoxy Today: Motives and Forms" (in Greek). In *To Emperistato tis Orthodoxias kai e Apostole tes sto Amesso Mellon: Pagkrito Theologiko Synedrio ypo ten Aigida tes Ieras Metropoleos Lampis kai Sfakion 21–23 October 1993*, edited by Nicholaos Markantonis, 218–32. Speli, Rethymnon: Ekdosis tou Patriarchikou Pneumatikou Kentrou "Agios Rafael," 1993.

"The Church as Communion." *St. Vladimir's Theological Quarterly* 38 (1994): 7–19.

"Communion and Otherness." *Sobornost* 16 (1994): 3–16.

"The Eucharist and the Kingdom of God (Part 1)." *Sourozh* 58 (November 1994): 1–12; (Part 2) 59 (February 1995): 22–38; and (Part 3) 60 (May 1995): 32–46. This article was originally published in Greek in *Synaxe* 49 (1994): 7–18; 51 (1994): 83–102; 52 (1994): 81–98.

"The Doctrine of the Holy Trinity: The Significance of the Cappadocian Contribution." In *Trinitarian Theology Today: Essays in Divine Being and Act*, edited by Christoph Schwöbel, 44–60. Edinburgh: T&T Clark, 1995.

"The Apocalypse and the Natural Environment" (in Greek). *Synaxe* 56 (1995): 13–22.

"What Does the Church Hope for from Theology?" (in Greek). In *Ekklessiastikos Kerykas* 7 (1995): 171–84.

"Man the Priest of Creation." In *Living Orthodoxy in the Modern World*, edited by A. Walker and C. Carras, 178–88. London: SPCK, 1996.

"Apostolic Continuity of the Church and Apostolic Succession in the First Five Centuries." In *Apostolic Continuity of the Church and Apostolic Succession*, edited by James F. Puglisi and Dennis J. Billy, 153–68. Louvain: Faculty of Theology Katholicke Universteit, 1996.

"The Self-Understanding of the Orthodox and Their Participation in the Ecumenical Movement." In *The Ecumenical Movement, the Churches and the World Council of Churches: An Orthodox Contribution to the Reflection Process on 'The Common Understanding and the Vision of the WCC*, edited by Gennadios Limouris, 37–46. Geneva: World Council of Churches, 1997.

"Ecological Asceticism: A Cultural Revolution." *Sourozh* 50 (1997): 22–25.

"Fr. Georges Florovsky: An Ecumenical Teacher" (in Greek). *Synaxe* 64 (1997): 12–26.

"Out of Nothing" (in Greek). *Diavasi* 10 (1997): 9–23.

"The Book of the Apocalypse and the Natural Environment" (in Greek). In *Apokalypse kai Periballon 95–1995 A.D. Symposio tes Patmou I, 20–27 Septembriou 1995*, edited by Sarah Hobson and Jane Lubchenco, 31–35. Ekdoseis Dafimiseis, 1997.

"Science and the Environment: A Theological Approach." In *Threskeia, Episteme kai Perivallon, Symposio 2. E Mavre Thalassa se Kindyno, Mia Syantese Pesteon: Enas koinos*

Antikeimenikos Skopos, 20–28 Septembriou 1997, edited by Sarah Hobson and Laurence David Mee, 61–66. Ekdoseis Diafimiseis, 1997.

"Primacy in the Church: An Orthodox Approach." *Eastern Churches Journal* 5, no. 2 (1998): 7–28. Reprinted in *Petrine Ministry and the Unity of the Church: Toward a Patient and Fraternal Dialogue: A Symposium Celebrating the 100th Anniversary of the Foundation of the Society of Atonement, Rome, December 4–6, 1997,* edited by James F. Puglisi, 115–25. Collegeville, MN: Liturgical Press, 1999. Also in *Sourozh* 84 (2001): 3–13.

"Illness and Healing in Orthodox Theology." In *Theologia kai Psychiatrike se Dialogo— Praktika Hmeridas,* 133–56. Athens: Apostoliki Diakonia, 1999.

"The International Initiatives of the Ecumenical Patriarchate for the Protection of the Environment." *Deltion Enosis Ellenikon Trapezon* 2 (1999): 96–99.

"Interview with His Eminence Metropolitan of Pergamum, John Zizioulas." In *2000 Chronia Meta,* 424–30. Athens: Akritas, 1999.

"Symbolism and Realism in Orthodox Worship." *Sourozh* 79 (2000): 3–17. This article first appeared in *Synaxe* 71 (1999): 6–21.

"The Orthodox Church and the Third Millenium." *Sourozh* 81 (2000): 20–31.

"Eschatologie et Societe." *Irenikon* 73 (2000): 278–97.

"The Theology of St. Silouan the Athonite" (in Greek). In *O Agios Silouanos tes Oikoumenes: Proseggise sten pneumatike kleronomia tou agiou Silouanou tou Athonite,* 31–48. Athens: Ekodoseis Akritas, 2001.

"Martyria and Diakonia of Orthodox Women within a United Europe: Presuppositions and Possibilities." In *E Orthodoxe Gynaika sten Enomene Europe: Praktika Diorthodoksou Europaikou Synedriou,* 85–108. Katerini: Epektasis, 2001.

"The Person and Genetic Interventions." *Indiktos* 14 (2001): 63–72.

Secondary Sources

On Lossky

Allchin, A. M. "Vladimir Lossky: The Witness of an Orthodox Theologian." *Theology* 72 (1969): 203–9.

Clément, Olivier. *Orient-Occident: Deux Passeurs: Vladimir Lossky et Paul Evdokimov.* Geneva: Labor et Fides, 1985.

Florovsky, Georges. "Review of *The Mystical Theology of the Eastern Church.*" *Journal of Religion* 38 (1958): 207–8.

Laats, Alar. *Doctrines of the Trinity in Eastern and Western Theologies: A Study with Special Reference to Karl Barth and Vladimir Lossky.* New York: Peter Lang, 1999.

Lossky, Nicholas. "Theology and Spirituality in the Work of Vladimir Lossky." *Ecumenical Review* 51 (1999): 288–93.

Morrel, George W. "Theology of Vladimir Lossky." *Anglican Theological Review* 41 (1959): 35–40.

Papanikolaou, Aristotle. "Divine Energies or Divine Personhood: Vladimir Lossky and John Zizioulas on Conceiving the Transcendent and Immanent God." *Modern Theology* 19, no. 3 (2003): 357–85.

Plekon, Michael. "Russian Theology and Theologians Revisited." *St. Vladimir's Theological Quarterly* 44 (2000): 409–19.

Schmemann, Alexander. "Lossky, Vladimir, 1903–58." *St. Vladimir's Seminary Quarterly* 2 (1958): 47–48.
Trethowan, Dom Illtyd. "Lossky on Mystical Theology." *The Downside Review* 92 (1974): 239–47.
Williams, Rowan G. *The Theology of Vladimir Nikolaievich Lossky: An Exposition and Critique*. Ph.D. diss., Oxford University, 1975.
———. "The Via Negativa and the Foundations of Theology: An Introduction to the Thought of V. N. Lossky." In *New Studies in Theology* edited by Stephen Sykes and Derek Holmes, 95–117. London: Duckworth, 1980.

On Zizioulas

Agoras, Constantin. "L'anthropologie théologique de Jean Zizioulas: A bref aperçu." *Contacts* 41 (1989): 6–23.
———. "Vision ecclésiale et ecclésiologie. À propos d'une lecture de l'oeuvre de Jean Zizioulas." *Contacts* 43 (1991): 106–23.
———. "Hellénisme et Christianisme: la question de l'histoire, de la personne et de sa liberté selon Jean Zizioulas." *Contacts* 44 (1992): 244–69.
———. *Personne et liberté ou 'etre comme communion', 'einai os kuinónia*. Ph.D. diss., Sorbonne, 1992. Abstract (in Greek) in *Synaxe* 48 (1993): 99.
Agourides, Savas. "Can the Persons of the Trinity Form the Basis for a Personalistic Understanding of the Human Being?" (in Greek). *Synaxe* 33 (1990): 67–78.
Baillargeon, Gaëtan. "Jean Zizioulas, porte-parole de l'Orthodoxie contemporaine." *Nouvelle Revue Théologique* 111 (1989): 176–93.
———. *Perspectives Orthodoxes sur l'Église Communion: L'oeuvre de Jean Zizioulas*. Montreal: Éditions Paulines & Médiaspaul, 1989.
Del Colle, Ralph. "'Person' and 'Being' in John Zizioulas' Trinitarian Theology: Conversations with Thomas Torrance and Thomas Aquinas." *Scottish Journal of Theology* 54, no. 1 (2001): 70–86.
Fermer, Richard M. "The Limits of Trinitarian Theology as a Methodological Paradigm." *Neue Zeitschrift für systematische Theologie und Religionsphilosophie* 41, no. 2 (1999): 158–86.
Fisher, David A. "Byzantine Ontology: Reflections on the Thought of John Zizioulas." *Diakonia* 29 (1996): 57–63.
Fontbona-I-Missé, Jaume. *Comunión y Sinodalidad. La eclesiología eucarística después de N. Afanasiev en I. Zizioulas y J. M. R. Tillard* (Sant Paciá, 52). Barcelona: Edicions de la Facultat de Teologia de Catalunya—Herder, 1994.
Fox, Patricia A. *God as Communion: John Zizioulas, Elizabeth Johnson, and the Retrieval of the Symbol of the Triune God*. Collegeville, MN: Liturgical Press, 2001.
Hankey, Wayne J. "*Theoria versus Poesis:* Neoplatonism and Trinitarian Difference in Aquinas, John Milbank, Jean-Luc Marion and John Zizioulas." *Modern Theology* 15, no. 4 (1999): 387–415.
Harrison, Nonna Verna. "Zizioulas on Communion and Otherness." *St. Vladimir's Theological Quarterly* 42 (1998): 273–300.
Ickert, Scott S. "The Missing Word in John Zizioulas' Ecumenical Theology." *Dialog* 37 (1998): 220–27.

Knight, Douglas. "John Zizioulas on the Eschatology of the Person." In *The Future as God's Gift: Explorations in Christian Eschatology,* edited by David Fergusson and Marcel Sarot, 189–97. Edinburgh: T&T Clark, 2000.

McPartlan, Paul. *The Eucharist Makes the Church: Henri de Lubac and John Zizioulas in Dialogue.* Edinburgh: T&T Clark, 1993.

Melissaris, Athanasios G. "The Challenge of Patristic Ontology in the Theology of Metropolitan John (Zizioulas) of Pergamon." *Greek Orthodox Theological Review* 44 (1999): 467–90.

———. *Personhood Re-Examined: Current Perspectives from Orthodox Anthropology and Archtypal Psychology: A Comparison of John Zizioulas and James Hillman.* Katerini: Epektasis Publications, 2002.

Panagopoulos, John. "Ontology or Theology of Person?" (in Greek). *Synaxe* 13–14 (1985): 63–79; 35–47.

Papanikolaou, Aristotle. "Divine Energies or Divine Personhood: Vladimir Lossky and John Zizioulas on Conceiving the Transcendent and Immanent God." *Modern Theology* 19, no. 3 (2003): 357–85.

———. "Is John Zizioulas an Existentialist in Disguise? Response to Lucian Turcescu." *Modern Theology* 20, no. 4 (2004): 587–93.

Pavlidou, Eleni. *Cristologia e pneumatologia tra Occidente cattolica e Orente ortodosso neo-greco: per una lettura integrata di W Kasper e J Zizioulas in prospettiva ecumenica.* Rome: Dehoniane, 1997.

Russell, Edward. "Reconsidering Relational Anthropology: A Critical Assessment of John Zizioulas's Theological Anthropology." *International Journal of Systematic Theology* 5, no.2 (2003): 168–86.

Schroeder, C. Paul. "Suffering towards Personhood: John Zizioulas and Fyodor Dostoevsky in Conversation on Freedom and the Human Person." *St. Vladimir's Theological Quarterly* 45, no. 3 (2001): 243–64.

Sherrard, Philip. Review of *E Ktisis os Eucharistia* (Creation as Eucharist) by John Zizioulas. *Epiphany* 13 (1993): 41–44.

Stavrou, Michel. *L'Approche Théologique de La Personne chez Vladimir Lossky et Jean Zizioulas: à L'Image et á La Ressemblance de Dieu.* Master's Thesis. Paris: Institute de Théologie Orthodoxe Saint-Serge, April 1996.

Turcescu, Lucian. "'Person' versus 'Individual', and Other Modern Misreadings of Gregory of Nyssa." *Modern Theology* 18, no. 4 (December 2002): 97–109.

Turner, Robert D. "Foundations for John Zizioulas' Approach to Ecclesial Communion." *Ephemerides Theologicae Lovanienses* 78 (2002): 438–67.

Volf, Miroslav. *After Our Likeness: The Church as the Image of the Trinity.* Grand Rapids, MI: Eerdmans, 1998.

Wilks, John G. F. "The Trinitarian Ontology of John Zizioulas." *Vox Evangelica* 25 (1995): 63–88.

Williams, Rowan D. Review of *Being as Communion. Scottish Journal of Theology* 42 (1989): 101–5.

General

Afanassieff, Nicholas. "The Church Which Presides in Love." In *The Primacy of Peter,* edited John Meyendorff et al., 57–110. London: Faith Press, 1963.

———. "Una Sancta: To the Memory of John XXIII, the Pope of Love." In *Tradition Alive: On the Church and the Christian Life in Our Time: Readings from the Eastern Church*, edited by Michael Plekon, 3–30. New York: Rowman & Littlefield, 2003.

Anatolios, Khaled. *Athanasius: The Coherency of His Thought*. London and New York: Routledge, 1998.

Armstrong, A. H. "Plotinus." In *The Cambridge History of Later Greek and Early Medieval Philosophy*, edited by A. H. Armstrong, 195–268. Cambridge: Cambridge University Press, 1967.

Behr, John. *The Nicene Faith*. Vol. 2 of *The Formation of Christian Theology*. Crestwood, NY: St. Vladimir's Seminary Press, 2004.

———. *The Way to Nicaea*. Vol. 1 of *The Formation of Christian Theology*. Crestwood, NY: St. Vladimir's Seminary Press, 2001.

Bobrinsky, Boris. *The Mystery of the Trinity: Trinitarian Experience and Vision in the Biblical and Patristic Tradition*. Translated by Anthony P. Gythiel. Crestwood, NY: St. Vladimir's Seminary Press, 1999.

———. "Présence réelle et communion eucharistique." *Revue des Sciences philosophiques et théologiques* 53 (1969): 402–20.

———. "Le Saint-Esprit dans la liturgie." *Studia Liturgia* 1 (1962): 47–60.

Bori, P. C. "Mélanges—l'unitè de l'Eglise durant les trois premiers siècles." *Revue d'histoire ecclésiastique* 65 (1970): 56–68.

Carabine, Deirdre. *The Unknown God: Negative Theology in the Platonic Tradition: Plato to Eriugena*. Louvain: Peters Press, 1995.

Carlson, Thomas A. *Indiscretion: Finitude and the Naming of God*. Chicago: University of Chicago Press, 1999.

Clapsis, Emmanuel. *Orthodoxy in Conversation*. Geneva: World Council of Churches, 2000.

Collins, Paul M. *Trinitarian Theology West and East: Karl Barth, the Cappadocian Fathers, and John Zizioulas*. Oxford: Oxford University Press, 2001.

Copleston, Frederick C. *Philosophy in Russia: From Herzen to Lenin and Berdyaev*. Notre Dame, IN: University of Notre Dame Press, 1986.

Cullman, Oscar, and F. J. Leenhardt. *Essays on the Lord's Supper*. Translated by J. G. Davies. Richmond, VA: John Knox Press, 1958.

Davies, Oliver, and Denys Turner, eds. *Silence and the Word: Negative Theology and Incarnation*. Cambridge: Cambridge University Press, 2002.

Edwards, Mark Julien. *Origen against Plato*. Hampshire: Ashgate, 2002.

Evdokimov, Paul. *The Art of the Icon: A Theology of Beauty*. Translated by Fr. Steven Bigham. Torrance, CA: Oakwood, 1990.

Fantino, Jacques. *La Théologie d'Irénée: Lecture des Écritures en réponse à l'exégèse gnostique: Une approche trinitaire*. Paris: Les Éditions du Cerf, 1994

Florovsky, Georges. "Creation and Creaturehood." In *Creation and Redemption*. Vol. 3 of *The Collected Works of Georges Florovsky*, 43–80. Belmont, MA: Nordland, 1976.

———. "Patristics and Modern Theology." In *Procès-verbaux du premier Congrès de Théologie Orthodoxe*, 238–42. Athens, 1939.

———. "St. Athanasius of Alexandria" and "St. Basil the Great." In *The Eastern Fathers of the Fourth Century*. Vol. 7 of *The Collected Works of Georges Florovsky*, 36–58, 72–107. Belmont, MS: Notable & Academic Books, 1987.

———. "St. Gregory Palamas and the Tradition of the Fathers." In *Bible, Church, Tradition: An Eastern Orthodox View*. Vol. 1 of *The Collected Works of Georges Florovsky*, 105–20. Belmont, MA: Nordland, 1972.

Giagkazoglou, Stavros. "Ousia, Hypostaseis, Personal Energies: The Teaching of St. Gregory Palamas on the Uncreated Energies" (in Greek). *Synaxe* 37–38 (1991): 71–78; 39–48.

Golitzin, Alexander. "Dionysius the Areopagite in the Words of Gregory Palamas: On the Question of a 'Christological Corrective' and Related Matters." *St. Vladimir's Theological Quarterly* 46, nos. 2–3 (2002): 163–90.

Grant, Robert. "Irenaeus and Hellenistic Culture." In *After the New Testament*. Philadelphia: Fortress Press, 1967.

de Halleux, André. "'L'église catholique' dans la lettre ignatienne aux Smyrnotes." *Ephemerides Theologicae Lovaniensis* 58 (1982): 5–24.

———. "'Hypostase' et 'personne' dans la formation du dogme trinitaire (ca. 375–81)." *Revue d'histoire ecclésiastique* 79 (1984): 313–69; 625–70.

———. "Personnalisme ou essentialisme trinitaire chez les Pères cappadociens? Une mauvaise controverse." *Revue théologique de Louvain* 17 (1986): 129–55; 265–92.

Harrison, Verna. "Perichoresis in the Greek Fathers." *St. Vladimir's Theological Quarterly* 35 (1991): 53–65.

Hayes, Zachary. *Visions of a Future: A Study of Christian Eschatology*. Wilmington, DE: Michael Glazier, 1989.

Hollywood, Amy. *Sensible Ecstasy: Mysticism, Sexual Difference, and the Demands of History*. Chicago: University of Chicago Press, 2002.

Jüngel, Eberhard. *God as the Mystery of the World*. Translated by Darrell L. Guder. Grand Rapids, MI: Eerdmans, 1983.

Khomiakov, A. S. *The Church is One*. Revised translation by Nicholas Zernov. London, 1968.

Kilmartin, Edward J. *The Eucharist in the Primitive Church*. Englewood Cliffs, NJ: Prentice-Hall, 1965.

Kilpatrick, G. D. *The Eucharist in Bible and Liturgy*. Cambridge: Cambridge University Press, 1983.

Kodell, Jerome. *The Eucharist in the New Testament*. Wilmington, DE: Michael Glazier, 1988.

LaCugna, Catherine Mowry. *God for Us: The Trinity and Christian Life*. New York: HarperCollins, 1991.

LaVerdiere, Eugene. *The Eucharist in the New Testament and the Early Church*. Collegeville, MN: Liturgical Press, 1996.

Leithart, Peter J. "'Framing' Sacramental Theology: Trinity and Symbol." *Westminster Theological Journal* 62, no. 1 (2000): 1–16.

Lewis, Alan E. "The Burial of God: Rupture and Resumption as the Story of Salvation." *Scottish Journal of Theology* 40 (1987): 335–62.

Lialine, Dom Clément. "The Theological Teaching of Gregory Palamas on the Divine Simplicity." *Eastern Churches Quarterly* 6 (1946): 266–87.

Lonergan, Bernard. *Method in Theology*. New York: Herder and Herder, 1972.

Louth, Andrew. *Denys the Areopagite*. London: Geoffrey Chapman, 1989.

Lynch, John J. "*Prosopon* in Gregory of Nyssa: A Theological Word in Transition." *Theological Studies* 40 (1979): 728–38.
McFague, Sallie. *Models of God*. Philadelphia: Fortress Press, 1987.
McGinn, Bernard. *The Foundations of Mysticism*. Vol. 1 of *The Presence of God: A History of Western Christian Mysticism*. New York: Crossroad, 1991.
———. "God as Eros: Metaphysical Foundations of Christian Mysticism." In *New Perspectives on Historical Theology: Essays in Memory of John Meyendorff*, edited by Bradley Nassif, 189–209. Grand Rapids, MI: Eerdmans, 1996.
McIntosh, Mark A. *Mystical Theology*. Oxford: Blackwell, 1998.
Marion, Jean-Luc. *God without Being*. Translated by Thomas Carlson. Chicago: University of Chicago Press, 1991.
———. *Being Given: Toward a Phenomenology of Givenness*. Translated by Jeffrey L. Kosky. Stanford, CA: Stanford University Press, 2002.
Marshall, Bruce D. "Action and Person: Do Palamas and Aquinas Agree about the Spirit?" *St. Vladimir's Theological Quarterly* 39, no. 4 (1995): 379–408.
Mascall, E. L. *Existence and Analogy*. New York: Longmans, Green, 1949.
May, Gerhard. *Creatio Ex Nihilo: The Doctrine of 'Creation out of Nothing' in Early Christian Thought*. Edinburgh: T&T Clark, 1994.
Meyendorff, John. *A Study of Gregory Palamas*. 2d. ed. Translated by George Lawrence. London: Faith Press, 1974.
Moltmann, Jürgen. *The Trinity and the Kingdom*. Translated by Margaret Kohl. San Francisco: HarperCollins, 1981.
Nichols, Aidan. *The Byzantine Gospel: Maximus the Confessor and Modern Scholarship*. Edinburgh: T & T Clark, 1993.
———. *Theology in the Russian Diaspora: Church, Fathers, Eucharist in Nikolai Afanas'ev*. Cambridge: Cambridge University Press, 1989.
Nissiotis, N. "The Importance of the Doctrine of the Trinity for Church Life and Theology." In *Orthodox Ethos*, edited by A. J. Philippou. Oxford: Holywell Press, 1964.
———. "Pneumatologie orthodoxe." In *Le Saint-Esprit*, edited by F. J. Leenhard et al. Geneva: Labor et Fides, 1963.
North American Orthodox-Catholic Theological Consultation. "The *Filioque:* A Church-Dividing Issue?" *St. Vladimir's Theological Quarterly* 48, no. 1 (2004): 93–123.
O'Leary, P. *The Triune Church: A Study in the Ecclesiology of A. S. Khomiakov*. Dublin, 1982.
Ouspensky, Leonid. *Theology of the Icon*. 2 vols. Translated by Anthony Gythiel. Crestwood, NY: St. Vladimir's Seminary Press, 1992.
Papanikolaou, Aristotle. "Byzantium, Orthodoxy, and Democracy." *Journal of the American Academy of Religion* 71, no. 1 (2003): 75–98.
———. "Person, *Kenosis* and Abuse: Hans Urs von Balthasar and Feminist Theologies in Conversation." *Modern Theology* 19, no. 1 (2003): 41–66.
———. "Reasonable Faith and Trinitarian Logic: Faith and Reason in Eastern Orthodox Theology." In *Restoring Faith in Reason*, edited by Laurence Paul Hemming and Susan Frank Parsons, 237–55. Notre Dame, IN: University of Notre Dame Press, 2003.
Pelikan, Jaroslav. "The Place of Maximus Confessor in the History of Christian Thought." In *Maximus Confessor: Actes du Symposium sur Maxime le Confesseur*, edited by F. Heinzer and C. Schönborn, 387–402. Fribourg: Editions Universitaires, 1982.

Perl, Eric D. "Metaphysics and Christology in Maximus Confessor and Eriugena." In *Eriugena: East and West,* edited by Bernard McGinn and Willemien Otten. Notre Dame, IN: University of Notre Dame Press, 1994.

Pettersen, Alvyn. *Athanasius.* Harrisburg, PA: Morehouse, 1995.

Plekon, Michael. *Living Icons: Persons of Faith in the Eastern Church.* Notre Dame, IN: University of Notre Dame Press, 2002.

———. ed. *Tradition Alive: On the Church and the Christian Life in Our Time: Readings from the Eastern Church.* New York: Rowman & Littlefield, 2003.

Rahner, Karl. *The Trinity.* translated by Joseph Donceel. New York: Crossroad, 1997.

Reid, Duncan. *Energies of the Spirit: Trinitarian Models in Eastern Orthodox and Western Theology.* Atlanta: Scholars Press, 1997.

Romanides, John. "Orthodox Ecclesiology According to Alexis Khomiakov." *Greek Orthodox Theological Review* 2 (1956): 57–73.

———. "The Theology of St. Ignatius of Antioch." *Greek Orthodox Theological Review* 7 (1961): 53–77.

Rorem, Paul. *Pseudo-Dionysius: A Commentary on the Texts and an Introduction to Their Influence.* New York: Oxford University Press, 1993.

Rubenstein, Mary-Jane. "Unknow Thyself: Apophaticism, Deconstruction, and Theology after Ontotheology." *Modern Theology* 19, no. 3 (2003): 387–417.

Schmemann, Alexander. *Introduction to Liturgical Theology.* Crestwood, NY: St. Vladimir's Seminary Press, 1986.

———. "Russian Theology: 1920–1972: An Introductory Survey." *St. Vladimir's Theological Quarterly* 16 (1972): 172–93.

Schoedel, William R. "Theological Method in Irenaeus (*Adversus Haereses* 2.25–28)." *Journal of Theological Studies* 35 (1984): 31–49.

Skira, Jaroslav Z. "The Synthesis between Christology and Pneumatology in Modern Orthodox Theology." *Orientalia Christiana Periodica* 68, no. 2 (2002): 435–65.

Smith, T. Allan. "A Century of Eastern Orthodox Theology in the West." *Religious Studies and Theology* 16 (1997): 60–77.

Stead, Christopher. *Philosophy in Christian Antiquity.* Cambridge: Cambridge University Press, 1994.

Taylor, Charles. *Sources of the Self: Toward the Making of Modern Identity.* Cambridge, MA: Harvard University Press, 1989.

Thunberg, Lars. *Man and the Cosmos: The Vision of St. Maximus the Confessor.* Crestwood, NY: St. Vladimir's Seminary Press, 1985.

———. *Microcosm and Mediator: The Theological Anthropology of Maximus the Confessor.* 2d ed. Chicago: Open Court, 1995.

Tillich, Paul. *Dynamics of Faith.* New York: Harper and Brothers, 1958.

Tracy, David. *Blessed Rage for Order: The New Pluralism in Theology,* with a New Preface. Chicago: University of Chicago Press, 1996.

———. *Plurality and Ambiguity.* San Francisco: Harper and Row, 1987.

Tremblay, Réal. *La manifestation et la vision de Dieu selon saint Irénée de Lyon.* Münster Westfalen: Aschendorffsche Buchdruckerei, 1978.

Torrance, Alan J. *Persons in Communion: An Essay on Trinitarian Description and Human Participation, with Special Reference to Volume One of Karl Barth's* Church Dogmatics. Edinburgh: T&T Clark, 1996.

Torrance, Thomas F. *The Christian Doctrine of God, One Being Three Persons.* Edinburgh: T&T Clark, 1996.

———. *The Trinitarian Faith: The Evangelical Theology of the Ancient Catholic Church.* Edinburgh: T&T Clark, 1988.

———. *Trinitarian Perspectives.* Edinburgh: T&T Clark, 1994.

Turner, Denys. *The Darkness of God: Negativity in Christian Mysticism.* Cambridge: Cambridge University Press, 1995.

Valliere, Paul. *Modern Russian Theology: Bukharev, Soloviev, Bulgakov: Orthodox Theology in a New Key.* Grand Rapids, MI: Eerdmans, 2000.

Wendebourg, Dorothea "From the Cappadocian Fathers to Gregory Palamas. The Defeat of Trinitarian Theology." *Studia Patristica* 17, no. 1 (1982): 194–98.

Widdicombe, Peter. *The Fatherhood of God from Origen to Athanasius.* Oxford: Oxford University Press, 1994.

Williams, Anna. *The Ground of Union: Deification in Aquinas and Palamas.* New York: Oxford University Press, 1999.

Williams, George H. "The Neo-Patristic Synthesis of Georges Florovsky." In *Georges Florovsky: Russian Intellectual and Orthodox Churchman,* edited by Andrew Blane, 287–340. Crestwood, NY: St. Vladimir's Seminary Press, 1993.

Williams, J. P. *Denying Divinity: Apophasis in the Patristic Tradition and Soto Zen Buddhist Traditions.* New York: Oxford University Press, 2000.

Williams, Rowan D. "The Deflections of Desire: Negative Theology and Trinitarian Discourse." In *Silence and the Word: Negative Theology and Incarnation,* edited by Oliver Davies and Denys Turner, 115–35. Cambridge: Cambridge University Press, 2002.

———. "The Philosophical Structures of Palamism." *Eastern Churches Review* 9 (1977): 27–44.

———. "*Sapientia* and the Trinity: Reflections on the *De Trinitate.*" In *Collectanea Augustiniana: Mélanges T. J. van Bavel,* edited by B. Bruing, M. Lamberigts, and J. van Houlm, 317–32. Louvain: Leuven University Press, 1990.

———. *Sergii Bulgakov: Towards a Russian Political Theology.* Edinburgh: T&T Clark, 1999.

Yannaras, Christos. "Theology in Present-Day Greece." *St. Vladimir's Theological Quarterly* 16 (1972): 195–214.

Index

Acts
  1:8, 35
  2:17, 172n.112
  2:18, 42
  10:38, 35
Afanasiev, Nicolas, 33
Agoras, Constantine, 95, 192n.27
Agourides, Savas, 94, 159, 204n.105
Akindynus, 168n.68
Anatolios, Khaled, 184n.139
Androutsos, Christos, 10
Anselm, St., 148, 182n.102
apophaticism
  apophatic knowledge, 12–15, 17–22, 25, 30, 101
  apophatic theology vs. apophatic method, 17–18
  and Derrida, 166n.36
  of Greek fathers, 94, 95, 97, 155
  and Heidegger, 166n.36
  of Lossky, 3, 4, 5, 6, 7, 11, 12–15, 17–21, 25, 29, 30, 31, 44, 49–50, 51–53, 58, 59, 62, 63, 4–65, 67–68, 70–71, 89–90, 91–93, 94–95, 98, 102, 102–3, 104–6, 113, 121, 122–24, 125, 126, 127, 130, 133–34, 140–41, 155, 166n.36, 167nn.39, 56, 177nn.4, 11, 13, 181n.93, 183n.124, 191n.227, 192n.18, 193nn.39, 47
  Zizioulas on, 3, 30, 31, 50, 90, 92–93, 94–96, 97, 101, 102–3, 104, 105–6, 133–34, 142, 191nn.1, 15, 192nn.18, 27, 193n.39
Aquinas, Thomas, 192n.27, 204n.104
  Lossky on, 10, 11, 13–14, 19, 21, 27, 29, 70, 155, 163n.2, 166n.36, 169n.82, 170n.88, 181n.101, 183n.114
  on simplicity of God, 27
  on the Trinity, 64, 66–67, 70, 140–41, 181n.101, 182nn.102, 103, 183n.114
Arianism, 73, 79–80, 127, 171n.97
Aristotle, 72, 140
  on substance/*ousia*, 56, 74, 79, 179n.45
Armstrong, A. H., 167n.54
Athanasius of Alexandria, 73–78
  vs. Cappadocian fathers, 5, 11, 21, 79, 80, 155, 187nn.170, 180, 202n.81
  Christology of, 75, 77, 127, 139, 171n.97
  on creation, 21, 75–77, 85, 127, 186n.167
  on divine substance as relational, 74, 79, 80
  on *hypostasis* and *ousia*, 187nn.170, 180
  on Incarnation, 75, 77, 139
  Lossky on, 61, 85
  on nature vs. will of God, 61, 73–75, 85–86, 189n.212
  on salvation, 75, 77, 139
  on the Trinity, 74, 79, 80, 202n.81
  Zizioulas on, 5, 11, 73–78, 79, 82, 171n.97, 184n.139, 186n.158, 187n.180
Augustine, St., 182n.102, 195n.78
  apophaticism of, 18–19
  Lossky on, 11, 18–19, 66, 155, 163n.2, 164n.6
  Zizioulas on, 11, 84, 155, 156, 163n.2, 164n.6

Baillargeon, Gaëtan, 173n.132, 176n.159, 192n.27
Balthasar, Hans Urs von, 10, 191n.227
baptism
  of Jesus Christ, 34, 172n.114
  Lossky on, 46, 117, 118–19, 124, 125
Barlaam, 25, 26, 27, 168n.68
Barnes, Michel René, 181n.101
Barth, Karl, 49, 148, 201n.74

Basil the Great, 25, 78
  Epistle 38, 204n.110
  Epistle 52, 82
  Epistle 236.6, 189n.202
  on *hypostasis*, 83–84, 87, 189n.202
  on *koinonia*, 83, 84, 188n.200, 204n.110
  on mode of existence (*tropos hyparxeos*), 181n.91
  On the Holy Spirit, 82, 100–101, 188n.200, 193n.31, 204n.110
  on *prosopon*, 83–84, 87, 189n.202
  on the Trinity, 82–84, 188nn.194, 200, 204n.110
  See also Cappadocian fathers
Berdyaev, Nicolai, 159–60
Bobrinsky, Boris, 33
Boethius, 115, 116, 156
Buber, Martin, 159–60, 205n.117
Bulgakov, Sergius, 1, 10, 62, 70, 181n.101

Cappadocian fathers
  vs. Athanasius, 5, 11, 21, 79, 80, 155, 187nn.170, 180, 202n.81
  Lossky on, 17, 94–95, 181n.101
  on the Trinity, 54, 73, 78–86, 94–95, 130, 156–57, 160, 177n.11, 181n.101, 187nn.170, 180, 198n.1, 202n.81
  Zizioulas on, 5, 11, 73, 75, 78–86, 90, 96–97, 100–101, 106, 126–27, 130, 134, 138, 156, 187nn.170, 180, 185, 188nn.193, 194, 197, 200, 189nn.202, 206, 193n.31, 198n.1, 204n.110, 205n.111
  See also Basil the Great; Greek fathers; Gregory of Nazianzus; Gregory of Nyssa
Carlson, Thomas, 166n.36, 170n.88
Chalcedon, Council of, 45, 47, 99, 107–8, 117, 119, 153, 192n.27
Char, René, 43
Clément, Olivier, 181nn.93, 96, 194n.64
Clement of Alexandria, 11, 17, 18, 21, 29, 71–72
Collins, Paul M., 201n.74
Congar, Yves, 2, 10, 170n.90

1 Corinthians
  2:4, 35
  15:44–45, 172n.112
2 Corinthians
  1:22, 172n.112
  13:13, 35
Corrigan, Kevin, 167n.54
Cullman, Oscar, 34

Daniélou, Jean, 2, 10
death
  Lossky on, 110, 114–15, 116, 195n.83, 197n.104
  relationship to personhood, 144, 145, 146
  Zizioulas on, 40, 41, 42, 76, 77, 121–22, 134–35, 141, 142, 144–45, 145, 146, 149–50, 157, 158, 188n.191
deification (*theosis*), 30, 76, 127, 194n.64
  Greek fathers on, 2, 5, 13, 25–27, 92, 106, 116, 165n.14, 196n.101
  Lossky on, 13, 25–27, 36, 45–46, 66, 69, 92, 106–7, 108, 111, 117, 118–19, 124, 125, 126, 172n.117, 177n.188, 181n.98
  of Theotokos, 45–46, 177n.188
Derrida, Jacques, 166n.36
Descartes, René, 105
Dionysius the Areopagite
  apophatic theology of, 17–18, 19, 21–22, 23, 192n.27
  cataphatic theology of, 15, 18
  darkness metaphor in, 23–24
  on energies of God (*proodoi/dunameis*), 15–16, 25
  on God as *hyperagathos*, 20
  Lossky on, 11, 13–20, 18, 21–22, 23–24, 25, 155, 165nn.14, 15, 20, 168n.65
  on unions (*enoseis*) and distinctions (*diakriseis*) in God, 15, 25
divine-human communion
  and Holy Spirit, 2, 8, 11, 31, 37–38
  Lossky on, 1, 2, 3–4, 5, 7–8, 10–11, 12, 13, 14, 18, 19–28, 29–30, 44, 45–46, 47, 49, 52, 59, 63–64, 69, 70–71, 89,

91, 93, 102–3, 104, 105, 106–8, 111–12, 114, 116, 118–19, 120, 122–25, 126, 139, 154–55, 158, 160–61, 166n.36, 167n.43, 176n.179, 196n.99, 197n.103
    relationship to theological epistemology, 3–4, 9, 11, 12, 13, 14–15, 18, 21–22, 30–31, 44, 46, 47–48, 49–50, 89, 104–5, 152
    Zizioulas on, 1, 2, 3–4, 5, 7–8, 32, 37–38, 40, 44, 45, 46–48, 49, 73, 74–75, 76, 77–78, 79, 88–89, 90, 91, 93, 96, 98, 102–3, 104, 117–20, 124, 125–27, 134, 139, 145, 146, 152, 153, 154–55, 157, 158, 160–61, 172n.117, 195n.95, 196n.101
Dostoevsky, Fyodor, 203n.95

ecclesiology
    the Church as Body of Christ, 33, 34, 35, 37, 38, 41, 44, 45, 46, 47, 111, 113, 118–19, 170n.89, 171n.98, 174nn.134, 140, 184n.135
    and Holy Spirit, 32–33, 34–35, 36
    of Lossky, 33, 47, 105, 111, 113, 118–19, 177nn.185, 187, 188, 194n.61
    of Zizioulas, 32–33, 34–35, 36–37, 38, 40–41, 42–43, 44, 45, 46–47, 101, 105, 118, 170nn.89, 94, 95, 171n.98, 173nn.125, 128, 132, 174nn.134, 136, 139, 175n.159, 184n.135
Eckhart, Meister, 165n.14
ecumenical movement, 1–2
ekstasis
    Heidegger on, 198n.5, 201n.69
    Lossky on, 5, 15, 18, 19–24, 92, 114, 132, 137–38, 198n.5
    Zizioulas on, 7, 86–87, 88, 100, 117, 132, 137–38, 142, 143–45, 146, 150, 153–54
Ephesians 1:14, 172n.112
eschatology
    and the eucharist, 31–32, 33, 36–37, 38
    and Holy Spirit, 34–35, 36–38, 41, 42, 45, 172nn.112, 117, 173n.132, 174n.139

    Kingdom of God, 31, 34, 36–37, 40, 42, 174n.139
    of Lossky, 24
    of Zizioulas, 31–32, 33, 34–35, 36–37, 38, 39–41, 42–43, 44, 45, 46, 71, 170nn.90, 95, 172n.112, 173n.132, 174n.139, 175nn.141, 143, 148, 149, 159, 206n.125
essence (*ousia/physis*)
    of God, 4–5, 6, 11, 15, 16, 19, 20, 21, 24–27, 28–29, 44, 50–65, 66–67, 68–69, 73–75, 79, 85–86, 87, 92, 96, 97–98, 101n.101, 103–4, 106, 114, 119–20, 121, 122, 123, 124, 126, 127, 131, 132, 135–36, 140–41, 155, 168nn.68, 71, 169n.82, 180n.82, 192n.18, 196nn.99, 100, 198n.3, 199n.18
    Greek fathers on, 54, 55, 79, 82–83, 96–97, 130, 157, 187n.170, 188n.197, 198n.1
    vs. *hypostasis*, 53–54, 55–59, 68–69, 81, 178n.33
eucharist, the
    and Body of Christ, 11, 31, 32, 33, 40, 41, 45, 46, 47, 50, 71, 72, 73, 83–84, 88, 98, 100, 104, 158, 170n.89, 175n.141, 184n.135
    and the eschaton, 31–32, 33, 36–37, 38
    and Holy Spirit, 31, 33, 34–35
    as icon, 39–41, 175n.141
    Ignatius on, 72, 73, 74, 171n.97, 184n.137
    Irenaeus on, 72, 73, 74, 171n.97, 184nn.135, 137, 139
    Zizioulas on, 3, 4, 5, 6, 11, 31–32, 33, 34–41, 42, 45, 46–47, 50, 71, 72, 73, 77–78, 83–84, 88–89, 90, 94, 96, 98, 100, 101, 104, 120, 126, 127, 134, 146, 147, 149–50, 152, 155, 158, 170nn.89, 92, 94, 95, 171n.97, 173nn.125, 132, 174nn.139, 140, 175nn.141, 143, 149, 176n.159, 184nn.135, 137, 139, 186n.169, 192n.27, 202n.89
Eunomianism, 78, 79–80, 133

Evagrius Ponticus, 21, 29
Every, George, 70
existentialism, 7, 129, 155, 159–60, 204n.105

faith, 28, 51, 69
Fantino, Jacques, 184n.135
Fermer, Richard M., 198n.2
Feuerbach, Ludwig, 105
filioque, the
   Lossky on, 50, 65–71, 93, 101–2, 106–7, 111–12, 113, 169n.82, 173n.128, 181nn.95, 96, 183n.120
   and Orthodox theology, 65–67, 68–69, 102, 183n.123
   Zizioulas on, 65, 93, 101–2, 181n.95
Florensky, Pavel, 95
Florovsky, Georges
   on Athanasius, 189n.212
   ecclesiology of, 33
   on Greek fathers, 1, 9
   on neo-scholasticism, 1
   relationship with Zizioulas, 1, 9

Gilson, Etienne, 165n.14, 169n.82
God
   as Creator, 5–6, 16, 17, 19–20, 25–26, 36, 51–52, 61, 71, 73–77, 85, 88–89, 106, 113, 120–21, 150, 152, 164n.9, 169n.82, 170n.90, 185n.149, 186nn.160, 161, 165, 167, 197n.105, 201n.71, 203n.93
   energies of, 4–5, 6, 11, 13, 15–17, 20, 24–27, 28–29, 44, 47–48, 50, 51, 63–64, 69, 92, 93, 96, 97, 98, 99, 100, 103–4, 106, 108, 109, 111, 117, 118–20, 121, 122, 123–25, 126, 155, 165n.14, 168n.68, 169n.82, 191n.227, 192n.18, 196nn.99, 100, 101, 197n.103
   essence of, 4–5, 6, 11, 15, 16, 19, 20, 21, 24–27, 28–29, 44, 50–65, 66–67, 68–69, 73–75, 79, 85–86, 87, 92, 95, 96, 97–98, 101n.101, 103–4, 106, 114, 119–20, 121, 122, 123, 124, 126, 127, 131, 132, 135–36, 140–41, 155, 168nn.68, 71, 169n.82, 180n.82, 192n.18, 196nn.99, 100, 198n.3, 199n.18
   existence of, 144, 146–47, 203nn.92, 93
   freedom of, 7, 16, 57–58, 60–61, 62–63, 64–65, 70, 71, 74–75, 76, 77–78, 79, 81–82, 84–87, 88, 89, 90, 92, 94, 95, 102, 103, 104, 107, 109, 110, 114, 117, 118, 120, 121, 122–24, 132, 133–35, 138, 142, 147–54, 157–58, 183n.124, 186nn.158, 161, 187n.170, 189nn.212, 222, 223, 195n.78, 198n.3, 199nn.17, 19, 202n.83, 203n.92, 205n.124, 206n.125
   grace of, 29, 46, 47, 196n.99
   human being as image of, 114, 115, 116, 117, 120, 139, 153, 195n.78, 202n.89, 204n.110
   immutability of, 75, 185n.151
   love of, 60–61, 62–63, 64–65, 70, 76, 77–78, 82, 84–85, 86–87, 88, 89, 90, 92, 103, 107, 109, 114, 121, 122–23, 132, 135, 136, 137–39, 141–42, 183n.124, 190nn.218, 222, 197n.103, 200n.44, 201n.58, 202n.83, 205n.113
   omnipotence of, 185n.151
   simplicity of, 26–27, 63, 79, 127, 168n.68
   as simultaneously transcendent and immanent, 2, 3, 4, 5–6, 11, 14–15, 19–21, 22, 24–25, 27–28, 29–31, 37–38, 44, 49, 50–53, 59, 70–71, 88–89, 90, 92, 104, 105, 123–24, 127, 131, 155, 166n.36
   and truth, 31, 32
   as unity-in-distinction, 4–5, 23, 52–53, 58–59, 65, 68–69, 70, 89, 131, 132–33, 202n.83
   will of, 51, 61–63, 64, 73–75, 77, 85–86, 116, 134, 138, 190n.214, 203nn.92, 93
   See also Holy Spirit; Jesus Christ; theological epistemology; Trinity, the
Grant, Robert, 184n.133
Greek fathers
   apophaticism of, 94, 95, 97, 155

and contemporary Orthodox
theologians, 1, 2, 7, 9–11, 129,
154–61, 204n.105
on deification (*theosis*), 2, 5, 13, 25–27,
92, 106, 116, 165n.14, 196n.101
eschatology in, 32
and the eucharist, 32
on *hypostasis*, 5, 7, 53–54, 55–57, 61, 79,
80–84, 90, 115, 116, 126–27, 130,
131, 135–36, 157, 178n.32, 179n.47,
187nn.170, 184, 185, 189n.202, 198n.1,
204n.110
Lossky on, 1, 7, 9–11, 12, 13, 17, 21, 24,
25, 29, 53–57, 58, 61, 94–95, 108, 115,
118, 129–32, 135, 140, 154–61, 164n.6,
165n.14, 179nn.47, 52, 187n.188,
193n.40, 195n.78, 198nn.1, 4
on mode of existence (*tropos hyparxeos*),
6, 27, 87–88, 104, 131, 181n.91,
191n.227, 204n.110
on monarchy of the Father, 82, 84–87,
90, 160, 205n.111
on *ousia*, 54, 55, 79, 82–83, 96–97, 130,
157, 187n.170, 188n.197, 198n.1
on *perichoresis*, 108, 193n.47
on *prosopon*, 53–55, 81–82, 83–84, 87, 130,
131, 157, 189n.202, 198n.1
on the Trinity, 32, 53–56, 58, 73, 78–86,
102, 129–30, 131–32, 134, 140, 156–57,
160, 177n.11, 181n.101, 187nn.170,
180, 184, 198n.1, 202n.81,
205n.111
Zizioulas on, 1, 5, 6, 7, 9–11, 32, 38,
40, 71–75, 78–88, 90, 94–95, 96–97,
102, 120, 122, 129–32, 134, 135, 138,
147, 154–61, 164nn.5, 6, 171n.97,
184nn.135, 137, 139, 185n.140,
186n.158, 187nn.180, 185, 188,
188nn.193, 194, 197, 200, 189nn.202,
206, 191n.227, 195n.78, 196n.101,
198nn.1, 4, 204n.110, 205n.111
Gregory of Nazianzus, 25, 78
on the Trinity, 84, 85–86, 157, 178n.37,
179n.60, 180n.72, 190n.214, 205n.111
See also Cappadocian fathers

Gregory of Nyssa, 78, 114, 156–57, 188n.197,
195n.78, 198n.1
Ad Ablabium, 205n.111
Epistle 38, 204n.110
See also Cappadocian fathers
Guichardan, S., 29

Halleux, A. de, 188n.194, 191n.1
Hankey, Wayne J., 191n.4
Harrison, Nonna Verna, 193n.47, 196n.101
Hayes, Zachary, 170n.90
Heidegger, Martin, 205n.116
on *Dasein,* 57, 198n.5
on *ekstasis,* 198n.5, 201n.69
on onto-theology, 166n.36
history
and Holy Spirit, 34, 35, 36–37, 38, 42
and icon, 39–40
Zizioulas on, 34, 35, 36–37, 38, 39–40,
42–43, 44, 71, 72–73, 158, 173nn.123,
132, 135, 175nn.149, 159
Holy Spirit
and divine-human communion, 2, 8,
11, 31, 37–38
and ecclesiology, 32–33, 34–35, 36
economy of, 36, 37–38
eschatological role of, 34–35, 36–38, 41,
42, 45, 172nn.112, 117, 173n.132,
174n.139
and the eucharist, 31, 33, 34–35
eucharistic-eschatological type of
pneumatology, 34–35
the *filioque,* 50, 65–71, 93, 101–2, 102,
106–7, 111–12, 113, 169n.82, 173n.128,
181nn.95, 96, 183nn.120, 123
and history, 34, 35, 36–37, 38, 42
Lossky on, 2, 33, 36, 37–38, 45, 46, 50,
65–71, 93, 106–7, 111–12, 118, 119,
124, 169n.82, 172n.117, 173n.128,
174n.135, 177nn.187, 188, 193nn.42,
76, 194nn.61, 65, 200n.39
missionary-historical type of
pneumatology, 34–35, 36, 173n.132
at Pentecost, 35, 46, 107, 112
procession of, 58, 61, 63, 64, 66–67, 85,

Holy Spirit (*cont.*)
    88, 102, 134, 140, 150–51, 157, 177n.10, 179n.58, 181nn.95, 96, 100, 101, 182n.103, 200n.39
    relationship to the Son, 32–38, 42, 43, 45, 46, 51, 65–71, 93, 100, 101–2, 106–7, 111–13, 118, 169n.82, 170n.89, 171n.99, 172n.114, 173nn.125, 128, 181nn.95, 96, 98, 183nn.120, 123, 200n.39
    Zizioulas on, 2, 31, 32–38, 41, 42–43, 45, 46, 50, 65, 93, 100, 101, 102, 106, 112, 118, 134, 150–51, 157, 158, 170n.89, 171n.95, 172nn.112, 114, 117, 173nn.125, 128, 174n.134, 139, 193n.42
    See also Trinity, the

hypostasis
    Basil on, 83–84, 87, 189n.202
    Greek fathers on, 5, 7, 53–54, 55–57, 61, 79, 80–84, 90, 115, 116, 126–27, 130, 131, 135–36, 157, 178n.32, 179n.47, 187nn.170, 184, 185, 189n.202, 198n.1, 204n.110
    of Jesus Christ, 43, 44, 46, 47, 111
    Lossky on, 6–7, 52, 55–56, 59, 65, 67, 68–69, 107, 115–16, 119, 130–31, 135–37, 138, 140, 159, 177n.2, 178nn.32, 33, 179nn.45, 49, 52, 196n.99, 198n.1, 199nn.18, 21
    vs. *ousia*, 53–54, 55–59, 68–69, 81, 178n.33
    and personhood, 43, 44, 46, 47, 56–57, 65, 68–69, 80–84, 130–32, 135–37, 138, 142, 144–45, 150, 159, 177n.2, 179n.47
    and *prosopon*, 81–82, 83–84, 130–31, 135, 157
    Zizioulas on, 5, 6–7, 43, 44, 80–84, 86, 87, 88, 98, 106, 117–18, 119, 126–27, 130, 135–37, 142, 143, 144–45, 150, 157, 158, 178n.32, 187n.184, 188n.200, 189n.208, 195n.83

icon
    iconoclastic controversy, 175n.141
    Marion on, 42, 43–44
    Zizioulas on, 31, 38–44, 45, 173n.132, 175nn.141, 143, 148, 149, 159, 176n.169

Ignatius of Antioch, 11, 78, 79, 155, 171n.98
    on the eucharist, 72, 73, 74, 171n.97, 184n.137
    on truth, 72, 73

Incarnation
    Athanasius on, 75, 77, 139
    as communication, 25
    Lossky on, 2, 4–5, 11, 12, 13, 14–15, 16, 17, 22, 25, 28, 29–30, 31, 36, 44, 45, 46, 50, 51, 53, 107–8, 112, 113, 116, 119, 124–25, 139, 164n.11, 165n.28
    Zizioulas on, 2, 30, 31, 36, 37, 38, 43, 44, 75, 77, 101, 117, 139, 153, 158

Irenaeus of Lyon, 11, 78, 79, 155, 186n.158
    on the eucharist, 72, 73, 74, 171n.97, 184nn.135, 137, 139
    on truth, 72, 73, 184n.133

Jesus Christ
    Athanasius on, 75, 77, 127, 139, 171n.97
    baptism of, 34, 172n.114
    birth of, 34
    the Church as Body of, 33, 34, 35, 37, 38, 41, 44, 45, 46, 47, 111, 113, 118–19, 170n.89, 171n.98, 174nn.134, 140, 184n.135
    corporate personality of, 37, 38, 71, 100, 171n.98
    the eucharist and the Body of, 11, 31, 32, 33, 40, 41, 45, 46, 47, 50, 71, 72, 73, 83–84, 88, 98, 100, 104, 158, 170n.89, 175n.141, 184n.135
    hypostasis/person of, 43, 44, 46, 47, 111
    as icon, 43–44, 45
    and *kenosis*, 7, 108–11, 113–14, 116, 152–54, 203n.98
    as *logos*, 51–52, 71–72
    Lossky on, 6, 33, 91–92, 106–11, 114, 115–17, 118–19, 124, 153, 169n.82, 173n.128, 177nn.185, 187, 191n.227, 193n.40, 194nn.64, 65, 203n.98
    Resurrection of, 34, 38, 43, 46, 47, 101, 184n.135
    as Savior, 43, 107

union of created and uncreated in, 13, 38, 43, 92, 96, 98, 153
union of divine and human in, 2, 8, 11, 12, 38, 45, 91–92, 96, 107–8, 111, 116, 117, 119, 124, 153
Zizioulas on, 6, 31, 32–38, 33, 36, 37, 42, 43–44, 45, 46–47, 50, 71, 77, 88–89, 90, 99, 100, 101, 102, 106, 117–18, 126, 127, 153, 157, 170nn.89, 95, 171n.98, 172n.114, 173n.125, 174nn.134, 135, 139, 191n.227, 192n.18, 195n.95
See also Incarnation; Theotokos; Trinity, the
John
1:6, 35
1:14, 40
John of Damascus, 11, 56, 61, 108, 138, 155, 175n.145
John Paul II, 183n.123
Jugie, M., 29
Justin Martyr, 11, 29, 71–72, 74

Kant, Immanuel, 105
kenosis
and Jesus Christ, 7, 108–11, 113–14, 116, 152–54, 203n.98
Lossky on, 7, 108–11, 113–15, 116–17, 129, 151, 152–54, 195n.76, 203n.98
relationship to personhood, 7, 108–11, 113–15, 116–17, 151, 152–54, 195n.76
Zizioulas on, 153
Khomiakov, A. S., 33
Kierkegaard, Søren, 159–60

Laats, Alar, 167n.56, 183n.120, 197nn.108, 109
LaCugna, Catherine Mowry, 178n.16
LaVerdiere, Eugene, 170n.94
law of non-contradiction, 27, 28–29, 30, 44
Levinas, Emmanuel, 205n.116
Lewis, Alan E., 203n.100
Lialine, Dom Clément, 169n.84
Liturgy of St. John the Chrysostom, 42
logic, law of non-contradiction, 27, 28–29, 30, 44

Lossky, Vladimir
on antinomic theology, 4–5, 11, 20–21, 27–30, 44, 49–50, 51–53, 54, 56, 59, 62, 63, 68–69, 70–71, 89–90, 125, 133–34, 164n.11
on apokatastasis, 121, 122
apophaticism of, 3, 4, 5, 6, 7, 11, 12–15, 17–21, 25, 29, 30, 31, 44, 49–50, 51–53, 58, 59, 62, 63, 64–65, 67–68, 70–71, 89–90, 91–93, 94–95, 98, 102, 102–3, 104–6, 113, 121, 122–24, 125, 126, 127, 130, 133–34, 140–41, 155, 166n.36, 167nn.39, 56, 177nn.4, 11, 13, 181n.93, 183n.124, 191n.227, 192n.18, 193nn.39, 47
on Aquinas, 10, 11, 13–14, 19, 21, 27, 29, 70, 155, 163n.2, 166n.36, 169n.82, 170n.88, 181n.101, 183n.114
on artists, 143, 200n.51
on Athanasius, 61, 85
on Augustine, 11, 18–19, 66, 155, 163n.2, 164n.6
on baptism, 46, 117, 118–19, 124, 125
on cataphatic theology, 12–20, 21, 25, 30, 44
Christology of, 6, 33, 91–92, 106–11, 114, 115–17, 118–19, 124, 153, 169n.82, 173n.128, 177nn.185, 187, 191n.227, 193n.40, 194nn.64, 65, 203n.98
creation theology of, 6, 106, 120–22, 191n.227, 197n.106
on death, 110, 114–15, 116, 195n.83, 197n.104
on deification (*theosis*), 13, 25–27, 36, 45–46, 66, 69, 92, 106–7, 108, 111, 117, 118–19, 124, 125, 126, 172n.117, 177n.188, 181n.98
on Dionysius, 11, 13–20, 18, 21–22, 23–24, 25, 155, 165nn.14, 15, 20, 168n.65
on divine-human communion, 1, 2, 3–4, 5, 7–8, 10–11, 12, 13, 14, 18, 19–28, 29–30, 44, 45–46, 47, 49, 52, 59, 63–64, 69, 70–71, 89, 91, 93, 102–3, 104, 105, 106–8, 111–12, 114, 116, 118–19, 120, 122–25, 126, 139,

Lossky, Vladimir (*cont.*)
    154–55, 158, 160–61, 166n.36,
    167n.43, 176n.179, 196n.99, 197n.103
on divine simplicity, 26–27
ecclesiology of, 33, 47, 105, 111, 113,
    118–19, 177nn.185, 187, 188, 194n.61
on economy of the Son, 106–12
on economy of the Spirit, 36, 37–38,
    111–12, 173n.128, 174n.135, 193n.42
and ecumenical movement, 1–2,
    181n.101
on *ekstasis*, 5, 15, 18, 19–24, 92, 114, 132,
    137–38, 198n.5
eschatology of, 24
on faith, 28, 51, 69
on the *filioque*, 50, 65–71, 93, 101–2,
    106–7, 111–12, 113, 169n.82, 173n.128,
    181nn.95, 96, 183n.120
on God's energies, 4–5, 6, 11, 15–16,
    24–27, 28–29, 44, 47–48, 50, 63–64,
    69, 92, 93, 98, 99, 100, 103–4, 106,
    107, 108, 109, 111, 117, 118–20, 121,
    122, 123–25, 126, 155, 169nn.82, 84,
    191n.227, 192n.18, 196nn.99, 100,
    197nn.103, 106
on God's essence, 4–5, 6, 11, 15–16, 19,
    24–27, 28–29, 44, 47–48, 50, 53, 56,
    62–64, 68, 69, 92, 93, 98, 99, 103–4,
    106, 119, 121, 122, 123, 124, 125, 126,
    131–33, 140–41, 155, 169nn.82, 84,
    192n.18, 196n.99, 198n.3, 199nn.18, 19
on God's freedom, 57–58, 60–61,
    62–63, 64–65, 70, 90, 92, 94, 95, 103,
    104, 118, 120, 121, 122–24, 132–33,
    135, 138, 139, 141, 183n.124, 195n.78,
    198nn.3, 5, 199n.19
on God's love, 60–61, 62–63, 64–65, 70,
    90, 92, 103, 104, 121, 122–23, 124, 132,
    138, 139, 183n.124, 197n.103
on God's will, 61–63, 64, 85
on Greek fathers, 1, 7, 9–11, 12, 13, 17,
    21, 25, 29, 53–57, 58, 61, 94–95, 108,
    115, 118, 129–32, 135, 140, 154–61,
    164n.6, 165n.14, 179nn.47, 52,
    181n.101, 187n.188, 193n.40, 195n.78,
    198nn.1, 4

on the Holy Spirit, 2, 33, 36, 37–38, 45,
    46, 50, 65–71, 93, 106–7, 111–12, 118,
    119, 124, 169n.82, 172n.117, 173n.128,
    174n.135, 177nn.187, 188, 193nn.42,
    76, 194nn.61, 65, 200n.39
on homoousios, 54
on human personhood, 103, 109, 111,
    114–17, 118–19, 139, 193n.40, 198n.2,
    200n.31
on *hyper*-essence/*hyperousia* of God, 6,
    15–16, 44, 50, 53, 56, 62–64, 68, 103,
    106, 114, 123
on *hypostasis*, 6–7, 52, 55–56, 59, 65, 67,
    68–69, 107, 115–16, 119, 130–31,
    135–37, 138, 140, 159, 177n.2,
    178nn.32, 33, 179nn.45, 49, 52,
    196n.99, 198n.1, 199nn.18, 21
on the Incarnation, 2, 4–5, 11, 12, 13,
    14–15, 16, 17, 22, 25, 28, 29–30, 31,
    36, 44, 45, 46, 50, 51, 53, 107–8, 112,
    113, 116, 119, 124–25, 139, 164n.11,
    165n.28
on Irenaeus, 11
on *kenosis* in human personhood,
    114–15, 116–17
on *kenosis* of the Son, 7, 108–11, 113–14,
    152–54, 203n.98
on *kenosis* of the Spirit, 113–14, 152–54,
    195n.76
on light and darkness, 23–24, 167n.56
on logical rules, 27, 28–29, 30, 44
on mode of existence (*tropos hyparxeos*),
    27, 64, 98, 104, 109, 180n.88, 181n.91,
    191n.227, 200n.39
on monarchy of the Father, 58–63,
    64–65, 68, 70, 89–90, 103, 132–34,
    135, 140, 181n.101
on nature/person distinction, 4–5,
    45–46, 50, 53–65, 68–69, 92, 107, 109,
    111, 114, 115–16, 117, 119, 124, 130,
    132–34, 135–36, 138, 139–41, 179n.52,
    181n.101, 183n.124, 194n.73, 198n.3,
    199n.18, 200n.31
on Origen, 11, 17, 18–19, 21, 29, 155,
    164n.6
on original sin, 114–15, 199n.23

on otherness, 44, 114
on *ousia,* 55–58, 178n.33, 198n.1, 198n.3, 199nn.18, 19
on Palamas, 11, 13, 16, 19, 23–24, 25, 26, 27, 29, 155, 168nn.65, 71, 169n.82, 169n.84, 196n.100
on personhood, 4–5, 6–7, 45–46, 50, 51–53, 56–63, 65, 66, 67, 68–69, 70, 89–90, 91–92, 93, 94–96, 103–5, 107, 109–11, 112, 113–17, 118–19, 121, 122–25, 127, 129–42, 155–61, 172n.117, 177n.13, 179nn.45, 52, 180n.72, 181nn.93, 101, 183n.124, 190n.215, 192nn.18, 27, 193nn.40, 47, 194nn.73, 83, 196n.100, 198nn.2, 4, 199nn.19, 21, 200n.31, 200n.51
on piety, 26, 168n.71
on *prosopon,* 54–55, 56, 130, 178nn.31, 32
on rationalism in theology, 1, 2, 10, 11, 13–14, 16, 19–20, 21–23, 26, 28–29, 51, 52–53, 66–67, 69–70, 90, 92, 95, 96, 101, 102, 103, 122, 133, 140–41, 154–55, 163n.2, 166n.36, 170n.88, 184n.133
on revelation, 12, 14–15, 22, 28, 50, 54, 56, 69, 70, 89, 92, 98, 101, 107, 164nn.9, 11, 180n.79
on Russian religious philosophy, 1, 10, 94, 95
on salvation, 24, 28, 63–64, 69, 91, 99, 103, 106, 107, 111, 112, 114–17, 118–20, 123, 124–25, 127, 139, 191n.227, 192n.18, 194nn.64, 65
on sexuality, 114–15, 195n.83
theological epistemology of, 3–4, 10, 11, 12–30, 29, 44, 45–46, 47–48, 49–50, 64–67, 92–93, 102–3, 104–6, 120, 172n.117, 181n.93
on the Theotokos, 45–46, 47, 177nn.185, 188
on the Trinity, 2–3, 4, 5–6, 7–8, 12, 16–17, 22, 23, 28, 36, 47–48, 49–71, 89–90, 91–102, 103–15, 117, 122–23, 126–27, 130–42, 164n.11, 165n.28, 177nn.2, 4, 10, 11, 13, 178n.37, 179nn.49, 52, 58, 180nn.72, 77, 80, 181nn.91, 93, 95, 96, 98, 101, 183n.124, 192n.27, 194n.73, 199n.18, 200nn.31, 39
on truth, 54, 69, 177n.188
Lossky vs. Zizioulas on:
apophaticism, 3, 30, 31, 50, 90, 92–93, 94–96, 102–3, 104–6, 126, 191n.227, 192n.18, 193n.39
Christology, 106, 117–18, 191n.227
creation theology, 120–22, 191n.227
divine-human communion, 2, 3–4, 5, 7–8, 9, 10–11, 30–31, 44–45, 46–48, 71, 89, 91, 93, 102–3, 104, 105, 118–20, 122, 124, 126–27, 131, 139, 154–55, 158, 160–61
ecclesiology, 33
ecumenical movement, 1–2
the *filioque,* 65, 101–2, 181n.95
God's energies, 6, 93, 100, 104, 119–20, 121, 122, 192n.18, 196n.100
Greek fathers, 7, 9–11, 129–30, 154–61, 164n.6, 198n.4
the Holy Spirit, 36, 37–38, 46, 65, 101–2, 106, 112, 118, 172n.117, 174n.135, 181n.95
mode of existence (*tropos hyparxeos*), 98, 180n.82, 181n.91, 191n.227
nothingness, 197n.106
personhood, 6–7, 91, 94–96, 103–5, 122, 129, 130–32, 135–42, 143, 154, 155–56, 158–59, 187n.188, 190n.215, 191n.227, 192nn.18, 27, 198n.4, 200n.51
prosopon, 178nn.31, 32
rationalism in theology, 1, 2, 10, 11, 154–55, 163n.2
salvation, 104, 106, 117–20, 126–27, 191n.227
theological epistemology, 3–4, 9, 11, 30, 44–45, 47–48, 49–50, 65, 91–93, 102–3, 104–5, 120, 172n.117
the Trinity, 2–3, 4, 5–6, 36, 37–38, 47–48, 49–50, 68, 70, 91–102, 103–5, 112, 118, 126–27, 130–33, 135, 139–42, 192n.27, 198n.3
Lubac, Henri de, 2, 10

Luke, gospel of
    4:14, 35
    24:49, 35
    birth narrative in, 34
Lynch, John, 187n.170, 198n.1

Macmurray, John, 159, 205n.117
Marcel, Gabriel, 2, 159–60
Marion, Jean-Luc, 93, 166n.36, 167n.39, 170n.88
    on icon, 42, 43–44
Maritain, Jacques, 159–60
Mark, gospel of, 172n.114
    birth narrative in, 34
Marshall, Bruce D., 204n.104
Mascall, E. L., *Existence and Analogy*, 169n.82
Maximus the Confessor, 11, 25, 155, 165n.14, 175n.141, 190n.214
    Christology of, 108, 165n.14
    on creation as the *idea thelemata* of God, 122
    diaphora (difference)/*diairesis* (division) distinction, 137, 200n.24
    on *gnomic* will vs. natural will, 110, 116
    on mode of existence (*tropos hyparxeos*), 87–88, 190n.224, 191n.227
    on the Trinity, 60, 87–88, 190n.224, 191n.227
McFague, Sallie, 176n.169
McGinn, Bernard, 166n.36, 167n.54
McPartlan, Paul, 171n.98, 173n.132, 192n.27, 193n.35, 199n.17
Meyendorff, John, 165nn.14, 20
Milbank, John, 93
mode of existence (*tropos hyparxeos*)
    Greek fathers on, 6, 27, 87–88, 104, 131, 181n.91, 191n.227, 204n.110
    Lossky on, 27, 64, 98, 104, 109, 180n.88, 181n.91, 191n.227, 200n.39
    Maximus on, 87–88, 190n.224, 191n.227
    Zizioulas on, 87–88, 89, 104, 131, 141, 153, 157–58, 180n.88, 181n.91, 186n.169, 190n.223
Moltmann, Jürgen, 203n.100

Monophysitism, 107
Mounier, E., 159–60

neo-platonism, 26, 94, 165n.15
    the One in, 13, 18–19, 23, 54, 81, 167n.54
Nestorianism, 107
Nichols, Aidan, 190n.214
Nissiotis, Nikos, 33, 204n.105
nothingness, 127
    Zizioulas on, 75–77, 88, 121–22, 197n.106
    Zizioulas on creation *ex nihilo*, 75–77, 121, 185n.149, 186nn.158, 160, 161, 165, 167, 169, 197n.105, 201n.71

onto-theology, 93, 166n.36, 170n.88
Origen, 80, 185n.151
    apophaticism of, 18–19
    Lossky on, 11, 17, 18–19, 21, 29, 155, 164n.6
    on the Trinity, 187nn.170, 184
    Zizioulas on, 11, 71–72, 74, 78, 155, 164n.6
Orthodox theology
    apokatastasis in, 121, 122
    deification in, 25–27, 30, 66
    divine-human communion in, 2, 5, 7–8, 13, 155
    ecclesiology in, 33
    and the *filioque*, 65–67, 68–69, 102, 183n.123
    God's energies in, 6, 13, 15–16, 25, 93, 106, 108, 119–20, 120, 155, 165n.14, 196nn.99, 100, 101
    God's essence in, 15, 25, 196nn.99, 1000
    and Greek fathers, 1, 2, 7, 9–11, 129, 154–61, 204n.105
otherness
    Lossky on, 44, 114
    relationship to personhood, 5, 96, 121–22, 130, 131, 136, 137, 138–40, 141–42, 145–46, 151, 153, 190n.218, 197n.111
    Zizioulas on, 38, 40, 74, 96, 97, 121–22, 130, 131, 137, 138–40, 141–42, 145–46, 151, 153, 190n.218, 197n.111
ousia. See essence (*ousia/physis*)

Palamas, Gregory, 204n.104
  Christology of, 165n.14
  on energies of God (*energia*), 16, 25, 26, 27, 29, 169nn.82, 84, 196nn.100, 101
  light metaphor in, 23–24
  Lossky on, 11, 13, 16, 19, 23–24, 25, 26, 27, 29, 155, 168nn.65, 71, 169nn.82, 84, 196n.100
  Zizioulas on, 196n.101
Panagopoulos, John, 94, 95, 159, 196n.100, 204n.105
Pannenberg, Wolfhart, 159, 182n.102, 183n.114, 205n.119
pantheism, 27, 38, 119, 126
patristic writings. *See* Greek fathers
personalism, modern, 7, 129, 154, 155, 158–60
personhood
  as *ekstatic*, 7, 86–87, 88, 117, 137–39, 142, 143–45, 146, 150, 153–54
  human vs. divine, 103, 109, 111, 114–15, 117–18, 119, 142–48, 193n.40, 198n.2, 200n.31
  and *hypostasis*, 56–57, 65, 68–69, 80–84, 130–32, 135–37, 138, 142, 144–45, 150, 159, 177n.2, 179n.47
  vs. individuality, 55–57, 115, 136–37, 145, 156–57, 179n.47, 190n.217, 201n.66
  Lossky on, 4–5, 6–7, 45–46, 50, 51–53, 56–63, 65, 66, 67, 68–69, 70, 89–90, 91–92, 93, 94–96, 103–5, 107, 109–11, 112, 113–17, 121, 122–25, 127, 129–42, 155–61, 172n.117, 177n.13, 179nn.45, 52, 180n.72, 181nn.93, 101, 183n.124, 190n.215, 192nn.18, 27, 193nn.40, 47, 194nn.73, 83, 196n.100, 198nn.2, 4, 199nn.19, 21, 200n.51
  and *prosopon*, 53–55, 56, 81–82, 83–84, 87, 88, 130–31, 135, 157, 178nn.31, 32, 189n.202, 198n.1
  relational character of, 5, 7, 74, 79, 80, 83–84, 86–90, 93, 126, 139–42, 155–61, 186n.169, 190n.218, 205n.113
  relationship to death, 144, 145, 146
  relationship to difference, 5, 52–53, 56, 61, 74, 84, 130, 131, 137, 138–39

relationship to freedom, 57–58, 60–61, 62–63, 64–65, 70, 81–82, 84–87, 88, 90, 92, 94, 103, 107, 109, 112, 114, 115, 116, 117, 118, 124, 132, 133–34, 137–38, 139, 142, 143, 144, 145, 146, 147, 148, 149, 150–54, 160, 183n.124, 187n.170, 190n.222, 195n.95, 197n.111, 199n.17, 205n.124
relationship to human being as image of God, 114, 115, 116, 117, 120, 139, 153, 195n.78, 202n.89, 204n.110
relationship to irreducibility, 55–57, 59, 65, 95, 96, 109, 115, 122, 123, 127, 130–31, 133, 138, 143, 179n.49
relationship to *kenosis*, 7, 108–11, 113–15, 116–17, 151, 152–54, 195n.76
relationship to love, 60–61, 62–63, 64–65, 70, 82, 84–85, 86–87, 88–89, 90, 92, 103, 109, 112, 114, 116, 124, 136, 137–38, 139, 145, 151, 152–54, 183n.124, 190n.218, 195n.95, 199n.21
relationship to otherness, 5, 96, 121–22, 130, 131, 136, 137, 138–40, 141–42, 145–46, 151, 153, 190n.218, 197n.111
relationship to tragedy, 143–45, 199n.17, 201nn.53, 66
relationship to uniqueness, 56–59, 80, 86, 112, 117, 118, 120, 122, 123, 133, 135–36, 138, 141–42, 143–44, 145, 156, 158, 160, 179n.52, 190n.218, 195nn.78, 95, 199n.21, 205n.113
Zizioulas on, 5, 6–7, 11, 43, 44, 79–88, 90, 91, 94–102, 117–22, 125–27, 129–48, 150–54, 155–61, 186n.169, 187nn.180, 181, 189n.208, 190nn.215, 218, 222, 191n.227, 192nn.18, 27, 195nn.78, 83, 95, 196n.100, 101, 197n.106, 111, 198nn.2, 4, 200n.33, 201nn.53, 55, 58, 66, 71, 205nn.117, 124, 206n.125
Pétau, Denis, 29
1 Peter, 1, 25, 197n.104
Peter, St., 196n.99
Pettersen, Alvyn, 189n.212
Philippians 2:1, 35

philosophy
- existentialism, 7, 129, 155, 159–60, 204n.105
- Greek philosophy, 13, 18–19, 23, 54, 71–72, 73, 74, 75, 76, 77, 79, 80, 81, 85, 88, 96, 129–30, 131, 132, 145–46, 155, 167n.54, 184n.136, 186n.158, 192n.27, 197n.105
- modern personalism, 7, 129, 154, 155, 158–60
- neo-platonism, 13, 18–19, 23, 26, 54, 81, 94, 165n.15, 167n.54
- Plotinus on the One, 13, 18–19, 23, 54, 167n.54
- relationship to theology, 7, 10, 26, 27–30, 51, 54, 65, 66, 69, 71–72, 105, 129, 147–48, 154, 155, 158–60, 170n.88, 177n.13, 192n.27, 205n.124
- Russian religious philosophy, 1, 10, 94, 95
- and Zizioulas's notion of person, 129, 142–48

Plotinus, on the One, 13, 18–19, 23, 54, 167n.54

prosopon
- Basil on, 83–84, 87, 189n.202
- Greek fathers on, 54–55, 81–82, 83–84, 87, 130, 131, 157, 189n.202, 198n.1
- and *hypostasis*, 81–82, 83–84, 130–31, 135, 157
- Lossky on, 54–55, 56, 130, 178nn.31, 32
- Zizioulas on, 81–82, 83–84, 88, 130, 135, 157, 178nn.31, 32, 198n.1

Rahner, Karl, on the Trinity, 3, 49, 93, 99–100

rationalism in theology
- contemporary Orthodox theology on, 2, 163n.2
- Lossky on, 1, 2, 10, 11, 13–14, 16, 19–20, 21–23, 26, 28–29, 51, 52–53, 66–67, 69–70, 90, 92, 95, 96, 101, 102, 103, 122, 133, 140–41, 154–55, 163n.2, 166n.36, 170n.88, 184n.133
- Zizioulas on, 1, 2, 10, 11, 73, 154–55, 163n.2, 164n.5, 170n.95, 184n.133

Régnon, Theodore de, 66, 181n.101, 182n.102
Richard of St. Victor, 187n.181
Robinson, H. Wheeler, 198n.1
Roman Catholic theology
- eschatology, 170n.90
- and the *filioque*, 183n.123
- ressourcement in, 10

Romans
- 8:23, 172n.112
- 15:13, 35

Rubenstein, Mary Jane, 166n.36
Russell, Edward, 199n.17

Sabellianism, 78–79, 80, 81, 82, 83, 130, 189n.202
salvation
- Athanasius on, 75, 77, 139
- Jesus as Savior, 43, 107
- Lossky on, 24, 28, 63–64, 69, 91, 99, 103, 106, 107, 111, 112, 114–17, 118–20, 123, 124–25, 127, 139, 191n.227, 192n.18, 194nn.64, 65
- Zizioulas on, 38, 72, 78, 91, 99, 100, 104, 106, 117–20, 125–26, 127, 134–35, 139, 149, 191n.227, 192n.18, 196n.101, 206n.125

Schoedel, William R., 184n.133
scholasticism/neo-scholasticism, 1, 21, 132, 135. See also Aquinas, Thomas; Thomism
Schroeder, C. Paul, 203n.95
Silence and the Word, 166n.36
Skira, Jaroslav Z., 171n.99
space, 75–76, 79
Spinoza, Benedict de, 105
Stavrou, Michel, 95, 192n.27, 194n.64
Stead, Christopher, 187n.185
Stoicism, 55
subordinationism, 51, 60, 126, 129, 148, 150–52, 202n.83, 203n.93

Theodoret of Cyrus, 56, 179n.45
Theokritoff, Elizabeth, 174n.140
theological epistemology
- apophatic knowledge, 12–15, 17–22, 25, 30, 44, 101

cataphatic knowledge, 12–20, 21, 25, 30, 44, 101
   of Lossky, 3–4, 10, 11, 12–30, 29, 44, 45–46, 47–48, 49–50, 64–67, 92–93, 102–3, 104–6, 120, 172n.117, 181n.93
   relationship to divine-human communion, 3–4, 9, 11, 12, 13, 14–15, 18, 21–22, 30–31, 44, 46, 47–48, 49–50, 89, 104–5, 152
   relationship to trinitarian theology, 91–93
   of Zizioulas, 3–4, 10, 11, 33, 38, 46, 47–48, 49, 92–93, 102–3, 120, 152, 172nn.105, 117, 191n.1
Theotokos, 45–46, 47, 112, 177nn.185, 188
1 Thessalonians 1:5, 35
Thomism, 10, 13, 19, 29, 66, 95, 140–41, 168n.68, 169n.82. *See also* Aquinas, Thomas
Thunberg, Lars, 200n.24
Tillich, Paul, 148, 176n.169
time, 39, 41, 75–76, 79
Torrance, Alan J., 147, 148–50, 151, 154, 201n.74, 202nn.81, 83, 89
Torrance, Thomas F., 151, 189n.206, 202n.81
Trembelas, Panagiotes, 10
Trethowan, Dom Illtyd, 196n.100
Trinity, the
   Aquinas on, 64, 66–67, 70, 140–41, 181n.101, 182nn.102, 103, 183n.114
   Athanasius on, 74, 79, 80, 202n.81
   Barth on, 49, 201n.74
   Basil on, 82–84, 188nn.194, 200, 204n.110
   causality within, 26, 29, 59, 84–85, 126, 129, 133–35, 146, 147, 148–52, 154, 202n.89, 203n.93
   communion within, 74–75, 80, 83, 86–87, 136, 137–39, 141–42, 148–49, 151, 153–54, 156–58, 188n.200, 189n.207, 200nn.33, 44, 201n.74, 204n.110
   as economic (*oikonomia*), 3, 5–6, 37, 50–53, 61, 65, 90, 92–93, 99–102, 103, 106–8, 110, 112–13, 115, 123, 141, 153, 174n.138, 177n.2, 193nn.30, 31
   economy of the Son, 37, 106–12
   economy of the Spirit, 36, 37–38, 111–12, 173n.128, 174n.135
   Eunomius on, 78, 79–80, 133
   the Father as source (*pege*), 84, 134, 152
   the *filioque*, 65–71, 93, 101–2, 106–7, 111–12, 113, 169n.82, 173n.128, 181nn.95, 96, 183nn.120, 123
   generation of the Son, 58, 61, 63, 64, 73–74, 75, 80, 85–86, 88, 102, 134, 140, 150–51, 157, 189n.212, 200n.39
   Greek fathers on, 32, 53–56, 58, 73, 78–86, 102, 129–30, 131–32, 140, 156–57, 160, 177n.11, 181n.101, 187nn.170, 180, 184, 198n.1, 202n.81, 205n.111
   as *homoousios*, 54, 80, 82, 83, 188n.200
   as immanent (*theologia*), 3, 5–6, 37, 50–53, 61, 62–63, 65, 70, 90, 92–93, 96, 99–102, 103, 104, 106, 109, 110, 112–13, 114, 115, 123–24, 141, 174n.138, 177nn.2, 10, 193nn.30, 31, 194n.73
   kenosis of the Son, 7, 108–11, 113–14, 153–54, 203n.98
   kenosis of the Spirit, 113–14, 153–54, 195n.76
   Lossky on, 2–3, 4, 5–6, 7–8, 12, 16–17, 22, 23, 28, 36, 47–48, 49–71, 89–90, 91–102, 103–15, 117, 122–23, 126–27, 130–42, 164n.11, 165n.28, 177nn.2, 4, 10, 11, 13, 178n.37, 179nn.49, 52, 58, 180nn.72, 77, 82, 181nn.91, 93, 95, 96, 98, 101, 183n.124, 192n.27, 194n.73, 199n.18, 200nn.31, 39
   monarchy of the Father, 5, 7, 58–63, 64–65, 68, 70, 82, 84–87, 89–90, 102, 103, 124, 126, 129, 132–35, 140, 147–55, 157–58, 160, 161, 181n.101, 189n.207, 191n.227, 199n.17, 202nn.81, 83, 203n.93, 206n.125
   necessity and contingency in, 61–63, 85–87, 95, 148–50, 152, 157–58, 180nn.77, 82, 187n.170, 198n.3, 203n.93

Trinity, the (*cont.*)
  procession of the Holy Spirit, 58, 61, 63, 64, 66–67, 85, 88, 102, 134, 140, 150–51, 157, 177n.10, 179n.58, 181nn.95, 96, 100, 101, 182n.103, 200n.39
  Rahner on, 3, 49, 93, 99–100
  relations of opposition in, 66–68, 140–41, 182n.103
  relations of origin in, 58–63, 64–65, 66–68, 70, 109, 140–41, 177n.10, 179n.58, 182n.103, 200n.39
  Sabellians on, 78–79, 80, 81, 82, 83, 130, 189n.202
  the Son as *Logos*/Wisdom, 51–52, 71–72
  Son-Holy Spirit relation, 32–38, 42, 43, 45, 46, 50, 51, 65–71, 93, 100, 101–2, 106–7, 111–13, 118, 169n.82, 170n.89, 171n.99, 172n.114, 173nn.125, 128, 181nn.95, 96, 98, 183nn.120, 123, 200n.39
  subordinationism regarding, 51, 60, 126, 129, 148, 150–52, 202n.83, 203n.93
  Zizioulas on, 2–3, 4, 5–6, 7–8, 32, 33, 36, 37, 47–48, 49–50, 73, 74, 78–89, 90, 92–102, 103–6, 126–27, 129, 130–54, 157–58, 160, 161, 174nn.136, 138, 184n.139, 189n.207, 191n.227, 193n.30, 199n.17, 201n.74, 202nn.81, 83, 89, 203nn.92, 93, 98, 205n.111, 206n.125. *See also* Holy Spirit; Jesus Christ
truth, 192n.27
  and God, 31, 32
  Ignatius on, 72, 73
  Irenaeus on, 72, 73, 184n.133
  as life, 72–73
  Lossky on, 54, 69, 177n.188
  Zizioulas on, 31–32, 40, 46, 71–73, 170n.95, 183n.125
Turcescu, Lucian, 129, 155–59, 204n.110, 205n.116
Turner, Denys, 166n.36
Turner, Robert, 197n.111

Vatican II, 170n.90
Virgin Mary, 45–46, 47, 112
Volf, Miroslav, 175n.159, 184n.139, 195n.95, 199n.17, 202n.83, 206n.125

Wendebourg, Dorothea, 197nn.108, 109
Williams, Anna, 204n.104
Williams, Rowan, 65, 66, 69, 70, 169n.84, 183nn.114, 124, 193n.41, 195n.78, 197nn.108, 109, 204nn.104, 105
World Council of Churches (WCC), 1

Yannaras, Christos, 198n.4, 204n.105

Zizioulas, John
  on apophaticism, 3, 30, 31, 50, 90, 92–93, 94–96, 97, 101, 102–3, 104, 105–6, 133–34, 142, 191nn.1, 15, 192nn.18, 27, 193n.39
  on Athanasius, 5, 11, 73–78, 79, 82, 171n.97, 184n.139, 186n.158, 187n.180
  on Augustine, 11, 84, 155, 156, 163n.2, 164n.6
  on Cappadocian fathers, 5, 11, 73, 75, 78–86, 90, 96–97, 100–101, 106, 126–27, 130, 134, 138, 156, 187nn.170, 180, 185, 188nn.193, 194, 197, 200, 189nn.202, 206, 193n.31, 198n.1, 204n.110, 205n.111
  Christology of, 6, 31, 32–38, 33, 36, 37, 42, 43–44, 45, 46–47, 50, 71, 77, 88–89, 90, 99, 100, 101, 102, 106, 117–18, 126, 127, 153, 157, 170nn.89, 95, 171n.98, 172n.114, 173n.125, 174nn.134, 135, 139, 191n.227, 192n.18, 195n.95
  on communion within God's trinitarian being, 74–75, 80, 83, 86–87, 136, 138–39, 141–42, 148–49, 151, 156–58, 188n.200, 189n.207, 200nn.33, 44, 201n.74, 204n.110
  on cosmos, 76, 186n.160
  on creation *ex nihilo*/creation theology, 6, 75–77, 106, 120–22, 185n.149, 186nn.158, 160, 161, 165, 167, 169, 191n.227, 197n.105, 201n.71

on death, 40, 41, 42, 76, 77, 121–22,
  134–35, 141, 142, 144–45, 146,
  149–50, 157, 158, 188n.191
on divine-human communion, 1, 2,
  3–4, 5, 7–8, 32, 36, 37–38, 40, 44,
  45, 46–48, 49, 73, 74–75, 76, 77–78,
  79, 88–89, 90, 91, 93, 96, 98, 102–3,
  104, 117–20, 124, 125–27, 134, 139,
  145, 146, 152, 153, 154–55, 157, 158,
  160–61, 172n.117, 195n.95,
  196n.101
ecclesiology of, 32–33, 34–35, 36–37, 38,
  40–41, 42–43, 44, 45, 46–47, 101, 105,
  118, 170nn.89, 94, 95, 171n.98,
  173nn.125, 128, 132, 174nn.134, 136,
  139, 175n.159, 184n.135
on economy of the Spirit, 36, 37,
  193n.42
and ecumenical movement, 1–2, 40,
  101–2, 175n.159
on *ekstasis*, 7, 86–87, 88, 100, 117, 132,
  137–38, 142, 143–45, 146, 150, 153–54
eschatology of, 31–32, 33, 34–35, 36–37,
  38, 39–41, 42–43, 44, 45, 46, 71,
  170nn.90, 95, 172n.112, 173n.132,
  174n.139, 175nn.141, 143, 148, 149,
  159, 206n.125
on the eucharist, 3, 4, 5, 6, 11, 31–32, 33,
  34–41, 42, 45, 46–47, 50, 71, 72, 73,
  77–78, 83–84, 88–89, 90, 94, 96, 98,
  100, 101, 104, 120, 126, 127, 134, 146,
  147, 149–50, 152, 155, 158, 170nn.89,
  92, 94, 95, 171n.97, 173nn.125, 132,
  174nn.139, 140, 175nn.141, 143, 149,
  176n.159, 184nn.135, 137, 139,
  186n.169, 192n.27, 202n.89
eucharistic eschatological type of
  pneumatology, 34–35
on the *filioque*, 65, 93, 101–2, 181n.95
on freedom from necessity and human
  existence, 81, 188n.191
on God's energies, 6, 93, 100, 104,
  117–18, 119–20, 121, 122, 192n.18,
  196nn.100, 101
on God's essence, 6, 96–98, 104, 126,
  131–32, 192nn.18, 27, 193n.35, 198n.3

on God's freedom, 7, 74–75, 76, 77–78,
  79, 81–82, 84–87, 88, 89, 100, 102,
  104, 117, 120, 121, 124, 132, 133–35,
  138, 139, 147–54, 149, 157–58,
  186nn.158, 222, 223, 198n.3, 199n.17,
  202n.83, 203nn.92, 93, 204n.110,
  205n.124, 206n.125
on God's love, 76, 77–78, 82, 84–85,
  86–87, 88, 89, 100, 104, 121, 122, 132,
  135, 138–39, 141–42, 190nn.218, 222,
  200n.44, 201n.58
on God's will, 73–75, 85–86
on Greek fathers, 1, 5, 6, 7, 9–11, 32,
  38, 40, 71–75, 76, 78–88, 90, 94–95,
  96–97, 102, 120, 122, 129–32, 134,
  135, 138, 147, 154–61, 164nn.5, 6,
  171n.97, 184nn.135, 137, 139, 185n.140,
  186n.158, 187nn.180, 185, 188,
  188nn.193, 194, 197, 200, 189nn.202,
  206, 191n.227, 195n.78, 196n.101,
  198nn.1, 4, 204n.110, 205n.111
on history, 34, 35, 36–37, 38, 39–40,
  42–43, 44, 71, 72–73, 158, 173nn.123,
  132, 135, 175nn.149, 159
on the Holy Spirit, 2, 31, 32–38, 41,
  42–43, 45, 46, 50, 65, 93, 100, 101, 102,
  106, 112, 118, 134, 150–51, 157, 158,
  170n.89, 171n.95, 172nn.112, 114, 117,
  173nn.125, 128, 174n.134, 139, 193n.42
on *hopos esti* (how God is), 6, 87–88,
  96–98, 99–101, 102, 104, 160,
  191n.227, 192n.27, 193nn.31, 35
on human creativity, 143, 147, 201n.53
on human personhood, 142–48, 198n.2,
  199n.17, 201n.55
on *hypostasis*, 5, 6–7, 43, 44, 80–84, 86,
  87, 88, 98, 106, 117–18, 119, 126–27,
  130, 135–37, 142, 143, 144–45, 150, 157,
  158, 178n.32, 187n.184, 188n.200,
  189n.208, 195n.83
on icon, 31, 38–44, 45, 173n.132,
  175nn.141, 143, 148, 149, 159, 176n.169
on the Incarnation, 2, 30, 31, 36, 37, 38,
  43, 44, 75, 77, 101, 117, 139, 153, 158
on Irenaeus, 11
on *kenosis*, 153

Zizioulas, John (*cont.*)
    197n.106
  on Origen, 11, 71–72, 74, 78, 155, 164n.6
  and Orthodox theology, 1, 2, 6,
    197n.106
  on otherness, 38, 40, 74, 96, 97, 121–22,
    130, 131, 137, 138–40, 141–42, 145–46,
    151, 153, 190n.218, 197n.111
  on particularity, 96, 97, 130, 131, 132,
    141–42, 145–46, 200n.33
  on personhood, 5, 6–7, 11, 43, 44,
    79–88, 90, 91, 94–102, 117–22,
    125–27, 129–48, 150–54, 155–61,
    186n.169, 187nn.180, 181, 189n.208,
    190nn.215, 218, 222, 191n.227,
    192nn.18, 27, 195nn.78, 83, 95,
    196n.100, 101, 197nn.106, 111, 198nn.2,
    4, 200n.33, 201nn.53, 55,
    58, 66, 71, 205nn.117, 124, 206n.125
  on philosophy and personhood, 129,
    142–48
  on the presence-in-absence paradox,
    143–45, 201nn.53, 55
  on *prosopon*, 81–82, 83–84, 88, 130, 135,
    157, 178nn.31, 32, 198n.1
  on rationalism in theology, 1, 2, 10, 11,
    73, 154–55, 163n.2, 164n.5, 170n.95,
    184n.133
  relationship with Florovsky, 1, 9
  on revelation, 97–98
  on sacraments, 40, 41, 42–43
  on salvation, 38, 72, 78, 91, 99, 100, 104,
    106, 117–20, 125–26, 127, 134–35, 139,
    149, 191n.227, 192n.18, 196n.101,
    206n.125
  on sexuality, 144–45, 195n.83

theological epistemology of, 3–4, 10, 11,
    33, 38, 46, 47–48, 49, 92–93,
    102–3, 120, 152, 172nn.105, 117, 191n.1
on the Trinity, 2–3, 4, 5–6, 7–8, 32, 33,
    36, 37, 47–48, 49–50, 73, 74, 78–89,
    90, 92–102, 103–6, 126–27, 129,
    130–54, 157–58, 160, 161, 174nn.136,
    138, 184n.139, 189n.207, 191n.227,
    193n.30, 199n.17, 201n.74, 202nn.81,
    83, 89, 203nn.92, 93, 98, 205n.111,
    206n.125
on *tropos hyparxeos*/mode of existence,
    6, 97–98, 180n.82, 181n.91,
    191n.227
on truth, 31–32, 40, 46, 71–73, 170n.95,
    183n.125
Zizioulas vs. Lossky. *See* Lossky vs.
    Zizioulas

ARISTOTLE PAPANIKOLAOU

is professor of theology and co-founding director of the Orthodox Christian Studies Center at Fordham University. He is the author and co-editor of a number of books, including *The Mystical as Political: Democracy and Non-Radical Orthodoxy* (University of Notre Dame Press, 2012).